Performance and
the Contemporary City
An Interdisciplinary Reader

Edited by
Nicolas Whybrow

palgrave
macmillan

First published 2010 by
PALGRAVE MACMILLAN

Palgrave Macmillan in the UK is an imprint of Macmillan Publishers Limited, registered in England, company number 785998, of Houndmills, Basingstoke, Hampshire RG21 6XS.

Palgrave Macmillan in the US is a division of St Martin's Press LLC, 175 Fifth Avenue, New York, NY 10010.

Palgrave Macmillan is the global academic imprint of the above companies and has companies and representatives throughout the world.

Palgrave® and Macmillan® are registered trademarks in the United States, the United Kingdom, Europe and other countries.

ISBN 978–0–230–52719–5   hardback
ISBN 978–0–230–52720–1   paperback

This book is printed on paper suitable for recycling and made from fully managed and sustained forest sources. Logging, pulping and manufacturing processes are expected to conform to the environmental regulations of the country of origin.

A catalogue record for this book is available from the British Library.

A catalog record for this book is available from the Library of Congress.

10   9   8   7   6   5   4   3   2   1
19   18   17   16   15   14   13   12   11   10

Printed and bound in China

In memory of my father John Whybrow (1931–2007), who would have read this book.

Contents

List of Illustrations

Acknowledgements

I would like to thank all authors and publishers of texts reprinted here, as well as respective photographers for the use of images. I am grateful in particular to those contributors who agreed to waive fees. Without their generosity the costs for this book would have become prohibitive. It should be made clear, moreover, that many sacrifices had to be made nevertheless, precisely because of overall copyright costs being too high. Thus a range of highly desirable texts by the likes of Michel de Certeau, Jane Jacobs, Bertolt Brecht, Jonathan Raban, Jon McGregor, W. G. Sebald, Alain de Botton, Jane McGonigal, Sophie Calle, Claire Doherty, Anthony Vidler and Doreen Massey have unfortunately had to be excluded.

Full details of the original sources of texts used are listed at the beginning of the part in which they appear. I would particularly like to mention Intellect Books for permitting several short passages from a previous book of mine – *Street Scenes: Brecht, Benjamin and Berlin* (2005) – to be reproduced, sometimes in slightly adjusted form, in some of the editorial introductions. Similarly, a paragraph appearing in an online article of mine on the artist Tomoko Takahashi, originally published in *Body, Space and Technology*, 6(2), 2006, has been inserted in Part 4. I am also grateful to the Humanities Research Centre at Warwick University for help from its research fund with the costs of permissions where they arose.

Thanks go to Kate Haines, my editor at Palgrave Macmillan, for encouraging the project in the first place and for responding extremely positively and constructively to any queries. I would also like to thank all my colleagues in the Theatre and Performance Studies department at Warwick for their all round support, often extended in implicit acts of generosity. The department's nurturing of research-based teaching in the third year of the undergraduate programme is what led to the development of a module bearing the same title as this publication. I am very grateful that this prompt was given and for the three classes of students who have opted to take the module since its devising, above all perhaps the very first 'guinea-pig' group, who really did suffer some ropey moments and did not have the benefit of the practical component that was added in subsequent years. All these groups have done so much to enrich the scope of the module, much of whose material is presented here. So, as a way of expressing my appreciation, I would like to list the names of each student (in no particular order): Becki Thompson, Mike Gill, Jenny Malenoir, Julia Austin, Jen Godwin, Hannah Gray, James Black, Lucy Norris, Bridget Gregory,

Laura Emberson, Kim Smith, Jon Stevens, David Moon, Jayne Dickinson, Emily Hudson, Simone Hancox, Helen Bradbury, Kate Madden, Laura Draper, Bethan Way, Tom Pullen, Hannah Morland, Matthew Runham, Claire Coffey, Melanie Gilbert, Rachael Harper, Lail Arad, Laura Doherty, Dominic Glynn, Sarah Kemp, Anna Cook, Lizzie Phillips, Louise Whiteley, Alexia Searle, Tory Frost, Gemma Smyth, Jeff Leach, Emily Brooks, Maxine Pemble, Alice Cadwgan, Nick Foster, Kezia Cole, Dean Murphy, Aimee Keith, Adam Alston, Sarah Benkalai, Esme Sparks, Claire Johnson, Chloe Hodge, Claire Read, Becky Greaves, Ellie Smith, Hannah Lane, Sam Chapman, Nicki Murphy, Sam Bevitt, Kay Polley, Nadia Lumley, Kim Pearce, Zac Russell and Cormac Brown.

The editor and publishers wish to thank the following for permission to reproduce copyright material:

Francis Alÿs for his illustrations in 'Rumours: A Conversation Between Francis Alÿs and James Lingwood', in Francis Alÿs Seven Walks, London 2004–5, Artangel (2005); Francis Alÿs and James Lingwood for pp. 16–22, an extract from 'Rumours: A Conversation Between Francis Alÿs and James Lingwood', in Francis Alÿs Seven Walks, London 2004–5, Artangel (2005); Birkhäuser Verlag AG for pp. 60–3, from Alex Coles, '"How Long I 'Been On?" Marc Dion's Performative Archaeology of the City', in N. Barley, ed., Breathing Cities: the Architecture of Movement (2000); Birkhäuser Verlag AG for pp. 198–9, from Bertrand Delanoë, 'Paris Plage', in F. Haydn and R. Temel, eds, Temporary Urban Spaces: Concepts for the Use of City Spaces (2006); Birkhäuser Verlag AG for pp. 105–12, from Ursula Hofbauer and Friedemann Derschmidt, 'Horror Vacui', in F. Haydn and R. Temel, eds, Temporary Urban Spaces: Concepts for the Use of City Spaces (2006); Birkhäuser Verlag AG for pp. 122–3, from LIGNA, 'Radioballett', in F. Haydn and R. Temel, eds, Temporary Urban Spaces: Concepts for the Use of City Spaces (2006); Birkhäuser Verlag AG for pp. 130–1, from Space Hijackers, 'Circle Line Party', in F. Haydn and R. Temel, eds, Temporary Urban Spaces: Concepts for the Use of City Spaces (2006); Cambridge University Press and the author, for Petra Kuppers, 'Moving in the Cityscape: Performance and the Embodied Experience of the Flâneur', in New Theatre Quarterly (1999), 15(04), © Cambridge University Press, reproduced with permission; Cambridge University Press and the author, for Carl Lavery, 'The Pepys of London E11: Graeme Miller and the Politics of Linked', in New Theatre Quarterly (2005), 21(02), © Cambridge University Press, reproduced with permission; The Continuum International Publishing Group for pp. 85–100, from Henri Lefebvre and Catherine

Régulier, 'Attempt at the Rhythmanalysis of Mediterranean Cities', in Rhythmanalysis: Space, Time and Everyday Life, intro. S. Eldon, trans. S. Eldon and G. More (2004), reprinted with the permission of the publisher, The Continuum International Publishing Group; Alice Debord for Guy Debord and Asger Jorn, The Naked City: illustration de l'hypothèse des plaques tournantes en psychogéographie, and Guy Debord, Paris Habité, © Alice Debord; Granta Books for pp. 1–4, from Iain Sinclair, 'Skating on Thin Eyes: the First Walk', in Lights Out for the Territory (1997); Guardian News & Media Ltd for Madeleine Bunting, 'Liberty and the state: the policing of the Artist', in The Guardian, 11 December 2007, Copyright Guardian News & Media Ltd 2007; Guardian News & Media Ltd for Geoff Dyer, 'An explosion of delight', in The Guardian, 14 October 2006, Copyright Guardian News & Media Ltd 2006; Guardian News & Media Ltd for Lyn Gardner, 'What a carry on', in The Guardian, 13 June 2007, Copyright Guardian News & Media Ltd 2007; Guardian News & Media Ltd for Jonathan Watts, 'How scratched car revealed the price of a peasant's life', in The Guardian, 8 April 2004, Copyright Guardian News & Media Ltd 2007; James Harkin for his article 'Saturday Interview: Cyborg city: James Harkin meets William J. Mitchell, advocate of the wireless world', in The Guardian, 26 November 2005; Intellect for Carl Lavery, '25 Instructions for Performance in Cities', in Studies in Theatre and Performance (2005) volume 25, issue 3, pp. 234–6; Liverpool University Press for pp. 215–18, from Andrew Hussey, '"The Map is Not the Territory": The Unfinished Journey of the Situationist International', in S. Speir, ed., Urban Visions: Experiencing and Envisioning the City (2002); The MIT press for images from Borden, Iain, Joe Kerr, and Jane Rendell, eds. Alicia Pivaro, The Unknown City: Contesting Architecture and Social Space, pp. file transfer of images contained within pages 388–406, © 2000 Massachusetts Institute of Technology, by permission of The MIT Press; The MIT Press for an extract from 'By Way of a Conclusion: One Place After Another', in Miwon Kwon, One Place after Another: Site-Specific Art and Locational Identity, pp. 160–4, © 2002 Massachusetts Institute of Technology, by permission of The MIT Press; The MIT Press for R. Wentworth, '"The Accident of Where I Live" – Journeys on the Caledonian Road', an interview with Joe Kerr, from Iain Borden, Joe Kerr and Jane Rendell, eds, with Alicia Pivaro, The Unknown City: Contesting Architecture and Social Space, text only from pp. 388–406, © Massachusetts Institute of Technology, by permission of The MIT Press; Keith Piper for his article, 'A Nigger in Cyberspace', pp. 38–43, in G. Tawadros, ed., Changing States: Contemporary Arts and Ideas in an Era of Globalisation, Iniva (2004); Sage Publications for pp. 40–56, from Nicholas Fyfe, 'Zero Tolerance, Maximum Surveillance?

Deviance, Difference and Crime Control in the Late Modern City',
reproduced by permission of Sage Publications, London, Los Angeles, New
Delhi and Singapore, from L. Lees, ed., The Emancipatory City? Paradoxes
and Possibilities, Copyright © Sage, 2004; Taylor & Francis Books for
pp. 76–83, 'Non-places', by Marc Augé, in A. Read, ed., Architecturally
Speaking: Practices of Art, Architecture and the Everyday, Copyright ©
2000 Routledge. Reproduced by permission of Taylor & Francis Books
UK; Taylor & Francis Books for 'Eight Fragments on Theatre and the
City', pp. 76–83 from Certain Fragments by Tim Etchells, Copyright ©
1999 Routledge. Reproduced by permission of Taylor & Francis Books
UK; Taylor & Francis Books for pp. 33–41, from Nick Kaye, 'Performing
the City: Krysztof Wodiczko', in Site-Specific Art: Performance, Place and
Documentation, Routledge (2000). Reproduced by permission of Taylor &
Francis Books UK; Taylor & Francis Books for pp. 86–9, 'Graffiti', by
Susan J. Smith, in Steven Pile, ed., City A–Z, Copyright © 2000 Routledge.
Reproduced by permission of Taylor & Francis Books UK; Taylor &
Francis Ltd for Sarah Gorman, 'Wandering and Wondering: Following Janet
Cardiff's Missing Voice', from Performance Research, Vol. 8:1, reprinted
by permission of the publisher, Taylor & Francis Ltd, http://www.infor-
maworld.com; Taylor & Francis Ltd for Carl Lavery, 'Situationism', from
Performance Research (2006), Vol. 11:3, reprinted by permission of the
publisher, Taylor & Francis Ltd, http://www.informaworld.com; Taylor &
Francis Ltd for Paul Rae and Low Kee Hong, 'Nosing Around: A Singapore
Scent Trail', adapted from Performance Research (2003), Vol. 8:3, reprinted
by permission of the publisher, Taylor & Francis Ltd, http://www.informa-
world.com; Taylor & Francis Ltd for Wrights and Sites, 'A Manifesto for a
New Walking Culture: "Dealing with the City"', adapted from Performance
Research (2006), Vol. 11:2, reprinted by permission of the publisher, Taylor
& Francis Ltd, http://www.informaworld.com; V2_Institute for the Unstable
Media for Arjun Appadurai (2001), 'The Right to Participate in the Work
of the Imagination' (interview with Arjen Mulder), TransUrbanism, eds
J. Brouwer, A. Mulder and L. Mertz, Rotterdam: V2_Publishing: pp. 32–
46; Verso for 'Naples', pp. 167–76 from Walter Benjamin and Asja Lacis,
One-Way Street and Other Writings, intro. S. Sontag, trans. E. Jephcott
and K. Shorter, London: Verso (1997); Richard Wentworth for photographs from R. Wentworth, '"The Accident of Where I Live" – Journeys
on the Caledonian Road', an interview with Joe Kerr, in I. Borden et al.,
The Unknown City: Contesting Architecture and Social Space, The MIT
Press (2000); Wiley-Blackwell for pp. 75–86, from Steve Pile, 'Sleepwalking
in the Modern City: Walter Benjamin and Sigmund Freud in the World
of Dreams', in G. Bridge and S. Watson, eds, A Companion to the City,

Blackwell Companions to Geography (2000); Jessica Winter for her article 'All the world's a car park', in The Guardian, 25 January 2005.

All texts have retained their original systems of referencing and annotation, so notes and references relating to a particular text are always given at the culmination of that text. Every effort has been made to trace rights holders, but if any have been inadvertently overlooked the publishers would be pleased to make the necessary arrangements at the first opportunity.

Preamble

Marco Polo: 'You take delight not in a city's seven or seventy wonders, but in the answer it gives to a question of yours.'

Kublai Khan: 'Or the question it asks you ...'

Italo Calvino, *Invisible Cities*

This book takes its cue from a research-based module I have been teaching to final year undergraduates at Warwick University for some three years now. I may be quite wrong, but I have always sensed there to be a mixture in students of trepidation and exhilaration when they embark on this module. On the one hand they are anxious about the way it is premised on venturing into uncharted territory – between art forms and disciplines – emphasising in its approach to material what appears to be a suggestive, associative strategy, coupled with first-hand experiencing 'on the street'. For how can you be assessed on something as vague and cavalier as that? On the other hand they are excited by the promise of enrichment in such encounters with the unknown as well as in the development of a form of creative criticality in their practical responses to the material. Not only may the students find themselves, then, having to drift far from the disciplinary moorings of theatre and performance, as they enter the multiplic*ity* of urban and spatial theory, human and cultural geography, architecture, philosophy, psychoanalysis, visual art and culture, anthropology, ethnography, sociology and so on, but they are also being asked to apply creative faculties – of thinking, writing and art-making – to their enquiry into performance's relationship with the contemporary city. And, as more and more questions bubble up, they are liable – as Kublai Khan's reply to Marco Polo implies – to feel personally implicated (Calvino 1997: 44). The city is not merely something you study, but a place you *inhabit*.

As their tutor the tension described makes me nervous, too. For what if the exploratory premise – which has, by definition, always to be subject to a failure that can have many causes – simply doesn't work out? How easy under those circumstances to find oneself, in a climate of enforced fidelity to benchmarks and outcomes, on the receiving end of accusations of engendering irresponsible risk-taking: of playing fast and loose with students' immediate prospects for their degrees and their futures. However, not wishing to overstate the 'radical departure' of the module in question, nor indeed to permit this discourse to evolve into a drawn out debate about creativity and learning in higher education – desirable and timely as that may be – I would simply maintain that in my experience students for the most part understand very well what they are signing up to. Indeed, they welcome the challenges and, even when things do not exactly 'work out', they recognise and accept the legitimacy of the terms and principles according to which they undertook those challenges in the first place. Failure or mistakes, moreover, while patently anathema to curricula couched in jargons of 'successful completion', are acknowledged frequently to emerge as productive catalysts, both in the sense of learning from them and as irregular factors: dissonances and ruptures that lead to creative insights and surprises.

But what I really mean to get round to suggesting is that the module concerned is conceived of as the performative enactment – and I use the expression advisedly – of that which it would set out to explore. In other words, it is premised in its form on opening a space of enquiry that figuratively replicates the stranger's encounter with the unknown terrain of the city. Walter Benjamin, whose spirit probably pervades every word of this publication, famously talked of the desirability 'to lose oneself in the city': a deceptively difficult 'art of straying', which calls in fact for 'a quite different schooling' (Benjamin 1997a: 298).[1] In effect, he was addressing the capacity to *perceive* or *experience* in the modern-day metropolis, urging vigilance and curiosity: to allow in the unknown by jolting perceptions of the familiar out of any banalising complacency. Hence, as the ethnographer Franco la Cecla has put it (though he signals no clear acknowledgement of Benjamin in doing so, as far as I can tell): the 'feeling of a possible and imminent danger is the sense of adventure'. For him getting lost in the city is, then, 'a condition of beginning, the need or the ground on which to start or resume getting orientated' (in Read 2000: 34). La Cecla also draws attention to the Socratean dictum that warns against 'taking yourself with you' on your travels and the danger, if you do, of 'colonising with [y]our presence every step of the journey [for] to know new places corresponds in this century with denying their difference' (ibid.: 39). Following from this, the architecture theorist Jane Rendell has drawn attention to Kaja Silverman's illuminating proposal of two diametrically opposed paradigms of identification when it comes to encountering the unknown. These are, on the one hand, '"heteropathic" where the subject aims to go outside the self, to identify with something/someone/somewhere different' and, on the other, '"cannibalistic" where the subject brings something other into the self to make it the same' (in Blamey 2002: 259).

While these various viewpoints relate to travel and identification, as well as to some extent to the physical act of walking in the city, they can perhaps be transposed metaphorically to the 'place or field of enquiry': moving in and around or *between* the spaces of the city emerges as a possible paradigm for interdisciplinary knowing, for the way in which we may come to know and be transformed by a variety of 'unknown things'. As Rendell (2007: 46) suggests, the recent search for new epistemological and ontological discourses has produced critical texts whose language 'is highly spatialised, with words such as "mapping", "locating", "situating", "positioning" and "boundaries" appearing frequently'. Concluding that 'positionality provides a way of understanding knowledge and being as contingent and strategic – where I am makes a difference to what I can know and who I can be. (But I am not going to be there for ever.)' (ibid.), she poses a series of powerfully rhetorical questions, which echo Silverman's contrasting modes of identification and clearly synthesises 'place' and 'knowing':

> Is the interdisciplinary operator one who straddles two places, one who maps the tears and rifts, the places where things have come apart, and the overlaps and the joins, the places where things come together? Or has s/he come from elsewhere, arrived as a stranger in town? Being someone new in town is a different experience altogether. Here one place has been left and a new unknown terrain entered. What do you do? Match the new to meet up with the standards of the old, or allow yourself to be changed by your new surroundings?
>
> (Ibid.: 47)

For literary theorist Greg Ulmer, the spatial mobility of discourse implied here – and manifest in the work of radical theorists as diverse as Montaigne, Heidegger, Wittgenstein and Derrida – is reminiscent of 'the ancient topos for rhetorical invention – the walk through the places' (1989: 167). For him it is no coincidence that these theorists 'all spoke of their method in this way, having to do with journeys, paths, maps – especially with journeys off the beaten track or highway' (ibid.: 168). Indeed, pre-figuring the postmodern turn of the latter half of the twentieth century – or arguably helping to bring it about, in fact – Benjamin conducted his own highly original experiments in a conjunction of urban walking, writing and discovery. His episodic 1928 publication *One-Way Street* is a kind of 'dream dictionary for the modern urban dweller' with entries that provide profound, revelatory readings of the so-called phantasmagoria of everyday city life.[2] It is dedicated obliquely to Asja Lacis (with whom Benjamin later co-authored the meditation on the city of Naples included in this volume) inasmuch as the mythical one-way street in question is declared at the beginning to be called Asja Lacis Street after the woman, an 'engineer', 'who cut it through the author' (Benjamin 1997a: 45). Thus, the irreversible and overwhelming effect of this infiltration into the Benjaminian body emerges for the reader in the form of an invitation to take a 'textual stroll' along that which sociologist David Frisby describes as this 'constellation or "construction" of aphorisms as a street' (in Tester 1994: 101). In a related vein, the point of Benjamin's magnum opus *The Arcades Project* was, as the political philosopher Susan Buck-Morss explains, precisely 'to bridge the gap between everyday experience and traditional academic concerns' (1989: 3). Made up effectively of a montage of reflections, aphorisms and quotations from a myriad of sources, which is organised into 36 'files' or so-called *Konvoluten* (bundles of papers) under a keyword heading, the project not only amounts to a replication of the architecture of the nineteenth-century (Parisian) arcade, and a meditation on its socio-cultural significance, but also proposes through its form an 'active writing' on the part of the reader, since it is not premised on any customary – and therefore reassuringly familiar – logics of linearity and chronology. It is a reading that presupposes a shock to the system: a deliberate disorientation that may eventually reap rewards via the startling or 'awakening' associations or, indeed, the jarring juxtapositions encountered by the meandering reader.

Benjamin's practice – for that is what it is – is certainly an inspiration. As such, it offers *something* of a model for the texts here: a portfolio (or bundle) of sometimes fragmentary documents, grouped in parts, which can be navigated in any number of ways. In fact, I would like to suggest that approaching this publication might be akin to approaching the space of the city, which, in turn, is akin to approaching the space of knowledge. As the reader, you will doubtless encounter the familiar as well as unfamiliar (to say nothing of the strangely or secretly familiar), making potential connections, it is hoped, as well as realising disjunctions. To set you on your way in the requisite frame of mind, I leave you with the writer Stephen Barber, for whom 'no city can be mapped except by the body' (2006: 24). In other words, as Benjamin too clearly believed, to know the city is to experience it physically. Having decided halfway through an epic journey from Los Angeles to Tokyo – described in his first-hand account *The Vanishing Map* – 'to spend the entirety of [the] winter traversing the cities of central Europe', Barber devises the following plan as he sits in a railway station café in Prague:

> I drew an itinerary at speed across a map of Europe torn from a magazine, tracing pencil-arrows at random through the empty gaps between cities: Budapest, Linz, Kraków, Vienna, Bratislava, Brno, determining the course of that journey without reflection, compulsively skimming the pencil over the surface space of Europe, and aware that any such mapping imposed on that surface would inevitably rectify itself into a set of diversions, deviations, pitfalls, descents and elevations. Nothing was discernable from ground level, where those cities appeared stultified and absent; instead any vision of Europe was located overhead and in its

subterranea, in movements through its altitudes and its ash-and-cinder skies, and through trackings of its urban underpasses and concealed spaces. As soon as the map of my itinerary was complete, I crumpled it in my fist, letting the nicks in my fingernails tear the paper, then carefully spread it out again, its surface now indented with a new landscape of rips, folds and furrows, the pencil lines linking the cities of Europe blurred and disjointed. That was the map I would follow.

(Barber 2006: 43–4)

Notes

1. See Part 2 for coverage of related Situationist practices of 'drifting'.
2. *The Dream Dictionary for the Modern Dreamer* (2001) is a publication by Tim Etchells, the director-cum-writer of the UK theatre company Forced Entertainment. An A–Z of entries presents a form of twenty-first century lexicon of 'everyday cultural artefacts', ranging from 'airport novels' to 'IKEA' to 'weeping on a game show'. Effectively premised on a 'writing over' of Freud's *Interpretation of Dreams* – as, indeed, was Benjamin's interpretation of the modern city as a dream world, according to Pile (in Bridge and Watson 2003: 81) – Etchells's definitions provide tongue-in-cheek takes on the symbolic significance of certain cultural phenomena hypothetically appearing to us in dreams. What is interesting is the tension that arises in these entries between an obviously ironic fictionality and the residual *potential* for the interpretations to ring true. In other words, though the observations are clearly made up for a laugh, something that can be said to chime with the experience of being immersed in 'western popular culture' frequently emerges unexpectedly. Thus, where Freud was preoccupied with rational explanations of the psyche of the individual – in which, for example, he fancied he could lead the dream appearance of a horse back to the domineering father that was meant in reality – Etchells is tapping into a form of collective or popular un/consciousness and implicitly demonstrating the extent to which this particular reality is dependent on the operation of a certain fictionality to come about. In fact, the title itself of the Forced Entertainment CD-Rom *Imaginary Evidence* (2003) perhaps best sums up the playful interdependency of what I am talking about. Moreover, one of the company's performance pieces, *The Travels* (2002), is also pertinent here: in effect its performance tells the story of how the piece itself came into being. The performers narrate how each one of them was tasked with visiting certain streets in the UK with particularly resonant names – Harmony Street, Cutthroat Alley, Love Lane, Rape Lane, and so on – as a form of first-hand research, and to bring back tales of their experiences (see Helmer and Malzacher 2004: 188). Hence, a form of 'getting lost as a condition of beginning', as discussed above, serves as the point of departure for what then evolves into 'evidence gathering' or 'witnessing the scene' – reminiscent perhaps of the practices of forensics or archaeology – emerging finally in performance almost as the 'relating of a bad dream' (or 'trip'), a kind of fictional documentary.

Introduction

> Most of us live in cities; it is the urban, the congregation of strangers, which defines our contemporary situation.
>
> Mike Pearson and Michael Shanks, *Theatre/Archaeology*

Urban populations

The simple observation above from Pearson and Shanks's interdisciplinary book is a useful point of departure, on several counts (2001: 147). For one thing, based on the assumption that the 'us' here is a universal one, it draws attention to the momentous fact that the majority of the world's population does indeed live in cities now: in 2007 the balance of urban to rural (or 'other') officially tipped irrevocably towards the former. By 2030, moreover, five billion out of a global population of just over eight billion is projected to be made up of city dwellers, with the major area of growth being in the so-called developing world. Thus, an 'exploding' city such as Lagos in Nigeria, with a current total of just over ten million, is expected to have doubled in size by 2020, making it the third largest city in the world.[1] By contrast, London will maintain the equilibrium of its present population of some eight million, and an advanced mega-city like Tokyo, which already has a staggering population of 35 million – the world's largest at the time of writing – is set to rise by a mere million in the same period (UN-HABITAT 2006: 8).

The global *differences* of growth rate are nowhere more marked than in the statistic that nearly a third of current city inhabitants live in slums, of which 90 per cent are in the developing world (ibid.: 11). The very nature of slums – officially defined *in part* as dwellings lacking sufficient living space (ibid.: 19) – makes clear, in turn, that one-third of the global urban population lives in circumstances of extremely high density. A high population in any one city of the developing world does not, therefore, imply a corresponding expanse of available space. Cities such as Cairo and Mumbai have residential densities of around 35,000 per km² as against 4,500 in London, for example. Mexico City by contrast, which has experienced a massive increase in population size since the mid-twentieth century – currently around 19 million, the bulk of which lives in poverty – has a density not that much higher than London's owing to its geographical positioning on a high plateau, which permits low-rise sprawl (*Global Cities* exhibition information, Tate Modern, London, 20 June to 27 August 2007). As such, it is important to bear in mind, on the one hand, that a rising urban demographic brings massive problems of overcrowding with it and, on the other, that contextual or local factors diverge enormously, producing quite distinct cities in terms of socio-economic and cultural/human geographic infrastructure.

The tension between a *perception* of trans-urban homogenisation in an age of globalisation and the *actual* specificities of local cultures is not one that should be suppressed then, as it might be, by reference to a universal 'us'. In the same way that it is still a majority of the world's population that does not in fact have the means to take advantage of digital communications technologies in all their various forms, so it is that there are vast discrepancies of wealth and amenities in urban centres around the globe. So, yes, most of us live in cities now, but most of 'us' are not even indirect beneficiaries of the first order of global finance and power. In fact, most of 'us' probably find ourselves at its mercy, so to speak: condemned as a member of 'the rest' or 'other world' to serve the interests and merely feed off the scraps of a dominant minority. (And I hasten to point out my own privileged position in sketching this scenario. Alone, the fact that I *can* sketch it in these perspectival terms is doubtless indicative of that.) Even within the 'secure confines' of, say, Europe there are considerable discrepancies of opportunity. Identifying the states of the former Soviet bloc as 'postmodern serfs, providing low-wage labour for the factories where the clothes, electronics and cars are produced for 20–25 per cent of the cost of making them in Europe', Naomi Klein describes the symbiotic mechanism of the new 'fortress continents' as

> a bloc of nations that joins forces to extract favourable trade terms from other countries, while patrolling their shared external borders to keep people from those countries out. But if a continent is serious about being a fortress, it also has to invite one or two poor countries within its walls, because somebody has to do the dirty work and heavy lifting.[2]

> (Klein 2003: 23)

As the sociologist Zygmunt Bauman reminds us, Klein's succinct analysis not only applies to Europe but is replicated in North America, for instance, where an arrangement between the USA and Mexico witnesses the latter 'policing its southern boundary to effectively stop the tide of impoverished human waste flowing to the US from Latin American countries' (Bauman 2004: 20). Thus, as Klein concludes, you stay *open for business* by expanding the perimeter and *closed to people* by subsequently locking down (Klein 2003: 23).

Urban bodies

The second main point to make, therefore, regarding Pearson/Shanks's quotation, is that it is the urban in all its *complexity* and *diversity* – more often than not produced by inequalities – which defines the contemporary circumstances of humanity as a whole. In fact, it may not be exaggerating the matter to say that the question of the city has superseded the preoccupation in recent decades of arts and humanities critical discourse generally with the signifying body as implicated and expressive, indeed performative, locus. Instead, so the argument might go, it is cities that have become the prime indices of a fast-changing super-modernity. Importantly, however, one should not lose sight in claiming this precisely of Pearson/Shanks's 'congregation of strangers': the body has not been replaced at all but *re-placed*, wandering en masse into the space of the city (not for the first time, of course), performing *in situ*, a relational body or 'switching station' that acts within and is acted upon by its urban surroundings. Thus bodies can be said to both *produce* and *be produced by* the city. And while cities obviously contain bodies, bodies also contain cities. In fact, the city itself functions as an ecological body, one that *facilitates* the circulation of particular socio-economic and cultural discourses while also thereby *delimiting* them. In other words, the various component parts of a city – its built environment, cultures, peoples, networks of communication and so on – operate interdependently, producing – but importantly also restricting or suppressing – possibilities of expression, identification and, in a more acute sense, survival via any number of visible and invisible interactions and overlaps.

In this sense cities can be said always to be 'on the move'; bodies, moreover, move because the city does, and vice versa. The notion of characterising cities according to their physical 'mobilisations' – how things and people moved or behaved within them – was a central concern of Walter Benjamin's in what might be called his dialectical 'thought experiments' (*Denkbilder*) relating to diverse European locations. For example, the improvisational 'porosity' of Naples, in which he observed a form of interchangeability between 'inside' and 'outside', private and public living; or Moscow's interpenetration of the technological on the one hand and the primitive on the other. Meanwhile, Benjamin's major work, the fragmentary *Arcades Project* – in the dual sense of being both unfinished and made up of fragments – centred on the nineteenth-century Parisian arcade as ruin. Once an architectural site promising the fulfilment of urban dwellers' desires, it had come to epitomise, for Benjamin, the transiency and inherent 'will to decay' of capitalism by the early twentieth century. Like the arcade itself, figures such as the *flâneur*, who seemed to operate on the cusp of such transitional 'moments', intrigued Benjamin for the way they embodied the contradictions of evolving urban conditions: a man immersed in the crowd, yet alienated from it. And the archetypal figure of the urban walker or 'wanderer' continues to have currency in the twenty-first century as the embodiment of the city's transiency. (Petra Küppers's contribution to Part 1 critiques the figure of the modern-day *flâneur*, specifically with regard to its gendering.)

As we have seen in relation to population figures specifically, cities change at differing rates and for a multitude of reasons, in some instances significantly revising their own physical or ecological constellations in the process. Like bodies they alter their appearance, growing and shrinking, renewing themselves, decaying 'naturally', being razed or 'quaked' to the ground, or dying out completely. Los Angeles is known to some as the hundred mile city, owing to the way it stretches endlessly along its smog-smothered valley, with no discernable single 'city centre' (Sudjic 1992). Another US city, Detroit, possessed a modern 'civilising centre' as little as half a century ago, but effectively lost it. With so-called 'white flight' in the 1960s and 1970s – a term which masks a plethora of complex, interconnected socio-economic and cultural factors – it deteriorated rapidly into a vast ghost town of abandoned civic, commercial and residential buildings as its white working- and middle-class demographic migrated to the city's suburbs: a modern industrial city with a large void at its core. The same can be said of Tokyo, but for very different reasons. Roland Barthes writes in his detailed account of the world's largest city – entitled *Empire of Signs* – that its spatial centre, the forbidden residential parklands of an unseen Emperor, are far from being an expression of power. Instead, having an 'evaporated notion' at the heart of the city has the function of 'giving the whole movement of the city the stabilising benefit of its central emptiness, permanently forcing traffic to be diverted. In this way … the system of the imaginary circulates via detours and return trips around an empty subject' (Barthes 1982: 30–2). Arguably there is a philosophical principle at stake here, which relates to notions of absence and presence as the respective progenitors of 'social being'. In both instances, though, a performative premise applies. In other words, the constellation of the urban installs constitutive effects and behaviours in the body of the citizenry. And these implicitly render ways of being in the city 'inconceivable' as much as they do conceivable. Barthes's concern is to contrast the discursive modes of the 'oriental void' and the (European) occidental one, which is built around 'space-filling plenitude' or presence: a holistic urban core in which certain identities are made available to or are sought by the citizen via the concentric arrangement of 'civilising institutions'. These are articulated through the built embodiments of spirituality (churches), power (offices), finance (banks), goods (shops) and general 'language flow' (cafés, bars). The implied security of that particular form can be violated, of course, in all kinds of ways: having been split down the middle for 28 Cold War years, Berlin is still engaged in a process of attempting to 'centre itself' again. When the Wall went up in 1961, it was West Berlin that ended up 'emasculated' in terms of those centralising institutions. As a result there was no up or down town to which one might take oneself. The tendency was for neighbourhood clusters to form and key civic amenities existed randomly in all parts of the enclave. When the Wall tumbled in 1989, the problem for the conjoining city was often how to negotiate the inevitable duplication of key institutions that had resulted.

I could go on when it comes to the performative morphology, texture or substance of cities: Venice by design the eternal floating city (just), New Orleans on the other hand by 'natural accident' – supposedly compounded by wanton political failure – the temporarily flooded one. But there are too many resonant examples to list, and I assume the sense of what is being said is probably clear by now. To make something of a theatrical analogy: cities take forms in which specific kinds of showing and looking, doing and interacting occur. In short, and at the risk of sounding trite, they are places in which things happen in a multitude of ways, and the ways in which they actually *do* happen are what determines how these cities and their inhabitants (are permitted to) *become what they are*, but they are not always going to remain that way.

Urban rights: theatre/play

In this respect I have always found a wholly irregular expansion of the German word *Schauplatz* quite useful. Meaning literally 'a place for viewing' and/or 'showing', and hence a kind of theatre, it signifies the 'event-site' or 'arena of operation' in everyday usage. In other words, it is where important things are 'going down', where spectacles take place, where the cut and thrust of 'battle' may occur. By usefully corrupting the term to *Schauspielplatz* you make explicit the degree to which performance is intrinsic to such 'scenes' or events. Thus, the urban *Schauspielplatz* or 'place of performance' is an integrated location in which there is both 'staged drama' or 'drama for show' (*Schauspiel*) and play(ing) (*spiel[en]*). Importantly, where the former may suggest it is conducted 'officially', for or on behalf of the spectator-citizen, the latter involves the spectator-citizen's participation in the playground (*Spielplatz*) that is the 'unofficial' or 'unaccounted for' city. Perhaps there is a tension in that relationship between the discursive enactment of that which is supposed to happen – or given to be enacted – and the unplanned, random, sometimes 'anarchic' play that arises as a consequence of the former's failure, inadequacy or inappropriateness. In other words, the former is premised on the idea – not dissimilar to the one that might apply to the upholding of a 'working society' of a stable, *functioning* city, one that serves its inhabitants' needs, interests and aspirations, and that is socially *just*. So, the city is built around the operation of certain agreements, a functional order that strives, moreover, to be moral as well as pragmatic. When it turns out not to be quite so – that is, when it turns out to be deluded about fulfilling its role in this regard, or when it implicitly disallows certain claims to or possibilities of existence – radical 'play' can assert itself in myriad ways, challenging the city's authority. (The appearance of phenomena such as graffiti and its offshoots is probably the most obvious example of this, as we shall see in Part 4.)

For Henri Lefebvre, that seminal theorist of the social production of urban space, the city 'revealed the contradictions of society' (Kofman and Lebas in Lefebvre 1996: 14). In particular, as Ben Highmore succinctly puts it, for Lefebvre 'the contemporary urban everyday of capitalism is characterised by the saturation of mass cultural forms ... penetrating everywhere as an act to cover and hide the discontinuities of everyday life'. But, Highmore goes on, such 'fissures in the urban fabric' – referring, for example, to 'spaces of different temporalities, outmoded spaces with distinct cultural characteristics' – existed and had the capacity precisely to 'interrupt the homogenising and hypnotising effects of capitalist standardisation through their cultural and historical differences' (Highmore 2002: 140–1). Central to a tactical, embodied response to a normative urban scene was the notion of the ludic city in the form of the 'festival' (*fête*) or 'collective game', which Lefebvre saw as the ultimate expression of social revolution. Staking his position on the city as the place in which use value is potentially preserved, resisting its subordination to exchange value – 'an urban reality for "users" and not for capitalist speculators' (1996: 167–8) – Lefebvre outlines his desire to 'restitute the *fête* by changing daily life' (ibid.: 168). In 'Right to the City', which, as the title suggests, polemically asserts the urban dweller's claim to participatory citizenship, he writes that such a 'renewed *fête*' was 'fundamentally linked to play' and involved 'subordinating to play rather than to subordinate play to the "seriousness" of culturalism. ... Only relatively recently and through institutions has theatre become "cultural", while play has lost its place and value in society' (ibid.: 171). 'Theatre', it is implied, has effectively been annexed and institutionalised by a privileged, complacent constituency of society when it ought to be both situated and sought (or encountered) on the street: 'to city people the urban centre is movement, the unpredictable, the possible, and encounters. For them it is either "spontaneous theatre" or nothing. ... Leaving aside representation, ornamentation and decoration, art can become *praxis* and *poiesis* on a social scale' (ibid.: 172–3). Thus, Lefebvre envisages a role for art that creatively produces the city in the interests of its citizens.

Consciously or not Lefebvre's anti-elitist proposal echoes the tenor of his compatriot Antonin Artaud's famous treatise 'No More Masterpieces', written some thirty or forty years previously. For Artaud, the urban public 'has the sense of what is true and always reacts to it when it appears. Today, however, we must look for it in the street, not on stage. And if the crowds in the street were given a chance to show their dignity as human beings, they would always do so' (Artaud 1974: 57–8). Moreover, Bertolt Brecht, that other pillar of twentieth-century theatre innovation, whose entire theory of epic theatre is premised on taking seriously 'that theatre whose setting is the street' (as the poem 'On Everyday Theatre', dated slightly earlier than Artaud's statement, puts it), is none too far from this impulse either, as we shall see (Brecht 1976: 176).

Psychogeography

If the likes of Lefebvre seem to be addressing the socio-political dimension of the *Schauspielplatz* of urban existence at the level of conscious engagement, a significant psycho-analytical and geographical aspect relating to this hybrid term is brought into play by Steve Pile via a well known Freudian anecdote. Employed as an example in the psychoanalyst's famous essay on the 'uncanny' to illustrate his personal experience of the so-called 'strangely familiar' within the space of an 'unknown city', Freud narrates the following tale of 'circular walking' on a hot summer afternoon in Genoa:

> I found myself in a quarter of whose character I could not long remain in doubt. Nothing but painted women were to be seen at the windows of the small houses, and I hastened to leave the narrow streets at the next turning. But after having wandered about for a time without inquiring my way, I suddenly found myself back in the same street, where my presence was now beginning to excite attention. I hurried away once more, only to arrive by another *détour* at the same place yet a third time. Now, however, a feeling overcame me which I can only describe as uncanny, and I was glad enough to find myself back at the piazza I had left a short while before, without any further voyages of discovery.
>
> (Freud 1990: 359)

The compulsive, subconscious return outlined in this event is understood as repeatedly performing the transition from desire to fear: 'his desire to know and his fear of knowing', as Pile describes it, adding: 'for Freud uncanniness is linked to boys' feelings about women's genitalia – both as archaic site/sight of desire and the site/sight of evidence of castration ... a desire to be (w)hole and a fear of being punished' (in Borden et al. 2002: 265–6). Be that as it may, the fear of punishment can alternatively, or simultaneously, be equated with the fear of public exposure: being outed as subconsciously desiring that which is morally frowned upon by society. Importantly, though,

Pile points elsewhere to the way in which 'The city becomes the "*show place*" of [Freud's] desire/fear. More than a stage on which the vicissitudes of mental life play out, *the city constructs the experience* (in mind and body)' [my emphases] (in Bridge and Watson 2003: 81). Although Pile's piece on 'Sleepwalking in the Modern City' features in Part 1 of this volume (for good reasons), the notion of place producing psychic responses naturally introduces the important realm of psychogeography, which is covered in Part 2 in specific relation to Situationism. As the introduction to this part strives to show, the Situationists' aims certainly had socio-political change in cities in mind, but their preoccupation was with the complex role of desire in the playing out of any such revolution. Rather than a rational blueprint for an improved urban ecology, the Situationists proposed 'disruptive mappings' premised on spontaneous encounters and events, as we shall see.

Between disciplines

Squeezing a further drop out of Pearson/Shanks – though less from the quote with which I began than their joint book as a whole – I would wish to ally the present volume with the interdisciplinary premise of their endeavour. The latter concentrates its energies on theatre and archaeology explicitly, but stretches beyond those fields to incorporate aspects of anthropology, architecture and myth, to whisper nothing of human/cultural geography and cartography. The tell-tale use of a forward slash in *Theatre/Archaeology*, moreover, already points graphically to some form of intersection or act of 'going over' (otherwise the link would have been made by 'and').[3] Like Benjamin's pertinent declaration that 'memory is not an instrument for exploring the past but its theatre' (1997a: 314), archaeology too is performed or 'given life' in and by its mobilisations in the present. In its attempt to calibrate that to which the past might amount, archaeology is dependent on performance for it to *come about* or *become*. Not only that, but the method of enquiry of *Theatre/Archaeology* clearly exploits the intersection of theory and practice, suggesting by implication that the former can indeed be the latter and vice versa, to the extent that the structural opposition of the two begins usefully to disintegrate. Pearson, strictly speaking the 'theatre' half of this authorial double-act – though I threaten to destroy precisely the position I have just established by asserting that – casts himself above all as an artist who, typically, might draw on his immediate experience of walking in the city (in this instance Copenhagen) 'as a kind of anthropological and archaeological enquiry ... to reveal the city through purposeful activity' (Pearson and Shanks 2001: 147). (The approach hinted at here is a central concern of Part 1, Walking/Theatres.)

Returning to the tenor of the present book's preamble for a moment (named so with deliberation in case you missed it), there are of course any number of ways of organising a reader relating to the city. As I have suggested, the plethora of possibilities is redolent of the multiplicitousness of cities themselves. Thus there are anthologies of texts that variously use culture, architecture, social sciences, gender, postmodernism, the 'unknown', hieroglyphics and so on as their conceptual or thematic framing devices for a critical contemplation of urban space. Striking in all of these publications is not only the range of disciplines officially represented by the contributors – even if it is billed, say, as a reader in architecture theory – but also the degree to which these writers are compelled to articulate themselves by recourse to fields outside of their supposed expertise: geographers on art and performance, anthropologists on the built environment and so on. In fact, it would be true to say that a primary motive in putting together a reader on performance and the contemporary city is, to some extent, to reclaim the term 'performance' for the field of performance given its frequent application in other discourses on urbanity, while simultaneously acknowledging the desirability of actively upholding the interdisciplinary methodology of much of this work.

One compilation of texts I am particularly fond of – in fact, I would go so far as to admit my considerable envy of the editors for the inventiveness of its conceit – is entitled simply *City A–Z*. Describing itself as being 'a contribution to a wave of experimentation which is concerned with writing the city' (Pile and Thrift 2000: xiii), the editors have collaged together a lexicon of entries – several per letter of the alphabet – relating to the urban experience (perhaps this too is a form of 'dream dictionary'). You can drift at your leisure from 'air' to 'airports', 'dream' to 'dust', 'tourists' to 'traffic lights', each entry penned by a different author. One of the several suggested modes of reading is provided by a metro map of 'entries-as-stops' inside the back cover of the book. These form specific urban 'themes-as-lines': for example, 'dis/order', 'nature', 'pleasure'. The approach is acknowledged to be influenced by Simon Patterson's well known rewriting of Harry Beck's London Underground map – entitled *The Great Bear* (1992) – in which, for example, the Victoria Line becomes 'Italian artists', the Circle Line 'philosophers' and the Jubilee Line 'footballers'. So a form of relationship to the publication is proposed in which the premise is placed on chance encounters occurring for the 'wandering reader' along the various routes or, more resonantly perhaps, at various intersections. Arguably, then, readers are positioned to experience an enhanced, affirmative sense of themselves assembling their own urban narratives in a form of 'textual drift'.

Following from this, and for the purposes of approaching the collection of texts presented here, I would wish to highlight two key determinants, both of which direct us – finally, I promise – to Pearson and Shanks. First, regarding the layout of the book, it is organised into parts relating to certain urban *phenomena*: aspects or features of the city, as well as actions or movements within it, rather than themes. So, on the one hand there are theatres, places, things, rhythms, flows, and on the other walking, drifting, sounding, playing and visioning. I have attempted as far as possible in this title selection to imply a linkage: 'walking theatres', 'drifting things', 'playing place' and so on. Inevitably there are overlaps between these diverse aspects of the city's make-up – in the same way that streets are not strictly separate from buildings, but a form of continuation – but the active binding factor and, therefore, rationale for this, is the spatio-temporal movement implied by *performance*. This second determinant provides both the all-encompassing framework for the book – the lens through which everything is viewed and weighed – and the conceptual dynamic that serves to interlink the phenomena in question. The writer Jonathan Raban's 1970s account of modern metropolitan existence *Soft City* recognised some time ago now not only the extent to which urban living was dependent on 'performances' but also that these were frequently fleeting and imperceptible:

> in every contact with every stranger, the self is projected and exhibited – or at least, a version of the self, a convenient mask which can be looked at and listened to, quickly comprehended, easily forgotten. … It does seem to me to be a logical product of the way in which cities make us live in them, of the urban necessity of playing many parts to a succession of short-order audiences.
>
> (Raban 1998: 72–3)

Thus, the 'hard city' or 'outer shell' of the built environment is sustained by the 'softness' of human movement and (inter)activity in all its variations. But arguably 'things' such as buildings can begin to *move* too as events begin to happen in and around them. One need only think in this regard of the enormously powerful impact of Christo's famous wrapping of the highly contested Reichstag building in Berlin six years after the fall of the Wall. The event attracted a staggering five million visitors within the period of a fortnight – which is as many as Tate Modern in London receives in a year (and *that* is considered overwhelming) – marking the transition of both the building and the German nation towards reunified democracy. As I have described elsewhere (in my book *Street Scenes: Brecht, Benjamin and Berlin*) in a passage worth quoting at length, what emerges as significant in Christo's piece is:

> first, at the interface between the formal functioning of the work; second, what it actually takes to bring it about; and, last, how it mobilises its

viewing constituency in the contextual circumstances – historical, political, topographical – in which it ultimately occurs. Each one of these aspects is premised on generating *movement*. Bureaucratic authorities are moved to negotiate, debate and legislate in what Christo refers to as the software stage. Spectators are moved to participate in the event physically – by being there and responding to it – and imaginatively, by speculating creatively over the broader significance of its impact. The formal act itself, finally, occurs as both a time and motion-based event. Lasting a fortnight and incorporating a three-phase process – the hardware stage – of *becoming*, then *being*, wrapped, as well as becoming unwrapped again, the estranged building also reproduces the remarkable sense of a breathing movement as the tied fabric envelops it and the wind gets under its skirts. The machinery of 'wrapping' corresponds formally in fact to the Brechtian sense of a 'staging of a veiling' in which a familiar object or circumstance is not just made strange but *shown* to be made so. The phenomenon in question both is and is not itself, replicating the Brechtian actor's *demonstration* of a character or situation and pointing to that character/situation's capacity to 'be otherwise'. Here a 'sick' building – one that is 'not quite itself' – is bandaged (or mummified), undergoing a two-week period of healing and convalescence in which it is 'wrapped as the Reichstag and unwrapped as the Bundestag' (Large 2002: 612). Effectively it has had 'the gift of life' breathed back into it, a repackaged present (or swaddled rebirthing) to the city from the artists. What you witness at each individual stage and as a whole is the ritualised performance of democracy in action.

(Whybrow 2005: 180–1)

Regarding the cultural/archaeological artefact, Shanks urges that the question, in evaluating it, be posed not in terms of ' "What is it?" Instead ask "What does it do?" Enquire of its social work. … The task is to establish the relationships which make an artefact what it is' (Pearson and Shanks 2001: 53). And the 'purposeful activity' of archaeology implies dealing also 'with the gaps between things – the dirt trapped between floor tiles – documented trivia – the result of slow processes of life and death' (ibid.: 44). There is, in fact, no better exemplification of this than a 'scientific artwork' by Gail Olding, which is documented in *Breathing Cities: The Architecture of Movement* (Barley 2000). Entitled *Dirt Analysis*, the work performs a kind of urban archaeology-cum-forensic practice. Olding collected scrapings of accumulated dirt from under her fingernails having spent a period of time in five separate European cities. These she placed in Petri dishes and sent off for formal forensic analysis. The results revealed distinctive differences that implicitly proposed 'the very singular presence of each city'. Thus, 'in Amsterdam diamond dust was detected. Traces of red, white and blue fibres were found in Paris, and residue from diesel fumes were prevalent in Berlin. … As the analysis shows, the city is ingested by us, consumed by the body' (in Barley 2000: 77).

For Shanks, then, attending to the materiality of the cultural artefact corresponds to maintaining

> a sensitivity to its historicity, its life and the way it gathers many sorts of things, people, feelings, aspirations. The assemblages respect no absolute distinctions between cultural categories, such as things and people, values and materials, strategies and resources, architectures and dispositions. And in this archaeological cyborg world we will have to talk a great deal of 'might' and 'if', of slippage and fluidity, of mess and what is missing, of gaps and bridges between different worlds, of time breaking up, moments lost and regained. We will need our dramaturgical imagination.
>
> (Pearson and Shanks 2001: 101)

So it is with the performance of the global cultural phenomenon that is the contemporary city, a living machine in which, as the artist Richard Wentworth once casually remarked to me, 'everything you see and hear is the consequence of a decision'. Thus, cities are *made* by human beings, even if the 'decisions' that have driven that making have often been unconscious ones. As cultural artefacts cities similarly recontextualise or 'write over' the relics and memories of their pasts in the present, while also constantly seeking out that which is new and generating material visions for the future. Of course, in making such a general claim, I realise that I may well be falling into the 'universal we' trap with which I began this introduction. I would wish the reader to keep in mind at all times, therefore, an assumption of geocultural diversity and difference in the way cities relate to performance. By the same token I am only too aware that this selection here reflects – simply because I cannot hope adequately to cover 'everywhere' – a bias towards events and phenomena relating to certain kinds of cities – London enjoying a particular prominence in this regard – as well as certain kinds of discourses around cities. Being based in a privileged UK/European context I fully acknowledge that this anthology will not manage to address directly all manner of relevant issues arising in cities around the world. One need only point out the lacking coverage of the 'broken city' that is Baghdad to underscore the point. However, I sincerely hope that there is much to be gained from the examples that *are* given, precisely because of the places to which they may refer but also over and above their specific localities.

Notes

1. Fascinated by the implications of this rapid expansion in Lagos, the architect Rem Koolhaas has engaged – as part of an investigation into the state of world urbanisation entitled the 'Harvard Project on the City' – in a long-term exploration of 'the hidden logic that makes a "dysfunctional" city function' (DVD notes, *Lagos Wide and Close: an Interactive Journey into an Exploding City*, Amsterdam: Submarine, 2005: 1).

2. In *The Vanishing Map* Stephen Barber describes the post-Cold War 'regime change' in Eastern Europe in more playful, quasi-allegorical terms: 'On one occasion, an authoritarian power based on the eastern edge of Europe grasped the entire eastern lands of the continent and rendered their inhabitants subject to a capricious regime in which vast monuments were revered, only for that initiative to be abruptly overturned, and the same lands seized by a satanic trade cartel based on the western edge of Europe; the liberated inhabitants began to celebrate the onset of their new masters' power, but before long, that euphoria turned to dismay' (2006: 42).

3. Pearson himself pointed this out, in fact citing his co-author as the original source, at the beginning of a keynote speech given at the University of Plymouth (conference entitled 'The Hidden City: Mythogeography and Writing for Site-Specific Performance', 4 October 2008). Observant readers will perhaps have noticed that the forward slash has been adopted for the titles of parts in this publication with a similar end in mind.

Part 1
Walking/Theatres

Text sources

1.1   Jonathan Watts (2004) 'How Scratched Car Revealed Price of a Peasant's Life', *Guardian*, 8 April: 17.

1.2   Walter Benjamin and Asja Lacis (1997) 'Naples', *One-Way Street*, intro. S. Sontag, trans. E. Jephcott and K. Shorter, London and New York: Verso: 167–76.

1.3   Tim Etchells (1999) 'Eight Fragments on Theatre and the City', *Certain Fragments*, London and New York: Routledge: 76–83.

1.4   Steve Pile (2000) 'Sleepwalking in the Modern City: Walter Benjamin and Sigmund Freud in the World of Dreams', *A Companion to the City*, ed. G. Bridge, and S. Watson, Oxford: Blackwell: 75–86.

1.5   Petra Küppers (1999) 'Moving in the Cityscape: Performance and the Embodied Experience of the *Flâneur*', *New Theatre Quarterly*, 15(4): 308–17.

1.6   Wrights and Sites (2006), 'A Manifesto for a New Walking Culture: "Dealing with the City"', *Performance Research*, 11(2): 115–22.

Introduction

> The artwork that turns us into witnesses leaves us, above all, unable to stop thinking, talking and reporting what we've seen. We're left like the people in Brecht's poem who've witnessed a road accident, still stood on the street corner discussing what happened, borne on by our responsibility to events.
>
> Tim Etchells, *Certain Fragments*

Urban encounters

In his discussion of contemporary performance's preoccupation with producing witnesses as opposed to spectators, the writer and director Tim Etchells talks of a relationship to the artwork premised on 'feel[ing] the weight of things and one's own place in them ... an invitation to be here and be now' (1999: 17–18). Ultimately, as the quotation at the top of the page indicates, he invokes an image of us 'left, like the people in Brecht's poem' (ibid.: 18), by which he means 'On Everyday Theatre'. The poem not only represents an early recognition of the performative nature of everyday life itself, but also argues for the imperative of art to seek a connection with the quotidian. Wittily Brecht identifies the stagehands as the true witnesses of the overblown spectacle that is the theatre. For they are the ones, positioned in the transitional space 'between dressing room and stage', who get a glimpse of the 'mysterious transformation' that occurs in that moment when 'an actor leaves the dressing room [and] a king appears on stage'. The performer on the street corner, by contrast, is 'no sleepwalker who must not be addressed [nor] high priest holding divine service' (Brecht 1976: 178). Instead, as the witness to incidents on the street, he or she is a demonstrator who, as Elizabeth Wright points out, 'must not identify with the bearing of the other but must "quote" him so the audience will see the split between who speaks and who is spoken' (1989: 32). The poem served, of course, as the prototype for Brecht's foundational model for an epic theatre, the 'Street Scene' (Brecht 1978: 121–9). For Brecht it signified 'a big step towards making the art of theatre profane and secular and stripping it of religious elements', a move that encroached upon the daily life realms of the erotic, business, politics, law, religion and, not least, 'the application of theatrical techniques to politics in fascism' (Brecht 1993: 115). And, as Etchells seems to be suggesting in his observation, the poem addresses the combined roles of both witness and reporter, of a spatio-temporal 'being here now', which feels 'exactly what it is to be in this place and this time' (Etchells 1999: 18).

What appears to be at stake in the crash scene is less the truth of what occurred than a form of opening up of possibilities or alternatives that induce participation in the event. It proposes the replication of that which the urban sociologist Richard Sennett has theorised (in Fyfe and Bannister's description) as the desirability of encountering disorderly, painful events in the city because of the way that they may force inhabitants to engage with 'otherness': to go beyond defined boundaries of self (in Fyfe 1998: 264). Sennett's concern is, in a sense, to 'naturalise' the experience of disruption on the streets of the city because without it our lives become alienated, intolerant of the concept of disorder to such an extent that our responses turn all the more aggressive when we *do* encounter situations of conflict. A forced engagement with 'otherness' serves then as the prelude to civilised and civilising social life, a notion endorsed by Robins (again in Fyfe and Bannister's words): 'the readiness to be out of control, combined with a maturity to handle the consequences [forms] the basis of an urban public and political culture' (ibid.: 264). As Brecht explains in the 'Street Scene' essay itself:

> The bystanders may not have observed what happened, or they may simply not agree with him, may 'see things a different way'; the point is that the demonstrator acts the behaviour of driver or victim or both in such a way that the bystanders are able to form an opinion about the accident.
>
> (Brecht 1978: 121)

Central to this mechanism operating successfully is that the 'demonstration admits it is a demonstration (and does not pretend to be the actual event)', in the same way that the theatre should not pretend *not* to be the construct that it is (ibid.: 122). Later in the essay Brecht establishes the relationship of the 'Street Scene' model to the notion of *Verfremdung* (or distanciation), arguing that 'The direct changeover from representation to commentary that is so characteristic of the epic theatre is still more easily recognised as one element of any street demonstration' (ibid.: 126). Referring to the 'Street Scene' model, Fredric Jameson describes the V-effect as the 'instant of intrusion into the everyday: it is what constantly demands to be explained and re-explained' (1998: 84). So, as witnesses of everyday life, but ultimately also of theatre, we are allotted positions not only of performing the act of distanciated seeing but, in a kind of double move, of recognising the self-reflective nature of that act of performance. As Jameson reiterates: 'The theory of estrangement ... must always estrange us from the everyday; the theory is thus itself an acting out of the process; the dramaturgy is itself a drama' (ibid.: 84).

As the poem 'On Everyday Theatre' goes on to discuss, the street scene situation ultimately has implications related to social justice. The demonstrator

'Knows that much depends on his exactness: whether the innocent man / Escapes ruin, whether the injured man is compensated' (Brecht 1976: 177). It is a matter not simply of establishing what may have happened but of allowing what may be at stake ideologically in a quotidian incident like this to emerge. In other words, the street scene encapsulates the form of the Brechtian *Gestus*: the 'pregnant moment' or act that crystallises social relations. And, in doing so, it sets up a clear link between the events of real life and their emerging or potential 'readability' as contradictory constructs, as revelatory of the way social processes can 'appear' in the detail of human behaviour. As Florian Vaßen observes, Brecht's 'philosophy of the street' 'reworks sociological and cultural analysis in a way which attempts to develop anticipatory behavioural lessons from necessary forms of response to the new realities of the city' (1998: 78). The street scene model also underlines the intended 'usability' of Brechtian production in its day. The spectacle of the 'accident' emerges not merely as an abstract model of an epic scene, a means of questioning the dangerously mesmeric 'traffic flow' of life as it is represented to us, but also as a significant marker for our personal experience of the street. Hence, as a trope or *gestic* moment that encapsulates the unexpected rupturing of the habitual and familiar necessary in the process of 'seeing', it prepares us for our implicated role in the encounter with the 'shock' of alterity in the streets of the city.

Urban scenes

An intriguingly literal and contemporary playing out of the Brechtian accident paradigm is presented in Part 1 via a 2004 *Guardian* newspaper report: 'How scratched car revealed the price of a peasant's life' (this volume *Performance and The Contemporary City*, hereafter PCC, pp. 26–7). With a delicious irony and retrospective affirmation of the validity of Brecht's thinking – given the context of the new, emergent China and the writer's own anti-capitalist politics – the article describes events surrounding the so-called 'BMW incident'. Having but scratched the wing-mirror of a BMW car belonging to the wife of one of China's new business tycoons as they passed by in their tractor laden with onions, a hapless peasant and his wife found a very Brechtian kind of 'class question' being screamed at them by the driver: 'How can you *afford* to scratch my car?' Without disclosing too much here, what followed this particular street scene would appear to supply all the ingredients for a perfect and real 'gestic parable'. A thoroughly modern Chinese drama of social inequality and rough justice unfolded, which included the peasant's wife being run over and killed, a retrial after accusations of bribery and, most significantly perhaps, in general terms, a mass debate about the incident on the 'new street corner': an Internet chatroom. With the participation of literally hundreds of thousands of Chinese citizens this witnessed a form of public performance of democracy, which for many of those involved represented perhaps the only 'affordable means' of expressing dissatisfaction with this particular enactment of so-called justice.

Walter Benjamin's 'Naples' essay (co-written with Asja Lacis), one of several 'city portraits' undertaken by him, also opens with a striking gestic moment at a street corner: a disgraced priest, being paraded through the streets, bumps into a wedding procession and promptly resumes authority over his 'mocking flock' as he offers his blessing to the newly-weds. Benjamin goes on to demonstrate how the 'rich barbarism' of social justice is performed in the symbiotic relationship between God-fearing Catholicism and the lawless Camorra clan that controls this city: 'Confession alone, not the police, is a match for the self-administration of the criminal world' (*PCC*, p. 28). In other words, the church is content for a gang of outlaws to act as regulator of both criminal and civic life in the city as long as the former can be perceived to be exercising overall, spiritual power. Every crime is justifiable as long as it admits to its sinfulness before God. Guilt may always be purged, thus extending full licence to the Camorra to go about its 'dirty work' with impunity.

While such a highly codified local way of life – closed, secretive, threatening – cannot easily accommodate the outsider, Benjamin's account is distinctive for its recognition of not only an inherent theatricality but also a so-called 'porosity' in the way the city functions. These two features intersect in fact in that porosity – 'the inexhaustible law of life in this city' (*PCC*, p. 31) – refers to the way in which the interiors of the built environment become exteriors and vice versa, producing 'innumerable, simultaneously animated theatres' (*PCC*, p. 30). Thus, the 'living room reappears on the street' and, once more echoing the Brechtian *Gestus*, 'each private attitude or act is permeated by streams of communal life' (*PCC*, p. 33). Extrapolated so as to serve as a general motif within the narrative of cities, the term 'porosity' points eventually 'to the relationship between architecture and action, and in particular the indeterminate, improvised character of everyday life as dramatic performance' (Gilloch 1997: 25). Moreover, if a governing 'collective deadly sin' can be identified for Naples – and Benjamin does precisely that – it is *indolence*. This plays itself out in the way general business is conducted in the city, which 'borders on a game of chance' (*PCC*, p. 32). Archetypical in this respect is the figure of the vendor standing on the street corner who employs all the improvisatory guile of the trickster to woo the crowd. Living off your wits in this way is the lazy option because it is easier; ultimately, however, in the same way as the city's own lottery trades on a fantasy of potential success, the reality is that you probably won't end up a winner in the long term.

A useful contrast to the fear-stricken regimen outlined in Benjamin's Naples portrait may be seen in the similarly unofficial but benign enactment of coexistence in the big city as described by the urban campaigner and architecture critic Jane Jacobs. Her 1960s portrayal of the 'sidewalk ballet' taking place on her Greenwich Village street in New York City is particularly well known (Jacobs 1993: 65–71). Importantly she observes in the everyday comings and goings on Hudson Street not only something that can be called an 'art form of the city' but also a kind of reassuring communication as well as informal security between neighbours, who may nevertheless remain strangers to one another: 'We nod; we each glance quickly up and down the street, then look back to each other and smile. We have done this many a morning for more than ten years, and we both know what it means: all is well' (ibid.: 61–2). Reminiscent of the 'phatic communication' invoked by de Certeau in his oft-cited discussion of walking in the city (1988: 91–110), this form of social enactment appears to have little purpose other than to acknowledge and thereby validate the presence of the other. Arguing against the regimentations of urban planning and policing, and for the diversity, randomness and informality of inner city neighbourhoods, Jacobs proposes, however, that such exchanges importantly bring with them their own implicit, but non-coercive, self-regulatory order.

If the accounts by Benjamin and Jacobs (the latter not included here) discover all manner of performances in the quotidian city, Tim Etchells's impulse in 'Eight Fragments on Theatre and the City' is perhaps rather to plunder and recycle the latter for its metaphorical artefacts. Etchells begins by referring to the clandestine arrival in a strange city and its exploration the following morning as 'acting out an allegory of knowledge' (*PCC*, p. 36). Continuing, seemingly in Benjaminian vein, moreover, he elaborates on the 'fascination of ruined places, of incomplete places' as 'the best places to play – stinking of previous use, ready for transgression' (*PCC*, p. 38). These liminal spaces are on the cusp of an eruption, a palimpsest-like 'writing over', which leads Etchells eventually to the striking conundrum: 'Do you have to have lived in a place a long time before you have the right to lie about it?' (*PCC*, p. 40). The paradoxical logic of that would seem to suggest, whether stranger or long-term inhabitant, the inescapable tendency, ultimately, is always already to be 'telling lies' in any account that is given of the city. In other words, the city can only begin to be grasped by the imperfect tales we have to tell of it.

Urban walking and writing

It was Walter Benjamin who articulated as well as enacted most comprehensively a praxis relating to the figure of the *flâneur*: the idle stroller, mingling with the urban masses on the streets, yet remaining a detached observer. Benjamin expounded his thinking chiefly in relation to Baudelaire and nineteenth-century Paris. But his other writings on cities, not least *One-Way Street* (1997a), can be seen as examples of the interactive conjunction of walking and reflecting embodied by the *flâneur*, a drifting figure, prone to distracted digression, to whom, supposedly, the detritus of modern life – from architectural ruins to banal 'things', 'the neglected and the chance ... the marginal and the forgotten' (Vidler 2000: 116) – throws the macroscopic into relief. In this view, as David Frisby reminds us, 'a neglected dimension of *flânerie* is revealed, namely the *flâneur* as producer (of texts, images, etc.)' (2001: 13). The practice implies the application of the collagist's or ragpicker's principle not only to that which is observed on the street but also to the process of reflection and writing: 'Diverse, incongruent elements are rudely dragged from their intellectual moorings to be reassembled in radical and illuminating configurations. The shock-like character of modern social life finds expression in this montage of heterogeneous fragments' (Gilloch 1997: 19). As the writer Iain Sinclair states at the onset of *Lights Out for the Territory*, a late twentieth-century exploration of a specific part of London's East End (from which a short extract is included in Part 4): 'Walking is the best way to explore and exploit the city' (1997: 4). Thus, urban walking continues to be viewed not only as a fundamental means in itself of engaging with the everyday city but also as possessing revelatory potential.

There is an important elusiveness in the action of the walker, which is redolent of the city's own unpredictable movement: I move as or because the city does and vice versa. The concept of characterising cities according to their 'mobilisations' was also one of Benjamin's preoccupations, as we have seen: the dialectic between how cities moved and how you moved in them. Speaking at a much later moment in the twentieth century, the architecture critic Neil Leach declares that: 'the "wanderer" represents the freedom and flux of the city ... [an] archetypal creature of our contemporary condition, a creature whose existence reflects the very transiency of the city' (1999: 159). Walking promises, moreover, a corporeal brushing with the 'real' and 'immediate' (as well as 'ever-shifting'), emphasising it as a *practice* that affords a particular sensibility to the detail of quotidian activity in the city.

As we saw earlier, the dislocation effected by the hypothetical occurrence of an accident on the street produces conditions in which unexpected perspectives present themselves. Brecht's model seeks not only to find theatre in everyday life, but also to emphasise the dual role of the witness as both compromised and responsible raconteur, character and performer. Arguably that function can be allied with Benjamin's preoccupations with the *flâneur*, a figure who is also both a spectator of and performer in 'scenes of the street', that 'dwelling place of the collective' (Benjamin 2002: 423).

At about the same point in history that Brecht was concerned with the articulation of the street scene model, the Austrian novelist Robert Musil was engaged in the writing of the first volume of his unfinished magnum opus, *The Man without Qualities* (1930). Keith Tester identifies 'Musil's use of the devices of *flânerie*' in the novel and 'his tendency to connect them to global problems of existence in cities' (1994: 10–11). According to Tester it is a generalising move that distinguishes his *flânerie* from the Baudelairean paradigm specific to nineteenth-century Paris. Tester's motive is to elucidate a 'dialectic of *flânerie*' between a narrator who observes and defines, but still seems subject to the enigma of the city, and the action of the narrative itself, 'the wandering along a city street of two individuals' (ibid.: 11). He maintains that there is a defining moment in the first, short chapter of the novel when the two individuals are suddenly faced with an accident in the street. Having earlier credited Musil with bringing the *flâneur* figure into the twentieth century through the generalisation suggested above, he now extrapolates this fictional incident into an emblematic comment on the *flâneur*'s fate. Essentially the twentieth century's introduction of technological urban rationalisation, of which 'the problem of traffic' is one effect, could imply the end of this form of 'knowing' the city given the threat posed: 'perhaps the man who is knocked down ... is, in fact, the last *flâneur*' (ibid.: 13).

Of course, as Tester acknowledges, Benjamin had already killed off the *flâneur* once in the streets of Hausmann's nineteenth-century Paris. That was a death associated specifically with the demise of the arcades (interior streets) – which provided both mystery and protection for the idle observer – and, more broadly, with the rationalising impulse of a fast-moving modernity. However, Frisby points at the same time to Benjamin's essay 'The Return of the *Flâneur*', in which he reviews his colleague Franz Hessel's 1929 book on *flânerie* in Berlin (Benjamin 1999: 262–7). The supposed 'decline of *flânerie*' was shown to have 'lacked finality', according to Frisby (2001: 13), who adds: 'If we have witnessed a renewed discourse on the *flâneur* and the practices of *flânerie* in recent decades, then in large part this must be due to our rediscovery of Walter Benjamin's own analysis of this urban figure in the late 1920s and 1930s' (ibid.: 304). So, 'the *flâneur* was back', as Esther Leslie agrees, and this one

> was not just one man in the crowd, but was part of the crowd. ... If the *flâneur* can be bothered to translate his viewing into reviewing, or his thought into theory, then this street furniture provides a bureau and drawing desk on which he can assemble the pieces of litter, the fragments of city lives, into images and narratives.
>
> (In Coles 1999: 85)

The evident resurrection occurring gestures towards an understanding of the role as a changing one in history, one, as Frisby makes clear, that may be attributed not only to Benjamin's critique of the figure, but also to the practice of his own writings (Frisby 2001: 34). As we saw in the Preamble to the present volume, Frisby indicates later in the same chapter that Benjamin's '*One-Way Street* is itself a constellation or "construction" of aphorisms as a street', a conjunction of the acts of walking and writing that invites the reader in turn to 'stroll along the textual one way street' (ibid.: 45). The historical shift to which claims may be made, then, is from 'the negative conception of the dandyish stroller and producer of harmless physiognomies to the notion of the more directed observer and investigator of the signifiers of the city' (ibid.: 35), indeed to the one who would bear witness.

Benjamin can be given credit, then, not only for a specific kind of attention to urban detail but also for a method that Susan Sontag identifies as the slowness of the Saturnine, melancholic temperament: 'things appear at a distance, come forward slowly' (Benjamin 1997a: 13–14). The speed of modernity is forced, effectively by the act of *noticing*, to slow down. It is a method that allows, as Benjamin himself puts it, 'the simultaneous perception of everything that potentially is happening in this single space' (2002: 418–19). Hence, as Gilloch summarises:

> For Benjamin, the buildings, spaces, monuments and objects that compose the urban environment both are a response to, and reflexively structure, patterns of human social activity. Architecture and action shape each other; they interpenetrate. The metropolis constitutes a frame or theatre of activity. The buildings of the city, and its interior setting in particular, form casings for action in which, or on which, human subjects leave 'traces', signs of their passing, markers or clues to their mode of existence.
>
> (Gilloch 1997: 6)

In a similar mode of 'deceleration', Brecht's so-called 'heir', the East German playwright Heiner Müller, seizes on the image of the pedestrian as a metaphor for the necessary process, as enacted by the writer, of slowing down contemporary life. In an interview he observes: 'in this modern, far more mobile society, the pedestrian – that's me – the pedestrian who, unlike the driver, has no bodyguard, is far more exposed to danger and has to be faster even than the cars in order to survive' (in Müller 1995: viii–ix). Paradoxically, it would seem, the pedestrian-writer of postmodernity approaching the turn of the millennium has to be 'quicker' in order to bring about a deceleration that might produce space: 'The terrible thing at present is of course that all that remains is time or velocity or the passage of time, but no more space. What one has to do now is to create and occupy spaces acting against this acceleration' (in Glendinning et al. 2000: 7). Hence, the pedestrian's physicality or 'presencing' within the spaces of the city is analogous to a writing that proves obstructive as well as slippery within the fast, saturated flow of mediated experiencing.

Such a perception of the city is perhaps what Steve Pile has in mind when he invokes the concept of 'sleepwalking', specifically with regard to the way Benjamin utilised dream analysis to interpret modernity and the city. The world of capitalist relations supposedly cast a phantasmagorical spell over people, producing a form of alienated, collective trance. Attention to dream-work, in particular the 'point of waking', provides Benjamin with a source of (revolutionary) hope, according to Pile. Probably influencing sentiments expressed by Tim Etchells earlier, 'Benjamin was most interested in those parts of the city that were being torn down or altered … temporary structures … the ruins of the city'. Such spaces were most likely to reveal the 'unconscious strivings of social and urban imagination' (*PCC*, p. 46). Since he is addressing the mechanism of dreams it makes sense for Pile to bring Freud into play, not least the account of his famous 'uncanny walk in Genoa' discussed in the main introduction to this book, and replayed here in Pile's article. Freud's experience is reminiscent of the 'shock of recognition' that Benjamin would seek. The former's commensurability with the latter is perfected then via a notion of uncovering 'the hidden desires and fears in the city's dreaming' (*PCC*, p. 47). Pile's concern, though, is to suggest that it is not only cities that are dream-like, but dreams that are city-like.

'Spatial practice'

Despite its obvious relevance Michel de Certeau's chapter 'Walking in the City' from *The Practice of Everyday Life* (1988) has been deemed too well known, if not 'of its time' (the original appeared a quarter of a century ago), to merit inclusion here. On the other hand there is also an argument to say that the chapter's startling opening image, the 'panoptic view' of the city offered from the 110th floor of the World Trade Centre in New York – which proves, of course, to be detached and partial – has taken on a particular resonance since the events of 9/11, beyond de Certeau's wildest dreams.

In other words, the supposed sense of omniscience and omnipotence evoked by both the vantage point and the sheer presence itself of the Twin Towers may be merely an illusion or empty sign – part of a 'rhetoric of excess', as de Certeau sets out to show (1988: 91) – but it is one that can 'work' with devastating effect. Ironically, spectacularly *taking out* the buildings in their entirety, as the terrorists of 9/11 did, is precisely the event that proves this most tellingly. Indeed, it is the recognition of the terrorist's role effectively as 'manipulator of images' that has inclined certain prominent artists to ally the spectacle of 9/11 controversially with that of an 'artwork'. It is also what leads the protagonist of Don DeLillo's 1992 novel *Mao II* – which explores the proximity of the writer's and terrorist's 'craft' – presciently to predict that 'Beckett is the last writer to shape the way we think and see. After him, the major work involves midair explosions and crumbled buildings. This is the new tragic narrative' (DeLillo 1992: 157).

Replicating some aspects of Jane Jacobs's objections to official strictures of urban planning, de Certeau's concern is to enable the 'effective thinking' – that is, *realisation* – of the city's actual plurality, and the act of walking epitomises for him such a move. Thus 'ordinary practitioners of the city live "down below", below the threshold at which visibility begins. They walk – an elementary form of this experience of the city' (de Certeau 1988: 93). And these walks, making use of 'spaces that cannot be seen', produce 'unrecognised poems … a manifold story that has neither author nor spectator' (ibid.). Perhaps most famously, then, de Certeau proceeds to draw an analogy between language and movement through urban space, specifically the speech act and the act of walking. The latter is seen as 'a space of enunciation … the walker transforms each spatial signifier into something else … the act of turning phrases finds an equivalent in an art of composing a path (*tourner un parcours*)' (ibid.: 98 and 100). The reference here to *parcours* – which implies the negotiation of an obstacle course – has acquired a particular contemporary resonance inasmuch as it is the term originally used (though usually spelt with a 'k') to describe the practice of free running. Exported from suburban France in the early years of the twenty-first century, this form of time-based 'spatial phrasing' – situated somewhere between athletics, gymnastics and dance – has become an extremely popular means of engaging with, if not aestheticising, the built environment and street furniture of cities.

New walkers

Returning us to the idea of the new *flâneur*, which, incidentally, de Certeau shows no interest in, Petra Küppers's article draws attention to some of the ways in which feminist critiques in particular have problematised the figure as representative of the privileged freedoms granted the white, European, educated, middle-class male. In particular she engages with questions, raised by several commentators, around the possibility of there being an equivalent female figure, the *flâneuse*. Concerned, however, to retain something of the Benjaminian 'body-in-the-street ... characterised as a modern, embodied participant-spectator' (pp. 57–9), Küppers believes Benjamin 'shows the *flâneur* as a distillation of recognisable body actions. The city is embodied in the staring eyes, idle hands, moving feet, casual touches of walls, expansive surveying of shop windows' (p. 63). Rather than constructing the possibility of a gendered alternative, then, the value of accepting the *flâneur* resides in the manner in which the figure's corporeality performs its subjection to and reiteration of socio-cultural forms: the body 'is present in a field of discursive lines that bind it to meaning. At the same time the body is the shared ground of meaning ... within which discursive difference is established' (p. 66).

Finally, the UK company Wrights and Sites, which has emerged in recent years as one of the foremost exponents of a creative walking practice, presents its 'Manifesto for a Walking Culture'. Though the title of this piece places it more or less firmly within this part of the book, it is positioned last because in many respects it is looking already to Part 2's implicit concerns with encountering and mapping. Moreover, Wrights and Sites' particular kind of walking arguably has far more to do with the productive, politicised drift of the Situationists than the apparently aimless dawdle of the *flâneur*, while still retaining an interest in the latter's principle of 'deliberately getting lost'. Having successfully produced a so-called mis-guide to its familiar home city of Exeter, the group was encouraged by its frequent travels to unknown cities to follow up with the *Mis-guide to Anywhere*, 'a utopian project for the recasting of a bitter world by disrupted walking' (Wrights and Sites 2007: cover notes). The mis-guide does not tell you about any one city but offers a methodological framework with which to approach *any* city. As such the experience is not mediated but assembled or performed by the user. The Manifesto included here is premised on a conference presentation delivered in Zürich and thus bears the traces of an encounter with that city. The notion of presenting the piece as a manifesto probably arose as a form of engagement with or rewriting of the Dadaist manifesto first read publicly in Zürich in 1918. However, where a manifesto would normally imply the clear assertion of radical positions, here its form has come about, with typical Wrights and Sites irony, as the product of a game of chance, a dealing of cards, and, as such, can only be viewed as provisional.

1.1   How Scratched Car Revealed the Price of a Peasant's Life
Jonathan Watts

It was the smallest of prangs, but the minor traffic accident between a top-of-the-range BMW and a rickety farmer's tractor has prompted the Chinese authorities to take drastic action to prevent a head-on collision between the top and bottom classes of its increasingly divided society.

'The BMW incident', as it is now widely known, forced the authorities to hold a retrial and made the propaganda ministry slam the brakes on internet chatrooms filled with public resentment.

This thoroughly modern Chinese tale of social inequality, dubious justice and appalling driving began innocuously one day last October when Liu Zhongxia, a peasant, and her husband Dai Yiquan were rattling through Harbin, in Heliongjiang province, in a tractor piled high with onions.

A few years ago they would have enjoyed the freedom of almost empty roads, but China's booming economy is increasing the traffic at the rate of more than 20% a year. In one of many changes of direction prompted by oncoming cars, Mr Liu scratched the wing mirror of a new BMW X5, prompting an altercation which has still to die down six months later.

The details of the road rage clash have become the stuff of myth, but according to the local media, the driver of the BMW, Su Xiuwen, hit Mrs Liu with her purse and screamed: 'How can you afford to scratch my car?'

The furious woman – the wife of a business tycoon – then got back in her car, slammed her foot on the accelerator and ran over Mrs Liu, killing her and injuring a dozen other bystanders.

Public anger at this display of petulance was only increased by the trial on December 20, when Mrs Su was cleared of manslaughter and given a suspended sentence. In a hearing that lasted only two hours, the court accepted her claim that she had accidentally put her car into the wrong gear.

But with little faith in the judicial system, many people are convinced that the case was decided by bribes.

Not one witness turned up to testify, not even Mr Dai, who accepted an out of court settlement of 80,000 yuan (£6,000) – equivalent of eight years' wages – for the death of his wife.

He told reporters he had had little choice: 'I told police that she drove into the crowd on purpose,' he said. 'But no one dared stand up as a witness. I had to give up because I was helpless. I have no money, no power.'

The same could not be said of Mrs Su, whose husband, Guan Mingbo, has earned a fortune as a property developer: As well as buying a car worth

£60,000, the couple splashed out on a personalised licence plate bearing the number 6666, which is considered auspicious in China. They also admitted buying Mrs Su's licence by paying an experienced driver to take the driving test on her behalf.

Millions were willing to believe the rumours circulating on the internet that Mrs Su had threatened to run people down before the accident, and that she had been able to escape punishment because her husband was related to a senior official in the local authority.

While such accusations lack evidence and have been denied by the parties involved, they fit a growing public belief that wealth equals corruption in a country that once prided itself on communist equality but is now racked by suspicions that officials are exploiting their control of land, the courts and the media to grow rich and escape justice.

The feeling is particularly strong in Harbin, the heart of the rust-belt in north-eastern China, where millions of workers have been laid off from state-owned enterprises since the switch to a market economy.

But it is spreading everywhere with the growing unease about the disparity between the urban rich and the rural poor, which rose last year to a record 4:1.

'If it were a rich family who lost a member like that, they would pursue justice in the courts,' a woman who gave her name as Mrs Yang said in Beijing yesterday.

'But the poor don't have the power to fight back.'

Public anger was apparent on the internet, which is now accessible by 78 million people and has become the main outlet for dissent. At the peak of interest after the trial, more than 200,000 comments were posted on chatroom sites.

Fearful that the BMW incident might become a cause celebre, the authorities ordered newspapers to play down or stop their coverage. The national propaganda department also instructed major chatrooms to tone down the contributions they were receiving.

To placate opinion, Heilongjiang province ordered a retrial. But it was reported this week that the outcome was the same. With newspaper and website editors now under orders to dampen the emotions aroused by the affair, the verdict has been given scant coverage. But experts said it was unlikely to be the last China heard of such disturbances.

'This case highlights the growing social concern about the gap in economic status,' said Qu Wenyong, a Heilongjiang University sociologist. 'People believe the rich can influence the law behind the scenes with money. More cases like the BMW furore are likely to happen in the future.'

1.2   Naples
Walter Benjamin and Asja Lacis

Some years ago a priest was drawn on a cart through the streets of Naples for indecent offences. He was followed by a crowd hurling maledictions. At a corner a wedding procession appeared. The priest stands up and makes the sign of a blessing, and the cart's pursuers fall on their knees. So absolutely, in this city, does Catholicism strive to reassert itself in every situation. Should it disappear from the face of the earth, its last foothold would perhaps not be Rome, but Naples.

Nowhere can this people live out its rich barbarism, which has its source in the heart of the city itself, more securely than in the lap of the Church. It needs Catholicism, for even its excesses are then legalized by a legend, the feast day of a martyr. Here Alfonso de Liguori was born, the saint who made the practice of the Catholic Church supple enough to accommodate the trade of the swindler and the whore, in order to control it with more or less rigorous penances in the confessional, for which he wrote a three-volume compendium. Confession alone, not the police, is a match for the self-administration of the criminal world, the *camorra*.

So it does not occur to an injured party to call the police if he is anxious to seek redress. Through civic or clerical mediators, if not personally, he approaches a *camorrista*. Through him he agrees on a ransom. From Naples to Castellamare, the length of the proletarian suburbs, run the headquarters of the mainland *camorra*. For these criminals avoid quarters in which they would be at the disposal of the police. They are dispersed over the city and the suburbs. That makes them dangerous. The travelling citizen who gropes his way as far as Rome from one work of art to the next, as along a stockade, loses his nerve in Naples.

No more grotesque demonstration of this could be provided than in the convocation of an international congress of philosophers. It disintegrated without trace in the fiery haze of this city, while the seventh-centennial celebration of the university, part of whose tinny halo it was intended to be, unfolded amid the uproar of a popular festival. Complaining guests, who had been instantly relieved of their money and identification papers, appeared at the secretariat. But the banal tourist fares no better. Even Baedeker cannot propitiate him. Here the churches cannot be found, the starred sculpture always stands in the locked wing of the museum, and the word 'mannerism' warns against the work of the native painters.

Nothing is enjoyable except the famous drinking water. Poverty and misery seem as contagious as they are pictured to be to children, and the foolish fear of being cheated is only a scanty rationalization for this feeling. It if is true, as Péladan said, that the nineteenth century inverted the medieval, the natural order of the vital needs of the poor, making shelter and clothing obligatory at the expense of food, such conventions have here been abolished. A beggar lies in the road propped against the sidewalk, waving his empty hat like a leave-taker at a station. Here poverty leads downward, as two thousand years ago it led down to the crypt: even today the way to the catacombs passes through a 'garden of agony'; in it, even today, the disinherited are the leaders. At the hospital San Gennaro dei Poveri the entrance is through a white complex of buildings that one passes via two courtyards. On either side of the road stand the benches for the invalids, who follow those going out with glances that do not reveal whether they are clinging to their garments to be liberated or to satisfy unimaginable desires. In the second courtyard the doorways of the chambers have gratings; behind them cripples put their deformities on show, and the shock given to day-dreaming passers-by is their joy.

One of the old men leads and holds the lantern close to a fragment of early Christian fresco. Now he utters the centuries-old magic word 'Pompeii'. Everything that the foreigner desires, admires, and pays for is 'Pompeii'. 'Pompeii' makes the plaster imitation of the temple ruins, the lava necklace, and the louse-ridden person of the guide irresistible. This fetish is all the more miraculous as only a small minority of those whom it sustains have ever seen it. It is understandable that the miracle-working Madonna enthroned there is receiving a brand-new, expensive church for pilgrims. In this building and not in that of the Vettii, Pompeii lives for the Neapolitans. And to it, again and again, swindling and wretchedness finally come home.

Fantastic reports by travellers have touched up the city. In reality it is grey: a grey-red or ochre, a grey-white. And entirely grey against sky and sea. It is this, not least, that disheartens the tourist. For anyone who is blind to forms sees little here. The city is craggy. Seen from a height not reached by the cries from below, from the Castell San Martino, it lies deserted in the dusk, grown into the rock. Only a strip of shore runs level; behind it buildings rise in tiers. Tenement blocks of six or seven stories, with staircases climbing their foundations, appear against the villas as skyscrapers. At the base of the cliff itself, where it touches the shore, caves have been hewn. As in the hermit pictures of the *Trecento*, a door is seen here and there in the rock. If it is open one can see into large cellars, which are at the same time sleeping places and storehouses. Farther on steps lead down to the sea, to fishermen's taverns installed in natural grottoes. Dim light and thin music come up from them in the evening.

As porous as this stone is the architecture. Building and action interpenetrate in the courtyards, arcades, and stairways. In everything they preserve the scope to become a theatre of new, unforseen constellations. The stamp of the definitive is avoided. No situation appears intended forever, no figure asserts its 'thus and not otherwise'. This is how architecture, the most binding part of the communal rhythm, comes into being here: civilized, private, and ordered only in the great hotel and warehouse buildings on the quays; anarchical, embroiled, village-like in the centre, into which large networks of streets were hacked only forty years ago. And only in these streets is the house, in the Nordic sense, the cell of the city's architecture. In contrast, within the tenement blocks, it seems held together at the corners, as if by iron clamps, by the murals of the Madonna.

No one orients himself by house numbers. Shops, wells, and churches are the reference points – and not always simple ones. For the typical Neapolitan church does not ostentatiously occupy a vast square, visible from afar, with transepts, gallery, and dome. It is hidden, built in; high domes are often to be seen only from a few places, and even then it is not easy to find one's way to them, impossible to distinguish the mass of the church from that of the neighbouring secular buildings. The stranger passes it by. The inconspicuous door, often only a curtain, is the secret gate for the initiate. A single step takes him from the humble of dirty courtyards into the pure solitude of a tall, whitewashed church interior. His private existence is the baroque opening of a heightened public sphere. For here his private self is not taken up by the four walls, among wife and children, but by devotion or by despair. Side alleys give glimpses of dirty stairs leading down to taverns, where three or four men, at intervals, hidden behind barrels as if behind church pillars, sit drinking.

In such corners one can scarcely discern where building is still in progress and where dilapidation has already set in. For nothing is included. Porosity results not only from the indolence of the Southern artisan, but also, above all, from the passion for improvisation, which demands that space and opportunity be at any price preserved. Buildings are used as a popular stage. They are all divided into innumerable, simultaneously animated theatres. Balcony, courtyard, window, gateway, staircase, roof are at the same time stage and boxes. Even the most wretched pauper is sovereign in the dim, dual awareness of participating, in all his destitution, in one of the pictures of Neapolitan street life that will never return, and of enjoying in all his poverty the leisure to follow the great panorama. What is enacted on the staircases is a high school of stage management. The stairs, never entirely exposed, but still less enclosed in the gloomy box of the Nordic house, erupt fragmentarily from the buildings, make an angular turn, and disappear, only to burst out again.

In their materials, too, the street decorations are closely related to those of the theatre. Paper plays the main part. Red, blue, and yellow fly-catchers, altars of coloured glossy paper on the walls, paper rosettes on the raw chunks of meat. Then the virtuosity of the variety show. Someone kneels on the asphalt, a little box beside him, and it is one of the busiest streets. With coloured chalk he draws the figure of Christ on the stone, below it perhaps the head of the Madonna. Meanwhile a circle has formed around him, the artist gets up, and while he waits beside his work for fifteen minutes or half an hour, sparse, counted-out coins fall from the onlookers onto the limbs, head, and trunk of his portrait. Until he gathers them up, everyone disperses, and in a few moments the picture is erased by feet.

Not the least example of such virtuosity is the art of eating macaroni with the hands. This is demonstrated to foreigners for remuneration. Other things are paid for according to tariffs. Vendors give a fixed price for the cigarette butts that, after a café closes, are culled from the chinks in the floor. (Earlier they were were sought by candlelight.) Alongside the leavings from restaurants, boiled cat skulls, and fish shells, they are sold at stalls in the harbour district. Music parades about: not mournful music for the courtyards, but brilliant sounds for the street. The broad cart, a kind of xylophone, is colourfully hung with song texts. Here they can be bought. One of the musicians turns the organ while the other, beside it, appears with his plate before anyone who stops dreamily to listen. So everything joyful is mobile: music, toys, ice cream circulate through the streets.

This music is both a residue of the last and a prelude to the next feast day. Irresistibly the festival penetrates each and every working day. Porosity is the inexhaustible law of the life of this city, reappearing everywhere. A grain of Sunday is hidden in each weekday, and how much weekday in this Sunday!

Nevertheless no city can fade, in the few hours of Sunday rest, more rapidly than Naples. It is crammed full of festal motifs nestling in the most inconspicuous places. When the blinds are taken down before a window, it is similar to flags being raised elsewhere. Brightly dressed boys fish in deep-blue streams and look up at rouged church steeples. High above the streets, washlines run, with garments suspended on them like rows of pennants. Faint suns shine from glass vats of iced drinks. Day and night the pavilions glow with the pale, aromatic juices that teach even the tongue what porosity can be.

If politics or the calendar offers the slightest pretext, however, this secret, scattered world condenses into a noisy feast. And regularly it is crowned with a fireworks display over the sea. From July to September, an unbroken band of fire runs, in the evenings, along the coast between Naples and Salerno. Now over Sorrento, now over Minori or Praiano, but always over Naples, stand fiery balls. Here fire is substance and shadow. It is subject to fashion and artifice. Each parish has to outdo the festival of its neighbour with new lighting effects.

In these festivals the oldest element of their Chinese origin, weather magic in the form of the rockets that spread like kites, proves far superior to terrestrial splendours: the earthbound suns and the crucifix surrounded by the glow of Saint Elmo's fire. At the beach the stone pines of the Giardino Pubblico form a cloister. Riding under them on a festival night, you see a rain of fire in every treetop. But here, too, nothing is dreamy. Only explosions win an apotheosis popular favour. At Piedigrotta, the Neapolitans' main holiday, this childish joy in tumult puts on a wild face. During the night of September 7, bands of men, up to a hundred strong, roam through every street. They blow on gigantic paper cornets, the orifice disguised with grotesque masks. Violently if necessary, one is encircled, and from countless pipes the hollow sound clamours in the ears. Whole trades are based on the spectacle. Newspaper boys drag out the names of their wares, *Roma* and the *Corriere di Napoli*, as though they were sticks of gum. Their trumpeting is part of urban manufacture.

Trade, deeply rooted in Naples, borders on a game of chance and adheres closely to the holiday. The well-known list of the seven deadly sins located pride in Genoa, avarice in Florence (the old Germans were of a different opinion and called what is known as Greek love *Florenzen*), voluptousness in Venice, anger in Bologna, greed in Milan, envy in Rome, and indolence in Naples. Lotto, alluring and consuming as nowhere else in Italy, remains the archetype of business life. Every Saturday at four o'clock, crowds form in front of the house where the numbers are drawn. Naples is one of the few cities with its own draw. With the pawnshop and lotto the state holds the proletariat in a vice: what it advances to them in one it takes back in the other. The more discreet and liberal intoxication of Hazard, in which the whole family takes part, replaces that of alcohol.

And business life is assimilated to it. A man stands in an unharnessed carriage on a street corner. People crowd around him. The lid of the coach-man's box is open, and from it the vendor takes something, singing its praises all the while. It disappears before one has caught sight of it into a piece of pink or green paper. When it is thus wrapped, he holds it aloft, and in a trice it is sold for a few *soldi*. With the same mysterious gesture he disposes of one article after another. Are there lots in this paper? Cakes with a coin in every tenth one? What makes the people so covetous and the man as inscrutable as Mograby? He is selling toothpaste.

A priceless example of such business manners is the auction. When, at eight in the morning, the street vendor has begun unpacking his goods – umbrellas, shirt material, shawls – presenting each item singly to his public, mistrustfully, as if he had first to test it himself; when, growing heated, he asks fantastic prices, and, while serenely folding up the large cloth that he has spread out for five hundred lire, drops the price at every fold, and finally, when it lies diminished on his arm, is ready to part with it for fifty, he has been true to the most ancient fairground practices. There are delightful stories of the Neapolitan's playful love of trade. In a busy piazza a fat lady drops her fan. She looks around helplessly; she is too unshapely to pick it up herself. A cavalier appears and is prepared to perform his service for fifty lire. They negotiate, and the lady receives her fan for ten.

Blissful confusion in the storehouses! For here they are still one with the vendor's stalls: they are bazaars. The long gangway is favoured. In a glass-roofed one there is a toyshop (in which perfume and liqueur glasses are also on sale) that would hold its own beside fairy-tale galleries. Like a gallery, too, is the main street of Naples, the Toledo. Its traffic is among the busiest on earth. On either side of this narrow alley all that has come together in the harbour city lies insolently, crudely, seductively displayed. Only in fairy tales are lanes so long that one must pass through without looking to left or right if one is not to fall prey to the devil. There is a department store, in other cities the rich, magnetic centre of purchasing. Here it is devoid of charm, outdone by the tightly packed multiplicity. But with a tiny offshoot – rubber balls, soap, chocolates – it re-emerges somewhere else among the small traders stalls.

Similarly dispersed, porous, and commingled is private life. What distinguishes Naples from other large cities is something it has in common with the African kraal; each private attitude or act is permeated by streams of communal life. To exist, for the Northern European the most private of affairs, is here, as in the kraal, a collective matter.

So the house is far less the refuge into which people retreat than the inexhaustible reservoir from which they flood out. Life bursts not only from doors, not only into front yards, where people on chairs do their work (for they have the faculty of making their bodies tables). Housekeeping utensils hang from balconies like potted plants. From the windows of the top floors come baskets on ropes for mail, fruit, and cabbage.

Just as the living room reappears on the street, with chairs, hearth, and altar, so, only much more loudly, the street migrates into the living room. Even the poorest one is as full of wax candles, biscuit saints, sheaves of photos on the wall, and iron bedsteads, as the street is of carts, people, and lights. Poverty has brought about a stretching of frontiers that mirrors the most radiant freedom of thought. There is no hour, often no place, for sleeping and eating.

The poorer the quarter, the more numerous the eating houses. From stoves in the open street, those who can do so fetch what they need. The same foods taste different at each stall; things are not done randomly but by proven recipes. In the way that, in the window of the smallest trattoria, fish and meat lie heaped up for inspection, there is a nuance that goes beyond the requirements of the connoisseur. In the fish market this seafaring people has created a marine sanctuary as grandiose as those of the Netherlands. Starfish, crayfish, cuttlefish from the gulf waters, which teem with creatures, cover the benches and are often devoured raw with a little lemon. Even the banal beasts of dry land become fantastic. In the fourth or fifth stories of these tenement blocks cows are kept. The animals never walk on the street, and their hoofs have become so long that they can no longer stand.

How could anyone sleep in such rooms? To be sure, there are beds, as many as the room will hold. But even if there are six or seven, there are often more than twice as many occupants. For this reason one sees children late at night – at twelve, even at two – still in the streets. At midday they then lie sleeping behind a shop counter or on a stairway. This sleep, which men and women also snatch in shady corners, is therefore not the protected Northern sleep. Here, too, there is interpenetration of day and night, noise and peace, outer light and inner darkness, street and home.

This extends even into toys. With the pale, watery colours of the Munich *Kindl*, the Madonna stands on the walls of the houses. The child that she holds away from her like a sceptre is to be found, just as stiff, wrapped and without arms or legs, as a wooden doll in the poorest shops of Santa Lucia. With these toys the urchins can hit whatever they like. A sceptre and a magic wand even in *their* fists; the Byzantine saviour still asserts himself today. Bare wood at the back; only the front is painted. A blue garment, white spots, red hem, and red cheeks.

But the demon of profligacy has entered some of these dolls that lie beneath cheap notepaper, clothespins, and tin sheep. In the overpopulated quarters children are also quickly acquainted with sex. But if their increase becomes devastating, if the father of a family dies or the mother wastes away, close or distant relatives are not needed. A neighbour takes a child to her table for a shorter or longer period, and thus families interpenetrate in relationships that can resemble adoption. True laboratories of this great process of intermingling are the cafés. Life is unable to sit down and stagnate in them. They are sober, open rooms resembling the political People's Café, and the opposite of everything Viennese, of the confined bourgeois, literary world. Neapolitan cafés are bluntly to the point. A prolonged stay is scarcely possible. A cup of excessively hot *caffe espresso* – in hot drinks this city is as unrivalled as in sherbets, spumoni, and ice cream – ushers the visitor out. The tables have a coppery shine, they are small and round, and a companion who is less than stalwart turns hesitantly on his heel in the doorway. Only a few people sit down briefly here. Three quick movements of the hand, and they have placed their order.

The language of gestures goes further here than anywhere else in Italy. The conversation is impenetrable to anyone from outside. Ears, nose, eyes, breast, and shoulders are signalling stations activated by the fingers. These configurations return in their fastidiously specialized eroticism. Helping gestures and impatient touches attract the stranger's attention through a regularity that excludes chance. Yes, here his cause would be hopelessly lost, but the Neapolitan benevolently sends him away, sends him a few kilometres farther on to Mori. '*Vedere Napoli e poi Mori*', he says, repeating an old pun. 'See Naples and die', says the foreigner after him.

1.3   Eight Fragments on Theatre and the City
Tim Etchells

This piece was written for and first published in the journal *Theaterschrift 10: City/Art/Cultural Identity*, and, as the title suggests, concerns itself with the relationship between the creative process and the myths, stories and practices of the urban everyday.

'It should all be considered like a letter – written to a long lost friend …'

Introduction

There is a great dream recounted in the book *Elvis after Life* in which a police officer whose son has gone missing receives help from the ghostly figure of Elvis Presley.

In the dream Elvis shows the cop where to find his missing son by taking him to the police station at night and pointing at a huge map of the city. Recounting the dream the cop says this: 'It's a map of San Fransicso – only it isn't San Francisco.'

It's that city, or one like it – this city, but not this one – that I'll write to you about here: eight fragments out of Not-England and nothing more.

1.   Exploration

One night when we were touring, somewhere far from home, we arrived in a place in the dead of night, found somewhere to park the van, found somewhere to sleep. Only when we woke the next morning did we realise that we were in a town right next to the sea and that the place where we had slept was right at the sea front itself. From our bedrooms we could hear the waves.

Harbisson writes about the experience of arriving in the city at night and starting to explore it in the morning – this process of veiled arrival and later exploration he calls 'acting out an allegory of knowledge'.

Walking in our own city we'd often employ a deliberate confusion about what we were trying to solve or understand – was it the latest show or the city itself? Right from the start this double act of walking and talking was a named part of our process, more important perhaps than anything that happened in the theatre itself. In the streets we'd see the crowds of cider-boys gathered laughing and muttering on the green grass outside Gateways supermarket. In the streets we'd see the old guy directing traffic, taking revenge on an order and an economy that had let him down; we'd see the bouncers stood in nightclub doorways, practising karate chops before the night of fighting had begun. The filthy polythene caught in trees, the cardboard houses under bridges, the boarded-up windows, buildings falling down. The neon signs, the old advertising slogans, the fragments of graffiti – all of these things made it into our shows.

2. Maintenance

There is a man that you see in this city – he's good-looking, well looked after, not like a street-crazy person at all. Each time that you see him he's walking on the pavement, through the crowds when he suddenly runs like a maniac, scattering people in confusion as he hurls himself at a building – shop front perhaps, or a tower block, or a multi-storey.

Thrown against a building like the whole thing is going to fall – body pressed flat, head thrown back and peering upwards, staring up to check for signs of movement in the concrete or the brick.

People say here that this man is keeping the city alive.

Some days when you see him he is calm but he's still leaning against buildings, palm flat against the walls, holding them up, checking for strength.

People say he used to be an architect and now he's a powerful magician who has slipped through the cracks in the welfare system. He walks a route through the city each day – holding and touching, same route day in and day out, same time every day, a route which is the maintenance of the city, a ritual system of good-luck checks which keeps the whole place from falling down.

Did I tell you that up on West Street someone has written on a burned-out building GET WELL SOON? Did I tell you that in some parts of the city the phones in the call boxes ring to empty streets at regular hours of the day and night?

Are these events connected? Are there persons here, working in concert?

In the city, as in all the best performance, I'm left joining dots, making my own connections, reasons, speculations.

3.   Mapping

Having so long created cities in our theatre work – implied, stolen from, talked of – we decided last year to make a whole one in a gallery installation/ performance piece called *Ground Plans for Paradise* (1995). Here a deserted model city – comprising nearly 1,000 balsa wood tower blocks – is laid out in a grid plan on top of a breeze-block plinth. Above the model are the faces of many people sleeping (photographed by Hugo Glendinning) – like angels looking after or dreaming of this world.

In *Ground Plans for Paradise* the city itself is both a map of space and a map of states of mind (like all real cities in fact) – only here the streets and buildings are named for the passions, fears and narrative echoes of the twentieth century: Love Street, Dave's Topless Chip Shop, Hope Street, The Blood Club, and the Institute for Darkness Research.

Looking down on the model the viewer is invited to speculate – wondering at the light which spills from inside the buildings – what kind of people might hang out at the Helium House or on Aluminium Square? What might happen at the corner of Transgression and Hesitation, or at the corner of Hata Street and Rain?

Here in Sheffield, Not-England are streets which I know by my own names – names dreamed up between the group of us when we first moved here – descriptive names, literal names, names that refer to the use we made of these streets and not their official function. We could visit the Street of Telephones or the Iqubal Brothers' Street; we could head for the ridge behind the city which we called simply the ridge, only to find out years later that it had a better name, a proper one: SKY EDGE.

I could talk to you about the views I have made mine here, the places that are now mine. I would write to you about the view of the city from the top deck of the bus coming off City Road and down towards the centre. The city itself is a model then, picked out in fairy lights, just like the crude wooden model in *Ground Plans for Paradise* – *a* space into which one astrally projects, a dream space. I think Foucault has given the desire for such views a bad name – after all, the panoptical view has in it both surveillance *and* imagining. To see the city from one's bed, from one's bath, from one's rooftop – how perfect to live in a city, like this one, with hills. Perhaps here sight is nine-tenths of ownership. What did we write in the text for one of our theatre pieces? 'A hill with a good view down onto the city is a good place to do deals, and discuss assassinations ...'

4.   Destruction / construction

We always loved the incomplete – from the building site to the demolition site, from the building that was used once and is no longer to the building that will be used. Did I tell you that Steve Rogers and I used to talk about this? The fascination of ruined places, of incomplete places. It seems unethical to admit – the strange charge of buildings left to run down – but they always were the best places to play – stinking of previous use, ready for transgression. Every piss you took in the corner and every window you broke and every game you played in the old factory, the old house was a writing over its everyday – a kind of actantial vandalism. And do you remember burying things in the foundations of new houses as they were being made? What a surprise for somebody – these traces of some inexplicable ritual? The cut-out pictures, the scribbled notes, the broken objects.

No surprise that the sets we made always looked half-finished. No surprise either that in recent works we always began the performance by building the sets, or ended by dismantling them. Always now this work of construction and deconstruction – letting no thing simply 'be' – seeing everything instead as a product, as the fruit of some labour, some desire, some ideology.

5.   Observation / coincidence

Did you understand that the city was always about glimpsing other lives? About the strange fragments and endless possibilities of people passing each other in the street. My thought is often – what if I went with that person or that person, what if I was that person or what if I went with them – what would my life then become? Where did I learn this fantasy, this way of surviving? Is there something about cities (the meeting point of crowds and of capital) which breeds the fantasy of human interchangeability? I think so. Perhaps the most extreme form of this is the escalator – where we pass each other as objects on a production line. (Remember the escalators up to heaven in the Powell and Press burger film *A Matter of Life and Death* with David Niven? I'm sure that for one project we stole dialogue from that film.) On the escalators we watch each other, getting closer, and then just when we could speak, or even touch, our eyes drop and the moment passes. There are these strange intimacies in the city – those moments on the escalator, those others in the lift, in the subway, or those moments when, stopped at the traffic lights, we glance to the car opposite and are close enough to speak, even touch. The fascination of these moments is simple – that our machines have brought us together and held us apart.

And isn't theatre now just an endless, rearticulation of this proxemics – the play between hereness and thereness – the play between presence and absence? No surprise that in this context I always love the moments of privacy in public – where theatre regrets itself and refuses to speak. Did you see Bobby Baker's *Drawing on a Mother's Experience*? She builds up to this moment where you feel sure she's going to 'tell you everything' and then she refuses – sprinkling the drawing that she's made with white flour until the whole thing is illegible and I'm left wondering what it was that she might have said. The city now is full of this – possibility, negation, guess-work.

6.   Shelter

In all our theatrical explorations of the city, perhaps it is no surprise that time after time we mark some part of the stage space as private space, as home.

In *200% & Bloody Thirsty* (1988) it is the skeletal structure of a building not yet built; in *Emanuelle Enchanted* (1992) and *Club of No Regrets* (1993/4) it is a series of flimsy and provisional rooms constructed from theatrical flats. In each case these structures cluster around an item or two of furniture – a bed perhaps, or a table and chairs – the structural tokens of interior space.

Beyond these crude houses or homes there is always an ambiguous zone – a zone that comprises two separate but interlocked 'outsides' – the real outside of the theatre with its piles of scaffolding, costumes and props and its brick walls, and the fictional outside of the protagonists world – a city implied and fragmented, which swirls around the private space, threatening always to intrude upon it.

The most extreme of these on-stage homes is that in *Hidden F*, where a four-walled plywood box is constructed at an angle to the audience and some way off from centre-stage. This house/room only affords us a view into it through a large rectangular window and is the most deeply private of these spaces, complete with curtains to block out our view inside, so that for some sections of the show performers talk, shout and weep from inside, invisible to those of us who watch.

Even allowing for such privacy, these crude homes offer little in the way of final or solid projection from the city beyond. When they are not being dismantled, they are massively permeable – guns, water, smoke, objects texts and swinging lights constantly invade the space in *Club of No Regrets* – thrust through crude windows and doorways or thrown over the walls by two surly stage-hands in a chaos orchestrated by a half-crazy woman in a blonde wig. In *Emanuelle Enchanted* even the walls of the room space will not stay still, eventually taking on a life of their own as they dance and thunder through the stage, erasing and revealing performers in a mad choreography – as if the city walls themselves become living, fluid, unreliable, malevolent.

Who wrote this: 'Each window a stage in the great drama of the city...'?

Were they thinking of the walk from my house to the shops where each living room I pass is bathed in TV-light which flickers and changes in rhythm to the changing of shots – the strange and synchronised dance of light on walls linking disparate houses, disparate lives?

These front rooms, these bodies in soft light, caught in postures and framed by their windows – we have striven for the perfect poise of these things.

7.   Gatekeepers / guides

When our model city was complete we began working on a project for a real one – here, in Sheffield, where we've always lived and worked. *Nights in This City* (1995) was a guided tour of the city with its audience and performers on board a bus – a guided tour which avoided facts in search of a different truth. Slipping through the centre of the city and out of control – off the beaten path, playing always to the differences between on-route and off-route, centre and periphery, legitimate and illegitimate. Playing always to the different histories written in urban space – the official historical, the personal, the mythical and the imaginary. This must've been the first guided tour of Sheffield which began with the words, 'Ladies and gentlemen, welcome to Paris...'. Come to think of it, it was probably more or less the first guided tour of Sheffield full stop. Do you have to have lived in a place for a long time before you have the right to tell lies about it? We enjoyed our *writing over* Sheffield, seeing the whole city as a sounding board, as a space that could be vandalised with love.

The text we created – pointing out buildings, street comers, carparks, patches of wasteground – was always overlaid with other texts – with the whispered or even shouted texts of other passengers ('That's where I used to work ...' 'That's the place where ...') and the silent text of actions created by those living and working in the city as the bus moved through it.

'We're off the route ...'. Isn't that the definition of liveness? When the thing which began as nothing more than a theatrical act has turned into an event? When the gatekeepers twitch nervously and the guides appear lost? Where safe passage back to the everyday is no longer assured?

8.   All taxi drivers are bastards

Returning from rehearsals late one night in 1989, overburdened with bags and video equipment I mistakenly left a small case in the boot of a taxi cab.

In the case is a notebook full of my work, a pile of script fragments and notes and an out-of print paperback book called *Elvis Presley Speaks from Beyond the Grave*. On the cover of the paperback Elvis's face is painted against a backdrop of pale blue sky and wispy cloud, his expression more than usually beatific. Despite all my attempts to track down that taxi, its driver and hence my belongings, none of these materially worthless things have ever been returned.

I think of the Elvis book, my notebook and scripts lying in that case somewhere, or cast out from it, in a taxi-driver's garage, or still in the boot of his cab, six years after the fact. I think of my notebooks travelling the city for eternity, in the dark hold of a taxi cab boot, with only the ghost of Elvis for company, riding always and forever through the streets of the night, like the city has taken back its own ...

1.4   Sleepwalking in the Modern City: Walter Benjamin and Sigmund Freud in the World of Dreams
Steve Pile

There were a hundred thousand slopes and substances of incompleteness, wildly mingled out of their places, upside down, burrowing in the earth, aspiring in the air, mouldering in the water, and unintelligible as any dream.

> Charles Dickens describing a suburb of London in 1848

The reform of consciousness consists *entirely* in making the world aware of its own consciousness, in arousing it from its dream of itself, in *explaining* its own actions to it.

> Karl Marx, in a letter to Arnold Ruge, 1843

A dream is an answer to a question we haven't learnt how to ask.

> Scully reminding Mulder of an observation he'd made in an earlier episode of the *X Files*, 1997

Never mind Charles, Karl, Dana, and Fox. In his novel *Invisible Cities*, Italo Calvino imagines a meeting between Marco Polo and Kublai Khan. In the course of their conversations, Marco Polo conjures up images of many fabulous and incredible cities. At one point, however, the Great Khan challenges Marco Polo. He has begun to notice that these cities have begun to resemble one another. The Khan's mind now sets out on its own journey. Interrupting Marco Polo, the Khan begins to describe a wondrous city. And he wonders whether it exists. But it appears the Khan had not been paying attention, for it seems that Marco Polo had been telling the Khan about precisely that city. Intrigued, or perhaps in disbelief, the Khan asks Marco Polo the name of the city:

> "It has neither name nor place. I shall repeat the reason why I was describing it to you: from the number of imaginable cities we must exclude those whose elements are assembled without a connecting thread, an inner rule, a perspective, a discourse. With cities, it is as with dreams: everything imaginable can be dreamed, but even the most unexpected dream is a rebus that conceals a desire or, its reverse, a fear. Cities, like dreams, are made of desires and fears, even if the thread of their discourse is secret, their rules are absurd, their perspectives deceitful, and everything conceals something else."
>
> "I have neither desires nor fears," the Khan declared, "and my dreams are composed either by my mind or by chance."
>
> "Cities also believe they are the work of the mind or of chance, but neither the one nor the other suffices to hold up their walls. You take delight not in a city's seven or seventy wonders, but in the answer it gives to a question of yours."
>
> (Calvino 1972: 37–8)

As with cities, so it is with dreams. Marco Polo's analysis is clear: the randomness of cities – their absurd or deceitful realities – has an inner meaning, an inner rule, a perspective, a discourse, in the same ways as dreams. Underlying the production of cities are the hidden workings of desire and fear. In other words, cities are desire and fear made concrete, but in deceitful, disguised, displaced ways. It is the same with dreams. Kublai Khan cannot accept this interpretation, either of dreams, or of the city. And, surely, dreams and cities have nothing to do with one another. Dreams are illusions, unreal. Cities are very real, the work of the conscious mind, not the random, absurd juxtaposition of astonishing images. But this chapter sides with Marco Polo. And not only Marco Polo. With Walter Benjamin and Sigmund Freud too. Out of these elements, it might be possible to discover the deceitful discourses, to uncover the hidden desires and fears, to dream again of/about the city. Let's start with Walter B.

Dreaming the modern city

Much has been said about Benjamin's use of dream analysis to interpret modernity and the city – the best commentators are Buck-Morss 1989;

Gilloch 1996 and Weigel 1996, and this chapter follows determinedly in their wake. However, rather than simply trail these analyses, I would like to demonstrate how Benjamin's ideas about dreams and his theory of revolution are provocatively combined in one of his best known (and loved) works, *One Way Street* (written between August 1925 and September 1926: Benjamin 1985).

We should start at the beginning. The title of *One Way Street* refers to the 'street' that his lover, Asja Lacis, had driven through him. The title is already a metaphor, one which evokes a one-way flow of ideas through Benjamin and through the city. But towards what? The work is filled with shorter and longer pieces of writing: each piece is an anecdote or metaphor, hewn from the natural history of modernity; each observation has its own heading, each heading is drawn from a detailed observation of the modern city. These fragments are bizarre, absurd, juxtaposed in odd, puzzling ways, their meaning not immediately apparent – and, when it is apparent, it becomes curious for being so obvious. The effect is deliberate. By juxtaposing these fragments in this way, Benjamin is attempting to bring seemingly unrelated things into a dialectical relationship. Through this process of dialectical imaging, Benjamin is seeking to use the tension between fragments to break them out of their isolation, their stasis. In this way, objects would be placed back in the flow of history, as if the dust had been shaken off them. The effect is almost city-like. Or, maybe, dreamlike. Marco Polo would be proud.

Let's take a closer look at the opening shots in Benjamin's analysis of the modern city (and it is important to remember that the pieces are named after features found in cities, since many of the pieces are seemingly not about cities). The first one is titled Filling Station. In it, Benjamin effectively introduces the work. It begins by talking about how the present is constructed out of facts, but facts that sterilize literary activity. The task of the critic, then, is to detonate this state of letters. In part, this is to be achieved through the use of opinions, which give writing both influence and the capacity to act. Such writing acts not in universal ways but through its specific, careful, accurate, and effective application – much as one applies oil to a complex machine (hence the title of the fragment). It can be easily surmised, then, that *One Way Street* is the drop-by-drop application of criticism to 'the vast apparatus of social existence' (1985: 45). Through this process, the work can become a significant literary work. Another lesson to draw is this: these fragments are not assembled without connecting threads, without a perspective. These fragments are a rebus. Locked in the puzzle are the desires and fears of the modern city. Let us proceed down the street.

The next observation is headed Breakfast Room. Benjamin begins:

> A popular tradition warns against recounting dreams on an empty stomach. In this state, though awake, one remains under the sway of the dream. For washing brings only the surface of the body and the visible motor functions into the light, while in the deeper strata, even during the morning ablution, the grey penumbra of dream persists and, indeed, in the solitude of the first waking hour.
>
> (1985: 45–6)

You might balk at this claim, but it is possible to glimpse Benjamin's understanding of modernity, cities and revolutionary practice in this tiny fragment of a fragment. Like a railroad station whose lines lead in many directions, so too we can tease out many themes from this apparently simple point of departure: the breakfast room.

In one direction, we can see that there is a tale about dreaming. Benjamin continues:

> The narration of dreams brings calamity, because a person still half in league with the dream world betrays it in his words and must incur its revenge. Expressed in more modern terms: he betrays himself.
>
> (1985: 46)

In a nutshell, it can be said that Benjamin is describing the alienation experienced by people in modernity. They betray themselves by articulating their dreams and the revenge that is wreaked on them is that they have to exist in the dreamworld of modernity. And from which they cannot awake:

> He has outgrown the protection of dreaming naïveté, and in laying clumsy hands on his dream visions he surrenders himself ... The fasting man tells his dream as if he were talking in his sleep.
>
> (1985: 46)

The 'moderns' – after betraying their (innermost) dreams – are doomed to walk in a gray, alienated dreamworld as if in their sleep. The problem is that they have no way of knowing that they are still half in league with the world of dreams. It is, therefore, the (revolutionary) task of the critic to shock the dreamers awake: to act as an alarm clock, to make the hammer strike the bell. For Benjamin, the desires and fears of the sleepwalker in the modern city have to be materialized, but this is not as easy as it might be. The modern individual is perfectly capable of articulating a whole series of needs and wants, fears, and anxieties. Indeed, the endless production of commodities taps directly into the conscious wishes of modern individuals.

Unfortunately, though commodities seemingly embody people's wishes, they remain unconnected to the desires and fears that surround them. It is as if the moderns are talking in their sleep: talking, asking, wishing, but unaware of the meaning of the words. In this sense, commodities become fetishes: they are worshipped, but no one knows why, nor what they stand for.

One might think that the late nineteenth-century city was terrible enough to wake anyone from their slumbers. But Simmel's analysis of the modern city and its effects on human psychology (1903) suggests exactly the opposite to be true. From Simmel, Benjamin learns that the urbanite becomes indifferent to the shocks of city life and blasé about the sheer number of – absurd and surprising, dreadful and exciting – things that cities bring into close proximity. Despite the clarion calls of injustice and inequality, then, the modern individual is indifferent. Worse, citydwellers become subject to the revenge of dreams, for once they learn indifference, their desires and fears become a secret discourse in which everything conceals something else. Though they can speak their wishes, the moderns have no way to make them real. The modern world becomes a never-ending cycle of dreamlike figures, none of which ever fulfills their promise. Fashions come and go, ever more rapidly, in ever more absurd forms. Buildings are put up and torn down, their façades become make-up in a clown's parade of architectural forms. Just admit it: nothing's shocking.

In Benjamin's analysis, 'dreaming' has two apparently contradictory meanings. It describes, on one hand, a state of sleeping and, on the other, a state of waking. Both asleep and awake, however, the mind dreams. So, Benjamin searches in the idea of the dream for a resource of (revolutionary) hope. He finds it in the possibility that the dreamer might awake: in a real way, dreams must anticipate a waking. Analytically, then, Benjamin was concerned to discover and interpret dreams, both past and present. He sought these in artifacts – especially old-fashioned objects (that embodied redundant dreams) – and in the sites that housed, or contained, dream-artifacts. It is worth looking in a little more detail at the dreamhouses of modernity, since this is where the dreamwork in the production of modern urban spaces is most apparent.

For Benjamin, the dream is most vivid at the point of waking. In practice, this means that Benjamin was most interested in those parts of the city that were being torn down or being altered, since it was as if people were waking up from the dreams that these spaces embodied. Such places included, famously, the once-fashionable arcades of Paris. But also the temporary structures put up for the great exhibitions of London and Paris. However, Benjamin also found modern dreams in museums (which contained artifacts – dreams – from the past) and railroad stations (where there were dreams of travel). He uncovered dreams of previous generations in the ruins of the city: in their castles and churches. Like an archeologist, he dug deeper and deeper into the historical layers of the city, to find the persistence of its dreams. Benjamin was searching for a memory. He was attempting to travel in time – *and space* – to recover the long history of a society's desires and fears. Through the labyrinths of the city's streets, through the journeys undertaken, Benjamin would piece by piece, piece together the unconscious strivings of social and urban imagination.

Benjamin was optimistic. If he could bring the pieces into tension, through 'dialectical imaging,' by putting the pieces side by side, Benjamin thought it would be possible to induce a shock that would wake up the moderns. In *One Way Street* this revolutionary task manifests itself in the juxtaposition of ideas within observations, but also in the juxtaposition of observations. Here, we see the world of dreams (significantly he recounts his dreams) and the world of waking (his analysis of the dreamlike connections between things) in direct relation to one another. The Breakfast Room, for example, becomes a space which contains two apparently unconnected ideas: the pre-modern folk-tale and an interior space in the bourgeois home set aside for the timed and localized activity of breakfasting, now regimented by capitalist labor relations.

Reading this work is almost like walking through a city: along any path, you find places built out of different stories, sometimes side by side, sometimes in the same place (say, as one use blends into another). So, in London today, if you go to the corner of Marlborough Crescent and Bedford Road, you can see two different dreamworlds: one is the bricks and gardens of the first garden suburbs built in the late nineteenth century, the other is the concrete and function dream of the 1960s high rise. Meanwhile, a local house in the same area now houses the local Victorian society, both appropriately (it's in a Victorian building) and ironically (since the Society has changed the use and look of the building). In this understanding, the city is an assemblage of absurdities that have lost their impact, and we can no longer see the dreams that are embodied in their bricks and concrete, their flowers and smells.

Through montage, through shocking juxtapositions, Benjamin was attempting to wake the modern world up, so that it could act on its dreams, rather than simply live in them. In this way, it might be possible to produce utopia, to make the dream real. Or so he hoped. But the dialectic of dreaming and awakening has never quite played itself out (at least, in Benjamin's terms). People seem to have remained relentlessly asleep, indifferent to the shocks of modernity. *But maybe the moderns are not sleep-walking in the city.* Maybe they have been walking open-eyed through the streets, fully aware of the poverty and brutality of modern life (like many of the chapters in this volume). So, it may be that Benjamin's understanding of dreams could usefully gain from another perspective. Benjamin was not adverse to psychoanalysis, though he knew very little about it (as Buck-Morss, Gilloch and Weigel have noted). Perhaps now is a good time to put Benjamin and Freud side by side. Let's see what Sigmund Freud might have to say about walking in the city, as if in a nightmare.

By another détour, the dreamcity

Freud is not renowned for his analyses of urban life (see Smith 1980). In fact, it is more common to complain about Freud's lack of appreciation of his own context (for a review of these criticisms, see Elliott 1998). Freud did use the city as a metaphor to describe mental life (Pile 1996, chapter 8), but it is more useful for this chapter that he described a walk in the city in his essay on the uncanny (1919). More generally, Freud's account of the uncanny has been taken up in many analyses of urban space (see, for example, Vidler 1992; Jacobs 1996 and Pile 2000). However, it is the dreamlike qualities of Freud's urban anecdote that concern us here, because this will allow us to pursue an interpretation of the dreamlike quality of cities and the city-like quality of dreams. In this way, it might be possible to progress Benjamin's project of uncovering the secret dis-courses of the city, the hidden desires and fears in the city's dreaming. First, let us examine Freud's uncanny story. While walking in Genoa,

> ... one hot summer afternoon, through the deserted streets of a provincial town in Italy which was unknown to me, I found myself in a quarter of whose charac-ter I could not long remain in doubt. Nothing but painted women were to be seen at the windows of the small houses, and I hastened to leave the narrow street at the next turning. But after having wandered about for a time without inquir-ing my way, I suddenly found myself back in the same street, where my presence was now beginning to excite attention. I hurried away once more, only to arrive by another *détour* at the same place yet a third time. Now, however, a feeling overcame me which I can only describe as uncanny, and I was glad enough to find myself back at the piazza I had left a short while before, without any further voyages of discovery.
>
> (Freud, [1919] 1985: 359)

Of course, we should realize quickly that this 'uncanny' experience is clearly the experience of a repressed bourgeois man who is afraid to be associated with 'painted women.' But Freud at least was prepared to admit a secret desire: to 'be with' the women whose character was not in doubt. Now, we can see in this tale how the return of a repressed desire might lead to a feeling of dread. It might be possible, quickly, to observe that the experience of the city – and perhaps of modernity in general – is ambivalent (about the interplay of desire and fear) or paradoxical (about the apparent contradiction between conscious desires and unconscious motivations). Among Victorian bourgeois men, this experience was certainly not unusual (see Walkowitz 1992). However, I would like to apply another form of interpretation to this situation, one derived from Freud's interpretation of dreams ([1900] 1976). In part, this is a legitimate move because it was this that Benjamin drew on in his interpretation of the dreamworld of the modern city, However, in Freudian terms, the move is illegal. So, let's proceed with enthusiasm!

Using Freud's story, it is possible to investigate the relationship between dreaming, waking and the geography of the city (for related discussions, see Pile 1998; 2000). To begin with, we can note that Freud's stance on dreams correlates quite nicely with Marco Polo's and Walter Benjamin's:

> ... in spite of everything, every dream has a meaning, though a hidden one, that dreams are designed to take the place of some other process of thought, and that we have only to undo the substitution correctly in order to arrive at this hidden meaning.
>
> ([1900] 1976: 169)

For Freud, dreams are the *'(disguised) fulfilment of a (suppressed or repressed) wish'* ([1900] 1976: 244). However, dreamwork responds to this imperative in such a way that the wish does not wake the dreamer. Dreams, therefore, are also 'the *GUARDIANS of sleep'* (1976: 330). It is presumed that the basic thought constituting the dream would trouble the dreamer enough to wake her/him up: so, the dream takes on a disguised form because the revelation of the dream's secret wish would, presumably, be disturbing and wake the dreamer up. This is certainly Benjamin's understanding of the modern individual, sleepwalking in the city. Thus, dreams are the guardians of a sleeping modern world.

In Freud's waking nightmare, we can see that he arrives at, then returns to, a place – with women – of a certain character. The scene is important. Freud carefully constructs a story out of a sequence of images, but his experience of uncanniness lies in the way in which time and space shift, dreadfully (in the city). Time becomes circular, while space is strangely connected. Both time and space take on character that is in doubt. Moreover, Freud's repeated returns to the same place indicate the labyrinthine nature both of the narrow streets of the city, and also of his unconscious wishes. The city becomes the 'show place' of his desire/fear. More than a stage on which the vicissitudes of mental life play out, the city constructs the experience (in mind and body). It was as if Freud had voyaged into some mythic labyrinth, only narrowly escaping intact. Perhaps this is more of a nightmare than a dream, but Freud found it hard to wake up from the torment.

For Freud dreams work mainly (though not only) through the use of images: 'Dreams construct a *situation* out of these images; they represent an event which is actually happening ... they "dramatize" an idea' (1976: 114). Such a view accords neatly with Benjamin's. The city is a collection of images, which can be produced in different forms. The city is put together as a situation – or series of situations – in which desire can be dramatized. However, these desires are dramatized in disguised ways. Thus, commodities represent a desire, but not directly. So it is, too, with physical infrastructure: homes, skyscrapers, overpasses, subways, piazzas, and the like. It is evident that, in the production of the dreamcity, some serious thinking has to take place: the wish has to be felt, then thought, then represented through images that disguise the thought, then the multifarious images have to be carefully assembled into a dream that has a (un)believable story line (however absurd the images and story seem). Freud calls this mental process dreamwork and identifies within it some key components: condensation, displacement, and the means of representation. It is this idea of dreamwork that might help us progress Benjamin's analysis of the work of modern cityspaces.

For Freud, dreamwork transcribes the dreamthought from one mode of expression (the desire/fear) into another mode of expression (the dream) by using images (or elements). Freud suggests that the process of transcription (dreamwork) allows for a complex (and duplicitous) interweaving of wishes, thoughts, and images:

> Not only are the elements of the dream determined by the dream-thoughts many times over, but the individual dream-thoughts are represented in the dream by several elements. Associative paths lead from one element of the dream to several dream-thoughts, and from one dream-thought to several elements of the dream. Thus ... a dream is constructed ... by the whole mass of dream-thoughts being submitted to a sort of manipulative process in which those elements which have the most numerous and strongest supports acquire the right of entry into the dream-content ...
>
> (1976: 389)

As for dreams, so it is for the city. As Freud walks through Genoa, he makes an element – the street – suddenly take on a character that he might not have noticed on another day. An associative path has been opened up that suddenly gives the place connotations it might not otherwise have had. A train of thought has been set in motion, at both a conscious and an unconscious level, each leading in opposite directions. Consciously, Freud wants to leave; unconsciously, he wants to return. Despite being fully awake, Freud would appear to be sleepwalking. This suggests that the street is dreamlike: a site of both condensation, displacement, and an image through which meaning comes to be represented – a meaning which is not immediately apparent. We can pick specific instances of this, though it should be remembered that these are just examples. In the street, we can see how one idea 'painted women' is substituted for another 'sex' and how 'the street' itself takes on this meaning, without it ever being said. In this way, the 'sexual energy' associated with the street is expressed only when the thought gains access to Freud's conscious thoughts, before that he was indifferent. However, the emotional intensity of city life can quickly make itself felt – and we see this in Freud's increasing discomfort.

Of course, Freud draws on a whole repertoire of images to tell his story and these contain or channel his story in particular ways. Others would tell Freud's story differently. Others, of course, have their own stories to tell. Their experiences would be different. Nevertheless, their experiences would also be partial, whether dream- or nightmare-like. This is an important point. This chapter stresses that people's experiences of the city – and of dreaming – are very differently located and localized. This point was paid insufficient attention by both Benjamin and Freud. Now, of course, it is less easy to make credible arguments about collective experiences, or collective dreams, of the city or modernity. Instead, we are more likely to see a crosscutting web of power relations, defining class, race, gender, sexuality, able-bodiedness, and so on. However, this should not allow us to ignore how 'dreaming' is bound up in the 'regulatory fictions' [fixions?] that determine how people are seen and how people see themselves, whether they feel at home, where they feel out of place, what mobilizes them, and so on.

Freud's story is significant not because his uncanny experience is *the* experience of cities, but because it suggests that the tension between ordinary indifference and shocking realization is all too rare. A view with which Benjamin would despairingly concur. In Benjamin's terms, this is a revolutionary moment: by putting two and two together, Freud is shocked to discover his own motivations and awakes to the secret discourse of his desires and fears. Indeed, it might be that the city affords the opportunity for such self-realizations, but for most these experiences will be privatized, cast in shadows, as if under an umbrella.

Even awake, the moderns talk – and walk – as if sleeping. The city is like a scene in a dream, not a passive backdrop, but an active constituent of the story itself. Indeed, the street activates the story. Each element a condensation of many meanings, a moment of intense indifference and potential shock, the full meaning of which is never quite realized. Dreams – and cities – remain the guardians of the moderns' sleep: an elaborate play of remembering and forgetting; showing and disguising. In this understanding, both displacement and condensation work (to make dreams; to make cities) by using associative paths to combine and recombine thoughts, and also to decenter both meanings and feelings. In this way, dreamcity-work enables the dreamcity to be woven out of seemingly desireless, fearless, and absurd elements.

Even awake, then, the most intricate structures (of dreams, of cities) are created, all of which are the points of articulation of many associative paths of meaning, all of which displace the intensity that realized them elsewhere. For sure, an understanding of the city must trace the social relations that produce 'things' (from buildings to emotions) – as political economists since Marx have pointed out. But now we must be sure that we understand that the 'things' that make (up) the city also have secret discourses of desire and fear, desires and fears that have been displaced along disparate paths. For Benjamin, as for Freud (and Marco Polo!) these paths can be reconstructed. And, in this reconstruction, it is possible to understand the paradoxical motivations that made the dreamcity possible; to map out the yearnings that cannot yet be realized – corporealized – in the dreamcity.

On another day Freud could have walked through the street in Genoa and been oblivious to its character. And he might have found his refuge piazza first time. Someone else walking the street would have experienced it very differently. And the 'painted women' were almost certainly having much more fun (at Freud's expense) than Freud! So, we can quickly surmise that *there is no one dream that articulates the city, nor one aspect of the city that defines its dreaming.* Instead, like a dream – or a city – the interpretation of cities must rely on the capacity to trace the lines of 'work' that emanate from urban spaces, an understanding of their production in multiple social relations and of how the dreamcity condenses and displaces meanings in their very form. But we know a little more than this too – and on this, I will conclude.

Conclusion

At the outset of this chapter, it was suggested that cities are like dreams, for both conceal secret desires and fears, for both are produced according to hidden rules which are only vaguely discernible in the disguised and deceitful forms (of dreams; of cities). There is of course a difference between the world of dreams and the waking world: to begin with, the world of dreams pays no attention to other people – a rare luxury in waking life! Nevertheless, Benjamin's allegory of the persistence of dreams, suggests that modernity – while constantly proclaiming its open-eyed objective gaze on the world – is just as prone to sleepwalking as the worlds of religion and the worlds of myths.

From Freud, it can be recognized that the mind, far from operating in completely incompatible and unrelated ways, in sleep and awake, works in parallel ways. Simmel was the first to suggest that mental life in cities is characterized by indifference, reserve, and a blasé attitude, but this only reinforces the idea that mental life in cities is characterized by displacement, condensation, and the use of images to represent *and effectively disguise* desires and fears – as in dreams. Freud's experience in Genoa suggests that elements of the city resemble dream elements – for not only can sites in cities be visited many times and the meanings of the locality change depending on the 'orientation' of the visit, but also cities bring together elements from different places and urban spaces are produced through the intersection of crosscutting social relations, which combine to produce meaningful places – whether these are Benjamin's arcades or multiplex cinemas, the Ministry of Defence or home sweet home. This is to say that, like the dream, the city is produced in time and space by fervently traced paths, made and unmade connections, and the composition and position of elements.

But to what purpose is all this musing? For Benjamin, we can see that his desire was to shock modernity into waking up. No such option would appear to exist in Freudian thought. Perhaps this means there is no future for cities. On the other hand, it is possible to draw other lessons from Benjamin, Freud, and co. In this, we can think again of the paradox of dreaming: that it occupies both our sleeping and waking worlds. Through dreaming, it might be possible to imagine different transformative possibilities (see also Robinson 1998). Thus, instead of waking (to realize those secret wishes), or, instead of returning to the dream (to find those hidden messages), the significant move may be to pursue with greater enthusiasm the unconscious logics of the city. These will not be singular, nor universal, nor capable of being circumscribed by a master narrative of urban development. Instead, we would be forced to recognize that cities will have contradictory, incommensurable logics. And perhaps this is why cities are like dreams, both because they are never simply works of the mind or of chance, and also because they embody paradoxical and ambivalent elements.

It still feels like musing, all this talk of dreams. The alarm bells are ringing loud and clear: cities are wrecked by earthquakes, riots, (not so) smart bombs, pervasive disease, abject poverty. The problems confronting cities are so vast that they seem absurd: Western-dominated neoliberal economic strictures force people off the land and into the shanty towns of the poorest countries of the world, so cities of 20 million plus are created where there isn't enough food. But it is important to remember that neoliberal dreamings are not the only ones, nor the inevitable ones. Perhaps the scale of the problem explains why it is so easy to forget what the dreams of the city are all about – what it means to live in cities, their freedoms and opportunities, their new communities and cosmopolitanism. This suggests a revolutionary practice that relies as much on imagining and mobilizing better stories as on shocks to the system. Collapsing neither into the waking world of rationalizations and instrumental logic, nor into the dreamworld of barbaric desires and satisfying fears, the transformation of urban space would instead necessitate an understanding of vicissitudes of the dreamcity.

References

Benjamin, W. 1985: *One Way Street and Other Writings*. London: Verso.

Buck-Morss, S. 1989: *The Dialectics of Seeing: Walter Benjamin and the Arcades Project*. Cambridge, MA: MIT Press.

Calvino, I. 1972: *Invisible Cities*. London: Faber and Faber.

Dickens, C. 1848: *Dombey and Son*. Harmondsworth: Penguin.

Elliott, A. 1998: Introduction. In A. Elliott (ed.), *Freud 2000*, Cambridge: Polity, 1–12.

Freud, S. [1900] 1976: *The Interpretation of Dreams*, vol. 4. Harmondsworth: Penguin Freud Library.

Freud, S. [1919] 1985: The 'uncanny'. In *Art and Literature: Jensen's 'Gradiva', Leonardo Da Vinci and other works*, vol. 14. Harmondsworth: Penguin Freud Library, 339–76.

Gilloch, G. 1996: *Myth and Metropolis: Walter Benjamin and the City*. Cambridge: Polity.

Jacobs, J. M. 1996: *Edge of Empire: Postcolonialism and the City*. London: Routledge.

Marx, K. [1843] 1975: Letters from the Franco-German Yearbooks. In K. Marx, *Early Writings*. Harmondsworth: Penguin, 199–209.

Pile, S. 1996: *The Body and The City: Psychoanalysis, Subjectivity and Space*. London. Routledge.

Pile, S. 1998: Freud, dreams and imaginative geographies. In A. Elliott (ed.), *Freud 2000*, Cambridge: Polity, 204–34.

Pile, S. 2000: The un(known)city ... or, an urban geography of what lies buried below the surface. In I. Borden, J. Kerr, A. Pivaro and J. Rendell (eds.), *The Unknown City*. Cambridge, MA: MIT Press.

Robinson, J. 1998: (Im)mobilizing space-dreaming (of) change. In H. Judin and I. Vladislavić (eds.), *Blank: Architecture apertheid and after* (Amsterdam: Netherlands Architecture Institute), 163–71.

Simmel, G. [1903] 1995: The metropolis and mental life. In P. Kasinitz (ed.), *Metropolis: Centre and Symbol of our Times*. Basingstoke: Macmillan, 30–45.

Smith, M. P. 1980: *The City and Social Theory*. Oxford: Basil Blackwell.

Vidler, A. 1992: *The Architectural Uncanny: Essays in the Modern Unhomely*. Cambridge, MA.: MIT Press.

Walkowitz, J. R. 1992: *City of Dreadful Delight: Narratives of Sexual Danger in Late-Victorian London*. London: Virago.

Weigel, S. 1996: *Body- and Image-Space: Re-reading Walter Benjamin*. London: Routledge.

1.5   Moving in the Cityscape: Performance and the Embodied Experience of the *Flâneur*
Petra Küppers

Cities are not just made out of concrete, glass and bricks, but live in the bodies, habits, and movements of their inhabitants. Here, I want to look at the embodied experience of the urban and trace the experience of 'being in the street' in contemporary performance works. In order to do so, I will focus on the interaction of the gaze and the moving body in three media: street theatre, film, and filmdance. The examples I use are moments from Kathryn Bigelow's film *Strange Days* (1996); a performance by the Austrian group Bilderwerfer, *Einblicke (Insights*, 1995); a performance by Francesca Vilalta-Ollé, *Orch-Skirt* (1998), which was part of the London event *Souvenirs;* and a camera-dance made for TV by director Katrina MacPherson and choreographer Marisa Zanotti, *Pace* (1995, transmitted 1996).

Two questions guide this investigation. How can I conceptualize historically specific embodiment in physical performance? And what is the position of gender in this field of embodiment? In considering them, I read Walter Benjamin and his concept of the *flâneur* to circumnavigate those aspects of contemporary theory that use the human body as metaphor rather than as physicality, a lived set of material practices and inscribed discourses. With this re-reading, the historicity of the performing body becomes the focal point for the performer/spectator relationships.[1]

Kathryn Bigelow's film *Strange Days* occupies a curious position in relation to conventional film narrative and documentation of physical performance. In the film, the city becomes a physical, bodily, choreographic presence. The narrative of the film centres on a new recording method, allowing visceral re-living of other people's lives. The characters gain 'fixes' by receiving the embodied imprint of another's experience: love-making, showering, being in different places, dying. These 'fixes' are short, and threaten to overload the sensory system.

When I first saw the film, its concert of montage, *mise-en-scène*, music, and the layering of sound-track and image reminded me of music video aesthetics and the club scene. I remember coming out of the cinema, gliding on an inner rhythm, as if I was just taking a breath of fresh air during a clubbing evening.

One of the actors in the film is Louise Lecavalier – the star dancer of the group *LaLaLaHuman Steps*, often quoted as the cyberdancing body (see Albright, 1997). Her muscular, post-punk presence in *Strange Days* further underlines the nearness of narrative (she plays a bodyguard) and contemporary theatre aesthetics (the kicks and strides of her role are highly reminiscent of her performances as dancer).

Towards the beginning of the film, the experience of living in a US city at the end of 1999 is established in a short scene. The male protagonist, slowly driving through mean streets, witnesses a bizarre mugging. The film focuses on his visual experience: the car window becomes like a cinema screen, the car radio music a sound-track to a 'mediated' form of living.[2] The driver scans his surroundings, but he is not seen to engage emotionally or physically with them. The camera portrays the happenings outside the car in a slow-motion rhythm, linked to the beat of the music, creating the sensation of a choreographed dance. Young women run towards and mug a Santa Claus, who slumps helplessly against a house wall as his victimizers run off.

These grotesque images are portrayed in a sensuous, lascivious format. When the events outside cease to be 'conventionally' viewed as filmic narrative, and instead become ordered into an aesthetic performance by the eyes and ears taking them in (by the driver as well as by the cinema audience who receive the aestheticized images), reactions change. Far from staying in the disinterested mode associated with postmodern citizenship, the effects on the driver become readable: but instead of open, public reactions they are private ones, impinging on consciousness rather than on conventional political action. The driver averts his eyes, but he does not open the car door to help. The reacting impetus is inwards, implicating him in the space and time witnessed. He becomes a witness of his own lived experience of seeing and not acting.

Ethical questions structure the film's moves towards its resolution: what can an individual do in a world that is dominated by electronic billboards and mass media information? The brief scene in the car lays down a challenge: it makes the distinction between being an active participant and being a witness. Ultimately, though, it shows that the mode of witnessing encouraged by the mediated performance (the live event viewed through a screen) does hail the spectator on the level of physicality.

The grotesqueness of the scene, the slow-motion delivery, and the distancing afforded by music and screen do not cover the fact that a shared knowledge exists between perpetrator, victim, and witness. All three groups mingle on the street, in the same temporal and spatial arrangement. The body motions of all members are known to all: it does not matter that the driver himself is not on the pavement. The choreographies of 'how to be on the street' – running, standing, mugging, and watching – are familiar to all.

The street scene in *Strange Days* is not so much created by architecture as by recognizable body actions. Most of the actions presented in this short sequence are probably familiar to most of us, and are ingrained in our physical memory. We all know about walking on the street, watching youngsters run by, witnessing violence, and feeling both helpless and cowardly in not acting. Most of us have the experience of framing our world-view 'through the car window' (or the TV screen), dissociating from the content of our surroundings and focusing on the dynamics, the format, and the aesthetics.

For choreographers, it is easy to create improvisational material out of street scenes, and it is equally easy for viewers to decode these familiar dances. *Objet-trouvé* movements could include the little dances of an old woman unsure whether she can cross the street in time to the hectic traffic-light beat, the skater with her expansive glide, out of sync with the walkers, the little steps of small dogs, the back-against-a-brick-wall stare. *Strange Days* is a film on the border-line between narrative and spectacle which plays with the effects and conse-quences of this 'lived knowledge' by bringing together the strangeness and the familiarity of these motions, and by asking for the ethics of the situation.

The motile interaction of these bodies with their spaces creates the urban, not the bricks and concrete themselves. This connection between physicality and space was recognized by Walter Benjamin in his readings of Baudelaire, and I am going to re-read his concept of the *flâneur* for traces of the complexities of being, moving and witnessing in the city.

Benjamin and the concept of the *flâneur*

Janet Woolf, pointing to the factors which make Benjamin such an interest-ing figure in the current situation, suggests that the

> interplay between the analytic and the subjective-personal is a major factor in the current interest in returning to Benjamin. There are three areas in particular where memoir is being taken seriously at the moment in cultural criticism: femi-nist literary theory, cultural history, and popular culture studies.
>
> (Woolf, 1993, p. 118)

Woolf sees as the main point of attraction Benjamin's micrological approach: the fascination with the concrete as source of metaphor, or Adorno's *concrète particular*. Woolf is suspicious of the true value of these politics of the personal, the concrete metaphor and its ability to capture social and cultural complexity. She sees Benjamin's inability to recognize the gendered nature of *the flâneur* as symptomatic of this methodology:

> In the case of 'thinking in images', we have to be especially alert to how these operate (since their 'immediate' character will not necessarily direct us to their theoretical orientation). This, I think, applies to all attempts to shortcut theory with images, tropes, chronotropes or metaphors.
>
> (Woolf, 1993, p. 122)

In this paper, I am trading in the 'concrete', the 'immediate': the experience of being a body inscribed by its specific historical position, with its specific movement vocabulary. The epistemological value of movement can be explored while being seen in a historical and cultural field of change and shift.

In the writings which I use, Benjamin indeed 'fleshes out' his historical analysis with personal (and poetic) anecdotes, but he also creates a multi-layered and complex experience of the effects of living – a 'way of living' which goes beyond the individual situation. If in literary theory the 'metaphor' of the fleshy writing has been explored and found tired with time, in dance and performance studies this flesh/body has (early phenomenological studies apart) only just started to emerge as a basis for theory.[3] Benjamin's body-in-the-street links effectively the body of metaphor and the body of movement, and this makes a re-reading fruitful.

Benjamin was interested in the ways in which the institution of the city shapes and interacts with human consciousness, and looked for raw material in the prose poems of Charles Baudelaire, who wrote about his city, Paris, and the changes that the wide boulevards of Hausmann and the arcades had brought. In response, Benjamin shaped the evocative figure of the *flâneur*.

The *flâneur* has been widely used to metaphorize the disinterested voyeur, the lonely figure haunting the streets of cities, the person who watches the spectacle of modern life. *The flâneur* has been seen as the shopper – someone whom modern work relations have freed to be the ultimate consumer, the person who provides the life-blood for the new shopping arcades. The *flâneur* has been seen as the mass being – the person for whom privacy is only available in the anonymity of the mass, the person who thinks his or her own thoughts while staring at the other passengers in a city bus.

The dance writer Valerie Briginshaw has reintroduced the *flâneur* and two writer/theorists of modernity, Baudelaire and Benjamin, to the study of dance. With this, she inserts a new note in the recent revival of Benjamin's writing.[4] Her interest is with the freedom of the *flâneur*.

> The *flâneur* was the hero of the modern city, enjoying the freedom to stroll in the boulevards and arcades, visit the cafés and department stores, get lost in the crowds but, importantly, 'to observe and be observed'.
>
> (Briginshaw, 1997, p. 41)

Questioning the blind spots of modernity writing, Janet Woolf has influentially interpreted the role of the *flâneur* as a gendered one (1990). She argues that women are not able to traverse the city anonymously and unimpeded; they do not carry the ability to look disinterestedly at a world dominated by male power:

> There is no question of inventing the *flâneuse*: the essential point is that such a character was rendered impossible by the sexual divisions of the nineteenth century. Nor is it appropriate to reject totally the existing literature on modernity, for the experiences it describes certainly defined a good deal of the lives of men, and also (but far less centrally) a part of the experience of women. What is missing in this literature is any account of life outside the public realm, of the experiences of 'the modern' in its private manifestations.
>
> (Woolf, 1990, p. 47)

After Woolf's intervention, the gendered, specific, historically situated, and inscribed figure of the *flâneur* has been used in a variety of contexts.[5] But I would like to step back from these uses of Benjamin's figure, and return, instead, to his writing.

'Botanizing on the asphalt'

In doing this, I am not arguing that the excavation of blind spots is not important, or that Benjamin's text doesn't get enriched by the variety of reproduction. My reading here points to the importance of the style with which *the flâneur* is evoked, the images used, and their specific, bodily resonance in the context of performances by women in the 1990s, which break open structures of private and public in the same way as did Baudelaire's *flâneur*.

I contend that the use of the *flâneur* by Baudelaire and Benjamin is already broken in many telling ways. In particular, I want to look at the 'situatedness' of the *flâneur* – Benjamin is already well aware of various socio-historical influences that frame his figure, and never theorizes an all-powerful, simplistic figure, instead creating his *flâneur* from moments of Baudelaire's actual person-in-the-street, moving through space, situated and specific.

Dance historian Lena Hammergren sees the value of the *flâneur* for her own project, 'The Re-turn of the Flâneuse':

> From Benjamin I have got the image of the *flânerie*, that is, to stroll through the streets of history, along the paths constructed by my intended research topic. I am trying to 'enter' a particular space to adjust the historian's body (my own) in that past space, and yield to recollections springing from a bodily memory that is mine, and yet belonged to strangers.
>
> (Hammergren, 1996, p. 54)

Whether conceived as supplementary or fundamental, an alternative source of knowledge can be found in *the flâneur* characterized as a modern, embodied participant-spectator.

For Benjamin, *the flâneur* is one embodied experience of the spaces of the urban. It is interesting in this respect to look at the difference between Benjamin and a theorist of postmodernity, Frederic Jameson, whose evocation of the experience of spatiality in modernity and postmodernity has focused on the Hotel Bonaventure in Los Angeles. Jameson describes an anti-spatial environment, a conceptual rather than an embodied, filled, physical space. The hotel 'transcend(s) the capacities of the individual human body to locate itself, ... to map its position in a mappable external world' (Jameson, 1988, p. 25).

It is illuminating to compare this sterilized vision to the images of the Bonaventure that TV documentaries or films depict: in these documents, the hotel is a thriving, moving, heaving space, peopled and traversed. Jameson's analysis does not take the lived physicality of the postmodern condition into account. Benjamin's words, on the other hand, are evocative, vivid, and convincing because they poetically conjure up the actuality of being-in-the-city. Our bodies and imaginations are malleable: we will find our way through the corridors of new hotels, and map anew our changing world. Some people are bound to make all micro-worlds, all new architectures, their home, no matter how abstract the theorist's views of these new environments.

The words Benjamin uses to establish the *flâneur* in the city space are evocative of bodily actions – the closely peering, bowed-shoulder activity of 'botanizing on the asphalt' (Benjamin, 1973, p. 36), which surely must remind us of people in our streets, scrutinizing passers-by from park benches. He talks about the privacy and intimacy of this city creature to its environment:

> The street becomes a dwelling for *the flâneur*, he is as much at home among the façades of houses as a citizen is in his four walls. To him the shiny, enamelled signs of businesses are at least as good a wall ornament as an oil painting is to a bourgeois in his salon. The walls are the desks against which he presses his notebooks: newsstands are his libraries and the terraces of cafés are the balconies from which he looks down on his household after his work is done.
>
> (Benjamin, 1973, p. 37)

Actions of living and breathing 'cityish' are clearly described, and create vivid images. This vision is intricately linked to a specific space and time – the Paris of the boulevards lit by gaslight – but the qualities of 'city moving' are clear to anyone who has either bodily felt out of place or recognized the country bumpkin on the main street.

Surreal but credible touches of fashion-writing enhance our image of the corporeal presence of the *flâneur*.

> Around 1840 it was briefly fashionable to take turtles for a walk in the arcades. The *flâneurs* liked to have the turtles set the pace for them. If they had their way, progress would have been obliged to accommodate itself to this pace.
>
> (Benjamin, 1973, p. 54)

Another facet of this ungraspable emblem of modernity is captured in this quotation by Benjamin from Edgar Allan Poe: 'He entered shop after shop, priced nothing, spoke no word, and looked at all objects with a wild and vacant stare' (Benjamin, 1973, p. 54). Poe is one of Benjamin's major sources, next to Baudelaire, and he sees *the flâneur* as a figure incorporating the modernity of detective fiction – 'developing forms of reactions that are in keeping with the pace of the big city. He catches things in flight; this enables him to dream that he is like an artist. Everyone praises the swift crayon of the artist' (Benjamin, 1973, p. 41).

Einblicke (*Insights*, 1995), a street performance by the Austrian performance group Bilderwerfer, may be linked to these vignettes of city seeing and living. In the performance, five solos, five monologues and one ensemble piece are enacted in a glass booth on the Naschmarkt, the biggest market-place in Vienna. Some members of the audience pay, and get a folding seat for their money, others wander by, stay, or hurry on.

'Einblicke': catching performance in flight

The dance and theatre pieces centre on the meetings of private thought and movement with public exposure, contact, and challenge. The audience is uneasy – the theatre context is referenced since seats are allocated and people perform for you, but you yourself become a part of the street theatre, as other passers-by watch you watching. The unease becomes deeper as the performers take to their curious stage. The performance space is a brightly lit metal cube, separating spectators and performers by walls of glass – an effect heightened when some of the monologues are delivered through video projection rather than 'in the flesh'.

The choreographies of difference are here accentuated in the bodies of the performers: two members of the company are wheelchair-users, and another is a young man with a learning disability. The objects of the gaze (of pity, embarrassment, and visible difference) look back, and challenge attempts to close their presence down to an easy narrative. Elisabeth Löffler, a wheelchair-using young woman, dances with herself and her tools (chair and crutches) on the floor in a shop window. Dressed in bright streetwise gear – red tights, yellow miniskirt, fake fur jacket, heavy make-up – she is moving her wheelchair over her body, and creates different spatial encounters with it.

Intimately familiar with her wheelchair, she spins it, handles it, and caresses it. She is private in the public space, using the shop as her 'salon'. Löffler investigates the reach of her crutches, and suggestively moves the crutch up and down her crotch. Finally, she comes up to the glass, staring through it at the audience beyond: but even here, at the limits between dance space and the outside, the blurring of the public and the private continues. Playing with weight and balance, Löffler uses the window as lever, partner, and a wall to bounce off.

Passers-by stop briefly and stare at the strange spectacle unfolding before them. Like the turn-of-the-century turtles, the performance is both 'normalized' as some walk on, leaving the scene of yet another unaccountable weirdness in the city, and 'made spectacular' – an effect of the narratives of disability, which would freak the disabled body as object of visual curiosity.[6]

The performance situation on the street means that everything is communicated quickly – the passers-by see a montage of differently filled shop windows, with this performance as one instance in a journey through the city. They can 'catch things in flight' – the disabled body is played both for its 'otherness' and for its familiarity (as the body of a young woman), sketching out new scenarios of disabled people as performers, participants in street scenes, people with fashion sense, 'extraordinary' as performers.

The encounters are framed in the shop windows: a mediation which can ensure the possibility of non-contact for the performer (the performers' work is often concentrated on the mechanics of moving body, crutches, and chair, the audience not always being acknowledged) and for the audience (who can choose to engage or not). During the original performance in Vienna, some members of the audience chose not to disengage, and so wrote complaining letters about a spectacle which 'used' disabled bodies as spectacle.[7]

'Orch-Skirt': the mechanics of self-display

This mixture of ethics, acknowledgements of gaze structures, and the concentration of presence in fleeting moments are the same elements at work in my earlier reading of *Strange Days*. The unexpected movements happening in the city space allow for challenge and for complacency, but both forms of audience/performer interactions require a shared understanding of the mechanics of shop-window displays, strolling, privacy in the masses – the mechanics of modernity which Benjamin describes.

A 1998 event in London equally acknowledges and plays with the lived knowledges that Benjamin describes: from 11 July to 9 August 1998, Museum Street, Bloomsbury, bore traces of the street event *Souvenirs*. One of the performances during this season was Francesca Vilalta-Ollé's

Orch-Skirt. Positioned in yet another shop window (the fashion shop Joie), another young woman took it upon herself to challenge both static audience and passers-by. The performance times were announced, and the theatre crowd could assemble on the pavement, but the tourists, shoppers, and strollers around the British Museum could chance on the show. The display window gave onto a busy street corner, and car drivers often had to stop for traffic and were able to take in the strange spectacle.

Vilalta-Ollé's self-display is that of the mannequin: arrayed in her tight silver ensemble, she could have mugged a plastic lady in one of the many surrounding show windows. Vilalta-Ollé's performance plays with the mechanics of being seen and seeing. In between the private action of putting on a silver skirt over her silver pants and the public action of moving her body invitingly, taking her gyrating hips through the motions of feminine display, she stares out and holds the eyes of whoever chances to see her.

Microphones are attached to her pants, and they capture and project through external speakers the sound of the skirt, which is hung with bells. This intimacy is channelled through technology, and is only what we are given to consume: it is projected, planned, public, reaching us through the mechanisms of amplification. The performer challenges our gaze not only through the confrontation of her gaze, but also through a pocket mirror with which she captures the light and bounces it off the opposite house walls, directing our gaze away from her. More aggressively, she flicks the light from her mirror into people's faces, obliterating her image in a flash of blinding light.[8]

But this direct challenge to the *flâneur*'s gaze is easily read back into the embodied choreographies of the street. 'Mad woman' or 'prostitute' are the names given to those women that look back. The *flâneur*'s gaze is easily averted – the *flâneur* gazes at things without making contact, making quick and instantaneous judgements. The challenge of the wrong body in the wrong position in the wrong space (the wheelchair-using woman in *Einblicke*) seems more upsetting than the right body in the right space, but with the wrong attitude (the living mannequin, starring back).

The distracted but frantic shopper, the person comfortable and unchallenged in the city space, the person with quick reactions and short attention-span – Benjamin's own descriptions, many of which remain apt and resonant for today's city living – are made with a fine eye for specific historic and local conditions. His description is situated in a very specific historic context. The embodied experiences of the shopper in the 1990s in London and Vienna are not the same as those of the Parisian *flâneur*, but by paying attention to the dynamics of time, space, gazes, and bodies, my analysis is able to point to new political engagements, new forms of challenges for performance. Bilderwerfer's play, with the various abilities of the *flâneur* combined with the expectations of a city audience, makes claims for socially engaging performance work.

Resistance and resilience

For me, the value of reading Benjamin's *flânerie* lies in the corporeal dimension of the descriptions. Benjamin doesn't just see the *flâneur* as some specific social, cultural, or economic entity (although he explores in depth the status of the *flâneur* in commodity production), he also shows the *flâneur* as a distillation of recognizable body actions. The city is embodied in the staring eyes, idle hands, moving feet, casual touches of walls, an expansive surveying of shop windows.

Instead of being merely represented in these activities, as an added set of movement characteristics, Benjamin's *flâneur* is crucially defined by them – they are his natural movements, just as the street is his natural home. Benjamin's writings about the historically located city-body foreshadow Foucault's on the constructive power at work in the creation of bodies. Feminist theorist Susan Bordo describes this conceptualization of knowledge as penetrating bodies:

> Marx and, later, Foucault [focused] on the 'direct grip' (as opposed to representational influence) that culture has on our bodies, through the practices and bodily habits of everyday life. Through routine, habitual activity, our bodies learn what is 'inner' and what is 'outer', which gestures are forbidden and which are required, how violable or inviolable are the boundaries of our bodies, how much space around the body may be claimed, and so on. These are often far more powerful lessons that those we learn consciously, through explicit instruction concerning the appropriate behaviour for your gender, race, and social class.
>
> (Bordo, 1993, p. 16)

Benjamin teased out some historical moments of this body technique, this cultural penetration of our bodily habits, in the description of *the flâneur*. Foucault writes:

> The body is moulded by a great many distinct regimes; it is broken down by the rhythms of work, rest, and holidays; it is poisoned by food or values, through eating habits or moral laws; it constructs resistances. ... Nothing in man – not even his body – is sufficiently stable to serve as a basis of self-recognition or for understanding other men.
>
> (Foucault, 1977, p. 153)

Of course, this does not mean that the body cannot serve as a vehicle of recognition: it is just not a stable, a-historic one. As I have shown in my analyses above, historically contingent body habits can indeed act as markers of meaning, of shared understanding, and even as a shared basis to challenge the status quo.

Foucault theorizes the moments of resistance, in-built in any alignment of knowledges in power. The feminist philosopher Elisabeth Grosz reads the scope of Foucault's resistance by pointing to its negativity:

> Foucault takes the body as a resistant yet fundamentally passive inertia whose internal features and forces are of little interest to the functioning of power. The body itself functions almost as a 'black box' in this account: it is acted upon, inscribed, peered into; information is extracted from it, and disciplinary regimes are imposed on it; yet its materiality, also entails a resilience and thus also (potential) modes of resistance to power's capillary alignments. It is a kind of passivity, capable of being mobilized according to the interests of power or in the forms of subversion, depending on its strategic position.
>
> (Grosz, 1994, p. 146–7)

These comments on the negativity of the physical body for Foucault are here made apropos Nietzsche's more positive image of the physical body as force, but I take Grosz's comments in order to point to a potential moment of incursion within the 'habituated' body movements of the urban. I think that the inertia of the corporeal might fundamentally upset the mobility of consciousness – upset it by pointing to the possibility of other channels of knowledges, producing alignments across other knowledges' dividing lines.

'Dancing cityish' in 'Pace'

Thus, an emphasis on the physical body might strategically undercut differences of gender, race, and class without romanticizing the hold that these distinctions have on embodied experience. To illustrate this tentative point, my last example of urban movement casts the woman outside the literal city space, but captures her in the execution of 'dancing cityish'.

The last two performance instances, of Bilderwerfer and Vilalta-Ollé, perceived the woman as object of the gaze, playing with the implications. In Katrina MacPherson's film-dance *Pace*, a woman (choreographer Marisa Zanotti) is the carrier of the *flâneur* meaning: the swift, sure, streetwise dance movement. At the same time, though, her movements are under surveillance: a camera captures the film-dance.

Pace is structured in three parts, moving from close-up, distorted images to a more 'realistic' presentation of the dancer and her space in medium shot, and again to brief, unlocated movement images. At the beginning of the video, all we see is quickly cut, abstract movement impressions; red swirls past us; white, a hand slashes downwards, red colour again. Slowly, the origin of the movements, their coherence in space and time become visible, as the time-distorted effect gives way to a more naturalistic but still close-up view of a dancing body.

We see a young woman in tracksuit trousers, sweatshirt, and trainers, moving on the floor, with the camera suspended just above her. The film cuts to her in the middle of a dance studio, dressed in a black and white sports tracksuit, upright now, her arms slashing into space. She stares briefly and aggressively into the camera, and continues her movement work.

Thus, the whole body in space becomes slowly visible, being pieced together from a mass of movement impressions captured for us. As a spectator, I can slowly tune into the movement, and learn the language of this encounter between camera and dancer. Eventually, I discern patterns and repetitions in the encounter, and I learn to make out the dimensions of the space presented. A foot clad in trainers slams into the floor, a leg glides purposefully over the floor and past the camera – a head shoves the camera out of the way, continuing the single-minded workout, assault, or exploration of the available space.

At the beginning of the dance it is hard to read the rather abstract, unlocated swirls, but the narrative of the interaction between camera and dancer teaches us the dimensions and movements of the body. Thus, when we return to the abstract in the last part of the film, we can feel the physicality and presence underneath, we have become knowledgeable in the movement quality of this mover, and we share the energy and dynamic of the dance: the effect of abstraction is broken.

The narrative of knowledge creation, of how we process input, has propelled us to a kinaesthetic affinity with the young woman. Just like Benjamin's *flâneur* who develops physically out of his surroundings, I, a 'nineties viewer, share cultural knowledge through embodied experience. The single-minded movement work combined with Philip Jeck's driving metal music does not shut me out.

Instead of reading this video through the mechanisms of postmodern fragmentation and alienation, I want to point to the embodied nature of our 'city' knowledge that allows me to see and tune in to the shared physicality between me and the 'other'. An aesthetic of fragmentation, close-ups, separated limbs, and isolated movement needs to be read against the audience's capacity to make meaning out of the material.

For contemporary film and TV viewers, the sound and image bites of MTV or the erratic camera work of the crime series *NYPD Blue* are no longer alienating – they are recognized and understood aesthetic strategies. Our eyes and bodies have become trained to read a fast-moving media world. We have to acknowledge that we have fully entered a commodity world.

This world is a shared one: the ethical dimension of watching and being in time and space is not lost. In *Pace*, the camera acquires a body: the city act of gazing, scanning, and focusing here becomes an embodied presence through the negotiations with physicality. Literally, the cameraperson recording the dance has to evade kicks and move quickly to capture feet and turns. This camera is no disembodied eye, but is held by somebody whose physical presence leaves traces on the recorded material.

The body, then, reasserts itself as always already there – not as something 'brute' or 'hindering' or 'essential', but as something that takes part in the act of watching, essential to the participation in culture. This physicality, the inertia, the being in time and space, can be an insertion point for resistances and re-inscriptions.

The paradoxes of knowing

In the shared body-knowledge, the paradoxes of knowing can become apparent, when the repetition of the same produces difference. Thus, the female body hunted by the camera, surveyed by the masculinized eye – the same old story – can hold difference when the shared embodiedness of the cultural field intrudes on the fantasy of pure vision. The camera has to side-step.

The *flâneur* is of the same as that which he or she surveys.[9] The positions change together, and gain mobility across cultural binaries together. Benjamin's *flâneur* hasn't become a *flâneuse* in my reading – instead, the position of the *flâneur* as limited, witnessing change, susceptible to cultural and social forces, and fragilely enacted in corporeality has become apparent.

As Foucault reminds us, gender is itself implicated in the construction of bodies through knowledge. Gender is not purely socially constructed, but neither is it essentially there. Sexuality

> is the name that can be given to a historical construct: not a furtive reality that is difficult to grasp, but a great surface network in which the stimulation of bodies, the intensification of pleasures, the incitement to discourse, the formation of special knowledges, the strengthening or controls and resistances, are linked to one another, in accordance with a few major strategies of knowledge and power.
>
> (Foucault, 1978, p. 105–6)

The body is not pre-gendered, but is present in a field of discursive lines that bind it to meaning. At the same time, the body is the shared ground of meaning. The *flâneur* is a specific alignment of bodies, discourses, habits, gaze structures, and gender identities at a specific time and place.

The binary inscription of the *flâneuse* is not necessary. To posit a *flâneuse* would not only reduce the historic specificity of the *flâneur*, but would also take away from the ground of commonality within which discursive difference is established. The *flâneur* is already a playing field of historical differences in body attitudes, gender inscriptions, and habits.

When I read Benjamin's *flâneur* as a specific and choreographically held position, I can open up performance possibilities on the limits of witnessing and watching. The corporeal presence of performer and audience in a shared time and space (if not necessarily in a literally shared time and space) can mobilize discursive inscriptions (such as the binaries of disabled/non-disabled or male/ female). As I have shown in my analyses of *Strange Days, Einblicke, Orch- Skirt,* and *Pace,* the embodied urban and the repetitions of the *flâneur*-moment in the cityscape can open up new choreographies for bodies and knowledges.

Notes

1. In the text, I am referring to the urban, being-in-the-city, and contemporary embodiment. I am using Benjamin's approach as a way to account for the lived experience of being in a specific historical environment. I am not entering into debates about the differences and continuities between modernity and postmodernity: my reading of Benjamin sees his figures as historically contingent, and his analysis as open to changes within the economic, social, and cultural environment.
2. Philip Auslander (1997) discussed the mediatization of performance, necessitating a non-essential vision of works of art and their origins. In this article, my focus is on the specific cultural meanings and messages that can be seen to adhere to specific performance instances, including the specific alignments of mediated and live forms. Benjamin's emphasis on the micro-politics of any work of art have alerted me to the complexities of the meetings of media, bodies, and spaces.
3. In particular, Luce Irigaray and Hélène Cixous's writings on the borderline of essentialism have moved feminists in performance studies. But the crux of imagining the concrete body as either pre-gendered, or as essentially gendered, is hard to overcome. At the same time, theorists who point to surface or body-knowledge as a second, 'other' category to 'discourse knowledge' and its binaries find themselves hard-pressed to articulate the effects of one on the other. Recent interventions into this field include Amelia Jones's *Body Art* and Rebecca Schneider's *The Explicit Body.*
4. Other highly evocative aspects of Benjamin's writing, such as the dialectical image and the gaze of the object, have been used by contemporary performance theorists (see Schneider, 1997). Benjamin's discussions of the aura and the aesthetics of material practice have influenced writers such as Alan Read (1993) in his discussion of the dialectical meeting of theatre and the everyday, and Auslander (1997) in his project to account for the proliferation of media in performance work.
5. Such instances of re-reading Benjamin are bel hooks's extension of Woolf's criticism: she points to the impossibility of black *flâneurs*/angels in her reading of Wim Wenders's *Wings of Desire* (1990) and S. Munt's appropriation in 'The Lesbian Flâneur' (1995). Within film studies, the most extended work on *flâneur* and the *flâneuse* can be found in Anne Friedberg's *Window Shopping: Cinema and the Postmodern* (1993). She focuses on disembodied *flânerie* in cinema – directly opposite to my emphasis on the embodied experience of being in the city leaving traces in performance.
6. The history of the disabled body in western culture is characterized by both its invisibility in the 'normal world' and its hypervisibility in the world of the side-show, the circus, or the medical performance platform. The dynamics of looking at a disabled woman in a space

which negotiates the public/private domain are charged with these histories of unequal visual power relations (see Thomson, 1997).

7. My source for this information is director Daniel Aschwanden, personal communication.

8. My description of the performance is indebted to Sorrel Muggridge, personal communication, and her review in *Liveartmagazine* (1998), p. 23–4.

9. This is not a Utopian moment of togetherness, but a recognition of being part of a commodity world: 'The *flâneur* is someone abandoned in the crowd. In this he shares the situation of commodity. ... The intoxication to which *the flâneur* surrenders is the intoxication of the commodity around which surges the stream of customers' (Benjamin, 1973, p. 55).

References

Philip Auslander, 'Against Ontology: Making Distinctions between the Live and the Mediatized', *Performance Research*, II, No. 3 (1997), p. 50–5.

Walter Benjamin, trans. H. Zohn, *Charles Baudelaire: a Lyric Poet in the Era of High Capitalism* (London: New Left Books, 1973).

Susan Bordo, *Unbearable Weight: Feminism, Western Culture, and the Body* (Berkeley: California University Press, 1993).

Valerie Briginshaw, '"Keep Your Great City Paris": the Lament of the Empress and Other Women', in *Dance in the City*, ed. Helen Thomas (Basingstoke: Macmillan, 1997), p. 34–49.

Ann Cooper Albright, *Choreographing Difference: the Body and Îdentity in Contemporary Dance* (Hanover: Wesleyan University Press, 1997).

Michel Foucault, trans. R. Hurley, *The History of Sexuality*, Vol. I (London: Allen Lane, 1978).

——, *Language, Counter-Memory, Practice: Selected Essays and Interviews*, ed. Donald Bouchard (Oxford: Blackwell, 1977).

Anne Friedberg, *Window Shopping: Cinema and the Postmodern* (Berkeley: University of California Press, 1993).

Elisabeth Grosz, *Volatile Bodies: Toward a Corporeal Feminism* (Bloomington: Indiana University Press, 1994).

Lena Hammergren, 'The Return of the Flâneuse', in *Corporealities: Dancing Knowledge, Culture and Power*, ed. Susan Leigh Foster (London: Routledge, 1996), p. 53–69.

bel hooks, 'Representing Whiteness: Seeing Wings of Desire', in *Yearning: Race, Gender, and Cultural Politics* (Boston: West End Press, 1990), p. 165–71.

Frederic Jameson, 'Postmodernism and Consumer Society', in *Postmodernism and its Discontents*, ed. E. A. Kaplan (London: Verso, 1988), p. 13–29.

Amelia Jones, *Body Art: Performing the Subject* (Minneapolis: University of Minnesota Press, 1998).

Sorrel Muggridge, 'Souvenirs', *Liveartmagazine*, No. 22 (5 October–30 November 1998), p. 23–4.

S. Munt, 'The Lesbian Flâneur', in *Mapping Desire*, ed. D. Bell and G. Valentine (London: Routledge, 1995).

Alan Read, *Theatre and Everyday Life: an Ethics of Performance* (London: Routledge, 1993).

Rebecca Schneider, *The Explicit Body in Performance* (London: Routledge, 1997).

Rosemarie Garland Thomson, ed., *Freakery: Cultural Spectacles of the Extraordinary Body* (New York: New York University Press, 1996).

Janet Woolf, 'The Invisible *Flâneuse*: Women and the Literature of Modernity', in *Feminine Sentences* (Cambridge: Polity Press, 1990), p. 34–50.

——, 'Memoirs and Micrologies: Walter Benjamin, Feminism, and Cultural Analysis', *New Formations*, No. 2 (Summer 1993), p. 113–22.

1.6   A Manifesto for a New Walking Culture: 'Dealing with the City'
Wrights and Sites

This manifesto was performed at a plenary session of a conference for urban planners, architects, activists and others interested in walking. Consistent with the site-specificity of our work at that time, it was created with the conference's Zürich venue, Kasino, in mind: it makes reference not only to the idea of the casino, but also to Zürich Dada and to Bertolt Brecht's brief period of exile in the city.

The idea of casino provided the structure of the manifesto, which is divided into four suits (as in a deck of playing cards). Each 'suit' was written by a different member of Wrights & Sites. For the 'court cards' (Jack, Queen, King) of each of these four suits, guest artists were invited to create short manifesto provocations. Fiona Templeton and Richard Layzell contributed short video statements, stills from which are presented here, while texts by Bess Lovejoy (with Damon Morris) and contemporaries of the Dada movement were projected.

The order of presentation was guided by a shuffle of a deck of cards by a croupier.

We had always liked the idea of writing a manifesto, though previous attempts to do so had spiralled into chaotic, lengthy documents or been forgotten, lost amid a plethora of other projects. The invitation to Zürich seemed an opportunity to realise this ambition, with a nod towards Dada's manifestos (or anti-manifestos). The structuring device of the deck of cards provided us with a formal strategy for layering the multiple perspectives in the manifesto.

The context of the manifesto was the making of site-specific perform-ance and art projects, with a particular emphasis on cities, carried out by Wrights & Sites since its formation in 1997. In 2003, we had produced *An Exeter Mis-Guide*, which encouraged new ways of exploring the city, making it strange and seeking out its 'mythogeography' (the personal, mythical, fictional and fanciful mappings that intertwine or subvert the official, municipal identities and histories of a place). Despite being made for a small city in the South-West of England, we were surprised by the interest in the book by people in other cities, countries and even continents. People were using *An Exeter Mis-Guide*, a book written for a city they would probably never even visit, in order to gather ideas for exploring their own locali-ties. In response to this, and disrupting the specificity of our own practice, we created a new publication, published shortly after this manifesto was written, but very much part of the same collection of work: *A Mis-Guide To Anywhere*, which plays with the absurd ambitions of its title and invites the reader to use it 'anywhere', thereby encouraging comparisons and imaginative links between diverse places. Alongside these publications and others (for example, *A Courtauld Mis-Guide*, created for the East Wing Collection at London's Courtauld Institute) we have worked with the 'drift' or 'dérive', the guided tour and other site-specific performance not only in Exeter but in other cities, islands and open spaces (Manchester, Münich, Herm, Bilbao, Paris, Naples, Winchester, Little Wittenham, New York, Milton Keynes, Ndola and Welcombe Barton to name a few).

Drawing on our urban exploratory work, this is a manifesto for the *active and creative* pedestrian. It envisions a walking that is neither a functional necessity (to shops, to work) nor a passive appreciation of (or complaint about) the urban environment. Instead this is a manifesto for a walking that engages with and changes the city, it recruits the arts not as passive expressions or appreciations of the city, but as the active changings of it.

Wrights & Sites would like to acknowledge support from the Centre for Creative Enterprise & Participation, Dartington College of Arts (now merged with University College Falmouth), the University of Exeter and the University of Winchester.

Q♦
'Our intent is to show walking not only as a directed movement from one place to another, but a wandering, an odyssey of sight and sound, a quest for knowledge and stimulation, a grand roaming expedition, and a living breathing work of art in its own right.' (Lovejoy & Morris 2005)

4♣

WALK: Attempt to redress, in a small way, the overabundance of hierarchical road signs established by our public servants.[1] 'They may, for example, tell you that there is only "one way" to navigate a particular area. Find other ways of walking, mapping and signing routes through these public spaces.' (Wrights & Sites 2003: 46)

3♠

To combat the functionalism of walking by having no particular place to go. To pick up on other walkers' varied paces from speedy to slow. To invent small or secret dances at bus stops and on railway platforms. To invite people to go for walks with you as a gift to be unwrapped with your feet. To use walking as an opportunity to greet neighbours and to break long-established silences. To write the city with your relationships.

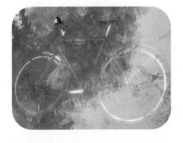

8♣

WALK: Abolish weather forecasts,[2] and consign the umbrella to the dissecting table.[3] Don't physically or mentally 'wrap yourself up against all weathers'. Unlike most municipal tour guides and their followers, be prepared to enjoy 'getting wet' along the way.

5♥

Guy Debord writes of the Situationist 'dérive' or 'drift', 'Written descriptions can be no more than passports to this great game.' (Debord 1995 [1958]: 53) We described our first Mis-Guide as 'a forged passport to your "other" city.' (Wrights & Sites 2003: back cover)

The passport gets us across a threshold, raises the curtain. The text of a misguide designates the city as a real, yet imaginary, space of play.

Brecht wrote that the only passport needed by theatre was fun: the invitation to a game. (Brecht 1964 [1949]: 180)

Our suggestions for walking make things strange, make the city 'other', as if the lighting state has suddenly altered. This is the half light, the 'candlelight' which, in the children's rhyme, gets us to Babylon and back.[4]

A♦

Is there any point in making walking safe if it only gets us to the hospice more efficiently?

J♦

'Most daily life in the westernized world involves pod-based living, from the home "pod" to the train or car "pod" to the work "pod", creating a closed-in sensorium that becomes one's sole experience. This is the antithesis of walking culture.' (Lovejoy & Morris 2005)

6♠

To go shopping without the intention to buy and to view shopping malls as hyper-real museums to consumerism. To travel the world in a supermarket making atlases from imported food placed in your basket or trolley. To write the city with conscious choices.

9♦

Hail the new citizen-octopus! – discovering sensations in the textures and secrets of their city, a city disrupted to meet the needs and desires of an evolving, mutating walking. Until the planners mutate we cannot submit our dreams to their permission, until then our plans will have momentum outside of legislation.

K♠

'This is a bus. They've only had buses in Tbilisi for three weeks. And I haven't taken one because nobody's quite sure where they go. It's much safer to walk.'[5]

K♦

'Different languages and moods float by, intermingling with sounds of industry, business, music, laughter, and the crying of children and seagulls. As the walker is drawn in by a friendly face, a startling art exhibit, or a secret path into strange lush grottos, we follow their experiences and are drawn in as well.' (Lovejoy & Morris 2005)

cabaret

Q♣

'...to be a Dadaist means to let oneself be thrown by things, to oppose all sedimentation; to sit in a chair for a single moment is to risk one's life ...' (Huelsenbeck 1989 [1920]: 246)

4♥

We aspire to games that are open to everyone, to the sky.

In Monte Carlo, I walked around the Grand Casino, fascinated by its doorways, its steps and arches. Security guards quietly hovered in the entrances. 'Members only' were invited up ornate steps. In the entrance hall there were photographs of Salvador Dali, kissing Princess Grace and speeding across the bay in a boat with Walt Disney.

I felt more at home with the herd of decorated cattle wandering the city centre: the *Cow Parade*, last seen in Manchester. Inelegant tourists, dressed in hearts and daisies, they seemed to look curiously at the casino, but remained sceptical.

A♠

Step on the cracks and find the gaps and make new tracks. Extend your walking territory becoming more aware of the restrictions being imposed upon you by signs and surfaces and the aggressive armoured invasion of the car. Extend your experience by habitually eroding the controls of speed and commerce. Walk a new walking culture to write the city with your bodies.

7♠

To give a word to each footstep so that a walk becomes a story or poem. To re-enact particular walks and styles of walking that you have found in books, plays and films and to write the city with your own associations.

J♠

'Somewhere here, six years ago, I broke my foot. But, when you break your foot, the hole is not the thing you remember. And it was dark. And I said I can walk in the dark, but I wasn't bargaining on the holes in the streets of Tbilisi.'[6]

6♣

'WALK: Abolish habitual walking patterns',[7] such as the home-to-work-and-back routine: those head-down journeys when the mind is focused elsewhere and 'elsewhen'. Walking artists, Lone Twin, for example, disrupted the byways of Colchester by carrying a telegraph pole in a straight line across the city, right through houses and shops, in their piece *Totem* (1998). 'I think we should get into the river … and walk from one side to the other', he said, Gary to Gregg. (Lone Twin 2001: 2)

4♠

To insist upon the rights of the pedestrian over the car. To dream of the day when you do not have to say 'Mind the road' to children. To continue laying flowers at the sites of pedestrian road accident fatalities. To regard wheelchair users as walkers not separate from ped-estrians. Take a chair into the Shopping Mall to see this point of view / this viewpoint. Break the taboo and travel by wheelchair for a day. To write the city with Human Rights.

2♦

Every walk is a potential planning – we can be planners or we can be artist's impressions.

7♥

Babylon is a dangerous place. Walking is the exercise of a freedom that does not exist everywhere or at all times or for all people. It is the exercise of a freedom to re-make the space by the ways in which we live it, perform it, play it.

10♥

We demand the right to linger. We are loiterers without intent. We are children taking the long way home from school.

J♥

'I think walking as part of my practice crept up on me: it was happening before I realised it.'[8]

10♠

To re-value public space with an eye more akin to the musings and perceptions of children so that we might gain a deeper insight into the 'poetics of space', inviting children's participation in the planning of their environments. To hold meetings, discussions, readings, and vigils on traffic islands or to make decisions on foot and on the streets instead of in airless committee meeting rooms. To write minutes, musings and decisions on paving stones.

K♣

'Leave everything. Leave Dada. Leave your wife. Leave your mistress. Leave your hopes and fears. Leave your children in the woods. Leave the substance for the shadow. Leave your easy life, leave what you are given for the future. Set off on the roads.' (Breton 1978 [1922]: 166)

5♦

We might change the meaning of 'excess' – from 'rubbish tip' to moving without a destination' – every seventh sign in our city will be a mystery, a metaphor or an absurdity.

10♦

In every city we will set up a Tourist Misinformation Office – to tell the truth about the city... to invite our visitors to re-make the city rather than consume it – we will stop tidying ruins and lighting the night sky, we will encourage public art to be made by the public – this will be funded by a subsidy equivalent to the city's spending on tranquilisers, weapons and automobiles.

K♥

'Now it's integrated into designing major events for 150 people to walk silently through a major city.'[9]

3♦

One architect-walker dreams of a city as delicate as flesh – where bodies are respected as pillars of stone once were. This architect will design the next landscapes as extended human organs.

Q♥

'Walking was becoming an art-form without really intending it to be.'[10]

9♠

Amble, ramble and de-ramble the city in search of wildlife, ancient tracks, sacred signs and paths of desire and fill abandoned roadside cars with earth and turn them into immobile gardens. To celebrate the growth of weeds, plants, flowers in the most hostile urban zones. To follow the journeys of insects as your guides. To write the city with cobwebs, tendrils and minute flora and fauna.

Zürich GPS map [detail]
Daniel Belasco Rogers

7♣

WALK: Abolish industrially-produced maps.[11] Walking can facilitate the construction of new, more personalised maps, as in the case of Daniel Belasco Rogers' *The daily practice of map making*. He's been using a handheld GPS device to record all of his journeys since April 2003.[12] 'If at the end of your life, you could look at the shapes your wanderings over the earth have made, what patterns would you see? What words may be formed that take a human lifetime to write?' he said in his piece *Unfallen* (2003).

5♠

To invite town planners on practical courses exploring trespass and paths of desire. To adopt public places for sitting as if they are an extension of your home and to recognise and respect the people whose furniture is the street. To write the city with your presence.

Q♠

'This is another dangerous spot to walk because usually there's water coming out of this spout here – because they don't really have gutters. It just pours out onto the street. So, I'm going to walk under it for safety – behind it.'[13]

8♥

Communists of international distinction have no business in our country any longer. Just because it is more comfortable to live in ... bourgeois Switzerland is no reason to let such foreigners take root here.

(Zürich foreign police, cited in Honegger 2005: 109)

And so the Zürich police refused a residence permit to Bertolt Brecht: his games were shifted elsewhere, his letters left in a forgotten suitcase, like so many others all over Europe. In spite of paranoid reactions to international terrorism, we propose to keep on welcoming strangers.

10♣

WALK: Believe absolutely that every walker is a potential mis-guide, every walk leads to anywhere.[14]

6♦

Another architect-walker will design a city of ideas where beliefs and differences of opinion blow the flags on an invisible town hall – yet another lets nature in, leaves spaces for miniature wildernesses, designs a monument to the glacier, wave or asteroid that will one day destroy us.

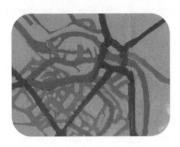

9♣

WALK: Abolish ETAs, predetermined destinations and thoughts of artistic outcomes.[15] Forget the future as you walk. Leave your watch at home. Drift for three or four months at a time as the psychogeographer, Ivan Chtcheglov, claimed to do. Like the artist, Richard Long, let the walk become the work. 'To walk a line is the easiest thing a human being can do to put his [or her] mark on a place,' he said. (Long 1991: 27)

8♦

Playfulness, disruption, gifts left for strangers, the sharing of visions, intelligent flash-mobbing, provocations at the tipping points of cities, making a scene so that the city performs itself, mis-guided tours, wireless on-line technology – combining phone, movie, digital design, camera, editing desk and ipod – sending routes, signs and stories in waves across spreading networks of uncontrollable walking, maps of atmospheres and basins of attraction, and festivals celebrating the reflections in windows and the glints in pedestrians' eyes – these are the instruments of the architect-walker – extraordinary changes will begin with disruptions in the ordinary.

A♥

Between one thing and another there hangs a curtain: let us draw it up!
(Brecht 1964 [1949]: 189)

J♣

'If you are ready to leave father and mother, and brother and sister, and wife and child and friends, and never see them again – if you have paid your debts, and made your will, and settled all your affairs, and are a free man – then you are ready to go for a walk.' (Thoreau 1994 [1862]: 4)

6♥

A 9 year old is quoted as saying: 'The most favourite game played in school is "Schools".' (Opie and Opie 1984: 333) As we walk the city, we like to play a game of 'cities'.

4♦

The pavements are our színház, our *stadt-theater*, our Institute of Contemporary Arts.

9♥

Wir wollen in den Garten gehn,
Wenn nur der böse Geist nicht wär!
(German children's rhyme,
cited in Opie and Opie 1984: 109)

A♣

WALK: Protest with your feet.[16]

2♣

WALK: Acquaint yourself with methods of urban exploration rejected by the good manners of the heritage and tourism industries.[17] 'What happens if you overlay a map of Moscow onto your own city? What do you find where the Kremlin should be? Look for coincidences or references to Russia. Stop in bars and drink vodka. What about Baghdad? ...' (Wrights & Sites 2006: 17)

3♥

On 9th November, 1947, the exiled Bertolt Brecht was in Zürich and drafted, with others, a manifesto for peace. While here, he also wrote his 'A Short Organum for the Theatre' (Brecht 1964 [1949]) in which he wished for a theatre that could help to change the world. We share Brecht's impulse to make the familiar strange, to engage in the movement of the world, to be flexible, to be open. However, in our work together, we have drawn different conclusions, finding it necessary to abandon the theatre space, however makeshift and temporary, and to walk with people, rather than perform in front of them. The acquisition of a theatre (as Brecht knew, or was to find out) is enmeshed in the conquest of territory. We wanted none of it.

Pas à Pas (Step by Step)

3♣

WALK: Abolish the Desk, home to scratching nibs and physical and mental stasis.[18] Erik Satie, for example, the only musician permitted access to the Dada 'club', used to compose during his daily walks to and from the centre of Paris, pausing under lamp-posts at night to write down his thoughts. Listen to his music and you will hear his footsteps. 'Before I compose a piece, I walk round it several times, accompanied by myself,' he said. (Satie 1980 [1913]: 79)

2♥

On Iona and Peter Opie's map (Opie and Opie 1984: 67), our city, Exeter, is replaced with the word 'Hit', while Dartmoor becomes 'Catchers'. North Devon is marked 'TIG'; Plymouth and Helston are both 'It' and Penzance becomes 'Hits'. This map of children's words for chasing games transforms the territory into the space of play we know it to be. We sneak into the grown-up spaces and steal our fun from under municipal noses:

> König, ich bin in deinem
> Land Ich stehl dir Gold und Silbersand.
> (German chasing rhyme,
> cited in Opie and Opie 1984: 86)

8♠

To reclaim the nights in the city. Walking through the streets at the dead of night is not a criminal offence. Insomniacs should not be made to feel guilty for being up and about. Walk where streets have become ghost corridors for somnambulists.

7♦

Anyone, anywhere can be an architect-walker – begin by mapping atmospheres and feelings – they are our foundations as we build from ideas and emotions outwards ...

2♠

To walk with a sense of not knowing anything about the city.

To walk as a constant experiment to discover the intricacies and individuality of your walk that is as distinctive as your handwriting.

> Now the city would move like a map you were drawing; now you would begin to live your life like a book you were writing.

Called forth by a street or a building, an ensemble of gestures might imply that a different street had to be found, that a building could be redesigned by the gestures performed within it, that new gestures had to be made, even that an unknown city had to be built or an old one overthrown ...

(Marcus 1990: 166)

5 ♣

WALK: Know that every object, all objects, feelings and obscurities, every apparition and the precise shock of parallel lines, are potential material for an artwork.[19] As you walk, gather found material, record the stories of the people that you encounter, encourage personal associations, generate mythogeographies, look for the extra-ordinary in the seemingly ordinal ...

Notes

1. See Tristan Tzara, *Dada Manifesto 1918*, originally read in the Salle Meise, Zürich, 23 March 1918 (1992 [1918]: 13): 'DADA; every hierarchy and social equation established for values by our valets'.
2. See Tzara (1992 [1918]: 13): 'DADA; the abolition of prophets'.
3. A reference to Lautréamont's oft-quoted, pre-Surrealist statement from *Maldoror* (1868-1869): 'As beautiful as the chance meeting on a dissecting table of a sewing machine and an umbrella.'
4. The rhyme goes as follows: 'How many miles to Babylon? / Three score and ten. / Can I get there by candlelight? / Yes, and back again.'
5. This text by Fiona Templeton was accompanied by a video extract of a research walk around Tbilisi (2005).
6. This text by Fiona Templeton was accompanied by a video extract of a research walk around Tbilisi (2005).
7. See Tzara (1992 [1918]: 13): 'DADA; the abolition of memory'.
8. This text by Richard Layzell was accompanied by a video extract of *Walking in Circles* (research in Wargrave, UK, 1999).
9. This text by Richard Layzell was accompanied by a video extract of *Sense Walk* (Project IS, Bristol, UK, 2005).
10. This text by Richard Layzell was accompanied by a video extract of *Talking to Tania 1* (Skyros, Greece, 2004).
11. See Tzara (1992 [1918]: 13): 'DADA; the abolition of archaeology'.
12. See http://www.planbperformance.net/dan/mapping.htm for further information.
13. This text by Fiona Templeton was accompanied by a video extract of a research walk around Tbilisi (2005).

14. See Tzara (1992 [1918]: 13): 'DADA; the absolute and indisputable belief in every god that is an immediate product of spontaneity'.
15. See Tzara (1992 [1918]: 13): 'DADA; the abolition of the future'.
16. See Tzara (1992 [1918]: 13): 'DADA; protest with the fists of one's whole being in destructive action'.
17. See Tzara (1992 [1918]: 13): 'DADA; acquaintance with all the means hitherto rejected by the sexual prudishness of easy compromise and good manners'.
18. See Tzara (1992 [1918]: 13): 'DADA; abolition of logic, dance of those who are incapable of creation'.
19. See Tzara (1992 [1918]: 13): 'DADA; every object, all objects, feelings and obscurities, every apparition and the precise shock of parallel lines, are means for the battle of'.

References

Brecht, Bertolt (1964) [1949], 'A Short Organum for the Theatre', in *Brecht on Theatre*, trans, and ed. John Willett, London: Methuen, pp. 179–208.

Breton, André (1978) [1922], 'Leave Everything', in *Dada and Surrealism Reviewed*, Dawn Ades, London: Arts Council of Great Britain, p.166.

Debord, Guy (1995) [1958], 'Theory of the Dérive', in *Situationist International Anthology*, trans. and ed. Ken Knabb, Berkeley (USA): Bureau of Public Secrets, pp. 50–54.

Honegger, Gitta (2005), 'Brecht, Switzerland, and the Hunt for the Lost Suitcase', *Theater*, 35: 1, March, pp. 109–113.

Huelsenbeck, Richard (1989) [1920], 'Collective Dada Manifesto', in *The Dada Painters and Poets: An Anthology*, ed. Robert Motherwell, Cambridge (Massachusetts) and London: The Belknap Press of Harvard University Press, pp. 242–246.

Lone Twin (2001), *Of Pigs & Lovers: A Lone Twin Research Companion*, London: Arts Council England.

Long, Richard (1991), *Walking In Circles*, London: Anthony d'Offay Gallery.

Lovejoy, Bess & Damon Morris (2005), *Going Anywhere*, unpublished artist's statement of intent.

Marcus, Greil (1990), *Lipstick Traces, A Secret History of the Twentieth Century*, London: Seeker & Warburg.

Opie, Iona and Peter Opie (1984), *Children's Games in Street and Playground*, Oxford and New York: Oxford University Press.

Satie, Erik (1980) [1913], 'Erik Satie', in *The Writings of Erik Satie*, trans. and ed. Nigel Wilkins, London: Eulenburg Books, p. 79.

Thoreau, Henry David 1994 [1862], *Walking*, San Francisco: HarperSanFrancisco.

Tzara, Tristan (1992) [1918], *Seven Dada Manifestos and Lampisteries*, trans. Barbara Wright, London, Paris and New York: Calder Publications.

Wrights & Sites (2003), *An Exeter Mis-Guide*, Exeter (UK): Local Heritage Initiative/Arts Council England.

—— (2006), *A Mis-Guide To Anywhere*, Exeter (UK): Arts Council England/Centre for Creative Enterprise & Participation.

Part 2
Drifting/Things

Text sources

2.1 Carl Lavery (2006) 'Situationism', *Performance Research*, 11(3): 111–13.

2.2 Andrew Hussey (2002) ' "The Map is Not the Territory": The Unfinished Journey of the Situationist International', *Urban Visions: Experiencing and Envisioning the City*, ed. S. Speir, Liverpool: Liverpool University Press and Tate Publishing: 215–28.

2.3 Richard Wentworth (2002) ' "The Accident of Where I Live" – Journeys on the Caledonian Road' (interview with Joe Kerr), *The Unknown City: Contesting Architecture and Social Space*, ed. I. Borden et al., London and Cambridge, MA: MIT Press: 386–405.

2.4 Alex Coles (2000) ' "How Long I 'Been On?": Marc Dion's Performative Archaeology of the City', *Breathing Cities: the Architecture of Movement*, ed. N. Barley, Basel, Boston and Berlin: Birkhäuser: 60–3.

2.5 Lyn Gardner (2007) 'What a Carry On', *Guardian*, 13 June: 26.

2.6 Paul Rae with Low Kee Hong (2003) 'Nosing Around: A Singapore Scent Trail', *Performance Research*, 8(3): 44–54.

Introduction

'We're off the route...we're off the route...'

Forced Entertainment, *Nights in This City*

Situationism

The inclusion of Situationism as one of the entries in a lexicon of key words relating to performance, recently published by *Performance Research* journal, serves as sufficient indication of the significance of this movement to the field. Historically curiosity has tended to flow one way, for, as the author of this entry points out: 'Although Situationism was definitely interested in performance, it rejected, with vehemence, all forms of organised theatre and was especially dismissive of Allan Kaprow's practice of happenings, which it regarded as depoliticised, exclusive and bourgeois' (*PCC*, p. 93). Carl Lavery cites several instances of contemporary practice that have been influenced by the ideas of the Situationist International, and he supplies a lucid summary of the way certain concepts relate to both performance and, importantly, the phenomenon of the city. (The line quoted above from a Forced Entertainment piece, involving a guided bus tour round the cities of Sheffield and Rotterdam respectively, encapsulates the idea of 'being lost' as a generative feature of both performing and encountering the city; in Kaye 2000: 13). Andrew Hussey's article meanwhile picks up the tab of this post-Situationist theme, pursuing the possibilities of what he identifies as the movement's 'unfinished business'.

The Situationist International, officially operational in Paris between 1957 and 1972, comprehensively developed the notion of 'drift' (*dérive*) as a form of reconception and remapping of the city based on a performative practice of 'walking without aim', as well as inducing impromptu 'diversions' (*détournement*): that is, triggering responses or 'situations' in public places that momentarily introduced ruptures into the urban everyday (or aspects of the so-called 'society of the spectacle'). In 'Theory of the Dérive', Guy Debord – doubtless the movement's principal player – is keen to play down the significance of chance as 'a less important factor in this activity than one might think: from a dérive point of view cities have psycho-geographical contours, with constant currents, fixed points and vortexes that strongly discourage entry into or exit from certain zones' (in Knabb 2006: 62). For Debord 'Progress means breaking through fields where chance holds sway by creating new conditions more favourable to our purposes' (ibid.: 63). Of other significant features to emerge from the practice the first is its varied durational aspect, a factor that surely pushes it towards the time-based conventions of performance: 'The average duration of a dérive is one day [but] one sequence of dérives was pursued without notable interruption for around two months' (ibid.: 64). A second aspect, of particular interest for this section, is the 'possible rendezvous' in which 'the subject is invited to come alone to a certain place at a specified time'. Ostensibly 'He is freed from the bothersome obligations of the ordinary rendezvous since there is no-one to wait for.' But 'It may be that the same spot has been specified for a "possible rendezvous" for someone else whose identity he has no way of knowing. Since he may never even have seen the other person before, he will be encouraged to start up conversations with various passers-by' (ibid.: 65).

The unattributed, shorter meditation on *détournement* as 'negation and prelude' that follows Debord's piece in Knabb's anthology is worth mentioning here too, primarily for its description of what sounds in many ways akin to the tactics of deconstruction. For Derrida, one of the options of the latter practice is 'to use against the edifice the instruments or stones available in the house' (1982: 135). The Situationists' 'negation and prelude' by comparison are premised on the 'loss of importance of each detourned autonomous element – which may go so far as to lose its original sense – and at the same time the organisation of another meaningful ensemble that confers on each element its new scope and effect' (in Knabb 2006: 67). Importantly, as Hussey makes clear in his article, it is the city that is seen as the 'future battleground for the conflict over the meaning of modernity', a battle that represents 'in many ways the defining moment in the development of Situationist strategy' (*PCC*, p. 96). Here a key distinction emerges between the latter and the apparently related practice of *flânerie*. Where the *flâneur* favours a form of ironic detachment from the 'society of the spectacle', Situationist practices are 'characterised by an active hostility to the representation of urban experience'. Instead, they are 'political acts which aim to reinstate lived experience as the true map of the city' (*PCC*, p. 97). If anything, Hussey points out (citing Patrick ffrench), the *dérive* is effectively a *détournement* of *flânerie*, according to the method of negation and prelude mentioned above (*PCC*, p. 97).

Collecting

The work of the artists Richard Wentworth and Mark Dion takes us into the realm of 'things': urban artefacts that tend to be overlooked or discarded as worthless, but that the artists retrieve and re-present in their respective ways.

In his interview with Wentworth, Joe Kerr sees this as a 'poetic engagement with observable reality ... not merely a task of recording' (*PCC*, p. 106), while the artist himself talks of 'calibrating our path through the city', which by extension can be said to correspond to 'how we gauge the calibre of a place' (*PCC*, p. 108). Wentworth's photographs of the Caledonian Road in North London, and, indeed, in many other cities of the world, are striking in that there are no people to be seen at all, merely traces of their presence, 'making do and getting by' (as one series of photographs was entitled): improvised signs of life in what are in fact densely populated urban environments; accidents of where and how people live. A displaced doormat draped on marble steps in Istanbul; a piece of paper stuck to the tarmac on a Barcelona street, bearing the tread-mark of the tyre that flattened it. These collected observations are what Walter Benjamin might have meant when he talked of a 'botanising of the asphalt' (1997b: 36). Ultimately it is the potential for 'visual riffs' to emerge from such found situations that seems to interest Wentworth: the poetry of coincidence, as well as the tactical disordering of order that is effected, which, in turn, produces its own quirky 'new order'. Despite the absence of people, Wentworth's reflections in the interview included here underline his interest in the streets as a 'kind of free theatre'. Importantly, he declares: 'the pleasure of the street for me is the fact that it's out of control' (*PCC*, p. 121). As such he is keen to rescue something positive from the voyeuristic notion of watching and being watched: 'it seems to me something that perhaps we ought to celebrate rather than try and prevent, because it's unpreventable' (*PCC*, p. 108). Without permitting the 'engine of curiosity' to run, the artist's process of looking, gathering, sifting and naming is halted.

Mark Dion's work could be said to subscribe to related precepts of collecting and cataloguing on the one hand, and of 'theatre' on the other. The event described here by Alex Coles, *Tate Thames Dig*, is referred to as a 'performative archaeology of the city' and involves several stages. Beginning with a process of beachcombing carried out by volunteers at two designated sites on the banks of the Thames river, it moves into an extended period of cleaning and classifying in tents sited outside the Tate Gallery, coupled with interaction with interested members of the public. This 'overlapping of the spaces of audience, volunteers and artists' produced an 'extremely engaging ... spontaneous choreography of the city'. The categorised detritus was then exhibited in a display cabinet (of curiosities) in the gallery, forming the final segment of this 'critical archaeology of the city' (*PCC*, p. 126).

Once again Walter Benjamin looms large in a contemplation of these artists' respective practices because of his preoccupation with the archetype of the itinerant rag-picker as a form of cultural historian or commentator.

Moreover, for Benjamin the 'promises of continual progress and endless improvement [were] among the mystifications of capitalism', with the 'endless stream of identical artefacts and the cyclical character of fashion' producing a phantasmagorical eternal return of the same, as we have seen (Gilloch 1997: 11–12). Rag-picking is 'the "career" of those who have been remaindered by capitalist modernization'; the transfigured rag-picker is then a cataloguer of 'the broken promises that have been abandoned in the everyday trash of history' (Highmore 2002: 63–5). As such, the archetype is emblematic of the fugitive or outsider, the rootless itinerant thrown 'hither and thither' by the effects of modernity. For Benjamin the activity of the rag-picker emerges, moreover, as a metaphorical figure of redemption: those things that have been rejected as worthless to humanity are salvaged as 'important to be deciphered' in order to understand, and thereby save, modernity (Gilloch 1997: 111).

Lone Twin's *Spiral*, featured in the article 'What a Carry On', is a durational site-specific piece that took place at London's Barbican Centre over a period of eight days in the summer of 2007. It too is based in part on collecting things, in this case a 'wonky table', which its two performers lug round the complex. However, as the company's name hints at, they are probably more interested in collecting people, or at least meeting them as the figurative fulfilment of the single twin's perception of there being 'something missing'. Thus the activity of carrying round a table containing donated objects, which they liken to 'a snowball gathering up everything in its path', serves as a form of elaborate pretext for bumping into strangers in unknown places: 'somebody said that what we do is go out into the city and look for love' (*PCC*, p. 128).

Paul Rae and Low Kee Hong are also in search of something in the city, but they rely on following their noses to track it down. As the final piece in the Drifting/Things section, this olfactory desire path through Singapore is already leading us to Part 3's specific preoccupation with another of the 'marginalised senses', that of hearing. Appropriately, my abiding memory of a recent stay in Singapore is precisely of its 'odours', be that the intense mix of spices and herbs in its Little India district or the pervasive whiff of mildew in some of the inadequately air-conditioned built environments of this tropical city. The authors' concern, though, is not merely to provide a 'scent map' of Singapore – paving the way for a 'perfumative drift' (*PCC*, p. 141) that, for a change, privileges the sense of smell over the visual – but to show how the performance of smell, above all its 're-' or 're-odorization', in a variety of contexts importantly constitutes the 'specific social, political and atmospheric conditions' of the new, independent Singapore (*PCC*, p. 130). In a way, then, Rae and Low conduct a form of scent analysis akin in its critical scope to Lefebvre's 'rhythmanalysis of cities', upon which Part 3 elaborates.

2.1   Situationism
Carl Lavery

Situationism describes the activities and ethos of the Situationist International (SI), a Paris-based **avant-garde** movement that existed from 1957 to 1972 and whose primary aim was to transform everyday life. Although it emerged from the experimental practices of post-second world war art groups such as Lettrism, Cobra and the Imaginist Bauhaus, the origins of Situationism can be traced back to Dadaism and Surrealism, both of which struggled to collapse rigid distinctions between art and politics. However unlike Dadaism, which wanted to abolish art in politics, and Surrealism, which sought to abolish politics in art, Situationism strove to resolve this dichotomy dialectically. In philosophical terms, this led Situationism to combine Marx's desire to change society with Nietszche's calls to treat life as a work of art. As a way of fulfilling this total revolution, Situationism violently rejected conventional forms of artistic expression and instead explored alternative, non-alienated modes of creativity. A favourite terrain for Situationism (at least in its early period in the 1950s) was the city, and contributors to the journal *Internationale Situationniste*, such as Ivan Chtcheglov, Michèle Bernstein and Ralph Rumney, explored the **practice** and theory of psycho-geography (registering how space affects consciousness) in an attempt to uncover the subtle connections of Paris, London and Venice. The aim behind this was to replace conventional urbanism with unitary urbanism, a playful form of city dwelling that was intended to undo the separation and aliena-tion produced by urban planners in the 1950s and 1960s. Although the Dutch architect Constant Nieuwenhuys sketched out plans for a Situationist city, the Situationists generally tried to realize their plans in more symbolic ways. The principal **technique** used was *la dérive* or drift, a planned walk in which a small group of adepts would consciously set out to register the psychogeographic effects or ambiences of certain areas and sites in the city. Drifting exemplified what the Situationists called *détournement*, a way of subverting the logic of the system by using the tools of the system against itself. Classic examples of *détournement* are found in the anti-art films of Guy Debord, as well as in the psychogeopraphic maps that he made with the Danish artist Asger Jorn.

The name Situationism can be traced back to Debord's essay 'Report on the Construction of Situations', in which he calls for 'constructed situations' to replace the passivity of art, and in particular theatre (2002: 46). However, an important influence that is often overlooked on the movement was Jean-Paul Sartre's populist brand of concrete existentialism.

According to Sartre, the human subject is always free to choose her freedom at any moment, and, for that reason, is always 'en situation'. Situationism reinterpreted Sartre's concept for its own purposes and deployed it for aesthetic and political ends rather than existential ones.

In the mid-1960s, Situationism entered its second, more theoretical phrase, and two key texts, one by Guy Debord (*The Society of the Spectacle*), the other by Raoul Vaneigem (*The Revolution of Everyday Life*), appeared in 1967. While there is no doubt that Situationism influenced the events of May 1968 in Paris, it is important to resist overestimating its real impact. The fall-out from May 1968 deflated the Situationists, and Debord disbanded the movement in 1972 but continued to criticize, with some validity, the increasing spectacularity of the world. While Situationism's theories can, from the vantage point of the present, certainly appear utopian, outdated and mistaken, concepts such as **spectacle**, everyday life and unitary urbanism remain pertinent. The movement has had a crucial influence on many performance artists and theorists, and it is very much in evidence in the work of experimental practitioners who use versions of *la dérive*, in an attempt to contest the spectacularity of everyday life in the city (see, for instance, Loading Deck, Graeme Miller, Mike Pearson, Fiona Templeton, Wrights & Sites). Nevertheless care needs to be taken here. Although Situationism was definitely interested in performance, it rejected, with vehemence, all forms of organized theatre and was especially dismissive of Allan Kaprow's **practice** of happenings, which it regarded as depoliticized, exclusive and bourgeois (see Vaneigem 2002: 147). This is not to say, however, that the spirit of Situationism is dead. On the contrary, it is embodied in the performative activism of movements such as Critical Mass and Reclaim the Streets, and in the interventionism of guerrilla theatre groups like ACT-UP and Billionaires for Bush. For these performer-activists, the **spectacle** is *détourné* (creatively hijacked) in an attempt to raise political awareness. Crucially, there is no product to consume in these performances, and the distinction between actors and spectators is often blurred.

References

Debord, Guy (2002) 'Report on the Construction of Situations and on the Terms of Organization and Action of the International Situationist Tendency', in Tom McDonough (ed.), *Guy Debord and the Situationist International: Texts and Documents*, Cambridge, Massachusetts: MIT Press, pp. 2–50.

Vaneigem, Raoul (2002), 'The Avant-garde of Presence', in Tom McDonough (ed.), *Guy Debord and the Situationist International: Texts and Documents*, Cambridge, Massachusetts: MIT Press, pp. 137–51.

Further reading

Bogad, L. M. (2005) *Electoral Guerrilla Theatre: Radical Ridicule and Social Movements*, London and New York: Routledge.

Hussey, Andrew (2002) 'The Map is not the Territory: The Unfinished Business of the Situationist International', in Steven Spier (ed.), *Urban Visions: Experiencing and Envisioning the City*, Liverpool: Liverpool University Press and Tate Liverpool, pp. 215–22.

Lavery, Carl (2005) 'The Pepys of London E11: Graeme Miller and the Politics of Linked', *New Theatre Quarterly* 21(2): 148–60.

Puchner, Martin (2004) 'Society of the Counter-Spectacle: Debord and the Theatre of the Situationists', *Theatre Research International* 29(1): 4–15.

Sadler, Simon (1998) *The Situationist City*, Cambridge, Massachusetts: MIT Press.

2.2 'The Map is Not the Territory': The Unfinished Journey of the Situationist International
Andrew Hussey

It is not by chance that the history of the Situationist International reads like an account of a military campaign. During their first, artistic phase (roughly speaking the period from 1957 to 1962), the Situationists declared a war of secession against what they contemptuously termed 'the civilisation of the image'.[1] They identified their enemies, in ascending order of importance, as work, leisure, boredom, advertising, modern art and, above all, the tendency of the present age to turn real life into an endless series of meaningless, frozen gestures or 'spectacles'. Their originality lay in the claim, delineated by the group's leading strategist Guy Debord, that 'the society of spectacle' could only be fought and defeated on its own terms.

Although the iconoclastic fury of the texts of this first period has remained undiminished by either the passage of time or academic scrutiny, it is the second, political phase, which has contributed most to the Situationists' legendary status. This period culminated in the 'revolutionary game' played out by the Situationists on the rue Gay-Lussac and in the Sorbonne during the events of May 1968. For a fleeting moment, as they engaged the enemy in the streets of Paris, the Situationists seemed to live up to their own expectations as avatars of the high point of post-war revolutionary theory. It is, therefore, a cruel irony that since 1968 the Situationist International has largely been considered no more than a footnote in the cultural history of post-war France and that, since his death in 1994, Guy Debord has been hailed in France less as a revolutionary thinker than as a master of French prose.[2]

What I want to propose here, however, is that the theses of the Situationist International still represent, more than any other revolutionary force this century, the potential to disrupt the organisation of society in a way which would be irreversible. For the Situationists following from Henri Lefebvre argue that pleasure, technology, and everyday life are in themselves transformative agents which can and should be used as weapons against the society of the spectacle, even in a world where – as Guy Debord emphasises in his later writings – real political activity has been inexorably and inevitably replaced by integrated spectacle (*spectacle integré*).[3] Most importantly, the Situationists sought to separate their activity from the dead language of classical French Marxism by privileging method and action over historical process. In this way the Situationist project can be read as not simply an attack on the shibboleths of Marxist orthodoxy, but also as a critical method which reintroduces a Hegelian vocabulary – negativity, labour, alienation – into debates about the theory and representation of revolution. In this sense, the Situationists offer a critique of the language of modern politics as well as of its essential content.

The first question to ask, therefore, is how Situationist theory, and in particular the Situationist critique of urbanism, emerges out of the development of practice or a series of practices which offer a concrete, non-metaphorical form of analysis. Secondly, what importance does this process have on the status of Situationist theories of urbanism within the framework of a larger critique which is founded on principles of negation rather than the logic of contradiction?

Finally, it is crucial for my argument to note that the demands made by the Situationists were not only political but aesthetic. Situationist politics emerged directly out of a preoccupation with reintegrating an aesthetic system into daily life. It is therefore of great significance that the opening shots fired by the Situationists in their war against culture were in the form of a critique of urbanism, and that the first site of Situationist guerrilla activity was the city itself.

'Strategies against architecture': the theory of the *dérive* and the fall of Paris

In some cases, the city meant London where, following the footsteps of their hero De Quincey and guided by a drug-addicted fellow traveller, the Scots writer Alex Trocchi, the Situationist International reported on the 'unitary ambience' of Limehouse and protested against the planned destruction of

Chinatown. It also meant Amsterdam, where the Dutch architect Constant Nieuwenhuys, who had originally coined the term 'situationist', collaborated with Guy Debord and experimented with an imaginary city he called New Babylon. It was also Venice, much admired by the Situationists for the dream-like quality of its architecture, where the English Situationist Ralph Rumney stalked Alan Ansen, Beat poet and intimate of William Burroughs, in a series of photographs which as a collage also form a map of the city. (Rumney returned to this theme for his major 1980s series 'The map is not the territory', also made in Venice.) Most importantly and most frequently, however, the city meant Paris.

Like Walter Benjamin, the Surrealists, or indeed Baudelaire, the Situationists saw Paris as a *topos*, which contained both poetic and political possibilities in its margins as well as at its centre. Unlike their precursors, however, the Situationists also saw the city as a future battleground for the conflict over the meaning of modernity. It is this battle for urban space, in a literal and metaphorical sense, which is in many ways the defining moment in the development of Situationist strategy.

Importantly, this battle was fought in real, practical terms as well as being a theoretical, speculative abstraction. The Situationists devoted a great deal of energy to developing techniques of 'psychogeography', varieties of what Iain Sinclair has recently termed ambulatory vandalism, which aimed at destabilising the spectacular organisation of the city. The most important of these techniques was the well-known practice of the drift, or *dérive*, in the course of which groups of Situationists would float across Paris in the pursuit of anarchy, play and poetry: Paris without spectacle. Their favoured places were those which, like the rue du Xavier-Privas, Square des Missions Étrangères, and the Canal Saint-Martin, moved observers, such as Michèle Bernstein, to 'salutary states of awe, melancholy, joy or terror'.[4]

The above is a well-documented version of Situationist practice and taken to be what is meant by 'Situationism'. For example, in *The Painting of Modern Life: Paris in the art of Manet and his followers*, the art historian T. J. Clark – now a Professor at Berkeley and briefly, in 1967, a member of the English Section of the Situationist International – argues, in strict Situationist terms, that what is termed Modern Art had its origins in the encounter between a newly consumerist society of late nineteenth-century Paris and a generation of artists who were deeply sceptical of the new city's Haussmannisation and pleasures. The ultimate situation for those who called themselves Situationists had been the Paris Commune, a moment when ordinary people seized control of their own lives in a revolutionary festival which actively negated the controlling principles of capital and consumerism. The failure of the Commune, the Situationists argued,

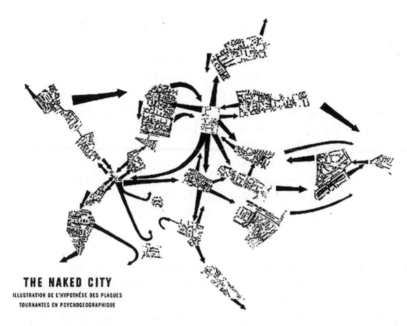

THE NAKED CITY
ILLUSTRATION DE L'HYPOTHÈSE DES PLAQUES
TOURNANTES EN PSYCHOGÉOGRAPHIQUE

Figure 2.1 Guy Debord and Asger John, *The Naked City: illustration de l'hypothèse des plaque tournantes en psychogéographie* (reproduced in *Documents rèlatifs à la foundation de l'internationale situationniste*, Paris, Allia, 1985).

and with which Clark agrees, was the moment when Paris began to be strangled by the demands of modernity.[5]

The *flânerie* which Clark describes in this book, and which he parallels to Situationist activity, is essentially, however, an ironic practice: the *flâneur* is a subject who remains at a fixed distance from the pleasures he (and it is always he) observes or consumes. The Situationist practice of *dérive*, on the other hand, is characterised by an active hostility to the representation of urban experience. The *dérive*, defined by the drunkenness of the subject and his relation to an environment which has lost shape, meaning or form, is a negation of the city as a site which invites the subject to remain detached from the object of its gaze. Unlike the intoxicated wanderings of Baudelaire, de Musset or Martin du Gard, Situationist practices are political acts which aim to reinstate lived experience as the true map of a city.

The theory of the *dérive* is indeed, as Patrick ffrench puts it, a '*détournement* of *flânerie* and its politicisation'. It reveals that 'the *flâneur* is at the mercy of reified social conditions without being aware of it and without any analysis'.[6] 'Haussmann's Paris', writes Debord, 'is a city built by an idiot, full of sound and fury, signifying nothing.' It is a city, which, in the name of rational organisation, has lost all sense of itself as a site for poetry, play, situations.

The *dérive*, as a practice that disorders and disorients the subject in the city, reveals for the Situationists the collision between poetry and its opposite. *Dérive* is an exercise in spatial projection, a rediscovery of the city as a labyrinth. Like Surrealist poetry, it is a collective practice which separates objects from their functions; as a fundamentally poetic game it reveals its opposite in an urban topography of fragmentation and dispersal. Paris, revealed in the analytic practice of *dérive*, is a fortress museum (*ville-musée gardée*). The fall of Paris as a spectacular city is therefore the necessary prelude to its reinvention as the *locus* of real creativity.[7]

The Naked City

The Situationists argue not only for an attack on the theory of urbanism, but most importantly for a defence of the meaning of Paris as a site which carries metaphorical and metonymic significance. This point is best demonstrated by one of the most well-known images associated with them, a screenprint by Guy Debord and Asger Jorn entitled *The Naked City: illustration de l'hypothèse des plaques tournantes en psychogéographie*.[8] The title of the piece, faithful to the Situationist practice of kidnapping (*détournement*), has been kidnapped from the famous American documentary of 1948 which portrayed hard-boiled cops at work in New York City. This film is particularly distinguished for the camera-work in its opening shot which swoops across the cityscape at night, focusing on incidental details before returning to the broad cinematic sweep of panoramic vision.

In their own version of *The Naked City* Debord and Jorn draw a picture of Paris which borrows from this technique and which negates it. This psycho-geographical map is an attempt to capture the movement of the city in time without freezing it into spectacle. It is therefore necessarily fluid, continuous and opposed to the static language and principles of conventional map-making. It is a map of experience rather than of activity.

The map which Debord and Jorn drew traverses the section of Paris which was designated for redevelopment in the late 1950s. *The Naked City* is the negative visual corollary of de Gaulle's programme – the so-called 'reconquest of Paris' – which aimed to evacuate the working classes from Saint-Lazare, Gare du Nord, and Place de la République and move them to the neo-Corbusian barracks of Sarcelles. It is a map of a city which is being emptied of human activity and which is in the process of becoming a dead site, a city without a *telos*.

Across this map, which runs roughly from the Gare de Lyon, on the right, to a limit marked by the Palais Royal and the Jardins du Luxembourg on the left, is a movement which designates sites which are absent – Rue Sauvage, the Halle aux Vins, rue du Xavier-Privas. The Situationists protested at the destruction of these places, which they identified as having magical or poetic significance and which were therefore essential to the metaphorical meaning of the city. (Many of these sites would disappear shortly after the map was drawn.) The map comes to function for the Situationists as a metonymic echo of the absence of those sites which first defined the city of Paris as metaphor and experience. With time the cliché of *The Naked City* has not only been *détourné* but also *détraqué*, that is to say upset, unhinged and broken down. *The Naked City* is a metaphor which undoes itself.

A metaphor which cannot sustain itself, by definition, functions no longer in the literal sense of the term but rather as an ironic comment on the possibility of its original meaning; it is an absolutely negative form of discourse. The Situationist critique of urbanism, founded on the negative principles of the *dérive*, which actively opposes the possibility of meaning in urbanism, is just such a form of discourse. This is how, I think, *The Naked City* and much of the Situationist critique of urbanism comes to be not only a map or series of maps which inform the development of a broader critique, but also a premonition.

Territory and city

In the section of *The Society of the Spectacle* devoted to 'Environmental Planning', Debord quotes two main sources, apart from Marx and Hegel, to support his theses. The first is Lewis Mumford, whose famous book *The City in History* was totemic for the Situationists. The second source is Machiavelli, whom Debord quotes as the *envoi* to this section:

> And he who becomes master of a city used to being free and does not destroy her can expect to be destroyed by her, because always she has as pretext in rebellion the name of liberty and her old customs, which through either length of time or benefits are forgotten, and in spite of anything that can be done or foreseen, unless citizens are disunited or dispersed, they do not forget that name and those institutions.[9]

Machiavelli represents for Debord an ideal of intellectual action and political reasoning. For Machiavelli politics and morality are inextricably linked and are, moreover, the defining criteria for the organisation of the state. This is not to say that morality must shape political life, or vice versa, but that there can be no divorce between the ethical imperatives of political behaviour and social existence. Machiavelli terms the coexistence of these conflicting demands *virtù*, and says that this principle is, in fact, the highest form of political morality.

Also important for Debord is Machiavelli's insistence that there should be no conflict between 'the morality of the souls and the morality of the city'. *Virtù* is, moreover, 'the quality of mind and action that creates, saves or maintains cities'. The opposite of *virtù* is *ozio*: indolence, stupidity or corruption, a quality which implies not only weakness but a dangerous lack of civic culture which destroys the soul of a people or citizenry.[10] It is important to note that *virtù*, although it comes from the Latin *vir* (man) and *virtus* (what is proper to a man), cannot be translated as virtue but as virtuosity. *Virtù* is not only a theory of action but a technique.

Virtù is the key concept which Debord applied to the map of his own life which he drew in two volumes of memoirs called *Panégyrique*. In the first volume, Debord presents us with an account of his life, art and politics with a series of quotations and references from Cardinal de Retz, Machiavelli, François Villon and Castiglione. In the second volume, the same account is given in a series of drawings, photographs and maps which correspond to or match the original text of the first volume.[11] Some of these have a clear meaning: 1953, for example, is represented by a photograph of Debord's graffiti from a wall on the rue de Seine in that year, 'Ne Travaillez Jamais' – a famous and ubiquitous slogan taken up in May 1968. Similarly, the year 1968 is announced by way of a detail from a press photograph showing Debord in charge of a Situationist delegation in the occupied Sorbonne. Other images celebrate the group of hooligans (*bande de voyous*) – Asger Jorn, Ivan Chtcheglov, Michèle Bernstein, Alice Becker-Ho – who were the lovers, friends and comrades who formed Debord's entourage during the heroic years of the Situationist adventure. There are maps of *Paris habité* and photographs of bars, cafés and apartments where a life was lived. There is also, most importantly, a photograph of the author's hand (*la main de l'auteur*); like his literary hero Laurence Sterne, Debord privileged the imprint of the author on his work as having an extra-literary value which marked the essential relation between life, art and subjectivity. Debord emphasised above all that these images have not been mediated by the commodity-spectacle and separated from their real meaning: they exist, instead, as iconographic proof of the Situationist notion that in the twentieth century life can be lived as an adventure within the city, outside of the all-pervasive, controlling narrative of the society of the spectacle.

It is, then, especially significant that the 'Environmental Planning' section of *Society of the Spectacle* is called in French *l'aménagement du territoire*. In French, and in Italian, *territoire* (territory) has a political meaning, which has not been fully translated into English. As Lewis Mumford notes, *territoire* is separate from the city in the sense that it is land, an area or a zone, which belongs to the state or government and not to its inhabitants. This makes it distinct from a political entity which makes the citizenry owners of the city. *Le territoire Français* refers not to land or people but is an abstraction defined by the organising administration to which the individual citizen stands in opposition. In *The City in History* Mumford describes the end of the Middle Ages and the onset of an early modern capital economy as emblematic of such an opposition: 'The age of free cities, with their widely diffused cultures and their relatively democratic modes of association, gave way to an age of absolute cities.'[12]

It is this tension between city and territory, says Mumford, which is the defining feature of the early modern world. In the same way for Debord it is the tension between the clandestine nature of private life (*la clandestinité de la vie privée*) and the spectacular society of surveillance and control which is the defining feature of the city in our age. If, however, as we infer from Debord, the Situationist city has already existed in the labyrinths and passages of the city-state of late medieval Italy, what chance can there be of its return in an era where the technology of separation – as the Situationists describe the occult powers of media hypnosis – reinforces daily what they call the powers of spectacular domination? The answer is that for Debord the Situationist city, like Thomas More's Amaraute, the city-state which lies at the heart of Utopia, is a city of the mind. This does not mean, however, that it does not exist: the maps of Barcelona, Florence and *Paris habité* are maps of cities defined by Debord and his *virtù*, that is to say historical life as opposed to historical lack. Debord quotes Paul deGondi, also known as Cardinal de Retz, active in the troubles of the Fronde, and follower of Machiavelli, improvising desperately his own panegyric before the Parlement de Paris: 'In bad times, I did not abandon the city; in good times, I had no private interests; in desperate times I feared nothing.'[13]

Historical life

In the film *Guy Debord son art et son temps*, Debord asserts his relationship to his time by quoting Baudelaire's famous poem *Le Cygne* in a scene which precedes his account of the final catastrophe unleashed by the technology of separation:

> *Le Vieux Paris n'est plus (La forme d'une ville*
> *change plus vite, hélas, que le cœur d'un mortel)*

> Old Paris is no more (the form of a city
> changes faster, alas, than the heart of mortal man)

Debord here compares himself to Baudelaire's swan, cut out of history and time by the relentless sweep of Haussmann's Boulevards, constructed not only to ease the movement of troops and arms across Paris in times of insurrection, but also to erase the historical memory of the proletariat. Debord thus places himself and his art, again like Baudelaire's swan, against a modernity which has been evacuated of historical sense.

Although Debord in his later years wrote as if the revolutionary moment had passed, I do not think that the Situationist critique of urbanism is in any sense anachronistic. Indeed, as debate about the structural meaning as well as the structural function of cities intensifies, the Situationist notions of history, space and subjectivity in the city are increasingly valid. The occupation of cities by historical absence is defined by Debord as the central fact of contemporary urbanism: 'Obviously, it is precisely because the liberation of history, which must take place in the cities, has not happened that forces of historical absence have set about their own exclusive landscape there.' Contemporary urbanism's main problem, therefore, is the

Figure 2.2   Guy Debord, *Paris Habité* (reproduced in *Panègyrique*, volume 2, Paris, Fayard, 1997).

movement of people, vehicles and commodities across a cityscape in which nothing happens and, as Debord writes, 'human movement is something to be consumed and deprived of its temporal aspect.'[14] Debord sees this as an abstract negativity which orders the controlling narrative of the spectacle: 'This society eliminates distance only to reap distance internally in the form of spectacular separation.'[15] Paul Virilio's assertion that 'social space is now constructed according to anti-terrorist strategies' is the most recent recognition of this situation. In post-modernity the city wall, whose modernist representation was the Parisian *boulevard périphérique*, has become, according to Virilio, 'the sensitiser installed in the doorways of shops, libraries, airports'.[16] 'A society that molds its entire surroundings has necessarily evolved its own techniques for working on the material basis of this set of tasks,' argued Debord in 1967. 'That material basis is the society's actual territory.'[17]

The Situationist project during its most artistic phase was conceived of as a series of tactics and strategies which would resist this technology of separation. In the writings of Debord and Raoul Vaneigem, the paintings and photographs of Asger Jorn, Pinot-Gallizio and Ralph Rumney, the Situationist ideas on psychogeography and the *dérive* are a critique of human geography which, as I have tried to suggest, necessarily imply the restoration of authentic value and meaning to the modern city, a *locus* of real experience rather than metaphorical activity. The later political impact of Situationist theory upon post-modernist debate is also shaped by this radical interrogation of urbanism. The Situationist critique of urbanism is not, however, simply a negation of the possibilities offered by modernism, but an active contradiction which withstands recuperation and defies the controlling logic of post-modernist attempts to explain away contemporary urbanism as subject to the demands of space and temporality.

Most importantly, a theory of urbanism must be judged as a promise of happiness for the Situationists. It is only as a map of Utopia that its failure can be measured. There is in this critique also a promise of romance, movement, passion: what Debord terms, with reference to Machiavelli and the late medieval notion of life as a journey towards the eternal, historical life. He writes of the Situationist city: 'the independence of places will be restored to us, along with authentic life understood as a journey containing its whole meaning within itself.'[18]

In *Mémoires*, his first attempt at autobiography, Debord quotes the *envoi* to Louis-Ferdinand Céline's novel *Voyage au bout de la nuit*. The *envoi* is apparently a regimental song of the Swiss Guard who were famously massacred in 1792 and in whose memory a chapel stands on the Boulevard Haussmann. It is an apt metaphor for the journey, without map or compass of the Situationist International: 'Our life is a journey in winter and night / We search for a way where there is no light.'[19]

The military metaphors used by the Situationists have a political as well as a poetic meaning. For Debord, in particular, it was significant that Carl von Clausewitz was a contemporary of Hegel and that von Clausewitz's critique of the shock waves sent round Europe by the French Revolution was founded in practical knowledge of the battlefield. The essential nature of combat, as described by von Clausewitz and defined by the Situationists, is that in war, as in politics, there can be no isolated act. It is this aspect of Situationist thinking which makes them our contemporaries rather than mere legends. In a world where a lack of ideology is the dominant value, the demand made by the Situationists for a political language which can express negation as well as contradiction is not anachronistic but rather an ever more relevant appeal for a return to real communication.

It may well be true, as the Situationists themselves believed, that the Situationist International offers the only authentic political language of the age, in fact the only living language of the century. It may even be true, as Guy Debord told us in his earliest works, that the time of the Situationist International has yet to come, in which case the Situationist adventure is literally an unfinished journey without maps.

Notes

1. This objective is indeed first delineated in the text 'La ligne générale', signed by Michèle Bernstein, M. Dahou, Véra and Gil J. Wolman in no. 14 of the 'pre-Situationist' journal *Potlatch*. See *Potlatch 1954/1957* (Paris, Allia, 1997), p. 51.
2. For accounts of Debord's current literary reputation in Paris see Andrew Hussey, 'Saint Guy de Paris', *Times Literary Supplement*, 4 October 1996, p. 10; Jacques-Emile Mireil, 'Les situs, précurseurs de mai 68', 'Éloge de la révolte', *Magazine littéraire* 365, May 1998, pp. 64–67; Francis Marmande, 'L'aube de l'internationale situationnniste', *Le Monde*, 22 June 1998, p. 12. An interesting perspective on Debord's legacy can be found in a text by Philippe Sollers, Debord's most prominent literary champion. See Philippe Sollers, 'La Guerre selon Guy Debord', in *La Guerre du Goût* (Paris, Gallimard, 1997), pp. 442–45.
3. Guy Debord, *Commentaires sur la société du spectacle* (Paris, Gallimard, 1992), p. 21.
4. The clearest delineation of a Situationist urban aesthetic as formulated by Bernstein can be found in the letter sent to *The Times* and reprinted in *Potlatch 23*, p. 107.
5. See T. J. Clark, *The Painting of Modern Life: Paris in the Art of Manet and his followers* (London, Thames & Hudson, 1996), pp. 68–69.
6. Patrick ffrench, 'Dérive: The détournement of the flâneur', in Andrew Hussey and Gavin Bowd (eds). *The Hacienda Must Be Built: On the Legacy of Situationist Revolt* (Manchester: AURA, 1997), p. 44.
7. Guy Debord, 'La Chute de Paris', *L'internationale situationniste* 4, 1960 (Paris, Éditions Gérard Lebovici, 1975). p. 7.
8. For a full description and account of this illustration see Simon Sadler, *The Situationist City* (Cambridge, MA, MIT Press, 1998), pp. 20–21.
9. Guy Debord, *The Society of the Spectacle*, translated by Donald Nicholson-Smith (New York, Zone, 1994), p. 119.

10. This fundamental distinction is described in Bernard Crick (ed.), *Machiavelli: The Discourses* (London, Penguin, 1970), pp. 41–45.

11. See *Panégyrique, tome premier* (Paris, Gallimard, 1993), and Patrick Mosconi (ed.), *Panégyrique, tome second*, (Paris, Fayard, 1997).

12. Lewis Mumford, *The City in History* (London, Duckworth, 1960), p. 134.

13. *Panégyrique, tome premier*, p. 32.

14. Debord, *The Society of the Spectacle*, p. 126.

15. Debord, *The Society of the Spectacle*, p. 120.

16. This is a reading of Virilio's relation to Situationism made by Patrick ffrench in 'Dérive', pp. 42–43. See also Paul Virilio, *L'Inertie Polaire* (Paris, Christian Bourgeois, 1990), p. 9.

17. ffrench, 'Dérive', p. 42.

18. Debord, *The Society of the Spectacle*, p. 126.

19. Guy Debord, *Mémoires* (Paris, Jean-Jacques Pauvert au Belles Lettres, 1993), unpaginated.

All translations are by the author unless otherwise noted.

2.3 'The Accident of Where I Live' – Journeys on the Caledonian Road: An Interview with Joe Kerr
Richard Wentworth

Artist Richard Wentworth has lived for twenty-five years just off the Caledonian Road, in North London. In his constant journeying along the 'Cally' he has investigated, and photographed, the many singularities and irregularities – pavement bubblegum sculptures, often useless but grandly titled shops, hapless dentists, and piles of 'building vomit' (the indigestible remnants of a bad postwar diet) – that for him make this decayed inner-city neighborhood an endlessly fascinating and genuinely unique fragment of the urban whole.

His photographs of the street, and the objects and people that inhabit it, illuminate his anecdotal accounts of the Cally, which together normally constitute a lecture performance of provoking originality. The following interview, which was conducted on and off the Caledonian Road, is intended partly to fix in a new and more permanent form this particular intertwining of word and image; but it also investigates how artistic practice is informed by urban experience and observation, and equally how this specific form of practice itself illuminates the understanding of architecture and of cities. Almost paradoxically, what makes Wentworth's work so original and insightful is its evocation of the surreal richness of mundanity, eccentricity, and accident that only city life, and a determinedly awkward artistic sensibility, can supply.

Figure 2.3

In particular, the perennial observation of the serial repetitions of every-day activity injects the sensation of lived time, and even perhaps of myth-making, into the more familiar structural understanding contained in the conventional 'snapshot' image of local life. Equally the close textural and textual study of the physical fabric – the accumulated flotsam of buildings and objects, the marks of pragmatic interventions – enables Wentworth to tease out a subjective and fleeting narrative, an intense and vivid testimony to the continuous relationship between people and the architecture they inhabit. However, this is not merely an uncritical celebration of life 'as it is,' for part of the process is to speculate, in the most imaginative and untram-meled manner, about the causes and purposes of what might otherwise be considered to be a wholly arbitrary collection and organization of diverse objects and phenomena. It is this poetic engagement with observable real-ity that distinguishes this as a creative process and not merely as a task of recording, while it is the freedom from the constraints of academic conven-tion that allows fresh insights into our discussions of urban experience.

This independence from such systems of thought permits the parameters – geographical and intellectual – of the urban study to be developed in subjec-tive and arbitrary terms. For Wentworth, the Cally is mapped in relation to his own participation in this environment; its structure is revealed when he discerns the underlying patterns of the landscape, and it is narrated by the successive act of photography.

Experience and practice

Joe Kerr:
So what status do we accord 'the Cally'; is it a definable concept?

Richard Wentworth:
Our habits of movement within cities are very telling – they may not be consistent but they are full of patterns based in accumulated choice and necessity. They contain preferred routes, whose whim may hinge on 'the sunny side of the street,' or an expectation of things or people to see or to avoid. The 'accident of where I live' presents me with one very specific option – a run of nearly a mile on a single road whose various characteristics combine under the one heading, 'the Cally.' This mile seems to contain the most significant phrases and measures of the Caledonian Road between the two landmarks of Pentonville Prison and King's Cross Station. Somehow it's a totality, a continuum.

It occurs to me that a roll of film is similar, and unavoidably any thirty-six exposures are a kind of diary, containing all kinds of oppositions mediated in linear form, a narrative frame by frame. Perhaps the length of a film is in some apposite relation to this length of road – a 'manageable' amount, readable but not epic. Terraced house construction is very similar (my street has thirty-six 'exposures' on either side). There is often that sense in London of a module which has had time to develop

Figure 2.4   The parallels of art and life.

sufficient variety, so that between any two we may compare and contrast. Just like the paving slabs of the pavement are for children, these are ways of *calibrating* our path through the city. By etymology we can extend it still further and say that this is how we gauge the *caliber* of a place.

I like my working process to be like the one which arranges the world anyway: the one which parks the cars so that they seem to have a kind of defined order about them, although you know there's no one out there with a peaked cap saying where they should be; the one that stacks up the washing-up to make a sculpture every time you do it. I am intrigued by all those practices which are actually world forming, and which in turn we respond to – how cars are parked affects how you are as a pedestrian – all those kinds of essentially urban conversations between people and objects. The problem of course is that those things that interest me are for the most part un-self-conscious; when you park the car you are not aware of making an image, but I come along and see the cars as imagery; I see three reds, a blue, two whites, a green, four blacks, and a brown, and I read it as an order, but the people who put the cars there weren't doing that.

JK: Presumably photography is an obvious way of actually making sense of that relationship between different objects in the world.

RW: I think these photographs are as near as I'll ever come to trying to pin down the moment of thinking that kind of thing, of revealing the potential of reverie.

JK: That's a very revealing idea, to talk about reverie in relation to your practice.

RW: But describing it creates one of those telling oppositions; if reverie is a beautiful engine, who would want to pin it down and reveal it? It's a typical human comedy, like saying 'Aren't butterflies wonderful, so bang a nail through them and stick them in a box.' But I like those spaces which seem to me to guarantee that they produce reverie, journeys sitting on the top of the bus, or speaking on the telephone: there's a completely different space that you occupy when you're on the telephone, which allows you to see the world as a sort of theater, like Jimmy Stewart does in *Rear Window*. I'm intrigued by the idea that humans are voyeuristic; it seems to me something that perhaps we ought to celebrate rather than try and prevent, because it's unpreventable. It seems to me that it's the engine of curiosity that you look, and as you look you name, and as you name you look more, and the whole process goes round.

JK: When you're actually walking on the street and seeing this striking relationship between the green and the white and the blue and the red object, to what extent is that something which just gives you pleasure for its own sake, or to what extent are you using it as a sketchbook, storing it up as something which will be useful in another place, to do something else – to make pieces, for instance?

RW: Well there's no obvious correspondence between the street and my work at all; the correspondence if there is any is that what I see on the street is a set of sympathies which I then try and allow in the work. The last thing I would want to do is to go to the studio and mimic, or mock up, or reengineer an event. I just want that apparent likeness, or banality, or set of oppositions, to come across.

JK: So why do you feel the need to create a fix of this?

RW: I feel rather ashamed, but I have realized recently that it's because I actually want to tell other people about it; it isn't enough for me to do it as an obsessive, private act. I want it to have other lives, even though if I died tomorrow nobody would know what to do with my slide photographs – most of them aren't even captioned – so I'm the only person who really knows anything about them. Some of these pictures are very articulate, and some of them are just about the voice-over, or the caption. But there is some sort of value there, and while there are comparable examples, it is not the work of Atget, it is not the work of Reyner Banham, nor is it the work of some freak in Islington civil engineering department, but it's in a space between all those, and thousands of other possibilities. Significantly, I don't actually like the transparencies as objects.

JK: But they're actually inert, except when they're being projected.

RW: Yes, and I love the idea that in much the same way the street is inert. Someone quoted Hamlet to me the other day, something like, 'There's neither good nor bad till it's thought.' It's only now when you look at the building opposite, which I've seen a thousand times, that you think, 'Aren't the afternoon shadows amazing'; because that's a north-facing street and it aligns itself with the setting sun at this time of the year. The rest of the time you might be merely saying, 'Oh they're stuccoed up to the first floor, and mostly they're painted white'; it's only where you are exhilarated that you name it.

JK: That was an intriguing list you gave of Atget, Banham, and others. So are you conscious of being in a tradition of urban commentary about lived experience, and of looking at the world in a certain way?

RW: No I don't think I am, and in a studied way I don't know anything about it, but I'm sensitive to that kind of idea. I remember that soon after leaving college, it was like throwing down a gauntlet to read Christopher Alexander's description of a newspaper-selling machine near a traffic light (I guess in Harvard); and the traffic light sequence allows you to stop at the newspaper machine, put the money in, and get the newspaper. He just pointed out that the sequence of the traffic lights gave that shop its economy. I thought this idea was just delicious, and it now seems terribly obvious, so for instance I know why the dry cleaners is by the bus stop, while ten doors up would not be a good site. I'm sure that particular dry cleaners legitimizes the incompetence of the bus service, so that people feel better about the wait, because there's a potential to do something in that space. It's not a traceable thing but I'm sure that part of that sense of waiting for the bus, the inconvenience of traveling by bus in London, is matched up with the idea 'well that's all right because I can combine it with going to the dry cleaners,' so that the two things are in a symbiotic relationship. Unlike nearby Logman Ltd., 'specialising in water melons,' who presumably doesn't need to be anywhere near any bus stop.

JK: Specializing in watermelons is a great idea, isn't it.
RW: It suggests that there are other things you can specialize in, like potatoes. ...
　　And the junk shop near here, I can't stand at the bus stop without surveying it, an automatic act of dawdling.

JK: That's like shopping malls, which are designed to hold you within one space for as long as possible to maximize the probability of purchase.
RW: Well in its horrible truth I can feel that it must be so. A friend of mine who is an art director says that the length of the feature film, an hour and a half, is based on the average 'bladder time.'

JK: So do you sympathize with Walter Benjamin's idea that it's from the fragments, the forgotten bits, that you actually read the world? He collected detritus, and said that this was the real museum.
RW: I think that idea relates to my work in one way, which is that the physical size of the most successful things I've made is very small, and in that sense aren't in the tradition of hefty sculpture – but I always think that there's an enormous space that comes with them, which is the space of imagination. If they're any good they can provoke that; they don't need to be huge. They're not in the American tradition of 'long and wide.' They don't come out of minimalism, which is a branch of the American landscape tradition, simply because I don't have any experience of that. In Europe there's nowhere we can go where someone hasn't been before, and you grow up knowing that. We don't have an idea about wilderness, except in the most conceptual way.

JK: And cities aren't as morally damaging or culturally impure in the European philosophical tradition as they are in the American one either. We don't live in the land of Thoreau or Whitman.

RW: Yes, I think that's so – and anyway we no longer have the space to make such tidy-minded distinctions.

On and off the Cally

RW: As to why the Cally means something to me, I'm one of those people who lives somewhere where I would never turn left outside my house, and that means I come down here. We all have those habits of bias. So in a way I'm obliged to see it, not like those places which you live very near, but which you never see. Thus in fact I do live near to Pentonville Prison but I'm not really a witness to the prison – and obviously you could read into that a kind of psychology. It's not that I don't want to live near the prison, I don't want to acknowledge it. It's as much part of being in a city as anything else, but I would be an odd person if I constantly went out and beat the bounds of the prison.

This view of the Cally causes even me to check; it's topographically correct, as it were, but then you think, 'Hey, this guy's going to die'; it's from a very high viewpoint. I was inspired by a fantastic radio broadcast by Cees Nooteboom from the top of a London bus. I've used the top of the bus much more since I heard that program; he reminded me that it's a very specific kind of place.

Figure 2.5   The view you can't have.

Figure 2.6

The Caledonian Road used to be much more 'butcher, baker, candlestick maker'; there was a wet fish shop here, a decent baker, Woolworth's, Boots, Tesco's, and they've all gone as they have in the whole country. But what is delightful here is that it's completely without any of the new orthodoxies of consumption – it's lost the old ones, but there's no Body Shop, no Sock Shop, no Pret à Manger, nobody wants to come here. The retail chains have somehow described an exclusion zone. The Cally hovers in the vacuum.

Surveying this, you have to ask who owns what and why. For people who think that there isn't a narrative, or that you shouldn't speak narratively, it is necessary to examine this landscape. You have here a circa 1972 conspiracy by the new middle-class occupiers of these residential streets to put barriers in the roads to make this side belong to us, and that side belong to them – just what Victorian London was like, I understand. Then you've got gestures to the Fire Brigade – they've put emergency access that looks like it couldn't possibly work: bollarding, some seats, private forecourts. If you came down here with a different color code for everything, this would be a psychedelic space, wouldn't it?

JK: Someone's organized this set of objects down the street, haven't they?
RW: Yes, this is the result of brief visitations by Islington Council, proposals that are completely blind in one eye, by somebody who probably just left architecture school, is still not really sure what it's all about, but who came here and laid this down.

I've often cited this particular bit of private space as not unlike the way we talk about the landscape, so that on a wet day the incredible hopelessness of this is actually very beautiful, this accumulation of knocked-up bits of mortar. It's a no-man's-land, but often when I'm walking through here I feel rather reassured; it's like the ruins of ancient Rome.

I've always felt there was something about trading on the street that was comparable to trading outside the city walls: there's always that strange collection of things that can't quite function inside the city, and part of that seems to be this collecting of fridges and freezers. A new thing that I've only seen for a year now is that you shrink-wrap them to somehow pull them back into being new, as if you've maintained a valued product, when in fact what you are doing is preventing anyone from looking inside to see if it works. Then symbolically you put the tall ones at the back and the short ones at the front and you make these walls, a process that's definitely been going on on the street for probably fifteen or twenty years (and this is done every day). These white parapets are built up each morning and dismantled at night, day-in day-out.

JK: You've got shops here which actually want to be a market, don't they? They set out their market stall every morning.

RW: I think that is the history of the street. They say that on a Sunday before the war this was somewhere you could come and buy absolutely anything. In a way it is like a disarranged Brick Lane [a famous Sunday secondhand market]; but there is something in the street which is deeply informal, unlike Brick Lane, which has a time to begin, a time to end, it's relatively structured – all anarchy will meet there for six hours. The Cally is in a much more flexible state.

Probably the undeclared fact of the street is that these were actually gardens and got paved over – so to the general user of the street it's all pavement, but in fact you can see it contains a legal demarcation: it's got crap care of Islington Council on one side, and crap care of the shopowner on the other side. And some people colonize in this way.

I often photograph this man's wall – he always makes these patterns, tries to order materials in this way. He has to try and arrange the fridges with the bed, with the bookshelves, but he always ends up with this row of fridges and cookers. I suspect it is their cubic-ness that's doing it – it's not that it's the kitchen section. It is the kind of order which could as likely be 'cooker/cooker/fridge/safe' as it could be 'cooker/cooker/filing cabinet/safe/fridge' – because 'that's how they go,' as a fruit seller on the Cally once justified a rotten punnet of fruit to my wife.

And this classification also happens with the smaller-scale objects, which rattle around together under some nominal order. Probably at

Figure 2.7   The city of fridges.

the small scale it guarantees a much better surrealism, this absolute stew of objects. When everything has been reduced to the scale of a shard, you get some pretty extraordinary combinations.

I think the owners, Lionel and his son Neville, may be the ultimate emblem for me: they don't live in the street, they come from Ilford every day, and they have a dog, Ben, which starts barking at Highbury Corner, it barks all the morning in the Cally, and in the afternoon it doesn't bark.

They don't have the interest, or the time, to do it otherwise – they're not antique dealers, which I think is incredibly important, and they know they're not antique dealers. They know what things are worth, within the big social-material possibility – like street sweeping; they're definitely dealing in the kind of stuff you push with a wide broom, rather than the refined, delicate stuff you'd sweep with a dustpan.

House clearance represents a very narrow vector of material. It's period limited, probably 1940s onwards, completely devoid of self-conscious value. If you want to get excited about the kind of blue china that we had the green version of when I was a child, you can. Tomorrow there'll be an Italian student who'll buy the lot and be delighted. But it's in a very narrow kind of space, and Neville uses that private space very vigorously. The display comes zooming out in the morning and he moves it all back much more sluggishly in the evening, like packing a suitcase. Every day a percentage gets left out – which I often photograph – of failure, the invalids, the three-legged beds. My children come down here if they want a 13-amp plug and chop it off the lame fridge with a Stanley knife.

Figure 2.8 *Turning your trash into cash.*

Figure 2.9

Figure 2.10

JK: This is an extraordinary arrangement of objects on the pavement!

RW: The interesting thing is about how you make an organization out of these disparate parts; we're looking at the moment at maybe basins from a builder who had gone bankrupt, weights from a weightlifter, school chairs, fridges, cookers, desks, hoovers [vacuum cleaners], old electric typewriters, all of these things which actually you can name but would never be found in that order domestically. Here there's a kind of battle to make sense of them. There are periods when he has a few boxes which he designates as the 'flawed' goods and then suddenly somebody will turn up and buy the whole lot, and then for a while there'll be a chaotic period when it's all in bins. So it hasn't got a finite form. And if you ask Neville why he does it he'll tell you he does it for people's pleasure; he loves the theater of it, he's quite open about that. It sustains him in some way.

JK: But it's also an archiving process of the objects?

RW: Yes, even though if I tell him that he says, 'Well I don't know, I just put them out'; but I think he knows incredibly well, but it's got nothing to do with that antique shop high self-consciousness.

JK: But objects are categorized as they would be in an antique shop, aren't they? The glasses are put together and so are the pots and the dumbbells.

RW: They are today.

Figure 2.11

There is a capacity for the Cally just to be permanently nauseated, which could obviously be traced to some economic condition, but I do sometimes imagine that round the back it is actually producing new products to spit out; but what comes out is always of a certain type and period. It's what I call the 'Valor/Ascot/Raleigh/Aladdin moment,' which is like a smell of 'Old London'; but also for my generation it's a diagram of 'the end of everything.' Even though those things were made very badly, they had the illusion of British Empire competence, and we found afterwards that we couldn't do it any more. There was a skip [large trash container] here this week full of large quantities of things that had obviously been shoveled out into a garden and left. It doesn't actually take a large quantity of this stuff to fill a skip, but visually it's amazing. I don't willfully photograph skips, but that one struck me as extraordinary.

This was Tesco's and is still a supermarket, but of its own kind, which is in the process of turning itself into 'student hostel with supermarket below.' Part of the design seems to have been to put in regularly spaced windows on the street face, and it's been my pleasure for about a month to witness a real predicament in actually inserting one of the windows, because it collides with some bit of interior structure; and I suppose the ultimate delight is that they've actually switched the windows to open the other way round. The more I look at it, the more wonderful it seems; I mean it's very inventive, and also stubborn, which is a characteristic of the street. No matter how stupid it is they

Figure 2.12   The afterlife of objects.

Figure 2.13 Transforming the ex-Tesco's.

wouldn't say 'Actually we won't have one there,' or shift the rhythm, they just carry on in this willful way.

I am in the process of gathering up all the adjectives, and perhaps imperatives to be found in the Cally, such as *Trust* and *Hot*. There's a President motor company and a Paradise grocers and the clean is *quick* and it's the Caledonian Superstore. Although you will find these elsewhere, I think there is a kind of collective knowledge on this street, of trying for self-elevation.

The jewellers and pawnbrokers

As far as I can remember the sign has always only had one golden ball, and it's funny how everyone comprehends it. I don't think it's part of any comedy; everybody just understands it's supposed to have three, and it's only got one. That's part of this absent, hyperpresent thing that the street has, which is that it's either missing something, but you understand what is absent and you just fill it in, or somebody isn't very sure about it so you see things which are numbered twice or named twice, or that are incredibly assertive.

How many times does it say café and restaurant and breakfast on one frontage? Except that having gone to some considerable effort to have proper signs put up, the *E* falls off and the *U* falls off, and have been off now for six months.

It's rather charming really, 'CAF RESTA RANT'!

Figure 2.14

Figure 2.15   The Caf.

Figure 2.16   The Caf.

JK: What about the possible accusation that with this work you are appropriating the city, aestheticizing it?

RW: There's a Barnet Newman quote, something about 'where art goes, property follows.' Given the very nature of doing what we're doing, which is to give attention to something and look at it, to turn it into an object, it seems probable to me that we're at the beginning of declaring the Caledonian Road as the Hoxton Square [a recently gentrified 'artists' quarter'] of the late '90s.

Eventualities

There's something that is to do with the experience of a city which is a continuum of experience, which no amount of diary keeping, or the cinema, or photography, can convey. It is a totality of continuous knowledge; so, for instance, in the case of the supermarket window there was a hole in the wall for a month with an awkward bit of structure behind it; it contained all the builder's head scratching and worries and insecurities about what he was going to do about it, which could not be represented by taking a snapshot of it afterwards.

The pleasure of the street for me is the fact that it's out of control. It occurred to me that this is comparable to our relationship to the outdoors. Why do we go for a walk and look at the landscape, given that we don't any longer live in it or have a daily experience of it, or own it? It's like

Figure 2.17

owning a cat: a half-wild furry thing, it's a kind of game with nature, it's a proposition about things beyond one's immediate control.

What I've probably done is to start to enjoy the city as a surrogate for that. Maybe there is a way you can enjoy the fear of the city, the fact that it's slightly out of control, and that people who live on the edge of the city are absolutely horrified by it and don't enjoy it the way you and I do. But because we're about as close to being in the middle as one can get without being either very poor or very rich, one gets a real sense of that pulse. It's a kind of free theater It's completely rewarding because there are so many eventualities, and you know that you are the sole witness of those particular eventualities. In twenty seconds' time the next person will get a completely different palette, or rather the same palette in a different order. It's incredibly stimulating, but what I'm supposed to do with it I don't quite know!

Note

Richard Wentworth was interviewed by Joe Kerr on and off the Caledonian Road in May/June 1997.

2.4   'How Long I 'Been On?' Mark Dion's Performative Archaeology of the City
Alex Coles

Mark Dion is often found deep in the rainforests of Venezuela collecting bugs and butterflies to be put to use in his installational tableaux. Decked out in khaki shorts, and gripping both a net and a large jar, every summer Dion chases after any number of jungle specimens. But simultaneously with undertaking these 'artistic safaris', Dion has been developing a body of work based on a very different type of jungle – the city.

The first of Dion's works to take the city as its 'site' was the aptly-titled *Concrete Jungle* (1992) (made in collaboration with Alexis Rockman). The work consisted of a mass of garbage cans, with many food cartons ooz-ing out under their lids; scattered around and perched on top of the cans were stuffed cats and pigeons, seemingly making the best of the situation. Despite its engagement with the city, this work – like the 'safaris' – belongs to Dion's 'Natural History' series. Alternatively, Dion's four archaeological digs, all undertaken over the past five years, zoom-in – through archaeo-logical method – on the material waste of the city. In other words, where *Concrete Jungle* focused on waste recently dumped on the surface of the city, the archaeology series grapples with the same fragments of our material culture after they have made their way beneath it.

So the first stage of these digs, then, must be to recover lost fragments that are embedded in just a few inches of mud. In *History Trash Dig* (1995) and *History Trash Scan* (1996) this meant undertaking a shallow exca-vation into a designated site, in the cities of Fribourg, Switzerland, and Perugin, Italy, respectively. In *Raiding Neptune's Vault* (1997) (also con-ducted in Italy, this time in Venice), a barge trawled the bottom of one of the canals and scooped a pile of sludge into a large container, from where it was cleaned and sorted. While the recovery technique employed on each dig alters according to the specifity of the site, all are equally archaic and intuitive – a far cry from the scientific rigour of contemporary archaeology. Moreover, unlike a true archaeology, the aim of Dion's digs is to retrieve both the civilisation that was lost hundreds of years ago along with the one that was lost just yesterday.

Tate Thames Dig is the most recent in the archaeology series, and by far the most complex. It consists of three stages. Together they establish the work's multi-layered relationship to London, as the dig simultaneously takes the city as its backdrop, subject and site of intervention. The first stage is the actual dig, consisting of beachcombing the banks of the Thames for ephemera. The second is the cleaning and classification of the finds, while the third consists of the display of the items in a purpose-built cabinet, a life-sized walk-through Wunderkammer. At each stage different stories about the city come to light. The assorted fragments recovered throughout *Tate Thames Dig* are metonyms of the lives of London's inhabitants – driving the dig is Dion's quest to unearth these hidden narratives. Because the fragments release something of London's lost texture, its overall ambience is constantly re-found through the sensation of tactility. Throughout the three stages of the dig, this is experienced in entirely different ways.

With its intuitive quasi-archaeological techniques, *Tate Thames Dig* supplies a very different story to that told by the Museum of London. That it is a more intuitive one means it can retain something of the dynamic of the city, which is too often frozen in museum displays. In this way, the heterogeneity of narrative sequences that constantly collide in the city – each one bursting with the energy of the chance encounters which make up the everyday – are given a new life. To undertake his pledged task, it is necessary that Dion excavate an area of the city rich in such narratives. So what better place for him to start an archaeology of London but at its heart, the Thames?

Beachcombing while they can

In the summer of 1999, Dion selected two sites next to the Thames for his volunteers (mostly recruited from local schools) to begin their detective work: one parallel to the Tate Gallery at Millbank, the other parallel to the new Tate Modem at Bankside. As each volunteer scoured the banks of their respective areas, using what archaeologists characterise as the 'scatter-gun' approach, they began to retrieve the narratives of their forebears. Crucial to this stage was the fact that Dion urged each volunteer to select flotsam and jetsam that appealed to them personally, thus ensuring that one-on-one connections were made. Ephemera recovered from the Millbank site revealed it to be rich with items such as clay pipes and broken ceramic shards; by contrast, finds in the Bankside area included an assortment of animal bones.

Tate Thames Dig gave a selected group of locals, especially those living near the Bankside site (in the borough of Southwark), the chance to present the public with their collective past before it is irretrievably lost. For when the Bankside branch of the Tate opens in May 2000, the process of gentrification which Southwark has progressively undergone over recent years will be complete. As a direct result of this change, many local residents will be forced out by rocketing food prices and housing costs. *Tate Thames Dig* thus attests to the fact that cities change in structure for predominately economic reasons. But, in the work itself, only the dialectical image conjured up by the placing of a mobile phone next to a broken shard of crockery (in the cabinet-stage of the project) gives this foreboding sense of the future.

Unbeknownst to them, Dion's volunteers were actually beachcombing the very same Thames-side sites once haunted by arch-detective Sherlock Holmes and his side-kick Watson, in Sir Arthur Conan Doyle's *The Sign of Four* (1892). Starting from the area around Millbank's prison (now the site of the Tate), in the story, the detective and the doctor track the footsteps of a murderer towards Southwark. Shots ring out and the murderer 'whirled round, threw up his arms, and, with a kind of choking cough, fell sideways in to the stream.' And so today 'somewhere in the dark ooze at the bottom of the Thames lie the bones of that strange visitor.' While Dion's assistants never recovered more than one or two human bones, they did find lots of conspicuous objects. Perhaps one of the long clay tubes was the exotic pea-shooter weapon with which Conan Doyle's murderer killed his victims by blowing poisoned darts at them? Besides this geographical correspondence, something of Holmes' method of elementary deduction also abounds in Dion's *Tate Thames Dig*. But where Holmes used it to foil criminals, Dion uses it to extract from the river's 'dark ooze' the submerged tales of the city.

The Mark Dion show

For almost a month at the end of the summer all the ephemera and detritus from the shore-side dig was stored in two tents pegged out on the front lawn of the Tate at Millbank. A third tent was established as an information point for the public. On two massive benches running parallel to the front end of the tents, a new set of volunteers were busy cleaning all the excavated objects. The entire set-up had the appearance of an outdoor theatre production, with cleaning brushes and lab-coats as props and costumes, and the Thames forming a sprawling, canvas-like backdrop.

From the very first day of cleaning a hungry audience turned up to peruse the sordid and the unfamiliar. In front of their eyes on the lawn, narratives of the city were being unleashed as Dion and his assistants cleaned the ephemera. The performative dimension to this stage of the dig – which resulted in the overlapping of the spaces of the audience, volunteer and artist – was extremely engaging. The montage effect produced by the interplay of people working and watching on the lawn fed back into the project something of the spontaneous choreography of the city that had been lost – rather than operating as dead metaphors, the fragments pulsate with the dynamic of the everyday.

While the analogy with theatre reveals much about the effects of the work on the viewer, Dion himself actually refers to the digs in terms analogous to cinema-going, suggesting that experiencing all the stages of the dig is like seeing 'not only the film but also [its] production.' Sticking both the reference to film and the one to theatre back-to-back leads to an even more felicitous analogy: to a filmed, but theatre-like, 'live' TV show Dion watched as he was growing up: *The Dean Martin Show* (1965–75). During each episode of the show, all the machinations of the televisual medium were revealed to the audience at home; Dino would read off cue-cards, gaze out and blink at the audience – even chancing to ask them, 'How long I 'been on?'

As Dion, dressed in a white lab coat and gripping a scrubbing brush, looks up from reading an archaeology text book and gazes-blankly out at the observing public, he recalls something of the dead-pan wit and deliberately-staged amateurishness of Dino's TV show. But unlike Dino, who sends up his audience glued to the TV screen by mocking their 'dumb' placidity, Dion engages his audience on the lawn. By inviting them to ask both himself and the volunteers questions and to sort through the detritus – both of which actively involve forming an opinion about what they see – they become part of the spectacle that the work produces.

A real museum of the city

In the final stage of the dig the interactive element that had unfolded outside the Tate was finally transferred inside the gallery, into a display cabinet designed to display the city's ephemera. This invited the viewer to take a close-up look at any number of the finds by opening the drawers, lined with rows of objects: bullets placed next to a sheep's teeth, bright shards of earthenware next to credit cards. Spliced together in this way – producing a montage-like effect quite different to the one on the lawn – new patterns emerged from the fragments, and formed new narrative sequences. With its three stages – the digging, the cleaning and the final display – Dion's *Tate Thames Dig* launches a critical archaeology of the city, providing an insight into the richness of the city's narratives – and the injustices that often accompany them.

2.5 What a Carry On
Lyn Gardner

High up on a desolate concrete walkway at London's Barbican, two men struggle to move a table. The table is wonky and won't stand up alone; its surface is covered with planks of woods, several Thermos flasks, cups and biscuits, and a large tool bag. Hanging down from the table are plastic bags. One is filled with dust. The few passers-by who walk past the duo eye them curiously and continue on. What they don't realise is that these two men struggling with a table are performance artists. What the passers-by have just witnessed is art in the act of being created.

Spiral, which began at 8am last Saturday and ends at 7pm next Saturday, is an impossible journey through the environs of the Barbican estate, a place that has been called the ugliest complex in Britain, but also admired for its brutal concrete beauty. Over the week, Gregg Whelan and Gary Winters, who make up Lone Twin, will attempt to navigate a spiral path that takes them from the tube station to the heart of the arts centre. The problem is that the designated spiral will take them through walls, under locked doors, through the middle of offices and through the City of London School for Girls. They are doomed to failure before they have walked a step. Oh, and there's another catch: along the way, they are asking the public to donate objects, which they will carry with them on their journey. They've already collected the table and the dust, and by next Saturday might well have acquired a three-piece suite and a fridge. Hence the tools with which they will try to fix everything together in one movable structure.

'It's a bit like a snowball gathering up everything in its path,' says Winter. He sets about attempting to fix some of the wood to the sides of table and grins: 'Is it live art or just bad carpentry?'

There may well be those who think they know the answer to that one, but as anyone who has ever seen any of the company's work will know, it has an ineffable sweetness as the pair undertake their chosen tasks to the bitter end in a way that makes them seem both supremely heroic and touchingly stupid. Often more Laurel and Hardy than Gilbert and George, Lone Twin's work takes the form of interventions in public spaces that change people's relationship with that space and with each other. Sometimes the work goes unwitnessed; more often, it creates instant communities. The oddity of the circumstances in which the encounters happen adds to their potency. To that end, they have spent 18 hours walking back and forth over a bridge in Denmark hoping that other people might join them; dressed up as cowboys and spent 12 hours linedancing; and carried a heavy wooden plank in a straight line through Colchester. Often, it ends in failure. They once stood on a bridge in northern Canada for 12 hours in the freezing cold inviting people to hold their hands. Nobody did.

Whelan doesn't see that as a failure. 'These attempts can go wrong, but they are still an event. The failure would be to stop because nobody is holding your hand. What we play with is possibility. We learned early on that once you've set out to do something you must stay with the primary engagement because you never know what might happen.' In *Ghost Dances*, when the pair dressed as cowboys and linedanced blindfolded for 12 hours, they never imagined that those who encountered them would join in. But they did. Sometimes for hours at a time, supporting the pair as exhaustion set in and the mock heroic cowboys became fragile, broken-down figures.

'You do have to just let it happen,' says Whelan. 'If we took off our blindfolds and asked people to dance, it would be something entirely different. The fact that they do walk or dance with you for hours, that they recognise that we need help to get through is often very moving. The world is full of acts of kindness, and we experience them all the time. We get paid to do what we do, but the people we encounter along the way and who help us, don't. But they still do it.'

'Our view has always been that if you go out into public spaces you should be positive. It is a waste of time not to look for the things that are hopeful, especially if you are engaged in an activity that is exhausting. Once, at a conference, somebody said that what we do is go out into the city and look for love. Yes, looking for love. That's what we do.'

2.6   Nosing Around: A Singapore Scent Trail
Paul Rae with Low Kee Hong

Stage 1: Changi

Let's say you arrive by plane, as 29 million do annually. The scent trail begins before you know it: high altitudes suppress the scent organs, and as you leave the gate for the first travellator, they're still struggling to adapt to the abrupt return to sea level. No matter. Maybe you can smell again by the time you hit immigration. But you wouldn't necessarily know it. Passport given, scanned, stamped, returned. Welcome to Singapore, where the only thing you can smell is yourself.

'While many new airports purport to symbolise the countries they welcome us to', boasts a glossy coffee-table book on the airport, 'few can claim to be icons amongst their own people. To Singapore's four million inhabitants, Changi *is* Singapore' (Kishnani 2002: 11). A straw poll of Singaporean friends reveals the degree of exaggeration here to be disconcertingly small. Air-conditioned, efficient, and squeaky squeaky clean: public-friendly private space. This is what Singaporeans think of when they equate 'Changi' with 'Singapore'. Orchids – the city-state's national flower – are in abundance here. Go closer, smell them – they are scentless, fake. Expecting plastic, you feel them, drop your nose down to the roots – their velvet texture and faint damp odour tell you otherwise. Flowers so real they look fake, something for Singapore's postmodern detractors to get their teeth into.[1] But it's the conjunction, not the inversion that is of interest. These orchids, planted in charcoal so their tentacular roots can gather moisture from the humid air, have been adapted to survive in significantly cooler, drier conditions at the cost of their scent and all that entails. Sterile. The central conceit of one of Singapore's most renowned plays, *Descendents of the Eunuch Admiral by* Kuo Pao Kun, is that Singaporeans have become modern castrati, emasculated by materialism and the state. If Changi is Singapore, are these orchids Singaporeans? Let's not get too glib, at least not yet. You've only just got off the plane.

But spend a bit more time in the terminal, to find out how such cleanliness comes about. Pick out a cleaner from the army that patrol the floors, and follow them. They circulate with their cleaning carts like lost luggage on a belt. Slowly. Disconsolately. At times, their eyes are glued to the gleaming floor, on the lookout for the tiniest scrap out of place. But often they are in a state of drift, animated only when their paths cross with colleagues, and they stop, briefly, to chat. Others, meanwhile, are at work cleaning the acres of glass separating travellers from relatives and friends,

Figure 2.18 Orchids at Changi Airport. Photo: Paul Rae.

and pulling apart the many lighting fixtures to wipe the grilles clean. And then it dawns on you that these tasks are only mock-Sisyphean: that in fact these cleaners have *nothing to do*. Changi is too clean, if such a condition is possible. Some kind of glitch in the system causes the cleaning turnaround to operate at a faster rate than the accumulation of dirt. The result: exponential efficiency that, ultimately, will be no efficiency at all, but, because of the self-erasing nature of the work, will take a while to become apparent. In the meantime, the excess manifests itself as performance.

A cleaner is on the move on an upper floor of one of the terminals (restaurants and viewing gallery). You observe, from a distance. He looks over the balcony for a while, and then, bored with doing nothing, attends to his work. He grabs his 'cleaning in progress' signs, paces out an area of tiled floor and begins to mop. Once finished, he packs up, and drifts off elsewhere. The area of floor selected for cleaning was apparently random: no less spotless than any around it, and now no more so for the extra attention lavished briefly upon it. What was important was not the effect, but the act. And yet the act achieved nothing demonstrable, let alone lasting. Far in excess of its apparent ends, but by no means ostentatiously done for public effect, it was a performance of which Richard Layzell, the British artist who has recently taken to acts of unbidden cleaning (in) a range of international sites, would be proud.

The cleaner's behaviour is indicative of two things. First, that tracking the ways in which people respond to and utilize smell invariably gives rise to questions of performance. Second, that the specific social, political and atmospheric conditions that constitute Singapore today make it a fascinating place to investigate the relationship between the two phenomena. Hovering between act and effect, deriving from an over-eager efficacy and a process of environmental control manifested as erasure, the performance of cleaning presents itself as supremely apt for this authoritarian republic. In this sense, at least, you can agree: Changi is Singapore.

Inevitably, then, there is little else to sniff out at the airport apart from the perfume outlets. Perhaps avail yourself of a bottle *of Raffles*, named after the British colonialist who 'founded' modern Singapore in 1819, or *Singapore Girl*, a scented tribute to one of Singapore Airlines' most renowned and resilient brands: their be-saronged female cabin crew. It's an intriguing choice. Who do you want to be today?

If you are not already in Terminal 2, take the skytrain from Terminal 1. From Terminal 2, take the Mass Rapid Transit (MRT, or Underground) train from Changi, change lines at City Hall, and alight at Orchard MRT station.

Stage 2: Orchard Road

Congratulations! You have managed to travel from wherever in the world you departed to the heart of Singapore without leaving the comfort of an air-conditioned environment. And your temperature-controlled experience need not end here. The fragrant fruit trees that gave the road above your head its name are long gone. Flanked by huge malls, Orchard Road now forms the backbone of Singapore's central commercial and civil district. At the subterranean station exit, you can take passageways south towards Wisma Atria, and the huge Ngee Ann City mall, or east, towards Tangs and Isetan without ever needing to expose yourself to the open air.

It is this preponderance of air-conditioning, and the resonances carried by the term, that gives context to the cleaner's performance you observed in the airport. When asked by the *Wall Street Journal* to name the most significant invention of the millennium, Singapore's revered 'founding father' Lee Kuan Yew named the air-conditioner, stating: 'Historically, advanced civilisations have flourished in the cooler climates. Now, lifestyles have become comparable to those in temperate zones and civilisation in the tropical zones need no longer lag behind' (quoted in George 2000: 14). Lee's blunt pragmatism is perfectly in evidence here, but for Singaporean commentator Cherian George 'there are few metaphors that more evocatively crystallise the essence of Singapore's politics'(15). The government exercises a high degree of 'conditioning' control, one of whose results is the affluent 'comfort' of the population: '[P]eople have mastered their environment, but at the cost of individual autonomy' (15).

Inevitably, that 'mastering of the environment' has increased in inverse proportion to the breadth of Singapore's olfactory spectrum. In 1965, after gaining independence first from Britain and then Malaysia, the city was notorious for its squalor, disease and over-crowding. Today, after 40 years of public housing and sanitation projects, social engineering and disciplinary hygiene campaigns, intensive infrastructure development and rapid economic growth, nowhere else in the world with such correspondingly high levels of humidity and population density smells so little. Anyone who has spent time in the equatorial capitals of the world will recognize the scale of the Singapore government's achievement the minute they stick their nose out of the door. George understates the case, for the metaphor goes full circle: it is Lee and his government that have been Singapore's air-conditioners. Literally.

The result, as the aspirational mimicry latent in Lee's quotation, above, suggests, is a certain kind of obligation to perform. Cooled and comfortable, the populace is generally willing, and a nose around the 'Home' department in the basement of Tangs department store indicates the degree to which such an obligation has been domesticated. With air-conditioning fitted as standard in all homes now, a new range of air-conditioning-conditioners is on sale and permanent demonstration, which are at every level surplus or excessive. Catch a hint of lemon or apple in the air? That will be one of the fruity water-based air fragrancers, which can be set to bubble away to themselves, and sporadically emit a waft of sweet scent to compensate for the arid olfactory desert your hermetically sealed home has become. And speaking of 'arid', was that a gentle puff of steam that just enveloped you as you walked past that oversized kettle? Why, that's no oversized kettle: it's a humidifier, because, after all, it may be 80% humidity *outside*, but how else can you guard against the skin-drying, sinus-ravaging effects of your air-conditioning system? And don't forget that the deluxe model comes with an aromatherapy option, which will infuse your home with 'exotic Asian scents', to soothe, heal and relax after a hard day in the office.

On top of Changi's forensic cleanliness, such high-street gadgets are further evidence that, at least as far as you, who are yet to surface, are concerned, Singapore has been comprehensively deodorized. It is an observation that Rem Koolhaas makes at the opening of his thoughtful mid-1990s article 'Singapore Songlines':

> I turned eight in the harbour of Singapore. We did not go ashore, but I remember the smell – sweetness and rot, both overwhelming.
> Last year I went again. The smell was gone. In fact, Singapore was gone, scraped, rebuilt. There was a completely new town there.
>
> (Koolhaas 1995: 1011)

For Koolhaas, writing about architecture and urban planning, the deodorization of Singapore is indicative of a broader project of radical modernization, which, over a period of 30 years, replaced all 'contextual remnants' with a 'potemkin metropolis' driven by 'pure intention'. It was precisely Singapore's pitiful social state at independence, he argues, that encouraged and enabled Lee's government to envision the island as a 'theater of the tabula rasa' and build the nation as if from scratch – including, it might be additionally observed, Lee's power base. The result is a city whose radical beginnings have left it haunted by its own potential impermanence. As such, it is 'a city without qualities', entirely subject to the whim of its leaders and planners: 'if there is chaos, it is *authored* chaos; if it is ugly, it is *designed* ugliness; if it is absurd, it is *willed* absurdity' (1011).

Back on the scent trail, the broad terms of Koolhaas's argument appear to be borne out. Deodorization to capitalist ends is inevitably followed by the controlled re-introduction of scent into the environment, as scent that *performs*. On Orchard Road, several smells are synthesized to bypass the cluttered visual field and arouse the busy shopper from their consumerist reverie. 'Free smells', announces the Famous Amos cookie store, further down the road at Centrepoint shopping centre. But it has been there too long – the joke has worn thin, and people are used to the smell. If you want to really go where the action is, step directly out of Tangs on Scotts Road, and follow your nose to 'Bread Talk': at time of writing, bakeries are all the rage in Singapore, due in no small measure to their canny placing of extractor fans above the doorway (as well, it has to be said, of their innovative and wildly popular 'pork floss bun'). Looking more carefully, you soon realize that the smells also compensate for an authenticity deficit elsewhere in the set-up. The 'bakers' may busy themselves endlessly around their eye-catching glass-fronted chromium kitchen. But the comically over-tall chefs' hats and the meagreness of their cooking activities reveal them to be nothing more than glorified heater-uppers. Indeed, as you chew disappointedly on the sweet, cloying dough of a pork floss bun, it dawns on you that perhaps the primary aim of the whole in-store 'cooking' rigmarole is, in fact, the creation of the smell that drew you there in the first place.

And so it goes on, with variations. A Bee Heng Liang stall offers the seasonal scent of *bah kua*: flat squares of processed, sweetened barbecued meat for Chinese New Year. Mac cosmetics deploy fragrant images to sell their latest range of floral shades. With nothing to sell but smell itself, Calvin Klein invert the process, with their new product, 'Crave', coming a poor fourth behind the video of the sexy guy falling off a skateboard, the interactive promo-editing computer game, and the allure of their sales team. 'It's starfruit', one of them mutters, as he jabs at your wrist with his atomizer, and when you realize that that's the closest Orchard Road is going to get to living up to its name, you know it's time for a change of scen(t)ery.

Step out of Tangs, and catch bus number 85, 106 or 111 down Orchard Road towards Serangoon Road. Ask someone to tell you when you get to 'Little India'. Alight accordingly. Should you wish to explore Little India while you are in the area, you are referred to the relevant literature published by the Singapore Tourist Board <www.stb.gov.sg>. We're not going to Little India today. We're going next door to ...

Stage 3: Tekka Market

If any public site remains imbued with the Singapore scent-scape that pervaded the city before it became, in Koolhaas's terms, a 'theater of the tabula rasa', it is the intensively smelly wet market. A tiled enclosure found in many parts of Singapore, the term 'wet market' connotes both the fresh produce on sale there, and the liquid run-offs and molten ice that accumulate on the floor over the course of the day. By contrast with Changi's overcautious cleaner-performers, the wet market revels in a hose-down at the end of the day that is both ebullient in its execution and perfunctory in its effects: for whatever is not washed away in the process thrives in the resulting dampness, and stinks. Rules are broken here: meat is left out; chiller cabinets remain open; stall-holders engage in practices of questionable hygienic merit. And by contrast with the pricier, but increasingly popular supermarkets, there is no air-conditioning. The atmosphere is warm and wet – possibly soupy, certainly close. Five minutes off the bus and you're sweating. Welcome to Singapore!

As you enter the wet market, the combined smells of meat, fruit and dried goods hit you from nose to stomach, and the attendant noise, chaos and action have a dizzying effect. Here, the smells are far in excess of those carefully produced and packaged scents on Orchard Road. Rather, they are released through direct action and real effort: chopping, grinding, skinning, peeling, slicing, dicing.

The market reconstitutes Singapore as the bustling contact zone it grew out of.[2] Colonized by Raffles for its strategic position on the trade routes between India to the West and the Spice Islands of Indonesia to the East, labour – forced, indentured and free – blew in with the trade winds: from China, India, Indonesia, Arabia and, of course, Britain and other Western European countries. It was a place of intensive buying, selling and ship chandlering between a highly cosmopolitan group of merchants, all engaged in the performance of cross-cultural bargaining, commerce and exchange.

Tekka market, at the northeast corner of the ethnic enclave known as 'Little India', captures this historical resonance more acutely than most. Its location means a greater-than-average ethnic diversity of patrons, stall-holders and produce, and the result is more action, more interaction, and a more strident clash of smells. Across the culture-gap, the performative element expands. In the absence of a sales patter, smell becomes a correspondingly more crucial way of deriving information about the produce, and the bargaining process begins with the customer's post-sniff reaction. Bargaining takes place with fingers, faces, and a combination of *pasar* (market) Malay and Singlish – the local pidgin English. In response the stall-holder deploys an entire repertoire of gesture, exaggeration and dexterity in the scent-releasing processes of display and the preparation of your selected cut.

Observing this, however, brings you up against a limit of participation. The undeniably performative quality of the transactions is clearest to you because you are a stranger here. Their mundane repetition is inaccessible to the casual observer, likewise the gradual 'naturalization' of the scent-scape to the nose of the daily visitor. To press on, you need to take a step back and look to your own place in the scheme of things. Amidst these most pungent practices of the everyday, it is you who are the performer. Play it up. Hitch a ride on a more available identification: the tourist.[3] Perform a little journey of your own, for to plot a scent-map round Tekka market is to smell your way through Singapore's history and place in the world. With Little India a popular tourist destination next door, you won't look too out of place in your shorts, ever so slightly loud shirt, and with a quizzical look upon your face. You carry a camera, too, but don't expect to get the pictures you want by asking: then people will nod their assent, and disappear, leaving the produce to pose alone. Being a tourist here has its merits though, because as soon as they realize you're not there to buy, the stall-holders will respond differently. The sales pitch recedes and you can apprehend it as it goes. They leave you to your own devices, or hang around to talk about football.

Start at the sweet-smelling southeast corner – the universally loved fruit stalls. Head north past the earthy bean-sprout and tofu displays and scent-less vegetables to the throat-pricking dried fish stalls, popular with the Chinese and the Malays. Cutting along the top, the unmistakable smell of pickled vegetables and bamboo shoots announces everything you could want for a Thai feast. Soon after, the sickly, heavy odour of ground coconut flesh draws your attention to the coconut milk outlets, a crucial stop for anyone contemplating a creamy, mild Southeast Asian curry. Heading south brings you past the only two pork stalls in the market to the specialist crab and fish stalls. People come from all over the city to buy Sri Lankan crab here, to make, amongst other things, the Singapore favourites chilli and black pepper crab. Further on, to the left, halal chicken, and to the right, beef, and then freshly ground spices: ginger, chilli, coriander, cumin, garlic. Finally, the most pungent of all: in the full glare of the sun, the *kambing* (goat meat) stalls, the smell thickening in your throat like curdled blood, the butchers hacking away, sweat pouring down their faces.

As you journey, you realize that you often smell something before you see it, especially when what you see is familiar, and what you smell is not. You cannot help but sniff out what you don't know. Standing amongst huge sacks of dried fish, squid and chillies, you ask the stall-keeper what he can smell. He answers in Singlish, with a grin: 'Nothing lah. Waste so much time here cannot smell already.' The comment is a telling one, hinting at reasons for desensitization other than sanitization, which has intriguing implications for Koolhaas's conspiracy theory.

Although opening with a first-person body memory, the planner's position Koolhaas subsequently adopts forecloses any further reflections on smell. For, as Jon McKenzie, following Marcuse, observes, smell is a 'proximity

Figure 2.19 Curry spices in Tekka Market. Photo: Low Kee Hong.

sense', which 'entails the disintegration of forms, the mixing of subjects and objects' (McKenzie 2001: 202). Within Koolhaas's architectural remit, this is not a position he is obliged to adopt, and his analysis reflects this. 'A city without qualities' would appear to posit performance as its basic condition of habitation. But such performance can only be apprehended up close, since it plays itself out in embodied and improvisatory ways. This does not necessarily undermine Koolhaas's overall point about 'authored chaos', but it does suggest that in ignoring how everyday meaning-making processes respond to such imperatives, he is missing a trick. If the synthesized scents of Orchard Road represent a controlled re-introduction into the deodorized environment, Tekka's soup of smells suggests an unruly reinfusion. In*scent*ives to buy on the shopping drag; blurred ethnicities in the market.

There is one smell, however, conspicuous by its absence even from the fruit stalls of Tekka. It infuses a still more complex scent environment in another part of town, and that's where you're going now. Take a deep breath!

> Get in a taxi and ask for 'the durian stalls at Geylang'. The driver will know
> where to take you.

Stage 4: Geylang

The durian stalls of the Geylang district announce themselves to nose and
eye like the checkpoint of some breakaway Republic of Stink in a land of
the bland. All that's missing is a flag flying over them, with the 'nefarious
fruit'[4] as its symbol. Under the glowing, pear-shaped bulbs that bedeck roadside stalls in this part of the world, the racks of spiky, green rugby balls are
resplendent in the night. And as you alight, the full force of the odour hits
you: it is not so much the *smell* – heavy, ripe, sweet – that is noxious, but
the way it infiltrates you as if through the pores, like a gas. It has the pervasive quality of hash smoke on a London street, and something of the same
illicit quality. For although the durian is not illegal, it *is* subject to a travel
ban: this fruit is under house arrest.

That's one of the two reasons the stalls are open until 5 am. Banned from
public transport because of its excessive and lingering stench, the durian is
invariably enjoyed on its own, *in situ*. As you watch, carloads of the dis-
cerning pile out for a bite. Irony of the durian: everything is hard work
apart from its savouring. At rough-hewn tables, next to bamboo baskets
for the detritus, sweating strong-men, stripped to the waist, shuck the fruits
with specially curved knives, as if they were industrial-sized oysters. For the
aficionado, within lies the pearl of pearls. Fist-shaped lumps of creamy yellow flesh, each wrapped round a hard seed. The taste is both heavenly and
volatile, a combination of ice cream and raw onion. As you eat, the smell
fades: or maybe you no longer notice it because your body has achieved
some state of olfactory equilibrium with its environment, equally pungent
both inside and out. There is something defiant in this unambiguous celebration of the pleasures of the flesh. Oh, and by the way, that's the other
reason the stalls are open until 5 am. Geylang only really 'works' at night. It
is Singapore's most popular red light district.

You are surprised perhaps to learn that, within designated areas, brothels
are legal in Singapore. Once again, history permeates the present, bringing
with it whiffs of a tropical port notorious for the services it could offer sail-
ors. Geylang, the largest of these areas, consists of rows of neon-lit detached
houses (backing onto teeming unlit alleys), and towering hourly-charging
hotels (prominent among them, the 'Fragrance' chain). Between the durian
stalls on Sims Avenue, and the red light *lorongs* (streets) to the south lie some
of the best late-opening food outlets in the city. Take a stroll. Past roasted

duck and chicken stalls; past the homely, steaming dim sum shop; past the first of many Thai massage parlours ('Herbal massage' extra); past porridge and soya bean; past chicken wings and frog's legs; past Chinese herbalists selling acrid aphrodisiacs; past beef noodles and oyster omelettes. 'Breakaway Republic of Stink' is not so very far off the mark. By contrast with the unruly but generic environment of food smells in Tekka and other wet markets, Geylang has a character all of its own, one that is not only gloriously pungent, but derives from a particularly potent mix: food, sex and superstition.

It doesn't take you long to notice the preponderance of other features in Geylang ostensibly unrelated to the sex industry, in particular the Buddhist institutes, lion dance headquarters, and clan associations. Merchants from China set up the latter in the 19th century as a way of safeguarding and representing the interests of the community. As the social geographer Brenda Yeoh points out, the clan associations played a key role in mediating between their members and the colonial administration, and were well placed to resist colonial initiatives when they saw fit:

> ... the conception of a municipal authority working towards the 'public good' was alien to Chinese society which revolved around a clan-centred culture visibly demonstrated in the urban landscape by the proliferation of *kongsi*, clan-owned temples, burial grounds, sick-receiving houses, schools and lodging houses catering exclusively to the needs of members and affiliates.
>
> (Yeoh 1996: 67)

In Geylang, this sense of alternative organization persists, asserting a diversified dialect-based sense of 'Chineseness' against the Anglophone and Mandarin cosmopolitan Confucianism of the state. Within the local scent environment, this manifests itself most directly in the pervasive smell of incense, ubiquitous in the *lorongs*. Every brothel has a Taoist altar outside, and several bored-looking men to oversee it, when not busy inviting you in.

The performance of ethnicity and faith is hugely complex in Singapore. Lily Kong has noted that Chinese Singaporeans observe many traditions that died out in China with the cultural revolution (after the Singaporeans' immigrant forebears had already departed). This sometimes causes them to regard themselves as 'more Chinese than the Chinese', which: 'underscores the importance of the recreation of rituals and performances in maintaining meaning and identity' (1999: 229). In Geylang, such rituals take on a more pressing aspect than elsewhere, for these men and women live on the perimeters of legality, and the hither side of social acceptance. With a traditionally close link between prostitution and Singapore's Triad-like Secret Societies – themselves subject to a panoply of superstitious observances – Geylang's altars and incense serve to maintain an identity that is at once brazenly displayed, and haunted by anxiety.

The same can be said for the area as a whole. At its most ebullient, Geylang revels in a *re*-odorization defiantly counter to the olfactory suppression that grips most of the city. Yet such defiance is anxious, and faltering. You pass through perfume, cigarette smoke, open drains stinking of urine. Behind you is where Geylang Stadium used to be – the last event there was a show by an experimental theatre company, the appropriately named *Exodus* by The Necessary Stage (you know a place is carrion when the site-specific vultures move in). On your left was Gay World amusement park. Also gone. Chinese *wayang* (street opera) is petering out. Only the clan or gangster-affiliated lion dance troupes remain, and the Chinese, Thai, Indian and local women of the *lorongs* sitting indolent behind glass in their ultra-violet 'fish tanks', waiting for custom. Nothing doing. Geylang stinks, but the theatre has gone elsewhere. Follow it.

From the durian stalls, hail a taxi and ask to go to 'the Durians'. The driver will know what you mean.

Stage 5: the Esplanade

From the taxi stand of the recently opened Esplanade – Theatres on the Bay, you are unable to take in the full effect of its distinctive architecture. You cross through to the waterside, and look back. This flagship performing arts centre is the brand new jewel in the crown of the government's 'Renaissance City' project, and such centres, like the Sydney Opera House, need an eye-catching aspect. In this case, the twin spiked domes that delineate the main theatre and concert hall (there are two other, smaller performance spaces) resemble bugs' eyes, or two halves of a durian. It's an identification that has been well taken by the brand managers who run the centre, and by their government paymasters. In the middle of a severe economic downturn, the Esplanade's price tag is a touchy subject, and any opportunity to endear it to the populace a welcome one. Accordingly, the official media, in particular *The Straits Times* (*ST*), Singapore's only English language broadsheet, has laboured long and hard to gain the sobriquet common currency. In addition to cooking up countless articles with durian-themed headlines, a leader column engaged in a spot of wishful projection when it opined that the term would have the effect of democratizing what was in effect an elitist institution (*ST* 11/10/02).

Well and good, but take a deep breath. Smell anything? (Democracy, perhaps?) Go inside, take a nose around. Observe the dull sheen of marble and granite in the monumentally bland main concourse. Browse the Asian exotica – futons, *cheong sum* dresses, Chinese teapots – in the shopping arcade. Catch if you can the fleeting scent of gourmet noodles and curries as they disappear up powerful extractor fans in expensive restaurants, and … wait, was that a faint whiff of durian you caught just there? Yes, but … that was you, residually 'durianed' – amongst other things – by Geylang, for, with a growing sense of *déjà vu*, you come to realize that *you* are the most pungent thing in this place: the Esplanade, like Changi, has no smell.

Even for a 'city without qualities', this is something of a coup. To appropriate the most potent symbol of Singapore's most pungent area, and to effect a complete deodorization in the process. It begs the question: what is the fate of performance – ostensibly 'the Durians' *raison d'être* – in all this? The answer lies in yet another serving from *The Straits Times*, which reported on attempts by the Acting Minister for Information, Communications and the Arts to 'sell' the centre to the masses by noting that many people were initially intimidated by personal computers, until they realized what they could do within three strokes (*ST* 20/10/02). The implicit functionality in the analogy enacts, in the terms suggested by Jon McKenzie in his provocative book *Perform or Else*, an almost complete overriding of 'cultural performance' by 'technological performance'. But you have been in Singapore long enough now not to be surprised by this. Just as, lacking a local precedent for an arts centre, the Esplanade is designed and run along corporate hospitality lines, so the absence of a widespread public discourse about the arts means that other paradigms must be brought to bear. For the technocrats of the Singaporean government, this is not simply a matter of improvised convenience. Here, more acutely than most other places in the world, the overlapping of McKenzie's three 'performance paradigms', cultural, technological and organizational (the latter epitomized by the Eplanade's hotelier CEO), constituting what he terms the 'performance stratum', is well advanced. First and foremost, the opening of the Esplanade signals Singapore's commitment to being a creative society, primed to perform innovatively and productively in a globalized knowledge economy.

Little point, then, in looking to the Esplanade programme for performances that will kick up a stink. However noxious their content or aesthetic – and to date, none has been – the effect lies circumscribed by a context that is less given to enacting conventional notions of normativity or resistance, than shuttling 'quickly between different evaluative grids, switching back and forth between divergent challenges to perform – or else' (McKenzic 2001: 19). In Singapore, the current mantra, and pressing reason for selling 'the Durians' to its people is: perform – or else be rendered economically obsolete by an emergent China.

And yet, you've been around. You've seen too much to conclude that *this* is the fate of performance in Singapore. Haven't you? Recall McKenzie's description of smell's effects: 'disintegration of forms, the mixing of subjects and objects'. He goes on to propose a 'funky' (in the scent sense of the term) riposte to the performance stratum which he terms 'perfumance':

> Unlike this formation [the performance stratum], where forms of discourse and practice are constructed and maintained, in the atmosphere of forces performatives and performances dissolve, disintegrate, become elemental. We're interested not only in the order, but in the odor of things and words.... [C]arrying the scent of exteriority, perfumance haunts the stratum's interior with odors emitted by certain incorporated remains.
>
> (McKenzie 2001: 203)

There you stand, inside 'the Durians', smelling of durian and all the other 'incorporated remains' that have accumulated about – and been secreted by – your person since you stepped off the plane at Changi. You have carried these odours into this scentless performance venue, and your journey is reconstituted as a perfumance. Maybe, dear reader, you've never been to Singapore, and even if you have, the trajectory you have performed at and upon each of the preceding stages has been vague: the only thing you know in precise detail is how to travel between them. But that vagueness is no accident, for it mimics the diffuse permeations of smell itself: in nosing around Singapore you have yourself enacted a perfumative drift. By sniffing out scent as an end in itself, you have engaged with Singapore's complex performance stratum without subjecting yourself entirely to its 'forms of discourse and practice'. You have played the observer, detective, consumer, tourist, client: but you are none of these things alone. The Singapore scent trail ends here. You are now free to follow your nose.

Notes

1. Cyberpunk writer William Gibson has famously described Singapore as 'Disneyland with the Death Penalty' (Deyan Sudjic, 'Virtual City'). For the most pristine take on Singapore's 'nationwide mise-en-scène', however, see Thomas 2Less (1998).
2. 'Contact zone' is a term introduced by Mary Louise Pratt to describe 'the places where cultures from disparate historical trajectories come into contact with each other' (Pratt 1996: 3). Pratt's own interest lies in the resultant heterogeneity of meanings and identities, often deriving from the asymmetrical relationships of the colonial context. James Clifford has brought the term to bear on contemporary 'border crossing' practices in *Routes: Travel and Translation in the Late Twentieth Century* (Clifford 1997).
3. You are not alone. American celebrity chef Anthony Bourdain glides past with camera crew in tow, poking his nose into things, filming the television series accompaniment to his book *A Cook's Tour*. Watch carefully when it is aired. You may see yourself there. Performing.
4. This was the term used by a spokesperson for the Queensland fire service when describing how the pungent smell of the durian had caused a full scale security alert aboard a passenger airliner due to fly from Brisbane to Adelaide (see *The Straits Times*, 17 January 2003).

References

Clifford, James (1997) *Routes: Travel and Translation in the Late Twentieth Century*, London: Harvard University Press.

George, Cherian (2000) *Singapore: The Air-Conditioned Nation: Essays on the Politics of Comfort and Control 1990–2000*, Singapore: Landmark Books.

Kishnani, Nirmal (2002) *Changi by Design: The Architecture of the World's Best Airport*, Singapore: Page One Publishers.

Kong, Lily (1999) 'Globalization, Transmigration and the Renegotiation of Ethnic Identity', in K. Olds, P. Dicken, P. F. Kelly, L. Kong and H. Wai-Cheung Yeung (eds) *Globalization and the Asia-Pacific: Contested Territories*, London: Routledge, pp. 219–36.

Koolhaas, Rem (1995) 'Singapore Songlines: Portrait of a Potemkin Metropolis ... or Thirty Years of Tabula Rasa', in R. Koolhaas and B. Mau, *S,M,L,XL*, New York/Cologne: Monacelli Press and Taschen.

McKenzie, Jon (2001) *Perform or Else: From Discipline to Performance*. London: Routledge.

Pratt, Mary Louise (1996) *Apocalypse in the Andes: Contact Zones and the Struggle for Interpretive Power*, Washington, DC: IDB Cultural Center.

2Less, Thomas (1998) 'Singapore ONE', *ctheory* <http://www.ctheory.net>

Yeoh, Brenda S. A. (1996) *Contesting Space: Power Relations and the Urban Built Environment in Colonial Singapore*, Oxford: Oxford University Press.

Part 3
Sounding/Rhythms

Text sources

3.1 Carl Lavery (2005) 'The Pepys of London E11: Graeme Miller and the Politics of *Linked*', *New Theatre Quarterly*, 21(2): 148–60.

3.2 Sarah Gorman (2003) 'Wandering and Wondering: Following Janet Cardiff's Missing Voice', *Performance Research*, 8(1): 83–92.

3.3 Henri Lefebvre and Catherine Régulier (2004) 'Attempt at the Rhythmanalysis of Mediterranean Cities', *Rhythmanalysis: Space, Time and Everyday Life*, intro. S.Eldon, trans. S. Eldon and G. Moore, London and New York: Continuum: 85–100.

3.4 Francis Alÿs and James Lingwood (2005) 'Rumours: A Conversation Between Francis Alÿs and James Lingwood', *Francis Alÿs Seven Walks, London, 2004–5*, London: Artangel: 16–22 (extract).

Introduction

[T]he 'rhythmanalyst' ... is strictly speaking neither psychologist, nor sociologist, nor anthropologist, nor economist; however he borders on each of these fields in turn and is able to draw on the instruments that the specialists use. He therefore adopts a transdisciplinary approach in relation to these different sciences. He is always 'listening out', but he does not only hear words, discourses, noises and sounds; he is capable of listening to a house, a street, a city as one listens to a symphony, an opera.

Henri Lefebvre and Catherine Régulier, in *Rhythmanalysis*

City silences

The opening of Jon McGregor's novel *If Nobody Speaks of Remarkable Things* (2003) urges the reader to listen to the city. Whether it is a symphony or an opera that is evoked, as Lefebvre and Régulier do above, or more a jazz improvisation is debatable (Lefebvre 2004: 87). What is undeniable, though – and, indeed, *remarkable* – is the way the author names a multiplicity of existing 'sound possibilities'. In other words, we *know* these sounds but we do not in the general course of living in the city *hear* them or isolate them amidst the everyday urban hum. This is why that chance moment in the dead of night when 'Everything has stopped momentarily', when 'there is silence and the whole city is still', is indeed 'a miracle' (McGregor 2003: 3–4). For it is an instant – perhaps one that occurs just for you – in which we hear the acuteness of our habitual 'not-hearing', a 'pause worth savouring, because the world will soon be complicated again' (ibid.: 5).[1]

As Carl Lavery tells us within the first paragraph of his article on Graeme Miller, the latter is a good example of someone who listens to that which Lefebvre calls 'the music of the city' (*PCC*, p. 150). Miller has set up a variety of 'observatories' in urban locations from which he collects sounds of the city. Often collaborating with the local inhabitants of these places – gathering testimonies, anecdotes and so on – Miller then devises soundscapes that are experienced by walking through designated sites. Spectators, wearing receivers as headphones, tune into transmitters that have been positioned strategically. Lavery's article concentrates on one piece, *Linked*, which had a particular resonance for Miller personally since it was based on his own neighbourhood in the East End of London. The piece is a response to the construction of, and prolonged protests around, the so-called M11 link road, which involved the forced eviction of countless residents – including the artist himself – and thus the break-up of long-established communities.

Premised upon what will turn out to be a recurring theme in Part 3, namely the notion of absence (whether momentarily or for good), *Linked* attempts to take soundings of and, indeed, actively *sound* that which has been silenced or voided: the lives of communities around a four-mile stretch of road. Weaving in many of the theorists represented elsewhere in this volume, Lavery delineates the way in which Miller provides a 'perform-ance map' with the help of which 'the city becomes a site for creative liv-ing and affective encounter, not simply something we pass through at speed' (*PCC*, p. 154). Two points of interest arise here: first, in writing about his own six-hour experience of walking the *Linked* route, he chooses delib-erately to do so 'as subjectively as possible', recognising that this corre-sponds to the logic of where the soundscape positions the walker-listener (*PCC*, p. 157). Second, his actual experience of the walk produces in him a sense of 'belonging to the world and yet being simultaneously outside it': in fact, 'I was dislocated' (*PCC*, p. 159). Thus, implicitly bringing into play territory relating to the 'impossibility of community' worked over by the likes of Jean-Luc Nancy in *The Inoperative Community* (1991) and Miwon Kwon in *One Place After Another* (2004), Lavery appears to be pointing to the operation of a form of 'un-belonging' or 'un-working' in the encoun-ter he describes. The 'work of mourning' that is *Linked* does not seek to indulge feelings of regretful nostalgia by rehearsing – for either the former inhabitant or the 'stranger' – the pain of an impossible return, but instead offers a 'critical unsiting', to apply Kwon's phrase (2004: 155). This pro-vides the means, first, to interrogate the terms by which a given social grouping establishes and maintains its legitimacy and, second, to identify with and reflect upon the ethical implications of what is at stake in the act of removal of such a community; in other words, a 'transformative recogni-tion' (*PCC*, p. 161). Returning us in conclusion to the philosophy of the Situationists, such an understanding uses the experience of the everyday to transcend art: 'to live is to create and to create is to live' (*PCC*, p. 164).

Janet Cardiff's audio walk-works also represent a form of sounding (out) the city. In *The Missing Voice (case study b)*, discussed in this section in Sarah Gorman's 'Wandering and Wondering' article, multiple narratives intertwine in a manner more akin to the structuring of a novel. Picking up a CD Walkman and handset from the local library, the spectator is taken on a form of guided tour round the Spitalfields, Brick Lane, Liverpool Street Station areas of London during which narrative modes and moods shift. Gorman identifies the piece as site-specific since 'the walk calls for participants to envision them-selves differently within this environment' (*PCC*, p. 171). It is not just other characters and story-fragments that are relayed to the listener but specific 'inter-active' instructions such as to follow a random member of the public, sit down on a particular bench or enter a church. Inevitably one of the most powerful narratives to emerge is an incidental – albeit 'planned' – one that can only occur for the particular participant concerned on that specific occasion. The 'missing narrative voice' it is implied, then, might be *yours*: the supposedly unmediated experience you compose for yourself, based on what you might be prompted to see, think and feel as you go along. For Gorman, however, this emerges as problematic because she chose to undertake the walk on 14 September 2001, and was unable to shake the events in New York of three days earlier from the field of experience that was opened out for her. So the immanence of 9/11 threw into sharp relief an ethical difficulty with the general principle of the work: that of relying on what and whom you happened to encounter – to say nothing of the baggage of that which you might have brought with you – in order to construct the experience. It made Gorman feel 'a bit of a fraud, a voyeur', since she was exploiting the fact that other people on the street had 'added an emotional depth to "my" narrative' (*PCC*, p. 173).

Rhythmanalysis

Henri Lefebvre is, as we have seen, one of the most prolific and original thinkers about the city and the everyday 'space of living' generally. Doubtless best known for his theorisation of 'the production of space' – the title in fact of his seminal book – in which he critiques the colonising abstraction of social space in the interests of bourgeois-capitalist ownership and consumption, Lefebvre develops a three-point definition of urban public space. This argues against its controlled, conceptualised homogenisation by the likes of planners and architects (representations of space), and has at its heart the recognition of the role of everyday life actions and behaviours in the construction of social space (spatial practices). The third component, spaces of representation, which complements the latter, corresponds to the embodied utilisation of public space for social expression, often taking forms that effectively subvert privatising tendencies, officialdom and regulation or that seek out possibilities of resistant spatial practice. Lefebvre's numerous writings on cities included attempting to articulate a theory of the citizen's 'right to the city', which among other things leads him to declare that 'the future of art is not artistic, but urban, because the future of "man" is not discovered in the cosmos, or in people, or in production, but in urban society' (1996: 173). Thus, the practice of urban social interaction itself is a creative act in an echo of Situationist sentiments applied to Graeme Miller's work by Lavery: the city as 'a site for creative living and affective encounter' (*PCC*, p. 154).

Lefebvre's development of a theory of rhythmanalysis was more or less the last project he undertook. An essay such as 'Seen from the Window' (2004: 27–37) almost seems to provide an abstracted 'sound and rhythm' counterpart to Jane Jacobs's account of the street ballet of Hudson Street. However, it is not merely the identification of an 'urban soundscape' that is at stake here but, as I have hinted at in relation to Paul Rae's Singapore 'scentanalysis', an understanding of urban rhythms as intrinsic to how cities constitute themselves. As Stuart Eldon writes in his introduction to the edited volume *Rhythmanalysis*, 'Lefebvre uses rhythm as a mode of analysis – a *tool* of analysis rather than just an *object* of it – to examine and re-examine a range of topics' (in Lefebvre 2004: xii). In Lefebvre's own words, then, 'Everywhere where there is interaction between a place, a time and an expenditure of energy, there is rhythm' (ibid.: 15). This is what he sets out to examine (in collaboration with Catherine Régulier) with specific regard to Mediterranean cities in the essay included here, discovering a difference in practice from

> social relations in Nordic towns [which] are founded on a contractual, and thus juridical, basis, which is to say on reciprocal good faith. Whereas relations in the Mediterranean would tend to be founded either on those tacit or explicit forms of alliance that go as far as the formation of clans (clientelism, mafias, etc.) or on the contrary on refusals of alliance that can lead as far as open struggle (vendettas, etc.).
>
> (*PCC*, p. 184)

Lefebvre and Régulier's view reveals shades of Benjamin's Naples analysis discussed in Part 1 of this book, not least in their subsequent use of theatrical terms: 'So what is particular about Mediterranean towns? It seems to us that in them, urban, which is to say public, space becomes the site of a vast staging where all ... these rhythms show and unfurl themselves. Rites, codes and relations ... act themselves out here' (*PCC*, p. 186). For Lefebvre/Régulier, though, it is Venice rather than Naples that is 'the example *par excellence*' of this: 'Is this city not a theatrical city, not to say a theatre-city, where the audience [*le public*] and the actors are the same, but in the multiplicity of their roles and relations?' (*PCC*, p. 186).

As it happens, one of the performances the artist Francis Alÿs talks about in his extended interview with James Lingwood – a short extract of which winds up Part 3 – took place in Venice:

> I entered the city by the train station and a friend of mine, the artist Honoré d'O arrived through Marco Polo airport. We arrived the same day, carrying the two different parts of a tuba, trying to find each other in the labyrinth of Venice. There was a basic dramatic construction to the piece, with the two protagonists needing to find each other. Eventually there was a happy end, maybe even a moral, to the story with the meeting and the physical reunion of the two halves, and the resulting production of a sound.
>
> (Alÿs et al. 2005: 28)

Alÿs's piece, entitled *Duett*, took its cue from a speech by Aristophanes in Plato's *Symposium* in which it is declared 'that it is in our nature to be incomplete, bisexual. There is always a missing half, a confusion, a split identity' (ibid.: 30). (Perhaps this is what it means to be a lone twin.) In a series of performances commissioned for London in 2004–5, the subject of this interview, Alÿs extrapolated the kernel of the Venice piece, this time incorporating a whole marching platoon of Coldstream Guards in the centre of the city. Similarly attempting to locate one another as individuals or sub-clusters, they eventually converge in a form of 'funnel action' – the outline of a funnel literally superimposed in the planning stages on to a ward map of central London (ibid.: 92–3) – which channels performers on to Southwark Bridge, where the formation disperses once more. The unlikely sight of Coldstream Guards being let loose on the streets of London's 'City' district implied a form of 'undoing' of British institutionalism: the Queen's personal guardians as anachronistic 'lost souls', searching for a home within the capital's financial heartland, whose ongoing wealth is founded on the exploitations of empire.

Following on from Lefebvre's rhythmanalysis, of particular interest here are Alÿs's 'street railings' works in which he runs a drum stick along railings in designated parts of London. Sometimes he lets the random rhythms produced predominate, at other times he attempts to impose a particular rhythm, and the 'railings function as an instrument. ... By just walking and running a stick against it, the details of the architecture automatically generate a sound pattern' (*PCC*, p. 193). For Alÿs, 'the simple act of touching the railings, of feeling the architecture with the drumstick acting as a kind of catalyst, was a way of making contact, of connecting to the physicality of place' (*PCC*, p. 193). In an echo of the theme of 'imperial London', moreover, alone the presence of railings in certain parts of the city is indicative of 'protected privilege'. Extracting ringing rhythms in this way clearly performs a provocation.

Not represented in this reader, owing to lack of space, but worth mentioning here is Iain Borden's exhaustive theorisation of skateboarding (fully realised in his book *Skateboarding, Space and the City*, 2001). Borden sees it as a 'critical practice ... directly confronting not only architecture but also the economic logic of capitalist abstract space' (in Borden et al. 2002: 179–80). Echoing many principles that might be applied to the much newer phenomenon of *parkour* or free running – whose exponents are *traceurs* (that is, tracers of urban textures and contours) – Borden's essay highlights that 'skateboarders implicitly realise the importance of the streets as a place to act'. Thus, a contemplation of the form as art does not by any means limit itself to the formal aesthetics of movement but is 'an attempt to write anew ... to insert meaning where precisely there was none' (ibid.: 182). Borden's prime example of this is the skateboarder's re-functioning of the handrail, ollie-ing up, then 'sliding down its length sideways [which] targets something to do with safety, with everyday security, and turns it into an object of risk' (ibid.: 186). In a similar way to Lefebvre's harnessing of rhythm – invoked by Borden as a point of reference – to 'sense' what is 'going on' in cities, the practice of skateboarding provides a tool for analysis: 'the continual performance of skateboarding ... *speaks* the city through utterance as bodily engagement. ... Skateboarders use themselves as reference to rethink the city' (ibid.: 195–6).

Note

1. For me the effect of a sudden heavy snow fall in the city is similar and accounts in part for the temporary playfulness and euphoria that breaks out: a suspension of the humdrum – for example, school and work stop early or are cancelled altogether – before the world 'gets complicated again'.

3.1   The Pepys of London E11: Graeme Miller and the Politics of *Linked*
Carl Lavery

Artists are meant to be that bit more resourceful, that bit better at lateral thinking, quicker to react, and they could have a useful role to play in the tiny acts of micropolitics that make a difference to the macropolitics that make a difference.

Graeme Miller[1]

Returning theatre to its urban context allows us to consider its function within a modern and contemporary urban practice.

Stanton B. Garner, Jr[2]

If he loves justice ... the 'scholar' of the future, the 'intellectual' of tomorrow should learn it and from the ghost. He should learn to live by learning not how to make conversation with the ghost but how to talk to him, with her, how to let them speak or to give them back speech, even if it is in oneself, in the other, in the other in oneself; they are always there, spectres, even if they do not exist, even if they are no longer, even if they are not yet.

Jacques Derrida[3]

Today everyone who values cities is disturbed by automobiles.

Jane Jacobs[4]

Although his practice resists easy definition, combining playwriting, composing, walking, and sonic installation art, Graeme Miller is consistent in his attempts to use performance as a barometer of the everyday, a way of gauging the temperature of the times. Much of his work is interventionist in a direct, site-specific sense. He has installed sound observatories to record what the Marxist philosopher Henri Lefebvre calls 'the music of the city';[5] collaborated with the inhabitants of these cities by making work from their experiences of space; and sent his audience (if we can still use that worn-out word in this context) on guided walks through a variety of urban landscapes.

Miller's interest in the city as a site of performance has much in common with contemporary currents in ethnology and sociology. In this essay I want to explore those parallels by focusing on *Linked*,[6] an on-going work that was commissioned by the Museum of London as part of its urban art collection in 2003.[7] The essay unfolds in three stages. In the first, I relate Miller's performance practice to developments in urban theory, paying particular attention to the concept of everyday life as theorized by Henri Lefebvre and Michel de Certeau. In the second, I provide a performative account of my experience of walking *Linked* in the summer of 2004.[8] In the third stage, I argue that *Linked* offers an alternative paradigm for political performance.

Siting *Linked*

Linked is part of a series of multi-disciplinary works on the city that Miller, a founding member of the influential Impact Theatre Co-operative, has been producing for more than a decade. These include *The Sound Observatory* (1992), a sonic map that traces the hidden rhythms and sounds of Birmingham; *The Desire Paths* (1993), a play in which five characters stumble through an apocalyptic urban wasteland with the help of an *A to Z*; *Feet of Memory, Boots of Nottingham* (1995), a sound installation documenting the memories of seventy citizens who walked the city in the course of a day; *Lost Sound* (2001), a film, made in collaboration with John Smith, in which Miller reconstructed his East London neighbourhood from cassette tapes discarded in the street;[9] *Dilston Grove* (2003), a photosynthetic work, commissioned by the London International Festival of Theatre (LIFT), where Miller's soundtrack accompanied Heather Ackroyd's and Dan Harvey's grass-filled church in Bermondsey, South London; and, most recently, *Bassline* (2004), which constructs an alternative map of Vienna from the recorded conversations of eleven participants who travelled through the city with a camera while followed by a double-bass player.

Like the performances mentioned above, *Linked* has no interest in fiction. Its purpose is to offer an alternative history of Miller's neighbourhood in East London, which was ravaged – indeed, literally torn apart – by the construction of the M11 link road in the early to mid-1990s. The work, then, is a form of resistance, a sonic memorial to the families who lived in the five hundred houses that were forcibly requisitioned and demolished so that commuters could reach the nearby City of London in time for work.

To combat the amnesia of the present, Miller lined the four-mile route of the link road with twenty transmitters that broadcast a haunting mixture of music, ambient sounds, and personal memories of those who once lived in the now vanished streets. To partake in the performance, the participant borrows a map and a receiver (a headset that looks and acts like a Walkman) from one of the local libraries in the boroughs of Hackney and Wanstead, and uses it to navigate his/her way through the urban landscape.

In the publicity that accompanies the work, *Linked* is defined as 'a landmark in sound, an invisible artwork, a walk'.[10] And it is not difficult to

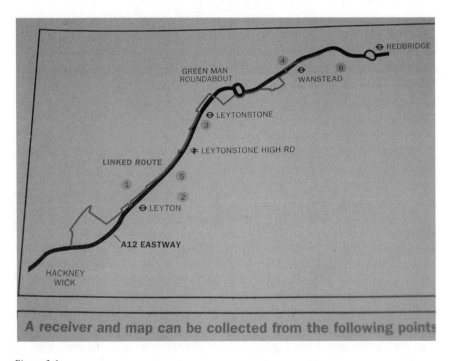

Figure 3.1

understand why. Although the work is rigorously sited – the location is the meaning – the site is absent, situated somewhere in the air above, or the ground beneath, the busy grey tarmac of the new road that rumbles noisily in the near distance. This invisibility, this erasure, is what Miller wants to contest. His sonic memorial haunts the road, reminding those who listen to the personal testimonies on the headset that this anonymous *passage de conduite* was once a dwelling place, a site of community. By making a visit to the site a prerequisite for the work, Miller transforms his performance into a civic practice in and by itself. To walk *Linked* is to become a part of the city, a witness to its processes, events, rhythms, and histories.

Performance, ethnography, and resistance

Miller's site-specific work encourages us to engage with the urban environment in which we are placed. Confronted with a performance like *Linked*, the vocabulary of theatre studies, with its emphasis on script, auditorium, and neat separation between actors and spectators, suddenly seems old, unable to deal with the collapse of boundaries that Miller insists on. If the discourse of drama studies can no longer account for Miller's work, then we need to look elsewhere. Ethnography provides a more suitable language for getting to grips with Miller's art. Contemporary ethnography, of the sort practised by James Clifford, is a discipline that tries to understand cultural processes 'from a standpoint of participant observation', 'situated knowledge', and 'self-reflexive writing'.[11] One way of understanding this self-reflexive and critical form of ethnography is to see it as a form of witnessing through empirical immersion, a means of arriving at the general through the particular, the macro through the micro.[12]

Ethnography's attempt to interpret ways of life and cultural trends through direct observation is exactly what Miller seeks to do when he sends his participants through the East End of London with a map and a headset.[13] As you walk along the route from Hackney to Wanstead, listening to the testimonies of the evicted and the re-located, it becomes impossible not to think about larger questions to do with life-style, public space, and what it means to be a citizen. To that extent, Miller invites us to practise – to perform – what Marc Augé calls 'an ethnology of supermodernity'.[14] According to Augé, such an ethnology can only ever be 'an ethnology of solitude', for, in today's society of retail parks, home entertainment systems, and 'real time', the subject is physically isolated from his/her community, and radically alone.

In the influential *Non-Places: an Introduction to an Anthropology of Supermodernity* (1992), Augé stresses the role that spatial practices have played in the production of super-modern *anomie*. For Augé, we live at a time in the West when place (the realm of history, identity, and dwelling) has been superseded by non-place (the realm of atemporality, anonymity and passage):

> In one form or another, ranging from the misery of refugee camps to the cosseted luxury of five-star hotels, some experience of non-place (indissociable from a more or less clear perception of the acceleration of history and the contraction of the planet) is today an essential component of all social existence. Hence the very particular and ultimately paradoxical character of what is sometimes regarded in the West as the fashion for 'cocooning', retreating into the self. ... The community of human destinies is experienced in the anonymity of non-place, and in solitude.[15]

If *Linked* is a performance that encourages its participants to reflect on contemporary spatial practices in the West, it also invites us to think about how that culture experiences time. According to Paul Virilio, the shift from place to non-place that Augé maps is consonant with our addiction to speed – our desire for faster roads, better computer servers, instant communication. In Virilio's view, speed institutes a process of collective forgetting. How can you find time to remember the past when things are so quick that you cannot deal with the present?

As a consequence of our obsession with speed, Virilio argues that we are on the brink of an apocalypse. Citing Walter Benjamin's well-known interpretation of Paul Klee's painting *Angelus Novus* (1920), Virilio depressingly concludes that 'today this theological vision no longer belongs to the angel of history. It has become the vision of each and every one of us.'[16]

While Miller's work encourages the participant to experience, and then reflect on, the cultural significance of space and time, he is not content to use performance merely to reveal these processes.[17] He wants to resist them. Speaking of his play *The Desire Paths* in an interview with the *Guardian* newspaper in 1993, Miller observes:

> We live at a time when people increasingly express the feeling that the world outside our windows is a dangerous and fragmented place. Once upon a time people walked through the city and it gave them a chance to name places and make contact with each other. Each individual has a different map of the city. But humans need to mark their lives against real space and other people. When they cease to walk, the real spaces become less plausible then than the centralized reality of the media and are increasingly witnessed as a passing blur from a car window. They become abandoned, the haunts of the disturbed.[18]

These comments provide an explicit insight into Miller's performance practice. If super-modernity deprives place of memory and community – and what could be more destructive of these things than a motorway? – then performance, Miller argues, ought to find a way of contesting this erasure by providing alternative methods for humanizing space.

Miller underlines his commitment to a politics of lived space in the essay 'Country Dance' (2000).[19] Crucially in this text he does not define himself as an artist, but as a cartographer interested in making the 'odd map to keep checking out what's what. To remind us that there is complex and subtle life out there. To reveal the singular, ineffable bits.'[20] His performance maps are designed for purposes of resistance. They are meant to reclaim place from the desert of non-place and, in the process, serve as monuments against forgetting. With the help of these maps, the city becomes a site for creative living and affective encounter, not simply something we pass through at top speed.

To that extent, Miller's performance work is part of an avant-garde tradition which, as Peter Bürger argues in *Theory of the Avant-Garde* (1974), attacks the Modernist idea of art as an activity or transcendence divorced from life itself. For Miller, as for Bürger, art is a social praxis:

> Having paced around the perimeter of a world which I questioned little and have spent years away from, I sense a yawning gap between Art and Culture. The City is built on the vernacular of shopping and now, Art is too. Art needs to be built on a thriving culture, not on its own ironic view of its own marketplace. Culture is the thick layer; Art the thin – the curious and beautiful distillation. The sooner Art gets itself a Culture on which to rest, the sooner it will feel good to be an artist and the less important whether you are one or not.[21]

The politics of pedestrian performance

Miller's attempt to re-appropriate urban space for humanist purposes situates his work in the non-heroic terrain of what Henri Lefebvre terms 'everyday life', the space where, in Lefebvre's view, alienation is most keenly felt because of its silent intimacy, its invisible proximity. Philip Wander provides a succinct definition of the Lefebvrian notion of everyday life in his 'Introduction' to the English translation of Lefebvre's key text *Everyday Life in the Modern World* (1968):

> 'Everyday life' refers to dull routine, the ongoing go-to-work, pay-the-bills, homeward trudge of daily existence. It indicates a sense of being in the world beyond philosophy, virtually beyond the capacity of language to describe, that we know simply as the grey reality enveloping all we do.[22]

Despite its seeming inconsequentiality – 'the grey reality enveloping all we do' – everyday life provides a privileged access to political reality.

The micro-acts and small-scale experiences that constitute the everyday reflect larger macro-processes that are occurring elsewhere.[23] The act of driving alone in a car, for instance, demonstrates the lonely isolation of the contemporary individual better than any theoretical text ever could: it provides empirical proof that supermodern individuality – the right to go where we want, when we want – entails separation from others and reinforces solitude.

To assent to that notion of individuality, then, is not just a personal act, it implicates the subject in a network of ideological meanings and assumptions. Or, as Augé puts it, 'never before have individual histories (because of their necessary relations with space, image, and consumption) been so deeply entangled with general history, with history, *tout court*'.[24] Yet if everyday life is the space where *anomie* is experienced concretely, it is equally, Lefebvre claims, the site where that *anomie* is best resisted. Revolting against the alienation of everyday life – in an urban context, reasserting what Lefebvre claims is our right to the city – is a liberating process: it releases us from the depressing drudgery and invisible discipline that pervades all aspects of everyday life.[25]

Miller's method for using art as an everyday strategy is to rely on the walk. Walking is well suited for this purpose because it allows us, as the French sociologist Michel de Certeau suggests in the influential *The Practice of Everyday Life* (1974), to see things at ground level and to experience events and sensations that maps and images of the city always miss in their quest for totality and spectacle:[26]

> The ordinary practitioners of the city live 'down below', below the thresholds at which visibility begins. They walk – an elementary form of this experience of the city; they are walkers, *Wandersmänner*, whose bodies follow the thins of an urban text they write without being able to read.[27]

The final line of this passage is important: it informs us that everyday life is not something that can be adequately represented in a text, or read passively at a distance. It is not an object to be consumed, a commodity, a spectacle. On the contrary, everyday life, in de Certeau's terms, is constituted through a series of practices: chance encounters, affective energy-flows, brief conversations, and ephemeral gestures. To get to grips with everyday life, we have to be part of it, to experience it, engage with it. Walking permits this type of embodied knowledge, this form of concrete participation, because it compels the walker to be physically present in the space s/he observes. In this way, everyday life reveals itself through smells, sounds, sights, tastes, intensities, and the rhythms of the body.[28]

As well as being an ideal strategy for witnessing, walking is also productive of everyday life. It is no coincidence, for instance, that de Certeau refers to walking as a speech act, a performative utterance: 'The act of walking is to the urban system what the speech act is to language or to statements uttered. ... It is a spatial acting-out of place.'[29] For de Certeau the city, like signification in general, is neither fixed nor stable: it is brought into being because it is practised, because people walk through it. To walk the city is to rewrite it, to appropriate it for yourself. Thus, no proper, official version of the city exists. We all own it:

> If it is true that forests of gestures are manifest in the street, their movement cannot be captured in a picture, nor can the meaning of their movements be circumscribed in a text. Their rhetorical transplantation carries away and displaces the analytical, coherent proper meanings of urbanism: it constitutes a 'wandering of the semantic' produced by masses that make some parts of the city disappear and exaggerate others, distorting it, fragmenting it, and diverting it from its immobile order.[30]

The similarities between de Certeau's utopian vision of pedestrianism and Miller's performance practice become evident when we look at how Miller understands the urban environment. Like de Certeau, Miller sees the city in linguistic terms as a text that is endlessly rewritten by the pedestrians moving through it:

> Everything is language and makes its own shapes and squiggles. The landscape throws out rushes of calligraphy and is constantly rewriting itself. Every moment we are composing ourselves and our world. A social culture is strings of these compositions which are agreed to be shared.[31]

For Miller, culture is spatial and space is produced through practice. So by sending his participants on a walk through the city, he allows them to engage in an act of *poiesis*, which, as de Certeau points out, means to 'create, invent, [and] generate'.[32] In the process, he troubles the logic of a society that associates art with the esoteric activities of 'specialists' (writers, painters, actors), not with the everyday practices of ordinary individuals. Or, to repeat Miller's comments from *Country Dance*: 'The sooner Art gets itself a Culture on which to rest, the sooner it will feel good to be an artist and the less important whether you are one or not.'

A note on representation

Miller's desire to engage the participant of *Linked* in a process of creative collaboration has important consequences for the objective writing, the impersonal voice of the third person, which is conventionally associated with academic discourse. For if Miller, like de Certeau, insists that the urban text is produced from the practices of individual *Wandersmänner*, then how can there be an objective and/or authoritative account of *Linked?* Surely, everybody will respond to the work differently and rewrite it according to his experiences and/or background?

In order to respect the logic of that position, I have tried to write about *Linked*, in the pages that follow, as subjectively as possible. I have done so by dividing my account into three separate sections: the way of the stranger; the way of the witness; and the way of the citizen. I use the word 'way' here to refer to (a) an act of walking; (b) a type of experience; and (c) a method of reflection.

This attempt to appropriate language, to write in the first person, is not motivated by a desire to obfuscate or to prevent dialogue. On the contrary, it is intended to enlarge meaning by encouraging the participants of *Linked* to compare and contrast their experience of the work with mine. The real, the dream of objectivity, is never abandoned. Rather it is re-imagined as something created through active dialogue, through difference. To that extent, my rewriting of *Linked* is a practice in itself, a method for remaking the everyday. A final point: the ways I have suggested below are my own. Other subjects will discover alternative paths and take different roads.

The way of the stranger (space)

Linked engaged me in a manner that conventional performance rarely does. Walking the four miles from the Lee Valley Park in Hackney to Redbridge Lane in Wanstead had more in common with an act of pilgrimage than with going to the theatre. There were no actors to gaze at, no building to enter, and no object to consume. The whole purpose of the performance was to bear witness to an act of real destruction, to listen to the voices of the departed, to resist the all-conquering claims of car culture.

Linked demands a sacrifice, an investment. You have to walk the route. You are obliged to put in the hours. Your feet suffer. You sweat. In a world of pure speed, a world where time is money, the six hours I spent walking, listening, and observing seemed extravagant, wasteful, sacred. I was part of a different economy, acutely aware of how this performance, this walk, was distancing me from the world of work, utility, and speed: the world of the car – the world of the link road. I felt alienated, marginalized, conscious of not working, of taking my time, of doing something different in the city. The performance had efficacy: it affected me. But why did it make me feel so strange?

The performance theorist Allan Kaprow provides a good explanation for this. According to him, performance that erases the boundaries between art and everyday life disturbs us more than performance that insists on maintaining its autonomy from the world. In happenings and invisible performance events, Kaprow argues, objects lose their meaning and migrate from their proper place. We realize then that reality is provisional and that what we do to space affects its meaning, its identity. Since existence is always sited in space and time, this inevitably affects the participant's sense of self:

> Such displacements of ordinary emphasis increase attentiveness ... to the peripheral parts of ourselves and our surroundings. Revealed in this way they are strange. Participants could feel momentarily separated from themselves.[33]

Kaprow was right. When I walked *Linked*, I felt self-conscious, not at home, 'separated from myself'. London had lost its 'hardness' and 'gone soft'. It had become a dream space, an 'unreal city' ...

The stories I heard on the receiver heightened the strangeness, fed the dream. The sonic skein that Miller spins over the city dislocates consciousness. The memories and sounds entering my ears conflicted with the data processed by my eyes. Where my ears recreated a vanished world of gardens, children playing in the streets, and snow in the city, my eye stubbornly insisted on what was still there: the motorway. Past and present merged; imaginative reality competed with everyday reality.

My disorientation was increased by the performance of the interviewees. Although the testimonies are about the past (hiding out in the Territorial Army Centre in Leytonstone in the 1950s, dancing to soul music at the Flamingo Club in the 1970s, protesting against the link road in the 1990s), they are all delivered as if they were happening just now, in the present.[34] This suspension of time is estranging: the past haunts the present, doubling it, and ultimately dislocating it from itself. The curator and writer Alan Read experienced a similar blast of strangeness:

> Charged with narrative yes, reminiscence maybe, gossip and rumour perhaps, but in *Linked* there is an invitation to come back down to earth, to walk, to encourage a pedestrian in the presence of the automobile, to engage with two presents. The present that is the first-person narrative of the speaker speaking, now in a present that must have been back then, at least eight years if the words are to be taken at face value. A second present that is the insistent present of the landscape transformed. And between these two presents a tension, held like a refrain from a faraway room, of the sound of memories coming into being just long enough for them to fail again in the forgetting of the insistent demands of time.[35]

Although Read talks of time, the voices on the headset affected me spatially. I had the sensation of belonging to the world and yet being simultaneously outside it. I felt liminal. Neither here nor there, betwixt and between. More attuned to absence (the voices on the headset) than presence (the pedestrians that passed me). I was dislocated.

The strangeness was not all about the voices, though. Throughout the performance I was acutely aware of being an outsider. Wearing a headset, carrying a map, and trying to tune in to a transmitter invariably transforms you into an object of attention. Passers-by looked at me strangely, trying to figure me out, seeking to understand what I was doing. In Leyton, a builder eyed me suspiciously as I was trying to tune into a transmitter at the junction between Colville Road and Grove Green Road; in Kingswood Road in Leytonstone, a young woman came out of her house to watch me, and in Wanstead, just off the ironically named Green Man Roundabout (there was nothing pagan or green about this roundabout), a mother and her three children scrutinized me sitting under a transmitter. I wondered if these people thought I was a policeman, a Department of Health and Social Security officer, a private detective, or a spy. I had become paranoid, unsure of my place.

In *Linked*, space is not a passive substance, a mere receptacle. It disorientates; it challenges your perspective on the world; it comes alive. You cannot consume it as a tourist would – that is to say, as an image or as

Figure 3.2

something passive. On the contrary, space affects you; it troubles your ego by positioning you as the stranger, the one who does not belong.[36] You are catapulted out of the known, forced to leave home, opened to the other. As with every act of pilgrimage, an event takes place in the four miles between Hackney and Wanstead. Something changes, alters, shifts ...

The way of the witness (ethics)

To perform *Linked* is to consent to a haunting, to agree to walk in a city of ghosts. The phantasmic voices broadcast by the transmitters weave a dream blanket of memory and reminiscence over the East End. They challenge reality as it is, reminding the solitary walker that the link road which now cuts through the neighbourhood was once filled with streets, houses, and trees, a place where people lived and shared experience.

Listening to these 'foreign correspondents from the past' unhinged me.[37] I felt melancholic, haunted by absence, surrounded by loss. I imagined the voices taking shape, filling space, living out an existence that had now gone. For all their distance, they seemed intimate, within reach. Their stories touched me. I was responsible for their memories, connected to them.

In the epigram from *Spectres of Marx: the State of the Debt, the Work of Mourning, and the New International* (1993) which opens this essay, Jacques Derrida talks about the special type of listening required if we are to communicate with ghosts. The striking thing about his injunction is that we are urged not to 'make conversation' with ghosts; rather he wants us 'to let them speak' so that we can discover 'the other in oneself'. For Derrida, the dislocation caused by the passing of the ghost is vital: it gets to the very core of ethics, which, in his view, is bound up with notions of inheritance and witnessing:

> That we are heirs does not mean that we have or that we receive this or that, some inheritance that enriches us one day with this or that, but that the being of what we are is first of all inheritance, whether we like it or know it or not. And that, as Hölderlin said so well, we can only bear witness to it. To bear witness would be to bear witness to what we are insofar as we inherit and that – here is the circle, here is the chance or finitude – we inherit the very thing that allows us to bear witness to it.[38]

Derrida's ideas provide a useful perspective on why *Linked* exerts such a strong if uncanny ethical pull. For if we accept Derrida's argument that the ghost's capacity to alter subjectivity is what transforms us from disinterested spectators into witnesses, then by placing us in contact with spectres, in this context, with people and places that are no longer there, Miller raises questions of value and justice. In Derrida's terms, he asks the naive, yet crucial question, of how to live.

> Someone, you or me, comes forward and says: I would like to learn to live finally. ... To learn to live: a strange watchword. Who would learn? From whom? To teach to live, but to whom. Will we ever know? Will we ever know how to live and first of all what to 'learn to live' means? And why 'finally'?[39]

In *Linked*, blunt questions have far-reaching consequences. I started to see the link road as something emblematic, which, like the purloined letter in Edgar Allan Poe's famous short story, conceals the very thing it makes manifest. Why, for instance, are individuals and communities routinely sacrificed for greater ease of access? Why this addiction to speed? Why the car? Why profit? How did we reach this point? Because it poses these questions, *Linked* stands as the conscience of capital, a performance that keeps the past alive, marking the traces of the dispatched and disappeared.

However, while *Linked* pays witness to what has gone, it is no exercise in nostalgia. I felt uplifted after walking *Linked*. As I left to take my train back to Kings Cross, the small pedestrianized square in front of Leytonstone Tube Station heaved with people in a riot of language and colour. The neighbourhood was on the mend, healing itself from the wounds inflicted by the road a mere fifty metres away across the bridge. This renewal of language, this rediscovery of community, is what Miller wants his spectral art, his conjuring trick, to contribute to:

> We read and write ourselves into the landscape, our own narrative overlapping with our neighbours. Yet I cannot fit my house back into its footprint (now space above the road). It is a surface that will no longer host my decade of life in Grove Green Road. As the particles of speech of *Linked* face the future there lies a hope that they will connect with triggered rememberings, counter-stories, and gross omissions and alternative versions of the same event that may renew the narrative tissue of the neighborhood.[40]

The futural hope that Miller places in memory, in the dislocated time of the spectre, brings to mind Derrida's claim in *Spectres of Marx* that to 'talk with or about some ghost' is to 'ask the question "where?", "where tomorrow?", "whither?"'[41] By inviting us to speak to ghosts, Miller opens his work to a different absence – the absence of those who have still to inherit. For reasons such as these, *Linked* can be profitably seen as a work of mourning. The sadness it evokes is galvanizing, producing what Avery Gordon calls 'transformative recognition'.[42] That is, recognition that alters the community allowing it to become something new, something different.

The way of the citizen (politics)

Linked is a profoundly political piece that bears witness to the attempts of the local community and a dedicated band of eco-warriors to block the construction of the M11 link road in the early to mid-1990s. Like *The Battle of Orgreave* (2001), Jeremy Deller's re-enactment of the pivotal clash between the miners and the police in the strike of 1984, *Linked* offers an alternative perspective on recent history: it reminds the listener that debate and protest, despite the claims of neo-liberal thinkers, have not disappeared in the last twenty years and that reality is still open to debate and change. The utopianism of the period is evident in the narrative of an activist who told how the local postman continued to deliver letters to his tree-house during the protests and how a retired RAF pilot, living in the houses opposite the common, left him half-bottles of whisky when it was cold.

Despite the failure of the protests – the presence of the link road is an all-too constant reminder of that – I was impressed by the exuberance and fortitude in the voices of the people recorded. It was apparent that the protest movement had been a defining moment in their lives. Deciding to resist government policy had politicized them, empowered them, made them more daring. The transmitter that stands sentinel on Wanstead Common, for instance, broadcasts the story of Jean, the Welsh lollipop lady, who, along with local schoolchildren and teachers, stopped the contractors from destroying a two-hundred-and-fifty-year-old chestnut tree on the common. Participating in a communal action allowed local residents like Jean to escape from the isolation of their living rooms – what Marc Augé calls 'cocooning' – and to constitute themselves as a civic body, a community. For citizens of the short-lived republics of Wanstonia and Leytonstonia, the city was exactly what the non-space of the link road was about to threaten: a public realm, a space where strangers were not only encountered but embraced.[43]

As I listened to these narratives, I became conscious of how they contradicted the spectacular images of metropolitan life that represent the inner city as a jungle, a landscape of danger and fear. In *Linked*, by contrast, the streets of Hackney and Wanstead are remembered by people who lived there as sites of openness and civility. To that extent, *Linked* echoes Jane Jacobs's warning about car culture in her classic book *The Death and Life of Great American Cities: the Failure of Town Planning* (1961). According to Jacobs, cities are not dangerous because they are filled with masses of strangers; rather, they are dangerous when they prevent people from meeting:

> Streets in cities serve many purposes besides carrying vehicles. ... Streets and their sidewalks, the main public places of a city, are its most vital organs. ... To keep the city safe is a fundamental task of a city's streets and its sidewalks.[44]

Jacobs's comments underline the sophistication of Miller's performance practice. *Linked* is not simply a political work because it represents an actual political event: its political value resides, ultimately, in its practical dimension. In *Linked*, stopping for a coffee, asking for directions *en route*, and buying food and water in local shops are significant acts: they provide an opportunity for conversation. And, as de Certeau reminds us, conversation is what socializes space:

> Conversation is a provisional and collective effect of competence in the art of manipulating 'commonplaces' and the inevitability of events in such a way as to make them 'habitable'.[45]

A paradigm for political performance

The speech that *Linked* inevitably gives rise to reveals the political essence of *civitas* to be neither dependent on juridical law nor on ideological consistency, but rather on our ability to live with – and respect – others who are not affiliated to us by ties of kinship or substantive notions of community *(Gemeinschaft)*. In this way, *Linked* practises what the urban sociologist Richard Sennett has argued in numerous publications from *The Fall of Public Man: on the Social Psychology of Capitalism* (1974) to *Respect in a World of Inequality* (2003): namely, that city living, the politics of the *polis*, is grounded in our ability to live with strangers in public spaces that encourage encounter and debate.

In the pages above, I have responded to Miller's invitation to rewrite *Linked* from a personal perspective. I have done so by stressing the existential, ethical, and political significance it had for me. In the final section, I want to argue that *Linked*'s practical dimension – the fact that the everyday is experienced as an empirical event – offers an alternative paradigm that has much in common with the aesthetic and political programme of the Situationists.

For the Situationists, art is neither a vicarious experience nor a mere functional tool. Rather, art – and in particular theatre – has the capacity to explode the logic of the society of the spectacle, which, according to Guy Debord, Situationism's main theorist, is based on the twin evils of separation (keeping people apart) and specialization (perpetuating hierarchies of people). Art that has renounced the page, stage, and gallery has the potential to be a revolutionary practice, argues Debord, because, in an age of abundance, cultural production is more important than economic production.[46] In a post-industrial, service economy, the crucial battle is for the mind of the masses, and this battle, Debord maintains, takes place at the level of the spectacle, the image: 'The spectacle is not a collection of images; rather, it is a social relationship between people that is mediated by images.'[47]

In the society 'mediated by images', spectatorship is politically reactionary, for it is this activity, above all else, claims Debord, that produces alienation and isolation:

> The spectacle's externality with respect to the acting subject is demonstrated by the fact that the individual's own gestures are no longer his own, but rather those of someone else who represents them to him.[48]

If controlling cultural consumption, situating the subject as spectator, is the essence of political domination, then activating cultural production on a mass scale, producing a society of performers, is, Debord believes, the key to cultural and political change. For how can the spectacle function if the masses prefer to remake the world actively rather than to watch it passively on the screen or monitor in front of them?

Debord contends that this shift from consumption to production can occur by subjecting everyday life to a process of *détournement* or imaginative hijacking. Situationists attempt to *détourner* the world by creating situations – public performances – that subvert reality from the inside, in the here and now. The crucial point about *détournement* is that art is not used to transcend the everyday; rather the everyday is used to transcend art. Or to put it differently: to live is to create and to create is to live. There is no need for a product or commodity, no space for a spectacle.

The notion of *détournement* describes, with some accuracy, what Miller is trying to do in *Linked*. By installing transmitters on a four-mile stretch of the M11 link road and inviting participants, many of whom are strangers to the area, to walk the route, Miller transforms a motorway into a work of art, a site where imaginative production takes place. In the process, he re-appropriates space (the place of encounter and dialogue) from the desert of non-space (the isolation caused by cars on a motorway).

The everyday is no longer a site of misery but a source of creativity. Just as importantly, the separation caused by the motorway – the fact that it physically blocks communication with other people – has been used to develop new forms of encounter with *Wandersmänner* who drift through the local community and produce social space with every step they take. *Linked* is a situation, an act of creative reclamation, a pedestrian performance that blurs the boundaries that link art and everyday life. To repeat a refrain from Miller that has run throughout this essay:

> The sooner Art gets itself a Culture on which to rest, the sooner it will feel good to be an artist and the less important whether you are one or not ...

Notes

I would like to thank Franc Chamberlain, Nicolas Whybrow and Ralph Yarrow for commenting on earlier drafts of this essay. Original dates are given in the main body of the text; dates of the editions I used are given in the notes.

1. Graeme Miller, 'Country Dance', in Alan Read, ed., *Architecturally Speaking: Practices of Art, Architecture, and the Everyday* (London: Routledge, 2000), p. 109–17 (117).
2. Stanton B. Garner, Jr, 'Urban Landscapes, Theatrical Encounters: Staging the City', in Elinor Fuchs and Una Chaudhuri, eds., *Land/Scape/Theater* (Ann Arbor: University of Michigan Press, 2002), p. 94–118 (96).
3. Jacques Derrida, *Spectres of Marx: the State of the Debt, the Work of Mourning, and the New International*, trans. Peggy Kamuf (London: Routledge, 1994), p. 176.
4. Jane Jacobs, *The Death and Life of Great American Cities: the Failure of Town Planning* (London: Penguin, 1972), p. 352.
5. Henri Lefebvre, *Rhythmanalysis: Space, Time, and Everyday Life*, trans. Stuart Elden and Gerald Moore (London: Continuum, 2004).
6. Cornelia Barker, *Linked* (London: Arts Admin, 2003), p. 2.
7. Note the comments of Cathy Ross, of the Museum of London, in *Linked* (p. 3): 'Linked will be the first site-specific artwork to enter the Museum's collections, but it is by no means our first piece of contemporary art. For the last fifteen years or so the Museum has been actively collecting what might be called 'urban art', work in some way engaged with the contemporary city. These works are collected very much as art, rather than topography, in that what the Museum looks for is an artist's subjective and individual vision of the city, rather than any objective record of what things looked like.'
8. I use the word performative here in the sense of Peggy Phelan's notion of performative writing which approaches performance from a joint theoretical and autobiographical perspective. See Peggy Phelan, *Mourning Sex* (London: Routledge, 1997). For a concrete example of performative writing, see Phelan's essay, 'On Seeing the Invisible: Marina Abramovi's *The House with the Ocean View*, in *Live: Art and Performance*, ed. Adrian Heathfield (London; Tate Publishing, 2004), p. 16–27.
9. See *Linked*, p. 16.
10. See <http://www.LinkedM11.net>.
11. James Clifford, *The Predicament of Culture: Twentieth-Century Ethnography, Literature, and Art* (Cambridge, MA: Harvard University Press, 1988), p. 9.
12. Speaking about how the modernist poet William Carlos Williams influenced his understanding of ethnography, Clifford notes: 'Williams's *Paterson* became a model, a provocation for a new kind of realism. This was situated knowledge, freed from the constraints of scientific objectivity and the Lukácsian "type", a path through even the most particular and subjective facts to a kind of general view, a "big enough" vision.' See James Clifford, 'An Ethnographer in the Field: James Clifford Interview', in Alex Cole, ed., *Site-Specificity: the Ethnographic Turn* (London: Black Dog, 2000), p. 52–71 (54).
13. This type of ethnography escapes the authoritarianism inherent in older anthropological models. Here, there is no desire to create a scientific object, existing beyond the observer: rather, it assumes that the observer is implicated in the production of knowledge, and, for that reason, offers an always already partial view. Hence the emphasis on self-reflexivity.
14. Marc Augé, *Non-Places: an Introduction to an Anthropology of Supermodernity*, trans. John Howe (London: Verso, 1995), p. 120.
15. Augé, p. 119–20.
16. Paul Virilio, *A Landscape of Events*, trans. Julie Rose (London: MIT Press, 2000), p. xii. Virilio's comments are based on the following remarks from Benjamin: 'A Klee painting named "Angelus Novus" shows an angel looking as though he is about to move away from something he is fixedly contemplating. His eyes are staring, his mouth is open, his

wings are spread. This is how one pictures the angel of history. His face is turned toward the past. Where we perceive a chain of events, he sees one single catastrophe which keeps piling wreckage upon wreckage and hurls it in front of his feet.' See Walter Benjamin, 'Theses on the Philosophy of History', in *Iluminations: Essays and Reflections*, trans. Harry Zohn, ed. Hannah Arendt (New York: Shocken, 1969), p. 253–64 (257).

17. Miller's performances are interventions in actual space and time. They encourage partici-pation and activation. To that extent, they differ from ethnography's page-bound critique. I am thinking here, in particular, of Marc Augé's essay, 'An Ethnologist in Disneyland', in *Site-Specificity: the Ethnographic Turn*, trans. Alexia Defert, p. 182–91.

18. Graeme Miller, *The Guardian*, 15 June 1993, p. 28.

19. This essay is a companion piece to Miller's production *Country Dance* (1999), a play that 'was conceived as a stage work about Dance, rather than as a dance work in itself'. See <http://www.mdx.ac.uk/rescen/Graeme_Miller/country.html>.

20. Miller, 'Country Dance', p. 116.

21. Ibid., p. 115.

22. Philip Wander, 'Introduction', in Henri Lefebvre, *Everyday Life in the Modern World*, trans. Sacha Rabinovitch (London: Transaction, 2002), p. vii–viii.

23. Lefebvre notes: 'The everyday can therefore be defined as a set of functions which con-nect and join together systems that might appear to be distinct. … A condition stipulated for the legibility of forms, ordained by means of functions, inscribed within structures, the everyday constitutes the platform upon which the bureaucratic society of controlled consumerism is erected.' See 'The Everyday and Everydayness', trans. Christine Levich, Alice Kaplan, and Kristin Ross, in Alice Kaplan and Kristin Ross, ed., *Everyday Life, Yale French Studies*, LXXIII (1987), p. 7–11 (9).

24. Augé, p. 119–20.

25. The urban sociologist Franco Bianchini defines four ways by which everyday alienation undermines creative living in the city: 'the dispersal of urban functions; the emergence of "non-places"; the reduction of leisure time for people in work; and the consequences of "information overload" and of the "audit explosion".' See 'A Crisis in Urban Creativity? Reflections on the Cultural Impacts of Globalization, and on the Potential of Urban Cultural Politics', paper presented at the International Symposium, 'The Age of the City: the Challenge for Creative Cities', Osaka, 7–10 February 2004.

26. Benjamin Rossiter and Katherine Gibson also stress the politics involved in pedestrian per-formance in their essay about the live performance *The Urban Dream Capsule*, performed by five 'art-stronauts' at the Melbourne International Arts Festival in 1996. They con-clude their essay thus: 'The poetics of walking permits encounters with city fragments and seemingly "unimportant" urban activities – the practices of urbanism that are not neatly folded into forceful stories of capitalist urbanization, social polarization, urban consolida-tion, and dead-city syndrome.' See Benjamin Rossiter and Katherine Gibson, 'Walking and Performing "The City": a Melbourne Chronicle', in *A Companion to the City*, ed. Gary Bridge and Sophie Watson (Oxford: Blackwell, 2003), p. 437–47 (445–6).

27. Michel de Certeau, *The Practice of Everyday Life*, trans. Steven F. Rendall (Berkeley: University of California Press, 1984), p. 93.

28. This is also how Lefebvre believes that everyday life gives up its secrets. For him, the 'truth' of the everyday is communicated in murmurs, sounds, and, especially, rhythms. See 'Elements of Rhythmanalysis: an Introduction to the Understanding of Rhythms' in *Rhythmanalyis: Space, Time, and the Everyday*, p. 1–69.

29. De Certeau, p. 97.

30. Ibid., p. 102.

31. Miller, 'Country Dance', p. 116.

32. De Certeau, p. 205.

33. Allan Kaprow, quoted in Sarah Gorman, 'Wandering and Wondering: Following Janet Cardiff's *Missing Voice*', *Performance Research*, VIII, No. 1 (2003), p. 83–92 (89).

34. The experience is not dissimilar to what Walter Benjamin calls *Jetztzeit:* a messianic moment that stops the flow of history. According to Benjamin, messianic time 'blasts' open 'the continuum of history' – and for that reason, it has the potential to deliver us from suffering, which, in Benjamin's opinion, teleologically driven notions of history are unable to do. See Benjamin, p. 261.

35. Alan Read, *Linked*, p. 5.

36. For a good account of how the tourist consumes space, see John Urry, *Consuming Places* (London: Routledge, 1995).

37. Miller, *Linked*, p. 2.

38. Derrida, p. 54.

39. Ibid., p. xvii.

40. Miller, *Linked*, p. 2.

41. Derrida, p. viiii–ix.

42. Avery Gordon notes: 'Being haunted draws us affectively, sometimes against our will and always a bit magically, into the structure of feeling we come to experience, not as cold knowledge, but as a transformative recognition.' See Avery F. Gordon, *Ghostly Matters: Haunting and the Sociological Imagination* (Minneapolis: University of Minnesota Press, 1997), p. 8.

43. As a form of protest against the government's refusal to listen to the democratic demands of its citizens, the free republics of Wanstonia and Leytonstonia were declared in January and February 1994.

44. Jacobs, p. 39.

45. de Certeau, p. xxii.

46. Alice Kaplan and Kristin Ross stress this aspect of Situationism: 'Staying within a specifically Marxist vocabulary, we might say that the Situationists shifted their attention from the relations of production within the factory to that basic yet undertheorized problem of social reproduction ... what we are here calling everyday life.' See Alice Kaplan and Kristin Ross, 'Introduction', in *Everyday Life*, p. 1–4 (2).

47. Guy Debord, trans. Donald Nicholson-Smith, *The Society of the Spectacle* (New York: Zone, 1995), p. 12.

48. Debord, p. 23.

3.2 Wandering and Wondering: Following Janet Cardiff's Missing Voice
Sarah Gorman

Three days after the US World Trade Center attack I took a walk in London's East End at the behest of Canadian artist Janet Cardiff, or at least guided by her absent voice. In 'The Missing Voice (Case Study B)', a piece described by Claire Bishop as an 'audio walk', Cardiff conflates ideas drawn from film-making and sound installation to produce a binaurally recorded sound track. Interweaving references to an absent *film noir* heroine with historical references to the local area, she reconceives the tourist audio-tour as sound art. Over the past 10 years Cardiff has made contemporary audio-tours for locations in Canada, the USA and Germany and from 1999 onwards her work has been sited at the Whitechapel Library in London and conceived as a walk around the locale. In pieces such as 'In Real Time' (1999) a piece produced for the Carnegie International and the German 'Walk Muenster' (1997) Cardiff also introduces a pre-recorded visual track viewed through a hand-held digital camera. When pointed in the designated direction the viewfinder image reveals figures who appear ominously absent from the participants' actual view. 'The Missing Voice' is her eleventh audio walk, commissioned by London's Artangel, an organization which invites artists to articulate their response to the city through site-specific work.

At 2.30 pm on 14 September I turned up at the library, exchanged a piece of ID for a CD Walkman and headset and entered the aural narrative of Cardiff's 'Missing Voice'. A comparative newcomer to London and unfamiliar with the local area, I was vaguely aware of the commercial 'Jack the Ripper' tours, which trace the path of a series of Victorian killings and which took a similar path to my own. However, 3 days after the World Trade Center attacks, the image of Jack the Ripper was not foremost in my mind. At that time UK media coverage of September 11[1] was largely dominated by reports of the incalculable loss of human life and undisciplined speculation about the identity of the perpetrators. During my own experience of 'doing' the 'Missing Voice' walk I felt that a certain sense of complacency about the nature of the urban street had been destabilized. My perceptions of street activity, the sounds around me and my sense of 'belonging' in that environment were heightened, I had a greater sense of visual stimulation, and was amused rather than irritated by the idiosyncrasies of people who passed by. But I felt more threatened than usual by the traffic as it appeared to be dangerously close, and I felt very aware of myself as a lone woman walking on the unfamiliar pavements of Whitechapel. On 14 September I was still in a state of shock, if not denial, about the terrorist attack, as I participated in the walk. I felt the activity around me was confirming my own sense that 'life must go on', but that as a community, people in London were reeling with shock at the idea of such an attack, and perhaps concerned about the implications of our ideological – if not geographical – proximity to North America.

In my discussion of 'The Missing Voice', I want to consider how Janet Cardiff's work seeks to alter viewing conventions more traditionally associated with tourist or educational audio-guides, and so to challenge epistemologies relating to representations of the cultural diversity of the city and of the self. But I also want to consider more subtle ways in which the work 'worked' for me on that day, as it could have on no other. My own heightened sense of awareness brought out feelings of dislocation, intuition, the uncanny and a kind of associative thinking that for me connected 'wandering' with 'wondering' as I attempted to negotiate the contradictory information contained within Cardiff's instructions. I want here to look at some of the ways in which cultural and artistic theories of walking, wandering and looking can help to understand and unpick these experiences.

Janet Cardiff's work is perhaps classically situated 'in between' genres. Perhaps coincidentally, but perhaps not, I write this work from a position of being 'in between' states of self-hood – an academic, a single woman, a western subject – states of consciousness that on the strange days after September 11 appeared to fracture and destabilize. While I said earlier that Janet Cardiff makes 'audio-visual art' this definition perhaps occludes the individual layers of 'meaning' activated through personal interaction. Much of her work requires the participant to engage in a walk close to an art or cultural location, in this case the Whitechapel Library in East London. It might additionally be described as 'site-specific', complying as it does with Miwon Kwon's definition of this genre of work:

> Site-specific art, whether interruptive or assimilative, [gives] itself up to its environmental context, being formally determined and directed by it. ... The art object or event in this context [has] to be singularly *experienced* in the here and now through the bodily presence of each viewing subject, in a sensorial immediacy of spatial extension and temporal duration.
>
> (Kwon 1997: 86)

After picking up the Walkman, the participant is given a brief introduction to the tour by one of the library attendants, who is required to make sure that she is aware that this is not a traditional tourist walk. Next, the participant is instructed to go and stand in front of the crime section of the library, to press 'play' and to follow the instructions on the Walkman. For the next 50 minutes the listener/participant is then instructed to carry out various tasks (opening a book, walking up stairs, opening doors, crossing the road, entering a church) before being finally abandoned on the concourse of Liverpool Street Station to make her own way back to the library.

The audio-track begins on the ground floor of the Library. Cardiff asks the participant to copy the activities of a man she is watching, to take a specific book off the shelf and read a certain paragraph. As Cardiff reads the paragraph aloud, backing music from a *film-noir* soundtrack increases in volume, ending with a high-pitched female shriek. The next instruction requires the participant to go upstairs into the music library to sit at a desk and look at a Magritte painting in an oversize art book. At this point the participant is told that she is being followed. As I registered this information, I remembered that I had been given instructions by Cardiff to follow someone myself.

A deliberate ambiguity about who is following and who is being followed continues throughout the piece as the participant is led around Brick Lane and Fashion Street then out towards The City, the financial district of London and Liverpool Street Station. The CD ends with Cardiff telling us that the young woman of the story had boarded a train and that her follower, the young man, was running along the platform to try to stop her from leaving. This imagined vignette provides a rare vision of clarity for the participant, who can possibly imagine the characters who have been filling her head for the past 50 minutes to have somehow materialized and to be leaving for a life beyond the narrative on a departing train.

The text constantly shifts in register, with Cardiff abandoning her conspiratorial, hushed, instructive voice, in favour of a confessional tone, or a pre-recorded voice replayed on dictaphone. At one point we hear Cardiff noting that the man she was following has gone into a pub, only to hear the same line rewound and replayed immediately over the dictaphone. The difference in sound quality is marked, moving from digital clarity to analogue hiss. One of Cardiff's personae tells us that she found a photograph of an auburn-haired woman on the floor; later on, we learn that she is disguised, wearing a red wig, so as to resemble the woman in the photograph. We learn that she has hired a private detective to find the woman in the photograph, who now appears to have gone missing. We hear a detective recite his findings with regard to this investigation on dictaphone. At times Cardiff appears to be conducting an investigation of her own, taking photographs and noting the proliferation of banana skins on the streets. Another male voice appears, apparently in love with one of the women in question.

The relationships between these characters are not stated explicitly, and their various narratives appear repetitive and even contradictory. However, they do appear to be linked by a discussion of disappearance on both a literal and metaphorical level. Kitty Scott has identified four different personae (or 'Cardiffs' as she refers to them), on the CD track:

> One speaks in a clipped voice and guides you through the city; another narrates in a confessional mode. Still another speaks in the detached third person; and yet another Cardiff sounds highly mediated as she talks into a portable recorder.
>
> (Scott in Cardiff 1999: 14)

Further confusion ensues as the established diegetic world of the London streets Cardiff guides us through appears to be displaced entirely. The customary description of shops and pedestrian crossings transmutes into a description of a war-torn landscape:

> There's a lime green car parked across the street, you can see the church steeple, scaffolding, graffiti on the wall, barbed wire, broken windows, men with guns in

black uniforms and face masks, fires all around me … there they saw hearses and coffins in the air, and there again, heaps of dead bodies lying unburied.

This is Commercial Street, there is a cross walk to the left, just around the corner, wait for the cars to stop and then cross over when you can.

(Cardiff 1999)

It becomes increasingly difficult for the participant to keep track of the stated relationship between the 'real' and 'fictional' landscape and to understand exactly who is speaking when, who desires to be, or to find, whom. The most prevalent voice appears to be that of Cardiff's conspiratorial presence who encourages the participant to cross the street and 'walk with me'. She points out geographical features and makes observations about the figures she notices in the street. The plot line of enigmatic, wayward heroine and concerned male detective is familiar enough territory from the generic *film-noir* narrative, but the position of the narrator as intra- or extra-diegetic is almost impossible for the participant to ascertain.

During my experience of the walk I found that the multiple narratives and apparently arbitrary nature of the journey gave so few pointers or indicators to Cardiff's intended 'meaning' that a kind of void or mental space opened up, into which my own thought processes flooded and into which, when these had been exhausted, ideas and perceptions from an over-stimulated mind began to flow. I reflected that while I might feel quite comfortable with such 'gaps' in a theatrical text, I felt a little apprehensive about these 'missing voices'. I was expecting this voice to guide me around London, and perhaps to reassure me as I entered unfamiliar territory. I began to go into self-reflexive overdrive: 'Could that be the pigeon man Cardiff referred to? … Well, of course not, it's an engineered moment of co-incidence, but then again, could it be?' The meanings I provided appeared crude and over-determined; I became incredibly self-conscious, over-aware of my relationship both to the text and to the city streets, attempting to theorize and fictionalize the 'real' surroundings pointed out by Cardiff.

Although the multiple narratives within Cardiff's audio-recording do not seem to rely solely upon the streets of East London for their fictional setting, I would suggest that the work could appropriately be described as site-specific as it appears to reorient the participant towards perceiving their environment in a different way. I might even go further, to suggest that the walk calls for participants to come to envision themselves differently within this environment, although I cannot trace exactly how this happens, and this is partly what intrigues me about this work. The process of following a prescribed journey, and of having to negotiate the conflicting information of 'real' environmental sounds of traffic and voices, alongside binaurally pre-recorded environmental sounds, appears to displace or disorient

Figure 3.3   Gun Street, London E1. Photo: Paul Brownridge.

traditional viewing conventions. Through a process of defamiliarization and disorientation it appears to ask the viewer to consider his or her place within the context of the changing environment.

Half way through the journey, Cardiff gives an instruction to sit on one of the benches tucked away behind a chapel off Bishopsgate; 14 September was a sunny day and a lot of people were lying on the grass, reading and eating lunch. I looked up and saw a plane fly behind an office block in front of me. I tried to imagine the plane flying into the building. I imagined what it would be like to see such an impact at close quarters, to experience it at first hand. I wasn't sure whether I felt connected to the 'real' horror of the experience or not, I think I felt very shocked, but also distanced from it all, so perhaps this was a guilty attempt to construct some kind of 'authentic' feeling of grief or horror at the event.

There are news-stands at regular intervals along Bishopsgate selling the *Evening Standard*, and Cardiff often gives an instruction to walk past, or turn after one such stand. She often reads a headline from one of the small advertising boards propped up against the stalls. One particular headline struck home. It may have been 'real' or 'fictional' from the period of her constructing the piece, it was impossible to tell: I became unnerved when, as I walked past a headline which read '20,000 presumed dead' in relation to the World Trade Center, Cardiff read out a similar headline, '20,000 tube delays'. I considered how the stark statistics of the news-stand work to remove all sense of human connection with the horror of such a loss. With this in mind I entered the church down the road and took my place towards the back, as instructed. The church was empty but for one suited young man who sat immobile, with his head bowed. It was impossible to tell whether he was praying, crying or sleeping. I felt a surge of sympathy for this young man even though I could not be certain about the cause of his distress, or even to establish whether he was in distress at all. The process of furnishing the bare bones of Cardiff's narratives with extra characters and extra meaning had permeated everything I did or saw. However, as with the office-block example, I also felt as if I was experimenting with experiencing this sympathy, I felt a bit of a fraud, a voyeur, somehow exploiting this young man's feelings and enjoying the fact that they added an emotional depth to 'my' narrative.

The World Trade Center attack also affected my experience of nearby Brick Lane, and I think it made me more aware than usual of my perception of the cultural differences between the Bangladeshi communities working there and the middle-class, predominantly white community working in the City. Whitechapel Library and the gallery close by are situated on the edge of London's financial district and the working-class communities of the East

End. Over the past century these streets have been lived and worked in first by Jewish immigrants from Eastern Europe and, more recently, by Muslim communities from Bangladesh and the Asian subcontinent. The locale is layered with histories and narratives, street names and historical sites, market stalls, clothing shops and eateries.

Cardiff had merely instructed me to follow a prescribed route which led me from Brick Lane to the City without foregrounding the difference in environment in any obvious way. I thought about the disparity in economic wealth, but then pitted that against a kind of spiritual wealth, as I saw men spilling out of the mosques, and compared this with the empty church on Bishopsgate, only half a mile away. I thought about my place within either community. How did the men I saw on Brick Lane perceive British women who were out walking alone? How would the hard-working city community conceive of someone with the time to 'wander' the city during the day without the imperative to return to the office? I became aware of being implicated by a number of contradictory, conflicting discourses. I caught a glimpse of the ideologies and discourses of power, which allowed me to conceptualize these two communities as 'different', and became aware of my comparatively privileged position in either context.

This journey did not clarify my feelings towards either community; rather it reinforced my sense of being an outsider to both. The entire route appeared to have raised questions about the complex network of relationships between commercial and interpersonal exchange in this part of London. This accidental discovery clarified for me de Certeau's understanding of walking in the city as a rhetorical practice.

Writing on the disruptive pleasures of the museum audio-guides of Sophie Calle, Janet Cardiff and Andrea Fraser, Jennifer Fisher sets out the 'sensory aesthetics of conventional audio-guides'. She states that the traditional 'goal of the audio-track is to record the curator's vision' or to give 'scholarly background' to the artwork (Fisher 1999:26). Certainly, this omniscient authorial voice was absent from Cardiff's walk. In relation to the possible expectations engendered by the tourist use of the audio-guide, I referred to John Urry's theory of 'the tourist gaze', which suggested that the tourist experience relied upon a denigration of the 'everyday' in order to celebrate the escape from the mundane and the quotidian. In contrast to traditional tourist guides, Cardiff's walk invited the spectator to look at and participate in everyday activities. The narrative offered no sense of escapism, nor could it be said to transport the (generic, British) participant out of their usual economic or cultural milieu. It is possible to consider here that Cardiff is deliberately playing with the conventions or 'sensory aesthetics' (Fisher 1999) of the audio-guide in order to confound the participant's expectations. It is interesting to consider the implications of a participant maintaining 'the tourist gaze' whilst looking at the everyday. For Urry, 'to be a tourist is one of the characteristics of the "modern" experience', an experience which presumably seeks to celebrate as 'exotic' or 'other', all that comes into view. Perhaps this attitude should also be considered in terms of Michel de Certeau's 'panoptic' view, as the tourist considers the object of his or her gaze with the same superior, detached objectivity as de Certeau suggests geographers and town-planners do in conceiving of the concept-city. Participating in Cardiff's walk with such an approach might result in an interesting inversion of the tourist gaze, whereby the participant comes to celebrate everyday practices as valuable within themselves, or to consider the approach of a stranger with a benign sense of curiosity rather than ambivalence or apprehension.

By asking the participants to perform an apparently mundane task (walking the streets, crossing the road) Cardiff is encouraging them to 'perform the everyday'. This sense of displacement which comes from 'consciously' performing the everyday has been suggested by Allan Kaprow to encourage a heightened awareness of environment,

> Such displacements of ordinary emphasis increase attentiveness ... to the peripheral parts of ourselves and our surroundings. Revealed in this way they are strange. Participants could feel momentarily separated from themselves.
>
> (Kaprow in Rawlinson 1966)

According to Kaprow's idea, the process of walking might encourage the participant to be more closely attuned towards considering how this particular environment makes them feel. In other words, they might experience an emotional or sensory response to an environment, which they might ordinarily sublimate in favour of a more factual or objective response.

If this were the case then it might be possible to consider the conceptual boundaries between cognitive and proprioceptive[2] reception to be temporarily eroded. In addition to an erosion of the modernist mind/body split, the spectator could be seen to experience an elision between external and internal spaces. The overlapping narratives and invocation of both visible and invisible spaces might lead the spectator to become confused as to whether the fiction lies in the external world of the street or the internal world of the fiction which appears to be going on in their head. They may borrow from personal experience to fill the gaps in the narrative. They may be told a 'fact' about their external world which corresponds to their proprioceptive sense of where they are and what they are doing, but in the next instant this continuity is disrupted, as key characters or aspects of the narrative appear to be 'absent' from the version they are experiencing.[3] 'The conventional relationship between values such as the real and the fictional, the subjective and objective, is displaced. As Fisher points out, Cardiff's work is not 'interpretative' or 'educational', but rather 'generative'. The participant furnishes his or her own 'meaning' and generates a text specific to the time and context of their walk.

I would suggest that Cardiff's audio walk encourages the participant to occupy what Urry has designated as a 'modernist' position, whilst maintaining an element of self-reflexivity about what they are seeing and experiencing. If we accept that such a gaze can be maintained, then the participant will conceive of their environment in terms of subject and object – the world or environment being a passive, knowable 'object' external to his or her active, interpreting self. The head-set, which destabilizes one aspect of sense perception, exaggerates the sense of 'separation' from the environment and yet, because the narrative being received through the head-set is not a coherent story, the participant is forced to draw upon the contingencies of the surrounding environment in order to complete the narrative. The vacuum created by the lack of coherence on the audio-track encourages the participant to look for 'meaning' in the context in which the information is received, to look to their immediate environment to furnish them with clues, or to even substitute themselves as one of the possible protagonists or personae participating in the fiction.

The view of the city from the ground made generalization about the city impossible, only a panoptic, lofty viewpoint could begin to simplify the confusion and separate the contradictions into palatable narratives. In critiquing

Figure 3.4   Fashion Street, London E1. Photo: Paul Brownridge.

the illusion of unity lent by his elevated viewpoint of New York from the 110th floor of the World Trade Center, de Certeau wrote:

> The figures of pedestrian rhetoric substitute trajectories that have a mythical structure, at least if one understands by 'myth' a discourse relative to the place/nowhere of concrete existence, for a story jerry-built out of elements taken from common sayings, an allusive and fragmentary story whose gaps mesh with the social practices it symbolizes.
>
> (de Certeau 1984:102)

Both Cardiff and de Certeau appear to be celebrating the indeterminacy of the city and of describing the self in the city. When describing the city de Certeau resists legibility, visibility, totalization, stability and interconnection. When compiling her walk around the city and the relationship between text and journey, Cardiff could be understood to similarly celebrate fragmentation, instability and incoherence. Both authors prize the subjective, localized practices of the individual in realizing a personal interpretation of the space of the city. Traditionally, when reading performance texts, the participant must negotiate between the real and fictional worlds of their own environment and the 'performed' environment being represented. However, in this instance there would appear to be slippage between the environment of the 'real' and the 'performed'; the disorientating references within Cardiff's text could be seen to persuade the participant to consider their 'real' world as simultaneously real and fictional, brought alive temporarily in a certain context, by a certain mode of activity. The 'missing voice' of Cardiff's text could be understood to be the absent authorial voice, or the supplier of the panoptic view, who describes, measures and explains away the contradictory and complex cultural relationships within any one society.

Coda

I presented a version of this article at the July 2002 International Federation of Theatre Research congress in Amsterdam. A number of other delegates presented papers that drew upon the attack upon New York's World Trade Center on September 11. The proliferation of references to this event provoked a debate about the problematics of engaging with this very 'real' event on a metaphorical level. For example, one delegate reprimanded Marvin Carlson for using 'Ground Zero' as a metaphor within his keynote speech on 'Haunted Houses'. In her paper on 'Place and Placelessness' Laurie Beth Clark also warned against the dangers of what Susan Bernstein has described as the 'promiscuous reading and identification' of trauma. I write this as an afterthought to a piece of work that for some may appear to collapse a gendered or xenophobic fear in relation to the WTC attack into the sense of apprehension I express in response to the audio-walk. I do acknowledge my distance from the 'real' effects of this attack within the body of the article, and recognize the problems with being seen to possibly appropriate the September 11 attack in any metaphorical sense.

Notes

1. I have chosen to refer to the date of September 11 in the British format with which I am most familiar. I recognise that both '9/11' and 'September 11' have become sedimented into 'titles' to refer to the specific event of the terrorist attacks on North America on that day in 2001, and that arguments are currently circulating within the academic community about the implications of a culturally specific date format becoming fixed as the generic title or name for this event.
2. Proptioceptive being a 'felt dimensionality' (Fisher) or a 'bodily' perception from the guts, nerve endings, muscle groups, etc.
3. Jen Harvie has written of a sense of 'absence' and 'presence' in the work of Janet Cardiff in her article 'Presence, Absence and Participation in the Art of Janet Cardiff and Tracey Emin'.

References

Bishop, Claire (1999) 'Missing Voice', *Flash Art* (November and December): 119.

Bernstein, Susan D. (forthcoming) 'Promiscuous Reading: the Problem of Identification and Anne Frank's Diary', in Michael Bernard-Donals and Richard Glezjer (eds) *Witnessing the Disaster: Essays on Representation and the Holocaust*, Madison: University of Wisconsin Press.

Carlson, Marvin (2002) 'Haunted Houses', Keynote speech presented to the 2002 Congress of the International Federation of Theatre Research, Amsterdam, July.

Clark, Laurie Beth (2002) 'Place and Placelessness in the Theatre of Memory', paper presented to the 2002 Congress of the International Federation of Theatre Research, Amsterdam, July.

De Certeau, Michel (1984) *The Practice of Everyday Life*, Steven Rendall (trans.), Berkeley: University of California Press.

Duncan, James and Ley, David (eds) (1993) *Place/Culture/Representation*, London and New York: Routledge.

Fisher, Jennifer (1999) 'Speeches of Display: The Museum Audioguides of Sophie Calle, Andrea Fraser and Janet Cardiff', *Parachute: Art Contemporaire/Contemporary Art* no. 94 (April–June): 24–31.

Kaye, Nick (2000) *Site Specific Art: Performance, Place and Documentation*, London and New York: Routledge.

Kwon, Miwon (1997) 'One Place after Another: Notes on Site Specificity', *October Magazine* no. 80 (Spring): 85–110.

Rawlinson, Ian (1996) 'Mugger Music', *Interelia: Journal of The European League of Institutes of the Arts* issue 2 (autumn): 24–31.

Scott, Kitty (1999) 'I Want You to Walk with Me', in James Lingwood and Gerrie Van Noord (eds) *The Missing Voice* (Case Study B) by Janet Cardiff, London: Artangel Afterlives, pp. 4–16.

Urry, John (1990) *The Tourist Gaze: Leisure and Travel in Contemporary Societies*, London: Sage Publications.

3.3 Attempt at the Rhythmanalysis of Mediterranean Cities

Henri Lefebvre and Catherine Régulier

This work is a fragment of a more complete study, or an introduction to this study. Mediterranean towns are striking, amazing, surprising, on account of their specific characteristics. We shall try, despite their differences, to tease out from their diversity some of their general traits. This evidently brings us to the largest cities, all of which are historical, often with a very ancient origin, stretching back as far as Ancient Greece. Like most historical towns in the world, they are destined either to decline or to break up by proliferating into suburbs and peripheries. Nonetheless historical traits seem to us to persist more in the Mediterranean than elsewhere, and with remarkable force. To these persistences, to this maintenance, rhythms – historical, but also everyday, 'at the heart of the lived [*au plus près du vécu*]'– are not, in our opinion, strangers. The question at least deserves to be posed.

It is impossible to understand urban rhythms without referring back to a general theory that focuses notably on these rhythms, but not solely on them, a general theory that we call 'Rhythmanalysis'.[1] This analysis of rhythms in all their magnitude 'from particles to galaxies' has a transdisciplinary character. It gives itself the objective, amongst others, of separating as little as possible the scientific from the poetic.

It is thus that we can try and draw the portrait of an enigmatic individual who strolls with his thoughts and his emotions, his impressions and his wonder, through the streets of large Mediterranean towns, and whom we shall call the 'rhythmanalyst'. More sensitive to times than to spaces, to moods than to images, to the atmosphere than to particular events, he is strictly speaking neither psychologist, nor sociologist, nor anthropologist, nor economist; however he borders on each of these fields in turn and is able to draw on the instruments that the specialists use. He therefore adopts a transdisciplinary approach in relation to these different sciences. He is always 'listening out', but he does not only hear words, discourses, noises and sounds; he is capable of listening to a house, a street, a town as one listens to a symphony, an opera. Of course, he seeks to know how this music is composed, who plays it and for whom. He will avoid characterising a town by a simple subjective trait, like some writer characterises New York by the howling of police sirens or London by the murmur of voices and the screaming of children in the squares. Attentive to time (to tempo) and consequently to repetitions and likewise to differences in time, he separates out through a mental act that which gives itself as linked to a whole: namely rhythms and their associations. He does not only observe human activities, he also hears [*entend*] (in the double sense of the word: noticing and understanding) the temporalities in which these activities unfold. On some occasions he rather resembles the physician (analyst) who examines functional disruptions in terms of malfunctions of rhythm, or of arrhythmia – on others, rather the poet who is able to say:

> O people that I know
> It is enough for me to hear the noise of their footsteps
> To be forever able to indicate the direction they have taken[2]

When rhythms are lived, they cannot be analysed. For example, we do not grasp the relations between the rhythms whose association constitutes our body: the heart, respiration, the senses, etc. We do not grasp even a single one of them separately, except when we are suffering. In order to analyse a rhythm, one must get outside it. Externality is necessary; and yet in order to grasp a rhythm one must have been grasped by it, have given or abandoned oneself 'inwardly' to the time that it rhythmed. Is it not like this in music and in dance? Just as, in order to understand a language and its rhythm, it is necessary to admit a principal that seems paradoxical. We only hear the sounds and frequencies that we produce in speaking – and vice versa, we can only produce those that we hear. This is called a circle …

If one observes a crowd attentively at peak times, and especially if one listens to its murmur, one will discern in the apparent disorder currents and an order that reveal themselves through rhythms: accidental or determined encounters, hurried carryings or nonchalant meanderings of people who go home in order to withdraw from the external world, or of those who leave their homes in order to make contact with the outside, business people and people of leisure [*gens d'affaires et gens vacants*]; as many elements that compose a polyrhythmia. The rhythmanalyst thus knows how to listen to a square, a market, an avenue.

In each of social practice, scientific knowledge and philosophical speculation, an ancient tradition separates time and space as two entities or two clearly distinct substances. This despite the contemporary theories that show a relation between time and space, or more exactly say how they are relative to one another. Despite these theories, in the social sciences we continue to divide up time into lived time, measured time, historical time, work time and free time, everyday time, etc., that are most often studied outside their spatial context. Now, concrete times have rhythms, or rather are rhythms – and all rhythms imply the relation of a time to a space, a localised time, or, if one prefers, a temporalised space. Rhythm is always linked to such and such a place, to its place, be that the heart, the fluttering of the eyelids, the movement of a street or the tempo of a waltz. This does not prevent it from being a time, which is to say an aspect of a movement or of a becoming.

Let us insist on the relativity of rhythms. They are not measured as the speed of a moving object on its trajectory is measured, beginning from a well-defined starting point (point zero) with a unit defined once and for all. A rhythm is only slow or fast in relation to other rhythms with which it finds itself associated in a more or less vast unity. For example, a living organism – our own body – or even a town (though, of course, without reducing the definition of the latter to that of a biological organism). This leads us to underline the plurality of rhythms, alongside that of their associations and their interactions or reciprocal actions.

Every more or less animate body and *a fortiori* every gathering of bodies is consequently polyrhythmic, which is to say composed of diverse rhythms, with each part, each organ or function having its own in a perpetual interaction that constitutes a set [*ensemble*] or a whole [*un tout*]. This last word does not signify a closed totality, but on the contrary an open totality. Such sets are always in a 'metastable' equilibrium, which is to say always compromised and most often recovered, except of course in cases of serious disruption or catastrophe.

Another important point: rhythms imply repetitions and can be defined as movements and differences within repetition. However, there are two types of repetition: cyclical repetition – linear repetition. Indissociable even if the analyst has the duty of distinguishing and separating them. It is thus that mathematicians distinguish cleanly between two types of movements, rotations and trajectories, and have different measures for these two types. Cyclical repetition is easily understood if one considers days and nights – hours and months – the seasons and years. And tides! The cyclical is generally of cosmic origin; it is not measured in the same way as the linear. The numbering systems best suited to it are duodecimal, which is to say base twelve: the twelve months of the year, the twelve hours of the clock-face, the 360° of the circumference (a multiple of twelve), the twelve signs of the zodiac and even a dozen eggs or oysters, which means to say that the measure by twelve extends itself to living matter in direct provenance from nature. Cyclical rhythms, each having a determined period or frequency, are also the rhythms of beginning again: of the 'returning' which does not oppose itself to the 'becoming', we could say, modifying a phrase of René Crevel. The dawn is always new. The linear, by contrast, defines itself through the consecution and reproduction of the same phenomenon, almost identical, if not identical, at roughly similar intervals; for example a series of hammer blows, a repetitive series into which are introduced harder and softer blows, and even silences, though at regular intervals. The metronome also provides an example of linear rhythm. It generally originates from human and social activities, and particularly from the movements [*gestes*] of work. It is the point of departure for all that is mechanical. Attaching themselves to the identity of that which returns, the linear and its rhythms have a tendency to oppose that which becomes. According to Crevel, 'the returning is opposed to the becoming'.[3] The linear, including lines, trajectories and repetitions in accordance with this schema are measured on the decimal base (the metric system). Therefore if the cyclical and the linear are clearly distinct, the analysis that separated them must join them back together because they enter into perpetual interaction and are even relative to one another, to the extent that one serves as the measure of the other. An example: so many days of work.

These several points being fixed beforehand, what will the rhythmanalyst say about Mediterranean towns? He has the duty of remaining attentive, let us insist again, to the relativity of rhythms. Every study of rhythms is necessarily comparative. We shall therefore begin by indicating briefly certain contrasts between Mediterranean and oceanic towns. These are governed by the cosmic rhythms of tides – lunar rhythms! With regard to Mediterranean towns, they lie alongside a sea with (almost) no tides; so the cyclical time of the sun takes on a predominant importance there. Lunar towns of the oceans? Solar towns of the Mediterranean? Why not?

But the shores of the Mediterranean are not homogeneous. Everyone knows that they differ in terms of people and population, ethnicities, history, specific features of the economy, in culture and in religion. How can we not distinguish between the oriental Mediterranean and the occidental Mediterranean, the Aegean and Adriatic Seas, the North Mediterranean that is part of Europe and that of the South, part of Africa? However, the Mediterranean itself imposes common characteristics on these towns, insofar as it is a relatively small, enclosed and limited sea. Anyone who has sailed, irrespective of how much, knows that the waves of the Mediterranean do not resemble those of oceans; a simple but significant detail, in that these waves have and are rhythms. The climate also seems to impose a certain homogeneity: olive trees, vines, etc., are found all around the Mediterranean. With regard to Mediterranean ports, they are marked by commercial relations that were the beginning of Greek civilisation. The resources available to most of these towns, which they draw from their hinterlands, are limited. Industrialisation was accomplished unevenly and with difficulty: it seems to have profoundly altered neither the traditions of exchange nor habits. On this basis of limited exchanges, power and political authorities that sought to dominate the town through the domination of space, were constituted very early. These powers drew and continue to draw on space as a means of control, as a political instrument.[4]

The shores of the Mediterranean gave rise, almost 2,500 years ago, to the city-state; it dominated a generally small territory but nonetheless protected trade that extended as far as was possible. In this trade, material exchange was always mixed with an extreme sociability but also, paradoxically, with piracy, pillage, naval wars and rivalries, with conquests and colonisations. Characteristics that are already found in Homer's *Odyssey*. Mediterranean towns are therefore political towns, but not in the same way as towns that border oceans. The state that dominates a city and its territory is both violent and weak. It always oscillates between democracy and tyranny. One could say that it tends toward arrhythmia; through its interventions in the life of the city, it finds itself at the heart of the city, but this heart beats in a manner at once brutal and discontinuous. In the city, public life organises itself around all kinds of exchange: material and non-material, objects and words, signs and products. If on the one hand, exchange and trade can never be reduced to a strictly economic and monetary dimension, on the other hand it seems that the life of the city seldom has a political objective – except in cases of revolt. In this public life, men are not tied together by the ties that made Nordic towns communities, guaranteed as such by oaths, pacts and charters; in such a way that all action there was perpetually civil and political. One can only note the foundational differences between large, independent Mediterranean towns and the free cities of Flanders, Germany, northern France and Europe. The large Mediterranean towns appear to have always lived and still to live in a regime of compromise between all the political powers. Such a 'metastable' state is the fact of the polyrhythmic. We cannot emphasise too much this form of alliance, of compromise, which differs historically from the 'Sworn Alliance'; this difference has had consequences up as far as our own era and influences, in our opinion, the rhythms of the city.

Without claiming to draw from it a complete theory, as a hypothesis we shall attribute a good deal of importance to these relations between towns, and especially ports, with space and (cosmic) time, with the sea and the world: to that which unites these towns with the world through the mediation of the sea. If it is true that Mediterranean towns are solar towns, one can expect from them a more intense urban life than in lunar towns, but also one richer in contrasts at the very heart of the town. While in Nordic and oceanic towns one can expect to find more regulated times, linked simultaneously to more restrictive, more disembodied and more abstract forms of (contractual rather than ritual) association. On the Atlantic and in the north, members of the urban community, engaged insofar as people in their relations of exchange, abandon a good deal of their availability, hence of their time, to these relations. While on the Mediterranean, state-political power manages space, dominates territories, controls, as we have already said, external relations without being able to prevent the townsfolk-citizens from making use of their time and consequently of the activities that rhythm it. This analysis enables us to understand that in the Mediterranean, the cradle of the city-state, the state, be it internal or external to the city, has always remained brutal and powerless – violent but weak – unificatory, but always shaky, threatened. Whereas in oceanic towns where the state and the political penetrated with fewer difficulties, therefore with fewer incidences of violence and dramas, they interfered profoundly with individual and social activities. The separation between the public and private, therefore between the external and the intimate, takes place everywhere where there is civil and political society, but it always has its own characteristics. The idea and reality of public-private separation are not everywhere identical. More concretely, what one conceals from, what one shows to and what one will see from the outside are not the same things.

If our hypothesis is exact, in the lived everyday, in practice, social relations in Nordic towns are founded on a contractual, therefore juridical, basis, which is to say on reciprocal good faith. Whereas relations in the Mediterranean would tend to be founded either on those tacit or explicit forms of alliance that go as far as the formation of clans (clientelisms, mafias, etc.) or on the contrary on refusals of alliance that can lead as far as open struggle (vendettas, etc.). Explications in terms of ancient history or in terms of the survival of peasant customs appear to us insufficient to explain the persistence and resurgence of these social relations. Codes function durably, more or less tacitly, more or less ritually; they rhythm time as they do relations. They are not strictly speaking rational laws, acceptable to if not accepted by all, that govern relations. The word 'code' does not here have the meaning that it takes in the north, and anyway it is we who are introducing it in order to designate a set of gestures, of conventions, of ways of being. Coding is complemented by ritual and vice versa.

The relations and refusals of alliance interest the rhythm analyst to the extent that they intervene in the production of social time. They take place and unfold in the inside of this social time that they contribute to producing (or reproducing) by impressing a rhythm upon it. Our hypothesis is therefore that every social, which is to say, collective, rhythm is determined by the forms of alliances that human groups give themselves. These forms of alliances are more varied and contradictory than is generally supposed, this being particularly, but not only, true of large towns where relations of class, relations of political force intervene.

Does the characteristic ambiguity of Mediterranean towns in relation to the state manifest itself in the rhythms of social life? It could be that the rhythmanalyst should seek the secret of rhythms around the Mediterranean, where ancient codes and strong rites are upheld. In fact, rites have a double relation with rhythms, each ritualisation creates its own time and particular rhythm, that of gestures, solemn words, acts prescribed in a certain sequence; but also rites and ritualisations intervening in everyday time, *punctuating* it. This occurs most frequently in the course of cyclical time, at fixed hours, dates or occasions. Let us note that there are several sorts of rites that punctuate everydayness:

a) Religious rites, their irruptions and also their interventions in everyday life; for example, fasting, prayers, ablutions, the muezzin, the angelus and the ringing of bells, etc.
b) Rites in the broadest sense, simultaneously sacred and profane such as festivals and carnivals that inaugurate a period or bring it to a close, rites of intimate convivialities or external sociability.
c) Finally, political rites, namely ceremonies, commemorations, votes, etc.

In short, we bring under this label everything that enters into the everyday in order to impress upon it an extra-everyday rhythm without interrupting it in so doing. The analysis of these multiple rhythms would, we claim, enable us to verify that the relation of the townsman to his town (to his neighbourhood) – notably in the Mediterranean – does not only consist in the sociological relation of the individual to the group; it is on the one hand a relation of the human being with his own body, with his tongue and his speech, with his gestures within a certain place, with an ensemble of gestures – and on the other hand, a relation with the largest public space, with the entire society and, beyond this, with the universe.

A hypothesis comes into place and takes shape here. The analysis of discourse discerns two sorts of expression: the one formal, rhetorical, frontal – the other more immediate, spontaneous. Just as the analysis of asocial time can discern two sorts of rhythms. We shall name these by borrowing terms from Robert Jaulin: 'rhythm of the self' and 'rhythm of the other'.[5] Rhythms 'of the other' would be the rhythms of activities turned outward, towards the public. One could also call them 'the rhythms of representation'; more restrained, more formalised, they would correspond to frontal expression in discourse. The rhythms 'of the self', in turn, are linked to more deeply inscribed rites, organising a time turned moreover towards private life, therefore opposing self-presence to representation and, as such, quieter, more intimate, forms of consciousness to the forms of discourse ...

This polar opposition should not lead us to forget that there are multiple transitions and imbrications between these poles: the bedroom, the apartment, the house, the street, the square and the district, finally the town – even the immediate family, the extended family, the neighbourhood, friendly relations and the city itself. The Self and the Other are not cut off from one another. The study of the space in a Muslim town shows these imbrications, these complex transitions and reciprocities between the public and the private.[6] In and around the body, the distinction between two sorts of rhythm is found as far as in movements [*gestes*], mannerisms and habits: and this from the most everyday (the way one eats and sleeps) to the most extra-everyday (the way one dances, sings, makes music, etc.). The extra-everyday rhythms the everyday and vice versa. No more than the linear and the cyclical can the rhythms 'of the self' and the rhythms 'of the other', those of presence and those of representation, be separated. Entangled with one another, they penetrate practice and are penetrated by it. This seems to us true of all times and spaces, urban or not. So what is particular about Mediterranean towns? It seems to us that in them, urban, which is to say public, space becomes the site of a vast staging where all these relations with their rhythms show and unfurl themselves. Rites, codes and relations make themselves visible here: they act themselves out here [*s'y miment*]. It is to be noted that a deserted street at four o'clock in the afternoon has as strong a significance as the swarming of a square at market or meeting times. In music, in poetry too, the silences have a meaning.

Isn't Venice the example *par excellence* of this? Is this city not a theatrical city, not to say a theatre-city, where the audience [*le public*] and the actors are the same, but in the multiplicity of their roles and their relations? Thus we imagine the Venice of Casanova, of Visconti's *Senso*, like the Venice of today.[7] Isn't that because a privileged form of civility, of liberty, founded on and in a dialectic of rhythms, gives itself free rein in this space? This liberty does not consist in the fact of being a free citizen within the state – but in being free in the city outside the state. Political power dominates or rather seeks to dominate space; whence the importance of monuments and squares, but if palaces and churches have a political meaning and goal, the townsfolk-citizens divert them from it; they appropriate this space in a non-political manner. Through a certain use of time the citizen resists the state. A struggle for appropriation is therefore unleashed, in which rhythms play a major role. Through them, civil, therefore social, time seeks to and succeeds in withdrawing itself from linear, unirhythmic, measuring/measured state time. Thus public space, the space of representation, becomes 'spontaneously' a place for walks and encounters, intrigues, diplomacy, deals and negotiations – it theatralises itself. Thus the time and the rhythms of the people who occupy this space are linked back to space.

The comparative analysis of urban rhythms only distinguishes between them in order to bring them closer together. In the case that concerns us, this analysis sometimes arrives at contrasts or strong oppositions, but more often at nuances. The analysis of the Spanish town evidently nuances that of the Islamic town or the Italian town. However, through the nuances and contrasts common aspects come to light. An illustration of this thesis: around the Mediterranean and irrespective of the country, many towns have been constructed on escarpments that dominate the sea. In these towns, a distinction is drawn between the lower town and the upper town: steps play a very important role. Generally, there is right around the Mediterranean a remarkable architecture of the stairway. A link between spaces, the stairway also ensures a link between times: between the time of architecture (the house, the enclosure) and urban time (the street, the open space, the square and the monuments). It links particular houses and dwellings back to their distribution in urban space. Now is the stairway not a localised time *par excellence*? Don't the steps in Venice rhythm the walk through the city, while serving simultaneously as a transition between different rhythms? Let us also evoke the steps of Gare Saint Charles in Marseille. They are for the traveller the obligatory – one could say initiatory – passage for the descent towards the city, towards the sea. More than that of a gate or an avenue, their screaming monumentality imposes on the body and on consciousness the requirement of passing from one rhythm to another, as yet unknown – to be discovered.

We have previously underlined the historical weaknesses of Mediterranean city-states. They were never able to form enduring alliances against common enemies, nor efficiently to oppose the great conquerors and the founders of great empires. The victory of Athens against the Persians remains an exceptional event. Whence the succession of empires that attempted to dominate or encircle the whole Mediterranean from antiquity to the present.[8] All the conquerors conquered the cities, but all the cities resisted. How and why? In our opinion, through time and rhythms. This underlines the consistent and solid character of urban times in the Mediterranean in relation to politically dominated space.

Some words here on tourism, a modern phenomenon that has become essential, and which in a curious way prolongs the historical problematic of conquests. Here too a paradox reveals itself: tourism is added to the traditional and customary use of space and time, of monumentality and rhythms 'of the other' without making it disappear. Tourism in Venice, for example, does not suppress the theatricality of the city: one would say that it reinforces it, even if it makes dramatic representation pass for something decidedly silly; it does not succeed in altering its profundity, in denying the principle. Whence this surprising fact: the most traditional towns accept modern tourism; they adapt themselves by resisting the loss of identity that these invasions could entail. Wouldn't this be the case, not only for Venice, but also for Syracuse, Barcelona, Palermo, Naples and Marseille, cities delivered over to tourism that fiercely resist homogenisation, linearity and the rhythms 'of the other'? Tourism can distort space without managing to deform lived time by rendering it a stranger to itself. In order to understand this situation, we have seen that it is necessary to appeal to the whole of history. It is necessary to remind oneself that the long predominance of commercial and cultural exchanges has produced a melting pot of diverse populations, migrations and cohabitations. This confirms that form of alliance found in the compromise that characterises the history of rhythm in these towns – and moreover maintains and consolidates clans. In other words, relations as solid and enduring in conflicts as in alliances. Which accentuates another paradox: how could such enduring historic compromises have been founded on such powerful Manicheanism? Answer: they were founded on the organisation of time and rhythms, an organisation at once public and private, sacred and profane, apparent and secret.

The state and the political are not alone in seeing themselves refused by the intimate, repressed or even expelled from their space by a strong rhythmicity, which does not prevent them from coming back, equally forcefully, towards that which refused them. All forms of hegemony and homogeneity are refused in the Mediterranean. It is not only the rhythms imposed by the state-political centre that might be resented as rhythms 'of the other'; it is the very idea of centrality that is refused, because each group, each entity, each religion and each culture considers itself as a centre. But what is a centre, if not a producer of rhythms in social time? The polyrhythmia of Mediterranean towns highlights their common character through their differences. Such urban practice raises a question: how does *each party* (individual–group–family, etc.) manage to insert its own rhythms amongst those of (different) others, including the rhythms imposed by authority? In this insertion of rhythms 'of the self' into rhythms 'of the other', what is the role of radical separation and compromises, of tolerance and violence? A well-known and banal fact, namely that in all large towns around the Mediterranean, everyone hears several languages from their childhood onwards, cannot not have consequences with regard to the 'spontaneous' or 'native' acceptance of diverse rhythms – with regard to the perception of the diversity of rhythms 'of the other'.

The enigma of practical and social life is therefore formulated in the following way: how are rhythms 'of the self' and rhythms 'of the other' determined, orientated and distributed? According to which principles do (civilian) townsfolk rule on the refusals and acceptances of alliances? Polyrhythmia always results from a contradiction, but also from resistance to this contradiction – resistance to a relation of force and an eventual conflict. Such a contradictory relation can be defined as the struggle between two tendencies: the tendency towards homogenisation and that towards diversity, the latter being particularly vigorous in the Mediterranean. This can be phrased in yet another way: there is a tendency towards the globalising domination of centres (capital cities, dominant cultures and countries, empires), which attacks the multidimensionality of the peripheries – which in turn perpetually threatens unity. In rhythmanalytic terms, let us say that there is a struggle between measured, imposed, external time and a more endogenous time. If it is true that in Mediterranean towns, diversity always takes its revenge, it does not succeed in defeating the opposite tendency towards political, organisational, cultural unity. Everything happens as if the Mediterranean could not renounce the unitary principle that founded and still founds its identity; however the ideologies of diversity oppose to the point of violence the structures of identity and unity. How can one not think of Beirut here? ...

When relations of power overcome relations of alliance, when rhythms 'of the other' make rhythms 'of the self' impossible, then total crisis breaks out, with the deregulation of all compromises, arrhythmia, the implosion – explosion of the town and the country. It seems to us that Beirut – this extreme case – cannot but take symbolic meaning and value. Fifteen or twenty years ago, Beirut was a place of compromise and alliance that today appears miraculous: the place of a polyrhythmia realised in an (apparent) harmony.

This brutal arrhythmia poses a question that concerns every Mediterranean project, every prospect of unity and globality in this region of the world. Does such a project founder before this drama? That is not for the rhythmanalyst to pronounce upon; at best he can maintain that the analysis of rhythms would contribute non-negligible elements to all questionings of this type.

The rhythmanalytical project applied to the urban can seem disparate, because it appeals to, in order to bring together, notions and aspects that analysis too often keeps separate: time and space, the public and the private, the state-political and the intimate; it places itself sometimes in one point of view and in a certain perspective, sometimes in another. Thus it can seem abstract, because it appeals to very general concepts. We could have avoided these reproaches and not left such an impression: either by painstakingly describing a known and privileged place – or by throwing ourselves into the lyricism that arouses the splendour of the cities evoked. But

this was not our purpose. We wanted to introduce concepts and a general idea – rhythmanalysis – into the debate. This concept has very diverse origins: the theory of measurement, the history of music, chronobiology and even cosmological theories. In proposing here several hypotheses in the hope that they would be taken up and carried further than before by others, we wanted to verify them as far as possible. We have therefore tried to tease out a paradigm: a table of oppositions constituting a whole; following this we have examined the specifically Mediterranean content of this form, the entry into practice of these oppositions. This has made evident virtual or actual conflicts, relations of force and threats of rupture. The paradigmatic table, when put into relation with practice, is dialecticised. The path marked out by these concepts thus opens itself onto finer analyses. To be undertaken.

Notes

1. Henri Lefebvre and Catherine Régulier, 'Le projet rythmanalytique', *Communications*, no. 41, 1985 [above pp. 73–83].
2. Guillaume Apollinaire, «Cortège», *Alcools*, 1920. [Translators' Note: reprinted in *Oeuvres complètes de Guillaume Apollinaire*, edited by Michel Décaudin, Paris: André Ballard & Jacques Lecat 1966, vol. 3, pp. 84–5. There is an English critical edition, not a translation, in Guillaume Apollinaire, *Alcools*, edited by Garnet Rees, London: The Athlone Press, University of London, 1975, p. 67. One of the notable things about *Alcools* is the complete absence of commas or periods. As Apollinaire wrote to Henry Martineau in 1913, 'as regards the punctuation, I cut it out simply because it seemed to me unnecessary; which in fact it is, for the rhythm itself and the division of the lines are the real punctuation, and nothing else is needed …'. The letter is found in *Apollinaire: Selected Poems*, translated by Oliver Bernard, London: Anvil Press Poetry, 1986, p. 6.]
3. Translator's Note: 'Le revenant s'oppose au devenant', also 'the ghost, that which returns, is opposed to that which becomes'. René Crevel (1900–35) was a French surrealist novelist and writer. The quote is from 'Individu et société', in *Le roman cassé et derniers écrits*, Paris: Pauvert, 1989, p. 147, although it actually reads 'Au revenant s'oppose le devenant'.
4. Fernand Braudel, *La Méditerranée et le monde méditerranéen au temps de Philippe II* [Translators' Note: Paris: Armand Colin, 2e édition, two volumes, 1967; translated by Siân Reynolds as *The Mediterranean and the Mediterranean World in the Age of Philip II*, New York: Harper & Row, two volumes, 1972].
5. Robert Jaulin, *Gens du soi, Gens de l'autre*, [Paris:] U.G.E. 10/18, 1973. [Translators' Note: Jaulin (1928–96) was a French ethnographer, the author of *Anthropologie et calcul* and *Géomancie et Islam*.]
6. Paul Vielle, 'L'État périphérique et son héritage', *Peuples Méditerranéens*, no. 27–28, avril–septembre 1984.
7. Translators' Note: Luchino Visconti (1906–76) was an Italian film and theatre director. *Senso* is set in Venice in the nineteenth century. He also directed the film version of *Death in Venice*.
8. Burhan Ghalioun, 'Dialectique de l'un et du multiple', *Peuples Méditerranéens*, no. 19, avril–juin 1982.

3.4   Rumours: A Conversation Between Francis Alÿs and James Lingwood

Francis Alÿs and James Lingwood

James Lingwood: How did you begin to work on the street railings?

Francis Alÿs: They are an omnipresent architectural device, more so than in other cities, I think. You see them all over London, in front of grand buildings, or humble houses, along streets or around parks and so on. They speak of a certain period in the city, maybe the Empire days, of a certain status in the world, they have/emanate a slightly nostalgic note.

James Lingwood: They are a motif you had worked with before, in drawings and animations? They are already part of your imaginary world as well as part of the city.

Francis Alÿs: It came as a natural expansion of a past obsession, plus the coincidence with my ongoing investigation around rhythmic

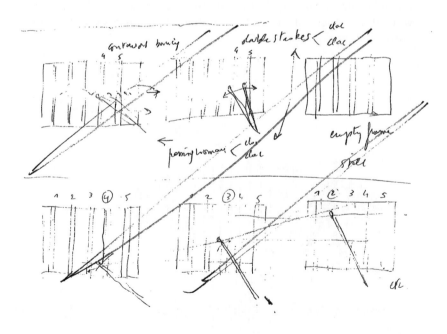

22

Figure 3.5

possibilities, which I had been working on in Mexico City although in a different way. More through the repetition, the space of the rehearsal, the ways of delaying the real momentum ...

James Lingwood: There's a direct correspondence with some of your paintings and animations – I'm thinking of a painting of a figure with a walking stick running along some railings. Where do they come from, these characters in your paintings?

Francis Alÿs: I would more call them 'personages' than specific characters. It's a coincidence of different factors. Definitely a lot of them have been inspired by real personages in urban life, people that I have witnessed or heard about. They then become the protagonist in a scenario that I'm trying to put into place. But there is no specific sequence in my work which means a painting precedes an action or vice-versa. They feed off each other – the studio and the street.

James Lingwood: Does your interest in railings come from a childhood memory, from growing up in Belgium?

Francis Alÿs: Maybe as a kid's game, you know, picking up a stick and running it along the railings. A lot of the walks have had that kind of echo, like kicking a bottle along the pavements, or dragging a magnet through the streets at the end of a string. ... I tried something similar in Mexico City – not on railings but on the metal shutters of shops in the old centre of the city. But the shutters in Mexico require more of a vertical movement of the stick, so it doesn't combine so well with the horizontal motion of the walker.

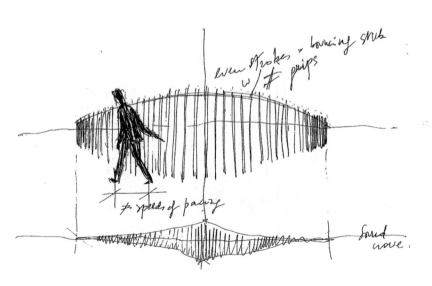

Figure 3.6

James Lingwood: The shutter is a barrier and a railing is also a barrier. It means you are obviously outside and the power and the wealth are inside.

Francis Alÿs: Richard Wentworth suggested to me that the railings are an echo of the moat around a castle. They play a role of protection, they are a filter.

James Lingwood: How did you decide on the different places to drum? They are all in grand, Establishment parts of the City.

Francis Alÿs: I think there were two requisites, they had to be representative of that social barrier we mentioned before, but they also had to have an acoustic quality. The railings function as an instrument, for example a free-standing railing gives out a richer, longer sound than one grounded in concrete. The architectural rhythms had a lot to do with the choice of locations: railings/column/entrance/column/railings etc. By just walking and running a stick against it, the details of the architecture automatically generate a sound pattern.

Now if I go back to the chronology of how the projects in London developed, the simple act of touching the railings, of feeling the architecture with the drumstick acting as a kind of catalyst, was a way of making contact, of connecting to the physicality of the place. ... As the drumming piece developed, a number of variations happened. The first moment was just walking with a stick bouncing on the architecture, there was no interaction, the architecture was entirely dictating the sound patterns, but the melody was generated by the motion of the walker.

James Lingwood: Architecture has been called 'frozen music'?

Francis Alÿs: The city is a kind of interlocutor. It was just about listening to the music of the city ... The second stage was to build some kind of archive of all the different sonorities that the railings and architectural patterns could offer, a kind of repertoire ... Once that had been done, the logical step was to start playing with the instrument, to improvise, to see how far this could get me. I am no musician, as you know, but the temptation was too great ... The different moments unfolded naturally, alongside discussions with Rafael Ortega, who was filming, and Mark Roberts who had given me a quick crash course in drumming.

James Lingwood: What kind of musical models did you have in mind?

Francis Alÿs: We talked about Steve Reich, John Cage, Ligeti about being open to the sounds of the city. All the incidental sounds a city can offer, an ambulance or a car, a police siren, a dog barking, they also became part of the piece. But we also talked about animated movies, like *Fantasia*, or films like *Berlin – Symphony of a City*.

Part 4

Playing/Place

Text sources

Introduction

We aren't blocking traffic. We are traffic.

Critical Mass slogan

Urban rights

Increasingly the centres of cities are becoming subject to privatisation and surveillance, not least in the UK, which has been officially identified currently as having 'the most intensive concentration of electronic "eyes on the street" in the world' (*PCC*, p. 269). Nicholas Fyfe's article in the final part of this book looks in detail at the ambivalent role of both closed circuit television (CCTV) surveillance and the phenomenon of zero tolerance policing (ZTP), teasing out the tension between safeguarding the enjoyment of public space without fear of violence on the one hand, and sacrificing freedoms, producing a 'criminology of intolerance', on the other (*PCC*, pp. 262–3). Part 4 here is concerned in a more general way with the contestation of public urban space, presenting a series of examples of 'unofficial' creative practices whose emergence, in a plethora of forms, is indicative, first, of the trend towards closing down or controlling the possibilities of space in the city and, second, of the degree of resistance to this shift. In many respects there is a Lefebvrian flavour to these spatial practices, since they are all driven by the question of the citizen's 'right to the city'. The interrogation taking place is based on the perception that increasingly the behaviour of individuals in urban space is becoming restricted in fact to little more than the 'right to shop' (or, as in the case of the cycling movement Critical Mass, whose slogan is cited above, the 'right to drive cars'). A recent study of a 'declining England' by Paul Kingsnorth, entitled *Real England: the Battle Against the Bland* (2008), has shown that it is not just enclosed shopping malls, with their private security forces, that will witness the eviction of members of the public for doing anything other than looking like they're shopping, but whole streets. One example given is of Liverpool, the European City of Culture for 2008, in which it is planned to bind in 33 city centre streets to so-called 'public realm agreements' granting limited access. When shops close at the end of the day, so will the street (ibid.: 172–81). So even the right-to-shop principle itself becomes subject to degrees of prohibition, though ultimately, of course, the limitation is imposed so as to safeguard the security of retail premises.

More significant, though, is the question: what if you possess neither the *means* nor the *desire* to shop? In general terms, the answer to the first part begins, of course, to take us towards criminality: that is, effectively asserting that 'right' even if you lack the means (shoplifting), or expressing your dissatisfaction at not being able to partake of such a shopping culture (violence). The answer to lacking *both* means and desire on the other hand may lead us to a further Lefebvrian preoccupation (touched on in the previous section's introduction), relating to the future of art being urban: 'Leaving aside representation, ornamentation and decoration, art can become *praxis* and *poesis* on a social scale: the art of living in the city as a work of art' (Lefebvre 1996: 173). Although Lefebvre is concerned here to acknowledge existing everyday urban practices as creative in themselves – 'to city people the urban centre is movement, the unpredictable, the possible and encounters. For them, it is either "spontaneous theatre" or nothing' (ibid.: 172) – he is also arguing for 'play(fulness)' precisely to 'come into play'. That is, to infiltrate spatial practices. Thus, art in the city, the 'right to the *oeuvre*, to participation and *appropriation* (clearly distinct from the right to property), [is] implied in the right to the city' (ibid.: 174).

Graffiti

Susan J. Smith's entry on 'Graffiti' for the *City A–Z* lexicon begins precisely by asking 'Whose city is this?' (*PCC*, p. 206). In a montage of citations and aphorisms, presented in various typefaces – the fact of which highlight graffiti's significance both as a *writing* of the city and as being spontaneous and fragmented in form – this is but the first of a series of key structural questions around ownership, art and vandalism. At the end she returns to the same question, twice; for Smith, the city is perhaps 'this place where we know the cost of so much and the value of so little' (*PCC*, p. 210). Graffiti itself, of course, costs nothing in its pure form – except to those who would like to remove it – arguably escaping the clutches of commodification, wherein lies one of its principal potencies.

The cultural geographer Tim Cresswell refers to graffiti as 'night discourse': 'subversive messages which appear in the morning after the secretive curtain of night has been raised' (in Fyfe 1998: 268). Supposedly, hardcore tagging, carried out by 'writers' or 'sprayers' known only within the confines of their specific tagging community, is intended not to impress – or offend – the general public, but to gain the 'respect' of fellow writers. In itself it isn't even particularly territorial, in the sense of demarcating a 'home patch' within the city, though it does sometimes cover vast expanses of surface, be that building or train. Its value to its executors lies more in a combination of quantity and risk, the latter being defined by both daringness of location and length of time spent completing a piece (which is consequently why quantity is prized). If graffiti-spraying of this sort can be called art – which according to van Treeck is a label writers themselves tend to reject (1999: 139) – surely it is one of *performance* rather than fine art. In fact, nothing could upset the impulse of the practice more than seeking to validate it on such a two-dimensional basis. For the impact of what writers leave behind is far less resonant for its intrinsic aesthetics (of painting or drawing) – though its stylistic features remain significant as signs of a specific metropolitan identity – than for the mystery of its executors' identity. You never see them. They're out there somewhere because their tags say they are, but you don't know who or where they are. So, what their pieces evoke – or *scream* might be more accurate – is the performance of their disappearance. That is the true moving force – perhaps threat – of their activity: their physical elusiveness.

I would argue, then, that writers *are* performing for the 'benefit' of a general public, as much as for their peers. Because, while the fact of their mark-making, its illegality in itself but also its execution in inaccessible, high-risk, forbidden locations, seeks an escape from surveillance, it nevertheless requires to be witnessed after the event. It must be sanctioned, if you will, as transgressive by those – everyday citizens – considered to be within the law. It has to be *dis*approved. As writing it *hurts*: it is the outlaw's expression of the pain of exclusion and dispossession, and it wounds what is 'in law'. Ultimately the act is, as John Berger says of the misunderstood terrorist or suicide martyr, 'a way of making sense of and thus transcending despair' (2001: 7). It is no coincidence, then, that taggers utilise the vocabulary of the terrorist: 'bombing' is to spray the whole expanse of a designated surface, and many will have seen the 'wholecar bombing' of trains. In spite of its non-specific territorial function within the context of the city, there is nevertheless a kind of necessary laying of claim to the built environment in operation in the application of graffiti. It is an irritant, an unwanted autograph or tattoo anonymously etched on to the body of official urban culture, reminding it perhaps – in contrast to Jane Jacobs's experience – that 'all is *not* well'.

The extract from Iain Sinclair's *Lights Out for the Territory* takes a less melancholic view of graffiti. Taken from the opening pages of his book about walking in the Hackney and Chingford areas of London 'reading the signs', the in-depth meditation on the nature of the practice is indicative not only of its prevalence – it cannot be ignored – but also of its high significance as mark-making, both to the psychogeographical method Sinclair would employ in most of his work and in itself, as a 'writing of the city'. Thus the 'crude V' cut 'into the sprawl of the city to vandalise dormant energies by an act of ambulant signmaking', which Sinclair sets out as the map he will follow, is itself a kind of 'metaphorical, lowest-common-denominator graffiti' (*PCC*, p. 211).

New urban practices

Inevitably the 'underground art form' that is graffiti has been jeopardised precisely by its widespread global visibility and accessibility. Not only has its imagery been shamelessly plundered, principally by 'youth culture orientated' corporations, but it has also been 'mainstreamed' as art, appearing in gallery spaces or other 'sanctioned sites'. The most famous embodiment of the 'is it still graffiti, though?' conundrum – certainly from a UK perspective – is, of course, Banksy, whose cultish suppression of his 'true identity' has become paradoxical: a kind of fetishisation of authorship by denial. In other words, anonymity is the new authorship according to Banksy. Be that as it may, his interventions – which some would cast doubt over as instances of graffiti – can certainly be viewed as witty, politically savvy contestations of the state-corporate control of public space. Unburdening the work of its need to be seen as graffiti (or not) would perhaps be doing it a useful service since it identifies this type of practice as being a more self-consciously engaged form of activity that has, in turn, spawned other 'new departures'. Francesca Gavin's recent book *Street Renegades: New Underground Art* has gathered an impressive range of practices that mark a shift by street artists towards not only greater self-awareness but also the dimensions of space. While I have tried to make the case for the supposed two dimensions of raw graffiti to be viewed in fact as 3-D performance, these artist-renegades are deliberately setting out to create 'performance-installations' in the city, 'manipulating urban architecture and interacting with the street furniture itself' (Gavin 2007: 6). Not represented in Gavin's book, but included here in the form of a newspaper article by Madeleine Bunting that addresses directly the 'new policing' to which much of this work is a subversive response, is the quirky practice of 'Chewing Gum Man' Ben Wilson. Picking up on the rash of discarded gum globules flattened permanently on to urban pavements, he has taken to painting on them in enamels: 'Each picture tells a story as recounted by a passer-by ... small signs of personal connection, a humanising of an anonymous environment' (*PCC*, p. 214). Crucially, Wilson 'paints the gum, not the pavement' and so cannot, theoretically, be charged with criminal damage. Arguably, then, used chewing gum takes on the virtual – or, indeed, actual – status of an 'independent republic'. Far from protecting him, however, the article describes the '500–600 encounters with police' the artist has experienced, including 'being punched and dragged across a police cell' and being forced to provide a DNA sample, which now sits in a national database (*PCC*, pp. 214–15).

Surfing the fine line between legality and guerrilla-like transgression as a means of calling into question the validity of the former is also at the heart of the widespread flash-mobbing phenomenon, as Jane McGonigal's online montage piece 'Dark Play in Public Spaces' (2004) suggests. The 'trick' with flash mobs seems essentially to be to engage in relatively harmless *legal* activities that take on the *appearance* of being illegal. So, it may be that some kind of infrastructural breakdown occurs in the city – the traffic gets stopped, for example – but it is not because anything transgressive of the law has been committed. It is merely because large numbers of people have opted to engage in the same activity and, in any case, it is only ever for a matter of minutes at most. Obliquely you might suggest the constructed event frequently draws attention to the escalating inability of urban amenities to cope with the global surge in population growth. But really it has more to do with a celebration of mobilising 'numbers of people with a common purpose', which, moreover, has its origins (and destination for that matter) in creating a temporary *electronic* community. McGonigal relates flash-mobbing to 'dark play', which involves both unwitting participation – so there are different kinds of witness to the event, some knowing, others not – and the coexistence of contradictory realities. Importantly, she points out the existence of two differing 'strains': the one of 'play' is intent on fun, while the other, of 'performance', is more concerned with instilling a deeper political consciousness. Perhaps most telling of all in McGonigal's account is the sheer global scale of the phenomenon now, with each local situation, from Singapore to Mumbai, revealing its own particularities.

Ursula Hofbauer and Friedemann Derschmidt's 'Horror Vacui' is taken from the publication *Temporary Urban Spaces* (Haydn and Temel 2006), which provides details of a plethora of sample projects undertaken in European and US cities. These are predicated either on performing temporary interventions into public space or in exploiting spaces whose status has been rendered 'in between'. The initiatives described – and some examples are included here – range from performance-based ventures to those where a particular social need – housing, for instance – is being addressed. As Hofbauer and Derschmidt show in their discussion of *Permanent Breakfast* – which began life at a highly symbolic, contested traffic intersection in Vienna, but has since migrated to many cities in the world – events typically take a hybrid form: '*Permanent Breakfast* is a game, an art project, art in a public space and public art, but also urban planning or a social project or a tool to test the quality of public spaces or, to put it another way, to ensure the public character of a certain space' (*PCC*, p. 216). In a way – and paradoxically – *Permanent Breakfast* can be said to replicate the instantaneous form of flash mobs, durationally. Based on a cascade effect, one breakfast set up in a city square for four guests (and for any passers-by that fancy it) leads to several others since guests are required, as a prerequisite of their participation, to follow up with their own breakfasts the following day, and so on.

All the examples included in Part 4 reveal highly inventive ways of legally negotiating the public's right to urban space via a kind of 'politics of fun', which prefers wit and subtlety to placards and marches. While there is always a danger of this brand of attempted subversion being dismissed as self-indulgent and ultimately 'not serious' or lasting in its impact, many of these examples can point to an actual difference being made. The *Paris Plage* initiative may merely be creating a temporary 'space of pleasure', but it is no mean feat to persuade a city council to turn an urban motorway into a beach for some five weeks every summer. Implicitly playing out via its very activity one of the popular slogans of the Paris revolts of 1968, 'beneath the pavement the beach' (a Lefebvrian coinage adopted by the first generation of skateboarders in California) – and precisely through such a historical echo acquiring a certain validity – stopping the traffic in this way simultaneously focuses public attention on city hall policies relating to issues around pedestrianisation. It also provides an interesting variation on the notion of 'closing down streets' as discussed above.

Finally, Geoff Dyer's reference to flash-mobbing as being 'predicated on its ingenious pointlessness' has the appearance of being a back-handed compliment (*PCC*, p. 225). He makes the comment in his report on an offshoot mobile clubbing event taking place at Liverpool Street Station in London – not part of *Temporary Urban Spaces* but related to the activities of LIGNA in its *Radioballett* performances (incorporated here) – but goes on to identify this silent rave in fact as a 'force for good' in the light of London stations being 'prime terrorist targets'. For him 'Mobile clubbing is a mirror image of a terrorist outrage', the similarly precise organisation of which also results in 'a detonation. Of joy' (*PCC*, p. 226). In the build up to this timed detonation, in which the 'feeling of conspiracy is palpable', Dyer also invokes a history of gay cruising he has read, which refers to the 'illicit thrill of gliding through the city, stealing glances at strangers, looking for a reciprocal sign that someone else is out for the same thing' (*PCC*, p. 225).

Urban disappearances

In an essay accompanying Patrick Keiller's DVD film *London* – itself perhaps the example *par excellence* of psychogeography as film, according to Pile (in Leach 2002: 203–16) – Iain Sinclair proposes that the future of urban cinema may be one of 'vagrancy':

> The truth of a city, divided against itself, can only be revealed, so Keiller believes, through a series of obscure pilgrimages, days spent crawling out on to the rim of things. The transcendent surrealism of airport perimeter roads, warehouses and reservoirs. J G Ballard. Shepperton.
>
> (in Keiller 2005: 10)

Based on this view one might say that where Keiller's film ends, Sinclair's own *London Orbital* begins. Originally a book but subsequently made into a film in collaboration with Chris Petit – which certainly stakes its claim to rival Keiller as optimum filmed psychogeography – it is predicated on a practice of walking-writing (Sinclair's prerogative) and driving-filming (Petit's) around the notoriously congested M25 motorway that encircles Greater London. Viewed as a kind of purgatory, a liminal non-place that trawls up all kinds of 'detritus' – including a seamy, menacing underworld element – the relentless, circulatory flow of motorway traffic past service stations and shopping malls epitomises the bland side of urban modernity. J. G. Ballard, who makes a cameo appearance, and who has become well known for his near-cultic fascination with the pain, failure and degeneration lurking behind the myth of technological progress, calls this bleak, 'negative space' of the M25 the new England: a transient space between decay and *noveau* wealth. Ironically perhaps Sinclair and Petit hope for a 'sublime moment' to occur amidst the monotonous flow of this motorway non-world, an instant of 'unbearable beauty' reminiscent perhaps of the *punctum* that Barthes always looked for in photographs, in which an element 'rises from the scene, shoots out of it like an arrow, and pierces me' (1993: 26). As a film-maker, Petit's joyless conclusion is that the M25 can only be adequately captured by CCTV. Anything he might articulate filmically is invariably haunted by loss, by that which it fails to capture. The impossibility of filming to which he refers appears to be replicated in Keiller's *London* where the walking protagonist, Robinson – also the title and main character, incidentally, of a crime novel by Petit – is quoted as claiming that 'the true identity of London … is in its absence. As a city, it no longer exists. In this alone, it is truly modern. London was the first metropolis to disappear.' As Pile suggests of *London*: 'At the point of discovery, it seems, the city disappears' (in Leach 2002: 214).

Another film-maker, Jem Cohen, has effectively picked up on the 'Ballardian horror story' evoked here (*PCC*, p. 231). According to Jessica Winter his film *Chain* 'takes as its subject the homogenous interzones of privately owned public space – shopping malls, hotel complexes, theme parks – that multinational corporations have remade in their own global-branded image, letting regional colour fade to a concrete grey' (*PCC*, p. 231). In fact, the film's title refers in part to its form, which assembles 'a mosaic of the worldwide urban sprawl'. Thus, as a way of interrogating not only the phenomenon of globalisation but also the degree to which America may, as Cohen himself says, 'be responsible for how a lot of the planet ends up looking', he began to chain together diverse cityscapes of everywhere and nowhere: 'I found that I could travel anywhere in the world and shoot footage that you couldn't identify in terms of where it came from. I thought I could join all that material together into a "superlandscape"' (*PCC*, p. 232).

Cohen's project – to say nothing of the 'London school' of Sinclair, Petit, Keiller and Ballard – displays clear affinities with the anthropologist Marc Augé's theorisation of the 'non-places of supermodernity', included here in a highly distilled version of his full-length monograph *Non-places: Introduction to an Anthropology of Supermodernity* (1995). Supermodernity is characterised by 'over-determination' visible in a trio of excesses: time (accelerating), space (shrinking) and individualisation (the consciousness that each of us can see everything and do nothing) (*PCC*, pp. 227–8). Non-places are locations in which the interplay between these component parts maximises itself; non-places, which 'begin with unrootedness' (*PCC*, p. 229), epitomise supermodernity. The locations Augé has in mind, then, are those of mainly urban circulation, information and communication. Essentially, though, they are zones that the public 'passes through': airports, service stations, shopping malls, supermarkets, fast-food outlets and so on. For Augé these are surroundings in which the individual is contained as one of many, but ends up temporarily without identity. Moreover, non-places project an 'overabundance of images' – often the well worn 'decals' of a global space of consumption – so that 'the more we get a chance to see everything, the less we can be sure we are still able to really look at them'. In this way the world becomes 'abstractly familiar' (*PCC*, p. 230).

Augé concludes that 'in the world of supermodernity people are always, and never at home' (1995: 109). Non-places not only produce a form of suspended identity (or temporary non-identity), they also – or therefore – preclude significant interaction with the subject's environment. Like white noise, they effect a 'blanding out', a state of alienation in which you cannot properly *sense*. Hence, the non-places of travel, for instance, can be said to promote an experience that is *forgettable*, in which no significant trace is left either in or by you although it may be a location to which you return repeatedly. In fact, Augé's non-places evoke a return that produces an absenting. Paradoxically, the traveller 'accedes to his anonymity only when he has given proof of his identity', a process that produces 'solitude and similitude':

> Alone, but one of many, the user of a non-place is in contractual relations with it (or with the powers that govern it). He is reminded, when necessary, that the contract exists. One element in this is the way the non-place is to be used. ... The contract always relates to the individual identity of the contracting party. To get into the departure lounge of an airport, a ticket – always inscribed with the passenger's name – must first be presented at the airport desk; proof that the contract has been respected comes at the immigration desk, with simultaneous presentation of the boarding pass and an identity document ... and checks are made at departure time to ensure that these will be properly fulfilled.
>
> (Ibid.: 101–3)

The English version of the French *non-lieu* (non-place) does not, as the translator of Augé's book points out, capture an important juridical application of the expression, namely 'no case to answer' or 'no grounds for prosecution'. In other words, it is 'a recognition that the accused is innocent [Tr.]'. As Augé himself states, 'In a way, the user of the non-place is always required to prove his innocence' (ibid.: 102) or, one might add to underline the paradox, to attest to his or her anonymity, to confirm their disappearance or absence.

Alain de Botton's take on such non-places – a term he would probably reject – is quite different, some might say romantic. In his book *The Art of Travel* (2003) he visits similar locations to the ones featuring so far – motorways, airports – but he finds in them a form not only of unexpected poetry – the sublime moments Sinclair and Petit waited for in vain? – but also (or therefore) of solace. They appear to be places of dreaming – a kind of 'nocturnal counterpoint' to the trials and tribulations of the urban everyday – to which he actively escapes when a mood of melancholy takes him. His source of inspiration in this respect is Benjamin's old *flâneur*-muse Charles Baudelaire who, when 'oppressed by the atmosphere in Paris ... would leave, "leave for leaving's sake", and travel to a harbor or train station' (ibid.: 35). Far from perceiving an abstract familiarity in the signage of terminal halls, de Botton finds, for instance, that the rows of arrivals and departures screens 'bear all the poetic resonance of the last line of James Joyce's *Ulysses*: at once a record of where the novel was written and, no less importantly, a symbol of the cosmopolitan spirit behind its composition: "Trieste, Zurich, Paris"' (ibid.: 39).

The conclusion – included in part here – to one of the principal books interrogating the relationship between site-specific art and locational identity, Miwon Kwon's *One Place After Another*, bases itself around one of Don DeLillo's works, the play *Valparaiso* (1999), which is premised effectively on a flying adventure arising from a misreading of those screens. The protagonist's trips to several cities of the same name are supposedly an accident, but turn out to be ones driven by the subconscious desire to give his existing life the *slip*: one might say a Freudian one of vast spatial proportions. On the face of it, Kwon's choice of example is surprising, on two counts: first, because DeLillo is not really known as a playwright and, second, because one of the radical impulses of site-specificity as a performative practice is, as Kwon's book makes clear (*and* as the term itself suggests), its disregard for both text as a point of departure and such institutional conventions as theatres (which traditionally stage plays). Thus, a play-text is unquestionably a strange place – if not the 'wrong place' – for Kwon to wind up. However, what intrigue her are the fortunes of the play's central character, Michael

Majeski, who finds himself en route to 'the wrong city', albeit with the right name (*PCC*, p. 234). What sets out as a trip to Valparaiso, Indiana, turns into one going to Valparaiso, Florida and ends in one to Valparaiso, Chile. One of Kwon's concerns is to highlight that what might appear to be sparked by 'an instance of locational misrecognition' at the airport of departure *evolves* inasmuch as Majeski submits to what has been accidentally set in train 'because he recognises a hitherto unknown logic of belonging, *a sense of belonging that is not bound to any specific location but to a system of movement*' (*PCC*, p. 236 emphasis added). As a result 'the disruption of a subject's habitual spatiotemporal experience propels the liberation and also the breakdown of its traditional sense of self' (*PCC*, p. 234). The extraordinary act of Majeski's translocation reveals the limitations of the city he would associate with belonging and identity – that is, 'home' – thus, Kwon infers, he is arguably escaping not *to* but '*from* a wrong place' (*PCC*, p. 237).

Unsited places

Our inclination may be to perceive buildings as immobile: fixed places made of solid materials that effectively 'hold their position'. But, as we have already witnessed in the example of Christo's wrapping of the Reichstag in Berlin, buildings can begin to *move* for a range of reasons. One of the factors contributing to that sense of movement involves the interaction with people. Another – strongly at play in Christo's piece – is the way in which buildings encapsulate and perform history. In other words: how they change, and are made to change, not only their functions but also what they stand for as events in time unfold. Moreover, as a character in Cees Nooteboom's novel *All Souls' Day* (set in post-Wall Berlin) suggests, 'buildings and voices make a city what it is. And that includes the buildings and voices that are no longer here (2002: 123).

Rachel Whiteread's infamous installation *House* (1993) provides a case in point in being a terraced house (in the East End of London) whose outer shell was stripped to reveal a form of 'petrified past' as well as 'negative space'. An illuminating article by Doreen Massey detects in the piece – torn down, of course, by Tower Hamlet's council not long after its unveiling – a 'disruption of ... social time-spaces' on three levels (in Lingwood 1995: 36). First, being 'the space of a house no longer there', it brought a familiar but absent past into the present (ibid.). Second, by turning space inside out, the 'private was opened to public view' (ibid.). And, third, by solidifying air *House* insisted 'on the impossibility of the recovery of [the] past' (ibid.: 43). Most importantly, perhaps, the work served as a form of blank canvas upon which were projected all kinds of contested meanings around those spatio-temporal axes. As Massey points out, references to a traditional past in the city's East End 'can bring to mind radicalism and ethnic diversity or racism and community closure' (ibid.: 46). One of her personal concerns is to highlight the double-edged nature for women of invoking memories of 'home' as a 'utopian place of safety and shelter for which we supposedly yearn' when it may also have been a place of work, conflict and entrapment (ibid.: 41). And, as a further example of the role of *House* as a projection screen for contentious issues, Massey cites the graffiti that was sprayed at one stage on the installation, calling attention to the situation of homelessness in the city: 'Homes for all, black and white' (ibid.: 49).

The artist Krzysztof Wodiczko has also engaged with the issue of homelessness in his work, though he is probably better known for his interrogations around the theme of migration, identity and communication, in which he has a particular personal interest as a Polish émigré to the USA. Where Whiteread's installations invite the public's implicit projections, as we have seen, Wodiczko indulges in explicit projections of film images on to the buildings and monuments of officialdom. As Nick Kaye proposes, in a comment that might equally apply to Whiteread, 'Wodiczko's points of departure are analyses of architecture and space as loci of power and authority' (*PCC*, p. 238). So, the artist 'works to expose the ideological complexities that underlie everyday readings and experiences of the city' (*PCC*, p. 238). The extract included as the conclusion to this section is from Kaye's book *Site-Specific Art* and draws attention to Rosalyn Deutsche's important identification of Wodiczko's interventions as being in fact 'projections on to projections' (*PCC*, p. 240). In her critique of a proposed project entitled *The Homeless Projection*, involving statues in New York's Union Square of 'heroes in American history', Deutsche herself explains the mechanism of reading one myth or semiotic code through another in a passage worth quoting here at length:

> To facilitate what I have interpreted as a democratic questioning of social unity, Wodiczko manipulates the statues' own language, breaking up its apparently stable and unitary meanings. He transforms the classical gestures, poses, and attitudes of the sculpted figures into the gestures, poses, and attitudes currently adopted by people begging on the streets: George Washington's left forearm presses down on a can of Windex and holds a cloth, so that the imperial gesture of his right arm is transformed into a signal made by the unemployed to stop cars, clean windshields, and obtain a street donation. Lincoln's stereotypically 'proud but humble' bearing is reconfigured, through the addition of a crutch and beggar's cup, into the posture of a homeless man soliciting money on a street corner. A bandage and cast change Lafayette's elegant stance and extended arm into the motions of a vagrant asking for alms, and the mother sheltering her children metamorphoses into a homeless family appealing for help.
>
> (Deutsche 1996: 42–3)

As this account might imply, Wodiczko's practice could be viewed as an instance of Situationist *détournement* in the way it reconfigures institutional signifiers 'against themselves' as a means of drawing attention to ironies and contradictions within public sculpture and built form. Kaye emphasises above all the significance of the body in the 'disruption of architecture's *place*. ... These projections attempt to provoke a *bodily* confrontation with architecture' (*PCC*, p. 242). As such the body effectively writes or performs the city: the body emerges 'as the site of the city's construction' (*PCC*, p. 242).

4.1   Graffiti
Susan J. Smith

Whose city is this?

Corporate identity shapes the skyline; commercial products line the streets. Faceless thousands surge through nameless spaces.

Whose place is this, and how do we know?

Look to the 'twilight zone of communication'.
The signs in the streets, the measures, the markings, the meanings, the movement. ...

Graffito: A drawing or writing scratched on a wall or other surface.

What's wrong with graffiti?

Graffito: ... scribblings or drawings, often indecent, found on public build-ings, in lavatories, etc.

What's wrong with graffiti?

> Tricia Rose knows, she writes in *Black Noise*:
> By the mid-1970s, graffiti emerged as a central example of the extent of urban decay and heightened already existing fears over a loss of control of the urban landscape.
> (1994, p. 44)

> And that's not all, as David Ley and Roman Cybriwsky observe in
> 'Urban graffiti as territorial markers':
> A zone of tension appeared, which is located exactly by the evidence of the walls. ... Diagnostic indicators of an invisible environment of attitudes and social processes ... far more than fears, threats and prejudices, they are a prelude and

a directive to open behaviour. ... The walls are more than an attitudinal tabloid;
they are a behavioural manifesto.
(1974, p. 503)

Graffiti is what they call an urban incivility. A signal that the social order is breaking down; a sign that some still scorn the forces for social control. Graffiti is the tip of the iceberg. If the writing is on the wall, it is only a matter of time before something worse will clamber from the hidden depths of the underworld, to threaten our well-being, steal our property, harm our loved ones, challenge our lifestyle. Graffiti is in our space, in our face. A blot on the landscape. Full stop.

Graffito; It. Graphein: to write, write: to record: to decree or foretell: to communicate.

A loss of control?

I started writing ... to prove to people where I was. You go
somewhere and get your name up there and people know you were
there, that you weren't afraid.
(Cool Earl)

Words out of place?

Spray painting ... is another solution to the incessant search for recognition,
identity and status in the inner city.
(Ley, 1974, p. 127)

Graffiti: words of despair ...

... or signs of hope?

Words function ... like chants, spells, incantations, curses, cheers,
raps, expletives. ... In some instances the most profound thing that can
be uttered is the most obscene thought one can think of, or the most violent.
(On Jean-Michel Basquiat, cited in the book of an exhibition mounted at the
Witney Museum of American Art, 1993, New York: Harvey N. Abrams, Inc.)

Is graffiti vandalism ...

... or could it be art?

Art: application of skill to production of beauty.

Writing names, symbols, images; working top to bottom; spreading colour along the length of the subway.

What is more interesting? Bare, twisted, rusting metal; bland advertisements, dusty floors and peeling walls? Or something surprising, colourful, words to hold your attention, changing each day, breaking the monotony of your life and its environment?

'Relax', says Tim Cresswell, as he explores the crucial 'where' of graffiti, and enjoy the visual bonus that comes these days with the purchase of a subway token (1996, p. 35). But city power brokers loathe these signs of life. Graffiti undermines their authority, usurps their space, encroaches on their territory. And so 'the graffiti problem was reconstructed as a central reason for the decline in quality of life in a fiscally fragile and rusting New York' (Rose, 1994, p. 44).

But theirs is not the only view; and soon:

> The level of municipal hostility exhibited towards graffiti art was
> matched only by the SoHo art scene's embrace of it.
> (Rose, 1994, p. 46)

Art matters ...

Aesthetics is the geography of every day life. As bell hooks puts it, 'more than a philosophy or theory of beauty, it is a way of inhabiting space' (1991, p. 104)

Art provides glimpses of otherness and elsewhere, frees desire from fantasy.

bell hooks again: 'in a democratic society art should be the location where everyone can witness the joy, pleasure and power that emerges when there is freedom of expression' (1995, p. 138)

Perhaps we should invest our radical aspirations in art, look to aesthetics to nurture the spirit, create the will to change the world?

That's what the street artists have done.

Experiencing art can enhance our understanding of what it means to live as free subjects in an unfree world. (hooks, 1995, p. 9)

So *Art* can tell us whose city this is, and why, and what it means!

Take, for example, the life and work of Jean-Michel Basquiat; graffiti artist and star; projecting signs from the street onto walls in the gallery. The more hostile New Yorkers became to urban graffiti, to words out of place; the more the art world gathered up these words, framed them, tamed them and accommodated them privately.

Not that Basquiat himself pandered to this distinction:

> In keeping with the codes of the street culture he loved so much, Basquiat's work is in-your-face.
> (hooks, 1995, p. 36)

> Basquiat often placed his work next to Soho art galleries on the night before an opening. Graffiti challenged the rigid *de facto* segregation of American cities by placing the work of outsiders where it could be seen by everyone.
> (Mirzoff, 1995, p. 164)

> 'Basquiat's work is in your face ... [it] holds no warm welcome for those who approach it with a narrow Eurocentric gaze.
> (hooks, 1995, p. 36)

Jean Michel Basquiat, American son of Haitian and Puerto Rican parents, dared to be 'black', dared to tap into the deep anxieties of his time, into the fear that 'the city was being "lost" by "us" ', that is to say by white European-Americans, and was being taken over by 'them', the African-Americans, Latinos, Chinese and others who were supposed to be neither seen nor heard, except in the appropriate venues' (Mirzoff, 1995, pp. 163–164).

> To make sense of Basquiat's language you have to first respect African people as language manipulators of the highest order, to respect the complexity of African cultures as series of overlapping texts, tongues and dialects, ranging from the in-joke to the alienated, from the colloquial to the schizophrenic.
> (On Jean-Michel Basquiat, cited in the book of an exhibition mounted at the Witney Museum of American Art, 1993, New York: Harvey N. Abrams, Inc.)

Basquiat dared to write, to paint, to project his words and pictures into the heart of whiteness: 'Basquiat's painting challenges folks who think that by merely looking they can "see" ' (hooks, 1995, p. 36).

You want to clean this graffiti up?

Get rid of this obscenity, this mess, this thing that is talked about as if it were a disease spread by madmen, these words that are nonsense, violent, barbaric, nonsense?

No civilised metropolis would endure a rash of graffiti; no decent city would let itself be so contaminated; what thinking person would want to read it, or reflect on it, or add to it?

Clean it up, then!

> Basquiat journeyed into the heart of whiteness ... a savage and brutal place.
> (hooks, 1995, p. 43)

> He tried to imagine a body that was not marked by race, while being constantly reminded of the racial mark inscribed on his own body by others.
> (Mirzoff, 1995, p. 189)

Like a graffiti tag sprayed on to the side of a subway carriage, the name 'Basquiat' circulated too publicly, too fast and across too many boundaries.

Vandal: a wilful or ignorant destroyer of anything beautiful, venerable or worthy of preservation.

Vandalism: ruthless destruction or spoiling of anything beautiful.

Whose city is this?
This place where we know the cost of so much and the value of so little?

Whose city is this?
We must learn to see.

References

Cresswell, T. (1996) *In Place/Out of Place: Geography, Ideology, and Transgression*, Minneapolis: University of Minnesota Press.

hooks, b. (1991) *Yearning*, London: Turnaround.

hooks, b. (1995) *Art on my Mind*, New York: The New Press.

Ley, D. (1974) *The Black Inner City as Frontier Outpost*, Washington, DC: Association of American Geographers.

Ley, D. and Cybriwsky, R. (1974) 'Urban graffiti as territorial markers', *Annals of the Association of American Geographers*, 64, 491–505.

Mirzoff, N. (1995) *Bodyscapes*, London: Routledge.

Rose, T. (1994) *Black Noise*, New England: Hanover University Press.

4.2   Skating on Thin Eyes: the First Walk
Iain Sinclair

the magus dee dreams of a stone island in force, dying in poverty, drunk on angelspeech, which paradoxically, he has not actually heard, the scales of music tripping upward to evade him in perpetual deferral to create open outward the place of definition.

Richard Makin

The notion was to cut a crude **V** into the sprawl of the city, to vandalise dormant energies by an act of ambulant signmaking. To walk out from Hackney to Greenwich Hill, and back along the River Lea to Chingford Mount, recording and retrieving the messages on walls, lampposts, doorjambs: the spites and spasms of an increasingly deranged populace. (I had developed this curious conceit while working on my novel *Radon Daughters*: that the physical movements of the characters across their territory might spell out the letters of a secret alphabet. Dynamic shapes, with ambitions to achieve a life of their own, quite independent of their supposed author. Railway to pub to hospital: trace the line on the map. These botched runes, burnt into the script in the heat of creation, offer an alternative reading – a subterranean, preconscious text capable of divination and prophecy. A sorcerer's grimoire that would function as a curse or a blessing.)

Armed with a cheap notebook, and accompanied by the photographer Marc Atkins, I would transcribe all the pictographs of venom that decorated our near-arbitrary route. The messages were, in truth, unimportant. Urban graffiti is all too often a signature without a document, an anonymous autograph. The tag is everything, as jealously defended as the Coke or Disney decals. Tags are the marginalia of corporate tribalism. Their offence is to parody the most visible aspect of high capitalist black magic. Spraycan bandits, like monks labouring on a Book of Hours, hold to their own patch, refining their art by infinite acts of repetition. The name, unnoticed except by fellow taggers, is a gesture, an assertion: it stands in place of the individual artist who, in giving up his freedom, becomes free. The public autograph is an announcement of nothingness, abdication, the swift erasure of the envelope of identity. It's like Salvador Dali in his twilight years putting his mark on hundreds of blank sheets of paper, authenticating chaos.

Serial composition: the city is the subject, a fiction that anyone can lay claim to. 'We are all artists,' they used to cry in the Sixties. Now, for the price of an aerosol, it's true. Pick your view and sign it. Sign events that have not yet happened. (Take a stroll down somewhere like Catherine

Wheel Alley, off Bishopsgate, and see the future revealed on a wall of white tiles. Superimposed fantasies. Scarlet swastikas swimming back to the surface. The Tourette's syndrome ravings of an outwardly reformed city. A private place, a narrow passage, in which to let out all the overtly disguised racist bile. The madness has to find somewhere to run wild. Obscene formulae incubating terrorist bombs. Runnels and enclosed ditches where unwaged scribes are at last free of the surveillance cameras.) Remember postal art, *Fluxus*? All that European and transatlantic bumf now consigned to a bunker beneath the Tate Gallery? Graffiti is the Year Zero version.

The tagger, the specialist who leaves his mark on a wall, is a hit and run calligrapher – probably young, MTV-grazing and male. His art is nomadic, a matter of quantity not quality. As often as not, the deed is carried out on the way back from a club in the early hours of the morning; the announcement of a jagged progress across home territory. Nothing too bulky to carry, a good black felt-tip pen in the pocket of your Pucca jeans will do the trick. The pseudonymous signature is rapidly perfected: Soxi, Coe, Sub, Hemp. Standards are rather more demanding than in Bond Street. Earlier efforts, already in place, if they are deemed inadequate, will be deleted with a single stroke. White boy business. Middle-class cultural diffusionism. The walls that have been set aside as open-air galleries, sites where aerosol activity is encouraged or at least tolerated, don't cut it. 'Sign Park' in an estate off Tufnell Park Road, although it features constantly evolving monster murals, is not considered a serious option. Your tag will all too soon be worked over, obliterated. Taggers can be solitaries, but, more frequently, they hang out in teams or crews. The tag represents a corporate identity; not so much a gang as a studio or 'school of'. Battles are not territorial; the climate here is clubbish, mildly hallucinogenic. Inner-city impressionists who have moved on from the posthumous representation of light and pleasure. Everything happens in the present tense. No history, no future. There is no interference with subject. Fragments of London are perceived as Polaroid epiphanies; signed and abandoned. The tag is the record of a fleeting instant of inspiration. 'Eas-y!' The more upwardly mobile careerists might attack a tube train, but most settle for walls and doorways, customised hoardings. Sprayed messages are meaningless, having no programme beyond the announcement of a non-presence. Night scrawls, minimal adjustments to the psychic skin of the city. The grander aerosol paintings, known as 'pieces', are altogether too flash, baroque, an art in decline. They draw attention to themselves, thereby neutralising their greatest strength – invisibility. They solicit photographic reproduction, a collaboration with Warhol-tendency vampires. The plain tag is a purist's form. Satisfaction is derived from getting your hit into some high risk location, a dangerous bridge climbed in heart-pumping, post-rave excitement. The clubbing tagger's E-vision is an authentic urban experience: an enforced homeward walk across a lucid wilderness from Barking or Brixton, sunrise over the industrial alps of Stratford East. That's as near as they are ever going to come to it, unsolicited satori. Hemp, an American exile, who arrived here from New York in the wake of a 500 dollar fine, enjoys a toke, a session with the chillum. In reflective mood, he meditates on the relationship between tagging and skate-boarding. He drifts backwards and forwards, enacting complicated figures, over a South London parking lot: 'If you're going to be around the city all the time, you'd better put your name up.'

As newspapers have atrophied into the playthings of grotesque megalomaniacs, uselessly shrill exercises in mind-control, so disenfranchised authors have been forced to adapt the walls to playful collages of argument and invective. Not the publicly displayed, and quietly absorbed, papers of the Chinese, but editorials of madness. Texts that nobody is going to stop and read. Unchallenged polemics. My own patch in Hackney has been mercilessly colonised by competing voices from elsewhere: Kurds, Peruvians, Irish, Russians, Africans. Contour lines of shorthand rhetoric asserting the borders between different areas of influence. Graffiti could, I hoped, be read like a tidemark. In the course of our walk we'd find precisely where the 'Freedom' of Dursan Karatas gave way to the 'Innocence' of George Davis – OK. (Yes, George is still getting a result, the benefit of the doubt from the railway bridges of East London – long after being caught in the act during a raid on the Bank of Cyprus in Seven Sisters Road, Holloway. For over twenty years Davis has woken to find himself framed by DS Mathews. Thus proving that graffiti has a half-life far in excess of the buildings on which they have been painted. Broken sentences and forgotten names wink like fossils among the ruins.)

Walking is the best way to explore and exploit the city; the changes, shifts, breaks in the cloud helmet, movement of light on water. Drifting purposefully is the recommended mode, tramping asphalted earth in alert reverie, allowing the fiction of an underlying pattern to reveal itself. To the no-bullshit materialist this sounds suspiciously like *fin-de-siècle* decadence, a poetic of entropy – but the born-again *flâneur* is a stubborn creature, less interested in texture and fabric, eavesdropping on philosophical conversation pieces, than in noticing *everything*. Alignments of telephone kiosks, maps made from moss on the slopes of Victorian sepulchres, collections of prostitutes' cards, torn and defaced promotional bills for cancelled events at York Hall, visits to the homes of dead writers, bronze casts on war memorials, plaster dogs, beer mats, concentrations of used condoms, the crystalline patterns of glass shards surrounding an imploded BMW quarter-light window, meditations on the relationship between the brain damage suffered by the super-middleweight boxer Gerald McClettan (lights out in the Royal London Hospital, Whitechapel) and the simultaneous collapse of Barings, bankers to the Queen. Walking, moving across a retreating townscape, stitches it all together: the illicit cocktail of bodily exhaustion and a raging carbon monoxide high.

4.3   The Policing of the Artist
Madeleine Bunting

Here's tale for our times. Over the last three years, it has been possible to catch the 'Chewing Gum Man' at work somewhere in London, crouched on a pavement. From a distance, he could be homeless or a drunk – his coat is spattered with paint – but as you near, you see that he is painting in enamels, with great delicacy, a picture on the discarded gum that litters urban pavements. When he moves on, the picture will catch passing eyes – particularly children's – for months to come. Each picture tells a story as recounted by a passer-by: this was the place where someone was knocked down or had their first kiss. The pictures are small signs of personal connection, a humanising of an anonymous urban environment; he doesn't want payment, it's a gift of recognition in the city's commercialised and often violent public space.

Romantic or eccentric, you many think, but surely no challenge to public order. The artist, Ben Wilson, estimates he has now clocked up about 500–600 encounters with the police during this project. Most have been amicable. Some local policemen came to recognise that buried in Wilson's purpose are ends not that dissimilar from their own about building a sense of connectedness, often among alienated groups such as teenagers.

It helps that Wilson is softly spoken, gentle, and clever enough to ensure that he is not breaking the law. He paints on the gum, not the pavement, and you can't be charged with criminal damage to litter. Unlike the graffiti artist, Banksy, who has had to remain anonymous or face criminal charges, Wilson wants to connect his public art with people.

He has sometimes run into more heavyhanded policing, but nothing prepared him for what happened a few months ago. Arrested and charged with criminal damage in front of a crowd of horrified tourists, he says he ended up being punched and dragged across a police cell. The story illustrates what little space is left for spontaneity, or even the gentlest subversion, on our streets.

The police now have extraordinarily broad powers for regulating behaviour in public space. The pretext for acquiring these was in part terrorism, in part anti-social behaviour. They can intervene with options such as imposing a fine, making an arrest, or stop and search. Absurd recent examples of how far these powers strech include a drunken Oxford student who said a police horse was gay and ended up with an £80 fixed-penalty fine. And the penalty fines handed to wearers of a 'Bollocks to Blair' T-shirt. The most egregious instance of this new civic conformity was Tony Blair's measure to ban political protests within a mile of Westminster. It led to the removal of anti-Iraq war placards, which, in their subsequent resurrection by artist Mark Wallinger as State Britain, won the Turner prize last week – a powerful indictment of how the messy, chaotic nature of protest is now tidied into the safe spaces of artistic institutions. The police have been made arbiters of our civic space, with unprecedented scope now to impose narrow definitions of conformity on the culture of the street – often places in desperate need of civilising with just the spontaneous human exchange Wilson initiates.

But Wilson's story didn't end there. Once at the station, he was told they wanted a DNA sample, which under a 2004 amendment, the police are entitled to take from everyone accused of a recordable offence. Even if the person is never convicted, or even charged, the DNA sits in a national database until they die, or their hundredth birthday. Wilson balked at this invasion of his privacy; he says he tried to reason with the police, and ended up on the floor being punched, as six or so hairs were taken for the DNA sample. Charges of obstructing police in the course of their duty, and criminal damage, were brought against him and then dropped.

The question left in Wilson's mind as he recovered from this shocking experience was how something so integral to his personhood and dignity as his DNA could now sit forever on a database, which is subcontracted to private laboratories. It is accessible by more than 50 other bodies and subject to the risks of being stolen or ... lost in the post.

The routine collection of DNA slipped through parliament with barely a murmur, while campaigning efforts were focused on anti-terrorism measures. The UK is accumulating the biggest DNA database in the world – and no one can be entirely sure of how this could be used in future, and by whom. What frustrates critics is that the government has yet to produce convincing evidence as to why it needs this vast database. Liberty, the human rights organisation, has a case challenging the way DNA is routinely collected and retained, due to reach the European court in March.

Has fear so cowed us that we are prepared to offer up so much – the culture of our streets, our very own DNA with the genetic code whose significance we are still unravelling – to the discretion of the police and the state?

4.4   Horror Vacui
Ursula Hofbauer and Friedemann Derschmidt

Permanent Breakfast is a game, an art project, art in a public space and public art, but also urban planning or a social project or a tool to test the quality of public spaces or, to put it another way, to ensure the public character of a certain space.

The game is begun when one or more people set up a breakfast table in a square, a street location or other public open space, offering, for example, coffee, rolls and jam and inviting passers-by to join them for breakfast. In the familiar, simple manner of a chain letter, the breakfasters are asked to organise a similar public breakfast the next day and invite the passers-by in turn. Ideally, everyone who organises the breakfast should invite at least four people, so that on the second day there are already sixteen, on the third day sixty-four and on the tenth day over a million people having breakfast in public.

Permanent Breakfast is renewed every year with a kick-off breakfast in Vienna's city centre. The goal of this initiation event is to invite as many people as possible to disseminate the game of a public breakfast over the course of the year: everywhere in the city but also beyond the municipal and national borders. In the ten years of its existence, the project has spread in the manner of a chain letter and taken root in most of the European metropolises. We ask all the breakfasters to send photos of their breakfasts, if possible. We have received hundreds of such reports back by mail, from nearly all the large cities of Europe but also from New York, Taiwan and the South Seas.

As a rule, the reactions to the public breakfast are positive. Passers-by readily sit down, drink coffee and chat. Even tourists and older people, who might at first be thought to have stricter ideas of order, overcame such behaviour. Many of them were probably appropriating some public space for their own objectives and needs for the first time. It helps that breakfasting is as harmless an activity as could be. No one would think it could be a kind of political rally, and yet public breakfasts are that as well: assemblies for the purpose of debate and exchange of opinions. The right to hold such assemblies – even without prior notification – has been guaranteed under German and Austrian law, for example, by their respective constitutional courts. That means that the right to have breakfast in public places ultimately derives from the right to assemble and demonstrate and the right of free expression of opinions.[1] One decidedly appealing effect of our efforts is that breakfast is politicised by taking it out of private contexts into the public sphere, but without losing its fun or sociable qualities.

Right of assembly and a culture of permits

Independently of legal questions, the act of breakfasting in public is an outstanding tool to expand other ideas and models to the use of public spaces on principle. The common culture of permits – that is, the assumption that only that which is explicitly permitted is not forbidden – usually draws the laws of one's own possibilities far more narrowly than necessary and prematurely avoids real or imaginary conflicts. This restraint vis-à-vis modes of behaviour that are not explicit permitted and pre-formulated, vis-à-vis models that have not (yet) been established is deeply anchored in the culture. We ourselves still experience a little stage fright when we breakfast in especially prominent places. Even though, after years of experience to the contrary, we ought to know better, sometimes we still think that this time the police might show up, and we would have to debate with them, or they would try to drive us away. For that reason, it is inevitable that the practice of Permanent Breakfast cannot avoid developing and stipulating a new model for behaving in public, for example, the model of breakfasting in public. It is not about teaching passers-by proper, perhaps more courageous civic behaviour. Rather the point is to open up and encourage a palette of possibilities, so that new uses of public space that are adequate to the needs in question can be designed and implemented.

This naturally places demands on space and its qualities. From our point of view, what is needed is not installing permanent facilities for our use in streets, squares or in parks – say, tables and chairs for breakfasting. What results from the practice of breakfasting, from the search for appropriate locations, is the need for flexible spaces that do not predetermine a particular use but rather permit many different uses as the users desire. That – and about this we do not want there to be any doubt – is a political challenge, for what could be more political than the question of who has control over resources, especially public resources and public spaces.

The public sphere and the pseudo-public sphere

In practice, people breakfasting in Austria rarely push the limits of what the executive branch tolerates and must tolerate. Far more frequently, however, one does make the acquaintance of private security services when one sets up tables, chairs and a coffee pot in the relevant places.[2] The reason for that is the fact that public spaces and public institutions are increasingly being privatised. This development is by no means limited to Austria; indeed, one finds such privatisations in all European countries in the wake of neo-liberal developments. Permanent Breakfast is a project that makes the concrete effects of these policies visible and questions how these trends towards privatisation will affect the use of public spaces, indeed how they will affect the concept of the public sphere in general. There is, of course, no right to stay and assemble in private or privatised spaces as there is in public ones.

At this point it could be helpful to illustrate once again what qualities distinguish private and public spaces in general. In our experience, there are three very different kinds of spaces: private spaces, public spaces and pseudo-public spaces. Private spaces are, of course, those in which the owners set the rules: I decide who can enter my living room when I send out invitations to my garden party; and the owners of a company decide who can enter their store or factory. By contrast, public spaces are those in which the rules are determined by the public. In a democratic state, that is supposed to be the sovereign – namely, the people, or at least a representative of the people. One of the essential features of public spaces is, of course, free access to all, the right to spend time there. The right to assemble, demonstrate and express one's own views there are also granted. Permanent Breakfast tries to encourage everyone to use their collective property.

We referred to the third kind of space as pseudo-public. These are private spaces or spaces administrated by private companies that are disguised as public spaces, where a kind of pseudo-publicness is staged. Shopping centres are a good example, as many of them are organised in imitation of European city centres, equipped with street signs, indoor plazas, fountains and the like.

Even in Europe, such malls tend to be based on American models. One of the most prominent examples is the Forum Shops in Caesars Palace in Las Vegas: an establishment that has both the familiar attributes of urbanity, such as organisation on a pedestrian scale, a central marketplace and a structure copied from streetscapes. It is a special form of imitating public open spaces: a ceiling with painted clouds that is intended to simulate the course of the sun by changing the incidence of light. When the history is examined more closely, however, it turns out that the vocabulary of these malls was indeed taken from the context of European city centres. For example, Michael Zinganel has recently demonstrated convincingly, that the Jewish architect and urban planner Victor Gruen, who was exiled from Vienna, had Vienna in mind when planning the details of the organisation of his shopping centres.[3] *The mall*, which in the context of American cities 'serves as a substitute for the neglected public space of the inner cities',[4] is now migrating back to the edges of European cities, competing with its own precursor and even threatening its existence.

The images of publicness that are evoked in shopping centres are clearly attractive and are used to draw in customers. These images can certainly obscure the fact that many essential aspects of publicness are lacking here, above all the simple right to stay in these spaces. Strictly speaking the private owners or operators do not even have to give a reason for expelling unwanted visitors form these locations. In these pseudo-public spaces, demonstrations are not permitted; homeless people cannot stay here and of course there is no right to assemble to exchange opinions freely. As long as one wants to shop, has a bank card and, in some cases, does not have an unwelcome skin colour, these limitations pose no problem. But apparently even the paying customers of the large shopping centres do not wish to be reduced to the role of pure consumers, so that one has to offer them an urban ambiance and at least a few signs of public space.

Another kind of pseudo-public space is the privatisation of formerly public institutions. The transformation of once public spaces like museums, railway stations and parks seems more problematic to us than the existence of shopping centres. One is used to thinking of them as public spaces and, if no occasion arises, one scarcely notices that they no longer are. For in the name of budget cutting or even tax savings, countless former public institutions have been sold or transformed into private companies in recent years. Gradually, an ideological reorientation is taking place that questions the concept of the public sphere per se. As formerly public spaces are stripped of universal access and use, and hence of their public character, it corroborates a point of view that wants to see state institutions reduced to the administration of private interests.

In contrast to that view, we think that the public sphere is more, and should be more, than the sum of private interests. The difference between the two viewpoints on how to approach public space can be clarified concretely: rights such as the right to use a space, the right to assemble, to debate, to demonstrate and to express one's own opinion are directly tied to the existence of public spaces. Private spaces are, however they may be designed, no substitute for that.

Disguising private, commercial spaces as public ones and the transformation of public locations into privately managed ones is making it increasingly difficult to tell what kind of space one is located in. Permanent Breakfast is a very handy litmus test to ensure oneself that a space is public. For breakfasting in public always means insisting on the right to assembly, to speak publicly and to use public resources. Any place one can have breakfast is therefore a public space, and vice versa: a space, or at least a free space, where one cannot have breakfast is not a real public space. The place and time of an assembly create a direct, socio-political field of tension between legislation regarding the use of public space and those using it. A breakfast in a public space should, therefore, always be seen as a political act as well.

Sovereignty

Fortunately, despite government austerity measures and a reorganisation of public institutions based on neo-conservative motives, there is still plenty of public space where one can have breakfast: streets, squares, parks, traffic islands, parking lots and so on.

Naturally, the beautiful locations, the successful plazas and especially the former spaces of the nobility should be used. Every year on 1 May we have breakfast on Heldenplatz in Vienna, in the former front garden of the imperial castle. An everyday action like having breakfast on the Hofburg grounds also plays with the image of the sovereign, who was once an emperor, and who could use the castle's extensive grounds to satisfy his private needs. In a democratic context, being sovereign could also mean appropriating the sensory pleasure of these spaces on a daily basis. Palace gardens for everyone, not just to be seen and photographed by tourists, but to be lived in. If one leaves the Vienna castle and heads to the old and new suburbs, it often becomes more restricted. It is not always the result of a lack of space. We refer to one phenomenon we often encounter as *horror vacui*, the fear of the empty place. One could almost formulate it as a rule: everywhere where space is particularly limited, you can be sure something will be standing in the way: a flowerbox, a bed of tulips, a bench, a fountain, some piece of art. In the middle of the plaza, as a rule. Perhaps these things were placed there to provide sensory pleasure for the sovereign, so that he didn't have to go to the Hofburg or to a museum every time he felt the need to see something beautiful. But perhaps these things are also there so that no one gets the idea that the plaza could be used. The sovereign, who on every halfway decent spring day seeks out in droves his former hunting grounds in Vienna's Prater park, to smell the grass, skate, play ball, play music or to picnic, might otherwise get the idea to do the same thing here. But perhaps it is also the case that very many of these people who spend their existences planning and beautifying such places suffer from a variety of *horror vacui* that prevents them from letting the object of their design be empty. Nothing is better suited to overcoming this fear than a full, well-placed breakfast table.

Notes

1. The Austrian Constitutional Court classifies a meeting of several people to be an assembly within the meaning of the Law of Assembly (Versammlungsgesetz; VersG 1867; 1953) if it is organised with the intention of bringing those present to a shared activity (debate, discussion, demonstration, etc.), such that a certain association of the assembled results (Austrian Constitutional Court, collections 4586/63, 5193/66, 5195/66, 8685/79, 9783/83,

10443/85, 10 608/85, 10 955, 11 651/88, 11 866/88, 11 904/88, 11 935/88, 12 161/89). In other words, an assembly is a temporary formation of a number of people in a non-institutional community or a meeting of people (even in the street) for a common goal of discussing opinions or expressing opinions to others in order to produce a common action (cf. German Constitutional Court, 11.6.1991, EvR772/90, EUGRZ 1991, S 363); or collective expression of opinion with the objective of intellectual debate.

2. A breakfast in the museum district of Vienna was expelled from the courtyard of a large museum complex that is public property but is administered by a private operating company. Unwanted people and actions are also removed from the grounds of railway stations in Vienna belonging to the Österreichische Bundesbahn (ÖBB, Austrian Federal Railway), which has also been transformed into a private company.

3. Michael Zinganel, 'Wien für Amerikaner', *dérive*, no. 3 (February 2001), pp. 4–6.

4. Ibid., p. 4.

4.5   Radioballett
LIGNA

Title	Radioballett
Type	an interventionist way of listening to the radio
Type of use	cultural
Location	many different public places, for example, a pedestrian precinct in Munich
Time	since 2002, for example, 9 February 2005 less than one hour each
Initiators	LIGNA (Ole Frahm, Michael Hueners, Torsten Michaelsen), radio builders
Temporary users	interventionist radio listeners
Role of city	none
Status	legal
Goals	LIGNA tries to change listeners to a temporary association through different models of radio use. This association can infiltrate the laws and standards of different public and private spaces and lay claim to its own space. Listening to the radio becomes intervention – and a practice of change.

www.radioballett.tk

The independent radio group LIGNA develops concepts that enable radio to intervene in controlled public spaces in such a way that their publicness appears to be an uncontrollable situation. If counter-publicness is essentially based on broadcasting the correct contents in traditional formats,

Radioballett is concerned with intervening in public spaces and thus creating a 'new format'– that of interventionist radio listening. If the concept of counter-publicness is concerned with listeners' development of political effectiveness outside the radio transmission, the concept of interventionist publicness is about allowing listening to the radio to become effective in itself. A Radioballett is not a gathering, but instead a dispersion. It has no consistent stage. It takes no particular shape and exists only in a concurrent, and yet dispersed gesture. It does not hinder passers-by, but instead irritates through its simultaneousness. No particular talent as a dancer is necessary to take part in this ballet. One only needs to have an attentive ear and a portable radio with earphones. Roughly distributed throughout a pedestrian precinct, participants, by listening to the radio, are instructed to carry out certain activities. The Radioballett can be received everywhere in the vicinity, just like any other radio programme, but is intended for a specific location. A Radioballett took place in Munich in 2005. As a prelude to protests against the NATO Security Conference approximately 300 radio ballet-dancers attended. The Munich Radioballett was broadcast by Radio Lora 92.4 and allowed people to dance for nearly a half an hour. They begged passers-by, stuck to the shop-windows at the temples of consumption, ran screaming or jumping through the crowd and moved at times in a serious fashion, at times in an amusing fashion through the pedestrain precinct. Because observers were confused at first, flyers were handed out to make the event more accessible to them.

4.6   Circle Line Party
Space Hijackers

Title	Circle Line Party
Type	temporary use of an underground train as a party room
Type of use	entertainment
Location	trains of the London Underground, Circle Line
Time	for the first time in March 1999, several times since then; the party described took place in 2003 several hours
Initiators	Space Hijackers, in existence since 1999
Temporary users	party guests
Role of city	none
Status	semi-legal

Goals   The idea behind the party was an expression of freedom and
                         protest against the repressive, war-like politics of greedy white
                         men who want to rule the world – an attempt to promote do-it-
                         yourself culture in an age of unrestrained consumerism, to create
                         a place for human interaction which is far from the clutches of
                         capitalism and finally, to play a nasty trick on those who destroy
                         civil rights and non-commercialised fun.

                         www.spacehijackers.org

The Circle Line Party is a celebration on the Circle Line, a circuitous
London underground line. A planning group was put together a few weeks
before the date of the party and a website started with tips about how to do
a round, have fun and not have any problems. Careful planning concerning
how people and equipment could be smuggled onto the train was necessary.
A stereo system, bar and podium for pole dancing had to be camouflaged
as normal luggage. In order to remain undiscovered for the longest possible
time the party should only take place in tunnels – in the stations everything
remained quiet, at least as long as no one was drunk. People were supposed to bring costumes with them that could be changed into and out of
quickly so that within an instant they could change from being commuters
in suits to party animals and back. When everything was ready there were
about 600 party-goers at the arranged meeting point. Initial access was at
the Liverpool Street Station, one of the few stations big enough to smug-
gle so many people in without becoming suspicious. The guard at the platform attempted to get everyone to spread out along its entire length, while
the party-goers wanted to stay as far back as possible so that the driver
wouldn't hear any music. The party crowd filled four complete carriages.
It took a few stations after departing before the music system was set up.
A samba band played in the last carriage, the DJ installed loudspeakers in
the second and third carriage and played music to fit the occasion, the pole
dancers danced and alcohol flowed like water. The trains were decorated:
colour transparencies were placed in front of the lights, mirrored balls
hung on the railings and a lot of balloons were used. After a time the party
got too loud and all of a sudden, during the second trip round, the British
Transport Police arrived on the scene. Instead of throwing all the party-
goers off the train, the trip was instead ended at Moorgate Station. Some
stayed behind in order to straighten things up.

4.7   Paris Plage
Bertrand Delanoë

Title	Paris Plage
Type	city event
Type of use	entertainment
Location	the centre of Paris
Time	every summer since 2002
	four to five weeks each time, mid-July to mid-August
Initiator	Bertrand Delanoë, Mayor of Paris
Temporary users	four million visitors annually
Role of city	organiser
Status	legal
Goals	making city hall traffic policies a theme, summer entertainment

At the initiative of Paris Mayor Bertrand Delanoë, the Georges Pompidou motorway in the city's centre has been replaced by a beach for four weeks every year since 2001. The beach lies on the right bank of the Seine between Pont Neuf and Pont de Sully. Because the river is not clean enough to swim in, a large temporary swimming pool is offered to visitors instead. Over a distance of 3.5 kilometres it is possible to lie in deck chairs and hammocks, go for a walk, play beach volleyball and visit cafés and concerts, as well as be cooled off by a fine mist from one of the popular *brumisateurs*. Approximately four million visitors come every year. For this purpose 3,000 tons of sand are poured onto the road, which is closed for the event. The project has an annual cost of two million euros, two-thirds of which are provided through sponsoring, and the occasion is a PR-event for the city hall's traffic policies, which envisage a future closing of the street. The idea has since been copied, without the political aspects, in a series of other European cities including Rome, Amsterdam, Berlin, Budapest, Prague and Vienna. In all of these cities the pure event therefore remains, which is certainly an essential sign of current urban policy in Europe and serves conversely, in the form of future event-like uses, exactly as a reason for urban planning decisions, instead of serving as a medium for urban planning suggestions which contain a social, cultural and, in any case, political background. The concept, incidentally, did not originate in Paris but in the small French city of St. Quentin, which has built a beach and swimming pool at the city hall plaza every summer since 1996.

4.8   An Explosion of Delight
Geoff Dyer

Everyone who was there – the dancers, the commuters; even I suspect, the police – would agree that this week's mobile clubbing event at Liverpool Street Station in London was magical. I'd heard about these happenings, and I loved the idea of hundreds of people freaking out to their own personal stereos – and their own choice of music – at a certain time and place, in silence. For one reason or another I'd never been able to get along to one, but on Wednesday things worked like a dream. An email instructed us to arrive at 7.15pm and then, as the clock struck 7.24, to start dancing 'like you've never danced before'. On Wednesdays I go to Norwich and get back to Liverpool Street at about 7pm, so I was a perfectly placed double agent: a signed-up mobile clubber *and* an authentic commuter.

By 7.05 there was already a subtle excitement in the air – or was it just me? In *Backward Glances*, his history of gay cruising, Mark Turner writes about the illicit thrill of gliding through the city, stealing glances at strangers, looking for a reciprocal sign that someone else is out for the same thing. That's how it was on Wednesday. Plenty of people had iPods, but that's normal. I'd dart a glance: were they here for *it* or were they just catching trains? And they'd look at me – that skinny, middle-aged, grey-haired guy with the rucksack? No, not him.

7.18: the station was definitely busier than usual. The proportion of people with headphones had risen. So had the number of young people wearing bright T-shirts. 7.20: half of those on the concourse were fiddling with their iPods, cueing up tracks. 7.21: I saw some of my friends. 7.23: everyone was looking at the clock. And at 7.24 the whole place went completely crazy.

Any worries about feeling self-conscious were obliterated by having your favourite music turned up sound-system-loud and by the fact that there were hundreds of others doing the same thing. I assumed that everyone was dancing to the same music as me – I'll keep that detail secret – but they could have been rocking out to Hendrix, Shostakovich or James Blunt. It really was like being in a nightclub – until you took off your headphones and saw that all these people were gyrating, smiling and jumping in virtual silence.

Mobile clubbing is an offshoot of flash-mobbing, a fad that was predicated on its ingenious pointlessness. The point of mobile clubbing is that an activity normally reserved for special occasions and places – parties, nightclubs – infiltrates daily life so thoroughly as to be indistinguishable from it. It has the guerrilla quality of illegal raves but is totally legal.

It is, in short, a force for good. This has become more pronounced since the London bombings last year. Stations are prime terrorist targets. You are going about your business and, in an instant – boom! – everything is changed terribly and irreparably. Mobile clubbing is a mirror image of a terrorist outrage. It's organised with similar precision, the feeling of conspiracy is palpable, and at the allotted time there is a detonation. Of joy.

Bystanders innocent of the plotting were caught up in this week's event at Liverpool Street to the extent that some with personal stereos joined in. Others looked on, bewildered but delighted. Quite a few missed their trains, but no one was inconvenienced. A shockwave of happiness spread through everyone in the vicinity. Most bizarrely of all, a few people danced *without* headphones.

It was still going strong when I had to leave at 8pm. I walked off, and within seconds I was just a guy walking home, listening to his iPod. A few friends stayed longer, but by 9pm it was all over. There was no mess to clear up. You could have been forgiven for thinking that nothing significant had happened.

4.9 Non-places
Marc Augé

In the last few years there has been continuous debate about the crisis of meaning. We have celebrated the demise of meta-narratives and of coherent explanation. The collapse of the Communist regime appeared as a symbol of the useless and dangerous pretensions of systems which claimed to speak and act in the name of totality, of definitive answers, of meanings. The horrors of this century – genocide, the death camps – have brought a rude jolt to the idea of progress on the moral level and, by a sort of contamination, on an intellectual level as well. In contrast with these factors of scepticism, if not pessimism, it should be acknowledged of course that there has been a certain progression in the world of the idea of democracy, and of a recognition of human rights. As for progress in science, it is not only incontestable but spectacular.

Even in these areas, however, a certain anxiety can surface, either in denouncing the characteristics of representative democracy, or in suspecting that the democratic ideal is simply a tool of the major powers whose interests are promoted by the idea of a New World Order. In the domain of science one can highlight the uselessness of new discoveries, or their threatening nature from moral or ethical points of view.

All of these factors have cast doubt on the concept of modernity. This idea, as it was defined in the nineteenth century, proceeded from history and developing events. It brought heritage and newness together in one movement which reconciled the two. Modernity is linked to the idea of an accumulation and progress, to the idea of synthesis.

Today the concept of postmodernity, at least in the way it is used by some of its exegetists, challenges the idea of movement which is linked to the idea of modernity. So far as it describes a world in which differences may co-exist in an arbitrary fashion, a patchwork world, the concept of postmodernity can be aptly applied to a society defined as multicultural. It can also, however, contribute to a fixing and rigidifying of difference, to a concretisation of the national culture and a break in the process of distinction and identification which is essential to all integration.

This cumulative vision of time, aligned with the idea of a progress, does not proceed by abrupt ruptures but by successive devolutions and combinations of various heritages. In the contrasting, but nonetheless united, spaces which correspond to this definition, to this conception of time, the feature of the 'other' always finds its place and remains both necessary and relative.

The idea of postmodermism disrupts this progressive scheme in affirming the brutal and sudden eruption of all others, of all otherness, at the very moment when the events of history seem to demonstrate the inanity of metanarratives or explanations which illustrate and succour the idea of progress.

Based on this view we have proclaimed in art, as elsewhere, the possibility and legitimacy of 'patchwork', not simply the mixing of genres but the end of genres. And the end of 'others' as well, if it is true that in the arbitrary synthesis of postmodernity 'the other' has no more consistency than the concept of 'the same'.

But the contemporary situation seems to me better explained by the word 'supermodernity', or perhaps I would prefer to say 'over-modernity'. I think in English one says 'over-determination', in the language of Freud or Lacan – and what I want to say echoing these constructions is 'over-modernity'. The current situation is better explained by these terms than by postmodernity. If I choose to employ the term 'super-' or 'over-modernity', it is because other words appear more marked by an acceleration of the cumulative process to which we have given the name modernity than by their disappearance.

I would characterise the super-modern by three types of excess:

1. An excess of time. We all have the impression that time is accelerating. The overloading of events in the world, which is obviously linked to the increased rule of the media and of the proliferation of information,

results in our immersion in history. However history itself catches up with us and becomes the news of the day.

2. An excess of space. The planet is shrinking, and while on the one hand we are becoming more and more conscious of our planetary identity, and the influence of the ecology movements is certainly linked to this new consciousness, on the other hand we are constantly projected to the four corners of the world through images and through the imagination.

3. An excess of individualisation, which is linked to the first two concepts. Under the weight of information and images, each one of us has a feeling of being not only a witness to the events of the world but somehow to western civilisation itself. This reaction produces a feeling of discomfort, of crisis, which is linked to the consciousness that each one of us can see everything and do nothing. And this is just as true in the case of the many individuals who have the conviction that it is up to them to give a meaning to life and to the world.

The cosmologies that ethnologists have organised in groups around powerful symbolic images become individual even when there are variations on a common theme. The important aspect from this point of view is not whether any particular individual has illusions about the originality of their own interpretation of life, their manner of believing in God, or of understanding politics, but the fact that they invent or implicitly adopt this reality of interpretation.

It should be clear that the outline of what I choose to call super-modernity includes a paradox and a contradiction. In one sense it opens each individual to the presence of others. It corresponds to a freer circulation of people, things and images. In another sense, however, it turns individuals back on themselves, making them more like witnesses than actors in contemporary life.

Today we have the illusion of being near everything and a feeling of increased individuality or loneliness. It is at this point perhaps that the notion of 'non-place' can help us to characterise the situation of over- or super-modernity.

I first developed the notion of non-space as a negation of the notion of place. Place, at least in the view of the anthropologist, is a space long taken over by human beings and where something is said about relationships which human beings have with their own history, their natural environment and with one another.

Anthropology has taught us that spatial organisation of the greatest refinement can be achieved in certain societies. For example, a single person is bound by the rules of residency to live with so and so, and so it goes from the cradle to the grave. Throughout each one of these social and biological periods of life – birth, marriage, procreation, old age – a change in status often brings about a change in the place of residence so that even the choice of a permanent place is given over to chance. From this point of view, non-places begin with unrootedness, nineteenth-century countrymen drawn from their land and thrown into human life, migrants, refugees – all of these people have direct experience of non-place, and the act of establishing colonies and of setting in new areas is related to the growth of turning space into place.

At this point, it is possible to see that the notion of non-places has an objective as well as a subjective dimension. A non-place comes into existence, even negatively, when human beings don't recognise themselves in it, or cease to recognise themselves in it, or have not yet recognised themselves in it. Deserts, islands, virgin forests, cannot be called non-places, for they were in fact spaces – and even tourist spaces – to be conquered, that is to say potential places.

The criteria for recognition is here essential, in which we recognise ourselves and in which others can recognise us as easily as we recognise them. Therefore it is possible to think that the same place can be looked upon as a place by some people and as a non-place by others, on a long-term or a short-term basis. For example, an airport space does not carry the same meaning for the passenger boarding the plane and for the employee who is working there.

In the full sense of the word, a place is a space where relationships are self evident and inter-recognition is at a maximum, and where each person knows where they and others belong. Therefore place is also interested in time. A village people, or indeed a village clock, has symbolic value in language, for we call home any place where we are understood by others, and in turn understand them, without having to spell things out. Anything that takes us away from a system of social relations takes us away from the place attached to it as well.

Today all of our circulation, information and communication spaces could be considered non-places. As a rule they don't serve as meeting places. They make very little use of language. Television screens carry all the information you need.

Through virtue of this temporal paradox one can be alone and, at the same time, in contact with everybody else around the world. This is a point of the greatest importance because of the inter-relatedness of the place/non-place opposition depending on our usage or subject. A place can become a non-place and vice versa.

Three major events may be called to our attention. First, that of the planet's urbanisation, certainly more dramatic in developing countries than in the most highly-developed countries, and its corollary, the unsymbolised characteristics of the new spaces thus occupied. These, of course, are of great interest to the urbanists and architects, being relatively indescribable, unqualifiable and uncontrolled intellectually. These are being designed as urban filaments.

We suppose that a strictly political question in global terms can be added to the aesthetic and sociological questions raised by this state of affairs. Traditional state borders are perhaps getting even more artificial as telecommunication's unprecedented development establishes the prerogative of instantaneity through which interconnected cities gain a rapidly-growing influence.

In fact, the conquest of space seems today more dedicated to the planet's technological and economical management than to exploring the unknown. The 'spectacular display of the world' is the expression I would suggest to give a sense of this second major event and its numerous aspects, in relation to the evolution of images and its consequences on the way we relate to reality. Everyday images are sent to us from around the world, to people living in the middle of nowhere, thousands of miles away from the nearest town, yet nevertheless belonging to the same planet, sometimes at their own expense, and caught in the same history.

This over-abundance of images has perverse consequences in so far as the more we get a chance to see everything, the less we can be sure we are still able to really look at them. The world becomes, one might say, abstractly familiar to us, so that, socially speaking, there are literally no more relations between the world and us, in so far as we are content with the images imparted to us, as is the case today for a lot of people. Other facts appear more enigmatic though they also promote, and participate, in the spectacular display of the world.

There has been such a growth in video technology that to view an event without its visual, or sometimes audiovisual, prolongations, has almost become unthinkable. Video recorders, as cameras, as images converted to processes, are processors of reality derivable only from this reality of images. World news is delivered to us fragmentarily with only a vague and faint familiarity. The television newscasters, the politicians, the heroes of TV series are indistinguishable from the actors and vice versa, and in the end, they turn out to share the reality and unreality factor to the same extent. Television reports on the Gulf War showed us images identical in source to video war games. The elimination of the real experience in tourism is particularly remarkable in France, though France is not exceptional; this form of theatricalisation being applicable, for example, to natural sites like the Niagara Falls and so on. It seems as if everything has to be done to turn the landscape into postcards so as to hold people's attention. A lot of tourists seem more eager to buy reproductions than to really look at the paintings they can only briefly glance at during their all-too-short visits to the museums.

In the so-called amusement park, the quintessential environment of this kind, the spectacle of display of the world is at its height, as what people come to see is mostly the spectacle of spectacle: for example Disney characters walking through a fake American street in a non-American region of the world, and filmed by real tourists hence restoring them to 'real' nature and making them again into movie characters. Through a process that is a reversal of Woody Allen in his film *The Purple Rose of Cairo* they inflict the same treatment on their families who, in turn, step into the screen to join their heroes.

This is a sad development, that one has every good reason to wish had never happened. Psychological and sociological factors might give us hope that its appearance will be postponed, or its manifestation negated. It is, however, already gaining ground on the street. I am speaking of the constitution of a totally fictional ego evolving through exposure to virtual reality networks, with the ego cast naked by images of images. The object of this fascination would be even less real than dreams and figments of imagination, obscuring how all traditional cultures have been made meaningful because they were the product of a given place and cosmology. We would then have gone from the edge of non-place to the edge of non-ego.

4.10   All the World's a Car Park
Jessica Winter

The full power of Jem Cohen's feature film *Chain* doesn't hit until the closing credits, which reveal that the movie's anonymous landscape of chain stores and highway interchanges was shot in seven countries and 11 American states.

Chain takes as its subject and setting the homogenised interzones of privately owned public space – shopping malls, hotel complexes, theme parks – that multinational corporations have remade in their own global-branded image, letting regional colour fade to a concrete grey. A hybrid of fiction and documentary, and a brilliantly discomfiting twist on the 'location shoot', *Chain* is also something of a Ballardian horror story.

'I was trying to get a grip on the nature of globalisation, which is such a hazy, amorphous term,' says the Brooklyn-based 42-year-old, who shot *Chain* on 16mm film over seven years. 'The film is not about America, but there's no question that we're primarily responsible for how a lot of the planet ends up looking. So much of the world becomes a mirror of American business and culture and iconography.' (None of *Chain* was shot in the UK, though the movie looks an awful lot like the Lakeside centre in Thurrock.)

Perhaps best-known for his music videos for REM and Elliott Smith, Cohen has spent much of his career compiling what he calls 'city portraits', including *This Is a History of New York* (1987) and the extraordinary east-European travelogue *Buried in Light* (1994). With *Chain*, however, he has assembled a mosaic of the worldwide urban sprawl. 'Whenever I would shoot places that I liked, often old neighbourhoods that were disappearing, I was always framing things out – putting McDonalds to my back or getting some billboard out of the frame – and I was starting to feel like I had to deal with the new stuff,' he says. 'In the mid-1990s, I started to collect these landscapes, and I found that I could travel anywhere in the world and shoot footage that you couldn't identify in terms of where it came from. I thought I could join all of that material together into a "superlandscape".'

Wandering this underpopulated superlandscape are *Chain's* two protagonists. Amanda (Mira Billotte) is a young American wanderer who lives in abandoned housing and floats between menial jobs; she keeps a diary in the form of the video-letter she composes for her sister. Tomiko (Miho Nikaido) is a businesswoman on a fact-finding mission for an unidentified Japanese company that wants to convert a steel mill into a leisure part; when the firm unaccountably ceases contact with Tomiko, she's left idling in her hotel room and roaming the edges of vast roads built solely for cars. 'She's like an astronaut in space on one of those tethers,' Cohen says, 'and the tether gets cut.'

The two women, equally alienated, take turns narrating *Chain* in tones as unnervingly flat and featureless as the spaces they inhabit. 'The movie was turned down by a lot of the major festivals, particularly the north American ones,' says Cohen, 'and I would get comments like: "Your characters are monotone and uninteresting." They completely missed the point. The characters have been forced into a monotone existence by circumstance.' As *Chain* proceeds, these women take on deeper hues of ambiguity and pathos, as when the quiet Amanda suddenly bashes out a song in a retail-park piano store before she's swiftly shown the door.

The dirge-like overture to *Chain* is a small masterpiece of controlled cacophony, provided by Canadian soundscapists Godspeed You! Black Emperor. 'The opening music had to be scary, like you're in a car headed for a slow-motion collision – this sense of impending catastrophe that doesn't come in any kind of Hollywood way,' the director says.

In a deftly incongruous move, Cohen also deploys the traditional *That Lonesome Valley*, performed by the Carolina Ramblers String Band. 'I wanted these little whispers of American folk music, this specifically regional music in a context where there's no regional character left.'

Chain's production was something of an underground operation. 'You're simply not allowed to shoot in any of these places,' Cohen says. 'It had to be done in, let's just say, a very discreet way. The nature of the production ties in with the subject matter of the movie, because you're dealing with surveillance and security and the degree to which the corporate presence is embedded in the landscape and controls people's activity, including that of the film-makers.

'You're not allowed to show logos, even in a documentary, which I find absurd because you can't film the world without showing logos. And you just can't shoot in a mall, any mall, particularly post-9/11 – everybody uses it as an excuse all the time.'

Cohen has become an archivist of public space at a time when much of that space has been colonised – and de-historicised – by corporations and transient consumer desires. But the heavy hand of the American fear factor is a new and unwelcome influence on his material, as he discovered on a recent train journey from Washington, DC, to New York.

'I've been shooting from train windows for 20 years, and recently I was stopped on a train and surrounded by cops who actually confiscated my footage for national security reasons,' Cohen recounts. 'I was really freaked out. I was shooting with an old hand-cranked 16mm Bolex, for God's sake. This kind of crackdown imposes a police-state mentality that is useful for public control. It's incredibly disturbing and it's happening to a lot of people: artists, tourists, anybody. And it's strange, because this incident has the effect of politicising this lyrical landscape footage.' (*Chain's* video footage of emptied-out office interiors takes on an added dimension when you discover the offices belonged to Enron.)

Since completing *Chain*, Cohen has taken his camera on the road with Amsterdam band the Ex, and is now 'getting little whispers of the next big project', he says. 'I have a pretty large archive of material of Times Square and 42nd Street, from the mid-1980s through the Disneyfication process to where it is now, and I'm starting to suspect that I could do a period feature film on the cheap by using that archive.'

If his Times Square project comes to fruition, it would mark Cohen's return to memorialising lost corners of urban life. *Chain*, meanwhile, documents commodified spaces so bland and omnipresent that we hardly bother to perceive them. 'I hoped that people would feel they were seeing these landscapes anew, because I find them so strangely invisible to us,' says Cohen. 'When I started *Chain* they were putting up a Wal-Mart about every four days, and when I finished it was about every day and a half. These places are so big, they're everywhere, but who really looks at them?'

4.11   By Way of a Conclusion:
One Place After Another
Miwon Kwon

I want to remember a particular lesson of a 'wrong' place described by novelist Don DeLillo in his recent two-act play *Valparaiso* (1999).[1] In the play, the protagonist, Michael Majeski, an average middle-class businessman (assumed to be white), on an ordinary business trip to Valparaiso, Indiana, ends up in another part of the world in Valparaiso, Chile, presumably by mistake, and then has to confront his own minor media celebrity on his return home. Majeski's extraordinary misadventure of falling off the track of his set itinerary and ending up in the wrong place (which isn't to say that he gets lost) is the starting point for DeLillo's fictional critique of the postmodern condition, in which the disruption of a subject's habitual spatiotemporal experience propels the liberation and also the breakdown of its traditional sense of self.

The play begins with Majeski recently returned from the unintended destination of his trip, the wrong Valparaiso in Chile (there are four Valparaisos in the world, so far as I am aware). Upon his return, he is confronted with numerous requests by the media – radio, television, newspapers, magazines, documentary film-makers – to recount his experience. It is a great human interest story, after all: we all want to know what happened. How could anyone make such a big mistake? Didn't he notice that he was headed for the wrong city? When did he notice? Why was he going to Valparaiso in the first place? What happened exactly? Who is Michael Majeski? What was he like as a child? What are his dreams? Does he love his wife? Submitting to such questions, he does 67 interviews in four and a half days in three and a half cities (at least we are told so by his wife), forced to repeat his narrative over and over in front of microphones and cameras, simultaneously constructing and confessing his identity and life history, including his struggles with alcoholism and the drunken car accident that disabled his only son.

With most of the scenes set in talk show 'living rooms,' DeLillo's primary concern is clearly the omnipresence of broadcast technology as an organizing force in our lives and minds. Indeed the collapse of traditional spatial and temporal modalities, and the fragmentation, discontinuity, and intensities presented by new modalities, are conveyed by the characters primarily through their use of language. The dialogue is full of truncated hesitations, random misfires, incomplete thoughts, and broken repetitions, as if the characters aren't really speaking to one another but through and past each other. There disjunctive conversations sound more like a set of uncoordinated soundtracks. Their words do not constitute even a monologue in that there are no real listeners, not even an inner self. Everyone speaks to, and answers to, an invisible ear, one that belongs to a phantom body of a televisual public.[2]

The fractured nature of DeLillo's language is not unlike that of Fredric Jameson's "schizophrenic" postmodern subject who, in the throes of an overwhelmingly intense or traumatic present, is unable to make coherent sense in any recognizable, conventional manner due to an utter breakdown of the basic temporality of narrative continuity.[3] But DeLillo's play has much to say on spatial issues, too, even if only implicitly. First, the space of our public conversations is now fully circumscribed by the camera or the media: life is footage waiting to be shot. Experience is not real unless it is recorded and validated through media representation. It is in this mediated virtual space that 'we talk to each other today. This is the way we tell each other things, in public, before listening millions, that we don't dare to say privately.'[4]

Secondly, spatial experience, like the broken temporality of language, is discontinuous and creepily disembodied. The words do not reach deep, they collage fleeting fragmentary impressions, and vision does not (cannot) distinguish between what is seen and the mediation of that scene. For example, Majeski describes the beginning of his journey to an interviewer: 'I'm watching the takeoff on live video. I'm on the plane, I'm in my seat. There's a monitor on the bulkhead. I look at the monitor and the plane is taking off. I look out the window and the plane is taking off. Then what. The plane is taking off outside the cabin and the plane is taking off inside the cabin. I look at the monitor, I look at the earth.'[5]

Thirdly, it is important to remember that the plot of the play is premised on an instance of locational misrecognition, on a character's temporarily losing his way in the world. How does this happen? Majeski leaves his house early in the morning to board a plane to Chicago. From there, he is to be picked up and driven to Valparaiso, Indiana, some forty miles away. But at the airport, the ticket counter attendant notices a discrepancy between his ticket (for Chicago) and his printed itinerary (for Miami). She tries to be helpful and finds him a seat on the Miami flight, about to take off; even though he was fully prepared for the Chicago flight, Majeski, not wanting to be discourteous to the attendant, makes a quick nondecision to head for Valparaiso, Florida, via Miami. Once in Miami, instead of boarding a chartered plane for this second Valparaiso, he somehow ends up on an international flight to Santiago, headed for Valparaiso, Chile. Details remain vague.

Majeski recalls the experience on a television talk show:

Yes. It was strange. The aircraft seemed too big, too wide-bodied for an intrastate flight. ... And I said nothing. I was intimidated by the systems. The enormous sense of power all around me. Heaving and breathing. How could I impose myself against this force? The electrical systems. The revving engines. ... The sense of life support. The oxygen in the oxygen masks. ... I felt submissive. I had to submit to the systems. They were all-powerful and all-knowing. If I was sitting in this assigned seat. Think about it. If the computers and metal detectors and uniformed personnel and bomb-sniffing dogs had allowed me to reach this assigned seat and given me this airline blanket that I could not rip out of its plastic shroud, then I must belong here. That's how I was thinking at the time.[6]

Majeski ends up in Chile not out of absentmindedness but because he recognizes a hitherto unknown logic of belonging, a sense of belonging that is not bound to any specific location but to a system of movement. Majeski does not resist the ways in which bodies are channeled through the sky along the prescribed trajectories of commercial air travel. He believes in its intimidating logic, has faith in its procedures, respects its timetables. He attributes almost mystical powers to the system. He might have ended up in the wrong city, but, in a sense, he was in the right place all along. So that when he reaches Santiago, fully aware of his mistake, it no longer matters how far he has strayed. He is calm. Instead of turning back, he is convinced to *complete* his mistake, to go all the way to Chile's Valparaiso. 'For the beauty and balance. The formal resolution.'[7] (Indeed, had Michael Majeski been an artist and his trip an art project, I would have been moved to think it a brilliant critique of site specificity.)

Often we are comforted by the thought that a place is ours, that we belong to it, even come from it, and therefore are tied to it in some fundamental way. Such places ('right' places?) are thought to reaffirm our sense of self, reflecting back to us an unthreatening picture of a grounded identity. This kind of continuous relationship between a place and a person is what many critics declare to be lost, and needed, in contemporary society. In contrast, the 'wrong' place is generally thought of as a place where one feels one does not belong – unfamiliar, disorienting, destabilizing, even threatening. This kind of stressful relationship to a place is, in turn, thought to be detrimental to a subject's capacity to constitute a coherent sense of self and the world.

Thanks to the perfection and formal beauty of Majeski's mistake, we can think about the 'wrong' place in altogether new ways. Rather than his 'losing himself' because he ends up in the wrong place, quite the opposite seems to happen in *Valparaiso*. Finding himself in an airplane headed for the wrong city, Majeski begins to recognise himself, or more precisely the conditions of his own estrangement, and is set on a journey to account for his identity. In the telling and retelling of the tale, his rather tragic and fractured sense of self is revealed not only to us, the audience, but to the character himself. It is the wrongness rather than rightness of place that brings Majeski into focus. As the play progresses, it become less and less clear whether Majeski was trapped in a journey headed for the wrong place or the trip was in fact an attempt to *escape from* a wrong place – his home, his job, his marriage, his family, his life, himself. An encounter with a 'wrong' place is likely to expose the instability of the 'right' place, and by extension the instability of the self. The price of such awakening is steep, however, as the concluding scenes of the play reveal. Suffice it to say that Majeski's psychological unmooring as a result of his trip both liberates and shatters him.

Notes

1. Don DeLillo, *Valparaiso* (New York: Scribner, 1999).
2. Here is a sample of such 'communication' in which Majeski is being interviewed by telephone: 'Yes. This is Michael Majeski. Hello, ABC Australia. Yes. I understand we are speaking live. What time is it there? No. What time is it there? Yes. I'm learning Spanish on tape. Yes. Some stranger had crept inside, like surreptitiously, to eat my airline food. No. The moment does not whisper the usual things. No. She brushes her teeth with baking soda. Yes. When I saw the towering mountains capped with snow. That's when I realized. Yes. That's when I realized. No. It was hugely and vastly comic. He had an unnamed rare disease. Pick up the white courtesy phone, please. Yes. But first I'm at the breakfast table staring at my eggs. No. What day is it there? No. What day is it there? Yes. When I saw the lowering mountains capped with snow. That's when I realized there was something terribly, terribly, wrong. No. She jerked me off in a taxi once. Yes. I was treated wonderfully, wonderfully well. They called me Miguel' (DeLillo, *Valparaiso*, 34).
3. See Jameson, *Postmodernism, or, the Cultural Logic of Late Capitalism* (Durham, NC: Duke University Press, 1991), 26–27.
4. Copy from the dust jacket of *Valparaiso*.
5. DeLillo, *Valparaiso*, 32.
6. Ibid., 86–87.
7. Ibid., 88.

4.12   Performing the City: Krzysztof Wodiczko
Nick Kaye

In contrast to the 'White Cube' gallery's signification of *emptiness*, the urban landscape offers a profusion and complexity of signs and spaces where the 'condition of reception' Crimp first identifies with site-specificity might be countered by an *excess* of information. Yet, although the city offers a text which is evidently very different to that into which the minimalist object intervenes, approaches to the city as site may still operate in the disjunctions between spaces, arising where the distinctions between spaces in which a work might establish its parameters are called into question.

Through his large-scale public projections, the émigré Polish artist Krzysztof Wodiczko works to expose the ideological complexities which underlie everyday readings and experiences of the city. Assuming that the built environment functions as a signifying system whose meanings can be destabilised, Wodiczko projects appropriated media-images of the body which, he suggests, are 'already carved into the memory of the viewers' (Wodiczko and Ferguson 1992: 48), on to specific buildings in order to reveal the languages of power and authority operating within the cityscape. Projecting images which might 'pervert or act as a parasite' (Wodiczko and Ferguson 1992: 62) on the buildings they illuminate, Wodiczko's interventions work to challenge and displace the architectural, ideological and visual languages he works through and on. In this sense, Wodiczko's strategy is overtly deconstructive and aligned with the 'post-modern' tactics of picture-theory artists such as Sherry Levine, Cindy Sherman, Barbara Kruger, Louise Lawler and Jenny Holzer. Yet where these artists' work exposes the instability of the pictorial and linguistic systems in which they are constituted, Wodiczko's points of departure are analyses of architecture and space as loci of power and authority. In *The Production of Space* Henri Lefebvre outlines an understanding of the function of the city's monuments which seems to underpin Wodiczko's position, stating that:

> Monumentality ... always embodies and imposes a clearly intelligible message. It says what it wishes to say – yet it hides a good deal more: being political, military, and ultimately fascist in character, monumental buildings mask the will to power and the arbitrariness of power beneath signs and surfaces which claim to express collective will and collective thought.
>
> (Lefebvre 1991: 143)

It is precisely against this masking function that Wodiczko's practice is directed. Inscribing on to the monument that which it hides or silences, Wodiczko unveils the complexity of its architectural, ideological or political subtexts, complicating a reading of the city's signs. His projections, he suggests, serve to expose 'meaningful silences which must be read. My projections are attempts to carve those silences into the monuments and spaces which propagate civic and dramatic fictions within the social sphere' (Wodiczko and Ferguson 1992: 51–2).

For Ewa Lajer-Burcharth, writing of Wodiczko's 'brilliantly illumi-
nated projection of a human hand' on to the AT&T building, New York,
in November 1984, in advance of Ronald Reagan's second inaugural
speech, the superimposition of this 'common and recognizable gesture of
the American political ritual: the pledge of allegiance' on to an overt symbol of corporate power 'suggested that these disparate elements are part
of the same body, signs in the same political spectacle' (Lajer-Burcharth
1987: 147). In graphically exposing this building's assertion of presence and
power by projecting upon it 'images in which the media present people like
buildings' (Wodiczko and Ferguson 1992: 51), Wodiczko produces a disjunctive relationship between the anthropomorphism of the built monument
and the monumental function of this iconic image. Thus, Lajer-Burcharth
argues, while asserting 'architecture's involvement in the maintenance of a
certain order' (Lajer-Burcharth 1987: 147), the AT&T projection has the
effect of 'introducing a foreign element into the original structure', as a consequence of which

> the spectator was left uncertain as to the naturalness of this new 'body.' The
> effect of interruption and ambiguity extended to the homogenous, bureaucratic
> cityscape of downtown Manhattan, where the fissured AT&T building suddenly
> struck a dissonant note [disturbing] that visual unity on which the function of the
> city as spectacle depends.
>
> (Lajer-Burcharth 1987: 148)

Such uncertainty is fundamental to the character of Wodiczko's procedures. Reproduced in such a way that they 'will have certain structural
qualities of the monument in order to make an organic counter-connection'
(Wodiczko and Ferguson 1992: 50), Wodiczko's projections work to revive
the very monuments they seek to disturb. Paradoxically, Wodiczko emphasises, by illuminating the monument, 'no matter what I project, no matter how critical I want to be, I bring it to its former glory, its presence'
(Wodiczko and Ferguson 1992: 62). Indeed, these projections not only rely
on a recuperation of the monuments they critique, but valorise the 'monumental function' of the media images through which this recuperation is
effected. Commenting on his projection of the caterpillar tracks and engine
of a tank, immediately below the image of a pair of hands caught in a gesture of hiding or masking, on to the plinth of the Duke of York Column,
near Admiralty Arch in central London in 1985, Wodiczko stressed that
his projections 'are not critical images, as you can see, they just belong
to a different repertoire of iconography', where, in the event of seeing
one 'myth' through another 'there is the possibility of challenging both'
(Wodiczko 1986).

Indeed, in grafting these appropriated 'media-images' of the body on to the 'official body' of the architectural façade (Wodiczko and Ferguson 1992: 51), Wodiczko's projections challenge the distinction between the 'built monument' and the 'projected image' by resolving the cityscape into a play of representations. It is in this context that Rosalyn Deutsche proposes, in her essay 'Architecture of the Evicted', that the concept of 'projection' in Wodiczko's work is best understood in terms of 'the procedural dimension of language', concluding that in 'calling attention to and manipulating architecture's language', Wodiczko's interventions reveal themselves to be 'projections on to projections' (Deutsche 1996: 31). Wodiczko has similarly invited a reading of his practice in terms of the intervention of one semiotic system into another, observing that 'photography, architecture, planning, advertising, painting, sculpture, film and television rely on existing codes. So, for me, there isn't a big difference in the end between the monument and the projected image' (Wodiczko and Ferguson 1992: 50).

This conflation of the functioning of art, architecture and these projected images also suggests that, in rendering the built environment as projections, Wodiczko's practices themselves become *part of* the city. Rather than establish a vantage point from which the city's 'text' might be read, or constituting a work explicitly 'other' to the cityscape, Wodiczko's ephemeral inscriptions produce 'a counter-image or counter-monument' (Wodiczko and Ferguson 1992: 50) which participates in the cityscape. Wodiczko states flatly that: 'In order to understand a public projection it must be recorded and announced as any significant urban event is. Events that project themselves on the city, even if they take place outside of it, are part of the experience of the city' (Wodiczko 1992: 196).

In being recorded and announced as an urban event, the projections function not only *in* the built environment, but are absorbed back into the media to become yet another repertoire of iconography in which the city's meanings are produced. Indeed, it is in this context that Wodiczko's work most obviously asserts the continuities between the eighteenth-century monument, the International Style corporate skyscraper and appropriated media-images, as these projections reveal, participate in, and become subject to, the signifying systems in which the city is continually being reproduced and so defined.

Such a participation in the cityscape, however, does not mean that Wodiczko's practices are simply absorbed back into the monumental function of the architecture and images they inhabit. In effecting a 'mobilisation of monuments' (Wodiczko 1996: 55), inherited and contemporary, one against the other, Wodiczko explicitly works in *excess* of the monumental function of the images he deploys and addresses. Engaging in strategies which Ewa Lajer-Burcharth characterises as 'visual disarticulation' (Lajer-Burcharth 1987: 148) where the languages he appropriates turn back against themselves, Wodiczko understands his projections to effect 'a disruption of a routine and passive perception of the ideological theatre of the built environment as well as a disruption of our imaginary place in it' (Wodiczko 1996: 55). Indeed, as Wodiczko implies, although effected through semiotic systems, these interventions are not limited in a simple way to a disruption of *reading*. In *The Production of Space*, and posing the question, 'Does it make sense to speak of a "reading" of space?', Lefebvre asserts that while both 'natural and urban spaces are, if anything, "over-inscribed" ... what one encounters here are directions – multifarious and overlapping instructions' (Lefebvre 1991: 142). He goes on to state, more categorically, that:

> Space lays down the law because it implies a certain order – and hence also a certain disorder ... Space commands bodies, prescribing or proscribing gestures, routes and distances to be covered ... The 'reading' of space is thus merely a secondary and practically irrelevant upshot, a rather superfluous reward to the individual for blind, spontaneous and *lived* obedience.
>
> (Lefebvre 1991: 143)

Indeed, as de Certeau tell us, the city does not function only as a text, even as it operates as a signifying system. Like de Certeau's street plan, architecture, in its various operations, constitutes a 'place' realised in the multiple and diverse practices of its users. It follows that Wodiczko's interventions must be located not simply in terms of *reading*, but in this very diversity of spatial practices: according to the 'pedestrian', the 'walker', in relation to this 'lived obedience'. It is here, too, that the significance of these projections' participation in the city becomes clearer.

In calling into question architecture's syntax, these counter-monuments not only complicate a reading of the city's signs, but create their own place, realised in a certain momentary disordering and disruption of the monument's authority. In this context, these projections' 'visual disarticulation', their disruption of architecture's *place*, is realised in spatial practices which subvert the monument's capacity to order, to 'command bodies'. Reflecting on the deconstructive effect of these superimpositions, Wodiczko emphasises that: 'My art must be understood, then, as a form of aesthetic politics; of making space within the space of political art (polis) ... my art, as politics, may then de-politicize this totally political art – this monument' (Wodiczko and Ferguson: 1992: 63–4).

Furthermore, in Wodiczko's equation between the body and the built environment, this disordering or disruption of the monument's place has a further and immediate effect for the user. Arguing, with reference to Michel Foucault, that 'our position in society is structured through bodily experience with architecture' (Wodiczko 1992: 199), Wodiczko's counter-monument works to reveal and so confront the reader with the body as the *hidden text* of the city's construction. In approaching a building, he emphasises that:

> I complete the body (the architectural form) after I learn what that body can do, what the ability of the body to speak is. This is a kind of phenomenological investigation ... I need to assign speech to each part of a particular building so that it will be able to speak in my terms, to speak in a more specific way than it already does.
>
> (Wodiczko 1992: 198)

In enacting the body as the site of the city's construction, Wodiczko assumes and addresses an intimate connection between the city's signs of the body and the construction of bodily experience. Thus, in animating this *textual* address to architecture's articulation of the effect upon the subject, these projections attempt to provoke a *bodily* confrontation with architecture. Through these large image projections, Wodiczko suggests: 'You can really match part of the body with part of the building, something that is hard to imagine without seeing it ... It's possible to see projected images as though they were projected from inside the body out, onto the building' (Wodiczko 1992: 202).

In this moment, Wodiczko's projections *work over* the disjunction between the city as text and as lived experience, and so the disjunction between the reading of 'ideal ... mental (mathematico-logical) categories' of space and the experience of 'real space ... the space of social practice' (Lefebvre 1991: 14). In doing so, Wodiczko calls into question the limits of his own artwork, the city as site, and the viewer's bodily confrontation with the building in order to reveal their construction in each other. It is here, too, that these counter-monuments' *disordering* of architecture's place addresses the individual's experience of the city and, through this, the construction of the individual in its spaces. Wodiczko emphasises that:

> My work attempts to enter and trespass this field of vision; the position of the individual as subject being constructed, or produced through the urban space in relation to others and in relation to monuments. I try to disrupt this continuous process of reproducing the individual in space.
>
> (Wodiczko and Ferguson 1992: 64)

Rather than effect a series of deconstructive moves upon the city's semiotic systems, Wodiczko's work addresses the city's architecture as a place which the individual realises in spatial practices, and through which she herself is realised. Treating architecture as this practiced place, Wodiczko's counter-monuments disrupt its 'orderly' performance, effecting a 'de-regulation' of the spatial practices in which the city's monuments are realised. Confronted, in this way, with architecture's displacement, Wodiczko notes:

> People speak with each other in front of this dialogue. People remember what they have seen, and what they have discussed, and with whom they discussed it ... When it is all remembered in this way, the Projection will stay, and the projected image will be seen as missing.
>
> (Wodiczko 1996: 56)

Finally, Wodiczko's work comes to define 'its' place in these dislocations, allowing its own spaces to remain elusive, realised in events and practices which *counter* the monument's authority and control rather than establish any separate identity. In this sense, Wodiczko's projections obtain a specificity to site by producing a kind of negative space, or lacuna, where the 'pedestrian' becomes aware of her own performance *in* and *of* the city.

Where Wodiczko's projections, in coming to the performance of 'real' space through the viewer's reading of the city's text, might seem antithetical to Morris' and Pistoletto's response to the 'deprived space' (Tschumi 1994: 42) of the 'White Cube' gallery, in fact both these strategies approach 'site' by *working over* the disjunction between the reading of space and the experience of space. In blurring the distinctions between the virtual space of a work and the real spaces in which the viewer acts, these strategies expose the performance of the places into which they intervene. Yet it is in contemporary architectural theory and practice, acting under the influence of both post-minimal explorations of the phenomenology of space and contemporary theories of the text, that this disjunction between 'spaces' is articulated most clearly.

References

Deutsche, R. (1996) *Evictions: Art and Spatial Politics*, Cambridge, MA: MIT Press.

Lajer-Burcharth, E. (1987) 'Urban Disturbances', *Art in America*, 75(11): 146–53, 197.

Lefebvre, H. (1991) *The Production of Space*, Oxford: Blackwell.

Tschumi, B. (1994) *Architecture and Disjunction*, London: MIT Press.

Wodiczko, K. (1986) 'Krzysztof Wodiczko', *Audio Arts Magazine*, side 1 (audio cassette).

Wodiczko, K. (1992) *Krzysztof Wodiczko: Instruments, Projeccions, Vehicles*, Barcelona: Fundacio Antoni Tapies.

Wodiczko, K. (1996) 'Projections', in Saskia Bos (ed.), *Krzysztof Wodiczko: De Appel Amsterdam 1996*, Amsterdam: De Appel Foundatin, 54–7.

Wodiczko, K. and Ferguson, B. W. (1992) 'A Conversation with Krzysztof Wodiczko', in Krzysztof *Wodiczko, Krzysztof Wodiczko: Instruments, Projeccions, Vehicles*, Barcelona: Fundacio Antoni Tapies, 47–66.

Part 5
Visioning/Flows

Text sources

5.1 Arjun Appadurai (2001) 'The Right to Participate in the Work of the Imagination' (interview with Arjen Mulder), *TransUrbanism*, ed. J. Brouwer, A. Mulder and L. Mertz, Amsterdam: V2_Publishing/NAI Publishers: 32–46.

5.2 Nicholas Fyfe (2004) 'Zero Tolerance, Maximum Surveillance? Deviance, Difference and Crime Control in the Late Modern City', *The Emancipatory City? Paradoxes and Possibilities*, ed. L. Lees, London: Sage Publications: 40–56.

5.3 Keith Piper (2004) 'A Nigger in Cyberspace', *Changing States: Contemporary Arts and Ideas in an Era of Globalisation*, ed. G. Tawadros, London: inIVA: 38–43.

5.4 James Harkin (2005) 'Cyborg City' (interview with William J. Mitchell), *Guardian*, 26 November: 31.

5.5 Carl Lavery (2005) '25 Instructions for Performance in Cities', *Studies in Theatre and Performance*, 25(3): 234–6 (extract).

Introduction

> Urbanity is transforming into an atmospheric condition which is no longer necessarily bound to place or space. ... It can certainly no longer be planned, for it occurs only if we perform it.
>
> Andreas Ruby, in *TransUrbanism*

New soft cities

The final part of this book does not have quite the same conceptual cohesion perhaps as previous ones. This is because it is looking to the future of the city – or futures of cities – and so its inclination is towards opening out a range of key areas of consideration – *visions* or projections – that may not necessarily be linked in an immediate sense. Having said that, I would refer the reader simultaneously to the implication of *flows* in Part 5's title, which suggests the intermingling or 'accidental inter-relatedness' of disparate phenomena within urban dimensions. As such, these various takes on the future, which are actually more like prescient readings of the present, *do* potentially share a certain collective perception, namely of the city's tendency to evolve away from a settled or 'sedimented' constitution – dependent on a notion of space and place (as Ruby observes at the top of the page; in Brouwer et al. 2002: 28) – and towards trans-urban networks involving perpetual *movement*. These take into account both migrations or displacements of peoples and advances in digital communications technologies on a global scale. The question, then, of where you are situated – of what your global coordinates happen to be – has acquired a paradoxical fluidity or multiplicity of intersecting possibilities. In other words, to be located somewhere is no longer necessarily to be in one place but rather 'here, there and elsewhere'. Indeed, one of the exercises I have conducted with my students is to ask them to list as many places as possible in which they can be said to *exist*, and this can range from the street in which they live, to their Facebook site, to being captured unwittingly on CCTV, minding their own business in some shopping mall (the possibilities are actually endless).

In a more global sense, as Arjen Mulder proposes in the introduction to *TransUrbanism*:

> A city produces a series of 'localities'. It is no longer a single public domain but a concatenation of diaspora-related public domains in which numerous 'cultures' or 'contexts' are settled but linked via the media to similar [ones] elsewhere. 'India' is located not only in India but also in the Gulf States, in London, in

the Caribbean and in your street. 'America' is to be found all over the world, although less and less often in the United States.

(In Brouwer et al. 2002: 9)

The Internet and electronic media generally have not just facilitated global communication networks but have, of course, become sites themselves. So, there is a vast range of constituencies that have gathered for any number of reasons: conglomerations of people reminiscent of urban concentrations and, therefore, worthy of consideration here as virtual or cyber cities. At the same time actual cities have been recreated virtually, again for a range of reasons, whether that be to replicate or enhance the tourist experience, as backdrop for game-playing scenarios, or for archaeo-historical research purposes.

Paul Virilio is nothing if not one of the foremost visionaries of our time, who – as is the fate of visionaries – has met with criticisms of exaggeration, utopianism, pessimism or simply incomprehension in the period of time in which it has taken the rest of us to catch up with him. 'The Overexposed City', first published in 1984, goes some way to vindicating the validity of his claims; many of the points raised appear to have come to pass or are still central to contemporary debates on the future of urbanism. Virilio's concern above all is with *speed distance*, which 'obliterates the notion of physical dimension' (1991: 18). As we have seen the likes of Augé and Müller observe, advances in telecommunications and mobility mean that space has shrunk rapidly. For Virilio 'distinctions of *here* and *there* no longer mean anything' (ibid.: 13), having been replaced by a certain 'overexposure in which the difference between "near" and "far" simply ceases to exist. ... The new technological time has no relation to any calendar of events nor to any collective memory. It is pure computer time, and as such helps construct a permanent present' (ibid.: 13 and 15). As such the city is now becoming part of an electronic topology in which entry to it is marked not by 'a gate nor [by] an *arc de triomphe* but rather [by] an electronic audience system. ... Where once the *polis* inaugurated a political theatre, with its *agora* and its *forum*, now there is only a cathode-ray system where the shadows and spectres of a community dance amid their processes of disappearance' (ibid.: 11 and 19).

Intersecting bodies

If the screen represents the new city square for Virilio, implying an increasing dematerialisation of corporeality, the anthropologist Arjun Appadurai – speaking at a much later point in time – attempts to retain the sense of a 'participating body' in his interview with Arjen Mulder. The abstraction of the 'electronic ether', of global cyberspace, is precisely the factor that calls for the need to ensure that a sense of 'hereness' remains, without thereby tying people to place: 'We don't necessarily need what used to be called face-to-face communities, but we need communities whose presence we can experience in a material, embodied, sensory manner. That's the key, rather than the idea that people need roots' (*PCC*, p. 251). As opposed to being seen as a single locality, cities should be recognised as a 'complex of localities', a circulatory nervous system of trans-local flows in which conventional lines of demarcation relating, for example, to nationhood or ethnicity dissolve or become porous. With the global growth of the city it can both absorb cultural diversity as a 'local site' and reach out across the world. Thus, as Mulder has already hinted, London exists in New York or Mumbai as much as it does in London, England. Above all it is 'in the work of the imagination ... that the cultural dimension now really lives. ... I inhabit a terrain of possibilities, constructed through the work of the imagination, in some social context which I inhabit, which allows me to infuse my life with meaning, with value, with belief' (*PCC*, p. 258). At the same time Appadurai is concerned to question whether such a perception of trans-urban fluidity, of inhabiting several 'places' simultaneously, is in fact a privilege: the urban poor of Mumbai, for instance, live lives of enforced mobility – 'floating material' – so 'for them something like secure tenure, even ten feet of land, is absolutely central ... a human claim to stability' (*PCC*, p. 253). For Appadurai, then, reconciling these two experiences is the principal challenge to imagining a global future for cities.

As already mentioned in the introduction to the Playing/Place part of this book, the surveillance and policing of urban space – implying a closing down of public freedoms – is an increasing phenomenon on a global scale but, above all, in the UK (as we speak). The geographer Nicholas Fyfe's piece engages with the twin strategies of zero tolerance and CCTV monitoring in urban centres. Intriguingly he does not opt for the 'easy' tactic of outright condemnation of such potential 'affronts' to individual rights by the hand of officialdom. Steering the possibility of 'reclaiming the streets' away from its association with the eponymous (dis)organisation, Fyfe wonders to what extent these strategies of control might serve a purpose that is in fact liberating and protective. Adopting a critical view that is less polarised between utopian or dystopian positions represents a start to a more nuanced and constructive negotiation of the politics of fear in cities. Fyfe's vision for the future takes him back in fact to the New York City of Jane Jacobs – 'probably the city's most infamous flâneur' (*PCC*, p. 274) – and a system of implicit neighbourhood cohesion premised on naturalising diversity and 'disorder': self-governing voluntary networks and associations in which context-specific values are taken into account and the intersection with the 'difference of strangers' comes to be seen not as a threat but as a productive imperative of living in a city.

As a form of creative counterpoint to the social scientific concerns of street surveillance and policing, Kate Adams's online article on Blast Theory's *Uncle Roy All Around You* – not included here but worth drawing attention to – investigates the interface of virtual and real city spaces. Participants in this urban performance game are placed in positions where they must make concrete decisions about the degree to which they are prepared to help, trust or make long-term commitments to complete strangers. Following instructions on a hand-held computer or mobile phone issued by online players, the participant sets out to look for Uncle Roy on the streets of the city. As well as 'exploring what we experience as trust in a world where community is dispersed, participation, here, is also about a confrontation with one's own behaviour and assumptions' (Adams 2006: n.p.). Effectively Blast Theory create a space within which participants are implicitly led to interrogate at a profound level their own part in creating the kind of city in which they wish to live:

> Blast Theory relinquish much of their control of how interactions develop and how the performance space – the city – is navigated. It is true that the basic structure of the narrative and the majority of clues are provided by Blast Theory, but where the participants go and what they see is under their own control. Their interaction with strangers in the street or over the net as they move through the city and how they perceive those interactions again is not determined. ... Most importantly, it is the participant who chooses how far the repercussions of the piece extend into their life afterwards.
>
> (Ibid.)

The artist Keith Piper's piece is similarly concerned with the intersection of the 'physical and social landscape of the city [and] the parallel landscape of cyberspace' (*PCC*, p. 278). Returning us also to forms of surveillance and policing, he is concerned above all to show how the 'new virtuality' replicates not only the 'orderly city' but also (or therefore) 'the social and economic interests of the enfranchised white status quo' (*PCC*, p. 279). Piper envisions such marginalisation as providing the tactical impetus with which to hack out a 'riot zone', as he puts it, which, ironically, brings about the 'digital equivalent of the disorderly black of urban chaos and transgressive behaviour', ensuring that 'treasured and privileged resources are redistributed and exclusive places are democratised' (*PCC*, p. 282).

Like Virilio, William J. Mitchell has achieved great success detecting and predicting the implications of global trends in electronic communications technology before anyone else. In *City of Bits* (1995) he drew attention to a new type of 'soft city' being created by the interlinked virtual spaces of the Internet, while in *e-topia* (2000) he extended his analysis to take into account the way the digital revolution will impact on how the urban infrastructure itself operates, proposing strategies for the creation of sustainable cities in an electronically networked world. Thus, where Piper sees cyberspace imitating urban forms, Mitchell witnesses the city changing its *modus operandi* as a consequence of cyberspace. Using an example that recalls Adams's adventures in search of Uncle Roy, he points – in this short newspaper profile based on a joint promenade with a journalist through a segment of central London – to the existence of 'a whole ragbag of new gadgets and wireless technologies hold[ing] up the promise of navigating our way through cities in exciting new ways' (*PCC*, p. 284). For Mitchell the 'real impact of all this ... is often better understood by culture and art'. And, in a tacit endorsement of Blast Theory's approach, what is needed in his view is a rewriting of *Ulysses* for the digital era in order to reproduce the way Joyce 'opens our eyes to ... the hidden possibilities of Dublin', a narrative that is 'sustained by random encounters' and characters 'forever jumping on tram cars, for example' (*PCC*, p. 284).

If Mitchell asks us to 'rewrite *Ulysses*' in our interactions with and understanding of the contemporary city, Carl Lavery's 'Instructions for Performances in Cities' offers 25 ways of doing just that. The module I teach at Warwick works its way through a swathe of theories, examples and practical exercises, its aim being to position students so that they may be inspired to make a piece of performance responding to and interrogating what living in the contemporary city means. An impressive range of innovative work has resulted in the short time the module has existed, including audio walking tours, graffiti trails, performances on (and between) buses and Vespas, or on the escalators of shopping malls. Lavery's 'instructions' leave the reader in a similar position, then, with a list that offers but the seeds of infinite possibilities.

5.1   The Right to Participate in the Work of the Imagination (interview with Arjen Mulder)
Arjun Appadurai

Arjen Mulder: In *Modernity at Large* you define a 'locality' not as a spatial structure but as a structure of feeling, and you mention a 'general technology for the production of locality.' How can this structure of feeling, this locality, be produced in a globalized world?

Arjun Appadurai: The impetus behind what I call the production of locality was, in the first place, to provide a counterpoint to the idea that was still very prevalent in anthropology in the early 1990s: that the local was somehow an inert canvas upon which global or other forces produced changes. This notion leads to all the contrasts between the local and the global that underlie a great many confusions and distortions in the way we analyze globalization. I wanted to unsettle the idea of the local as somehow given, and draw attention to the fact that any form of local social life requires agency, purpose, vision, design. The local is as much a process and a project as anything else.

The second point was to somewhat despatialize the local, and to get some initial distance from the idea of scale and scalar understandings of locality and globality. It's six years since the book appeared, and now that I've thought more about all these issues, I still think the issue of multiple scales, as well as the related issue of scales and forms – social forms, spatial forms – is by no means unimportant, but we shouldn't start with any mechanical idea of scales, or reduce the problem of the local and the global to a scalar problem. I talk about the local as a structure of feeling – a phrase I borrow from Raymond Williams – to try to slightly dematerialize it.

The final point in this approach to locality connects up with the emphasis in *Modernity at Large*, and in my other work after that, on the idea of the imagination as a social practice. This is the point on which I like to focus here. In the book I describe the imagination as something more than a kind of individual faculty, and something other than a mechanism for escaping the real. It's actually a collective tool for the transformation of the real, for the creation of multiple horizons of possibility. The production of locality is as much a work of the imagination as a work of material social construction.

Of course locality has a spatial dimension, a scalar dimension, a material dimension and a kind of embodied dimension, but I want to infuse them with the idea that in the world in which we live the imagination actually can reach into multiple scales and spaces and forms and possibilities. These then can become part of the toolkit through which the structure of feeling can be produced locally. Locality, in the end, may still have something to do with scale and place, and with the body (and without that it loses all its meaning) – but with the difference that the horizons of globality, through media and the work of the imagination and migration, can become part of the material through which specific groups of actors can envision, project, design and produce whatever kind of local feeling they wish to produce. I'm talking here, of course, about the more liberatory sense of the production of locality. There are other productions of locality which are much more confined and confining, but here I'm trying to emphasize the global as a kind of expansion of the horizon of the local.

AM: This brings us to the question of why we as human beings need a locality to live in. The postmodernist philosophers were always talking about being nomads and floating around through the world.

AA: Sure. But the nature of the human concern with intimacy, with friendship, with attachment, with predictability, with routine, and even with what we may call ordinary life, or everyday life, is such that it simply cannot work with entirely abstract, or virtual, or mediated, or imagined communities, to use the Anderson phrase. We seem to need things to which we have access of an embodied type. We don't necessarily need what used to be called face-to-face communities, but we need communities whose presence we can experience in a material, embodied, sensory manner. That's the key, rather than the idea that people need roots, which I think is a more dangerous and ambiguous and also inaccurate idea about what the needs here are.

Insofar as we're not merely actors and subjects, but also embodied or bodily subjects, we feel the need for some kind of sense of social productivity and collectivity whose imagined qualities echo with some sensory qualities. The social group can be very large, but it's one thing to be in a very large city of which you may know very little directly, and another to say that you're a citizen of the world, or a netizen – terms which clearly have some partial metaphoric meanings to them, but don't resolve the human need for linking intimacy with the everyday. That's why we need some spatialized local, which cannot in the end be tossed away.

AM: A fascinating aspect of your notion of locality is that cities are no longer one locality, but a complex of localities. This raises a difficult problem for urbanists: how to plan a city that's no longer homogeneous, but consists of all sorts of groups that want their own locality somehow produced or reproduced?

AA: We know two or three things are happening in this context. First of all, we know that by almost every measure that exist, the population of the world is moving into cities at an amazing rate. We also know that many of these cities are going to be megacities – there's not going to be hundreds of smaller cities, but a smaller number of very big cities. And thirdly, we know that these cities are going to be, on the whole, sites of dramatic inequalities. These three things, almost everybody agrees, are within the next thirty years non-negotiable probabilities. Of course we're not in an iron cage, and so there are possibilities to intervene, both in the number and the nature and the size of these cities. People involved in housing issues, in design issues, progressive architects and others are thinking very hard about how not to simply say, 'Well, this is going to happen, and what do we do?' and throw up their hands. But the force is there. The fact that as many as half the human population will be living in these huge cities is a reality that's clearly going to be among the two or three most important social facts of the first half of this century.

So the question of how to imagine cities as a site for the structure of feeling is a challenge, both conceptually and epistemologically and also practically in terms of urban planning and urban design and urban form. It would be a complete fantasy to think of a single design for cities like Bombay or Manila, of the sort that unfortunately still dominates a lot of urban planning. At the same time, activists, architects, planners, academics rightly don't want to open up a free market and say: 'Well, we'll design something, and then the next neighbor can do what they want.' We're caught between a top-down, state-like planning approach, and on the other hand a bottom-up, market, laissez-faire approach.

I think the beginning of an approach to this problem is not to reify the idea that cities are collections of subcultures or 'multicultures,' each of which needs it own forms and expressions and in a sense it own spaces. In such cases, we hope that those are safe and benign, as they actually turn out to be in some European cities, either by design or by accident. In Stockholm, for example, many people of non-Swedish origin are living in working-class suburbs solely devoted to non-Swedish migrants. But even when this approach works out very well and there's no conflict, my feeling is that this isn't the way to go, because it always carries the element of the ghetto in it, which isn't consistent with the pluralities, intersections, crossings, traffics that the modern world is capable of producing. In my view we should change our fundamental emphasis to the flows, rather than to the spaces and structures.

It's these traffics that make up the new, huge, complex cities, and the way to read these cities is something like the way I try and read the world as a globalized space. For cities that are expanding, like Mexico City, Bombay, Manila, Lagos (the list is long), as well as cities in the Northern Atlantic zone, which are growing at a very fast pace – thinking of them as 'global spaces' may not be a bad idea, in the sense that globalization is about flows, flows of mediated messages and actual flows of bodies. Even in terms of infrastructure, like electricity, sewage and so on, cities are all about movement, flow and transportation, rather than about settlement. This approach puts your attention not so much upon buildings or on the organization of particular neighborhoods, or on housing developments, or colonies, or on particular industrial parks, in other words: chunks of lived space. Instantly it puts you in touch with the circulatory system or the nervous system of the city as the object of planning and design.

This is difficult, however, because it requires an engagement which challenges not only the architectural imagination, but also the geographical imagination, the urban planner's imagination, and also the social scientist's imagination, because you have to get away from the distinction between what one might call 'sedimented space' and 'trafficked (or traversed) space.' Sedimented space is what all our specialties are about; even in social science, research is much easier once a population has precipitated or sedimented itself. But to look at the circulatory system through which forms are moving, through which bodies are moving and identities are moving and material, infrastructural stuff is moving, from electricity to cars to roads and postal services, etc., and then turn to more secure locational forms, is difficult.

Again, we shouldn't go too far with this circulatory, flow-based imagery, because especially if you take the point of view of the urban poor, and the poorest of the poor with whom I've been working for the last three years or so, I'm aware that for them something like secure tenure, even to ten feet of land, is absolutely central. So to speak of movement, flows, linkages, etc., may seem a bit remote to them. But if you speak with the poorest of the poor in a city like Bombay, they're extremely sensitive to the question of trains, the movement to jobs, to not being relocated to areas where they have to go ten miles to work. It's not that they're indifferent to movements of traffic, of bodies, of energies, of electricity, for they know about these things. But because they have been victims of unfree mobility, and have been pushed from place to place, they have a different investment in the places, sites and techniques of stability. They want a building, they want a flat, they want a room. They want full rights.

The biggest movement in urban housing today is the global campaign for what is called 'secure tenure.' It doesn't matter where you are, even if you're living under a lamppost, but you need the right to say, 'This is my place, I cannot just be kicked out.' We have rights for tenants, but the urban poor are basically seen as floating material, and they're asserting a human claim to stability. This comes back to your earlier question: even in a globalized world, we shouldn't ignore that people want points of reference. If you go to the urban world, it's very important to take the circulatory image, but negotiate it with the reality for the poorest of the poor: motion alone will not be the key, because motion for them has often been a nightmare. So how to combine these two things, I think, is the central challenge in the world we're creating.

AM: Let's move on to another notion in *Modernity at Large*, the concept of 'translocality.' There's this incredible example of translocality, the Indian call centers that exist in Bombay. The Indian employees there phone Americans in Texas or Alabama to ask when they're going to pay their bills and loans and so on. Their Indian names are changed into American names like John and Sally, and they even learn to speak with an American accent. There seem to be two sides to their job. First of all they earn a living, but secondly they learn that America is not the paradise that it's supposed to be, and that there are a lot of poor people there too.

AA: A similar example in Europe is Dublin, which is a great place for these call centers. I was told that the Irish accent was favored in Europe over the American accent. Somehow it has a certain charm. And this is related to the growth of Dublin and Ireland as an offshore service place in relation to the European Union. So we see it not just in India.

AM: Of course this is all possible because today the telephone is so cheap, and basically media are cheap. This is also an important reason why localities in the spatial sense are not that important anymore.

AA: In the Indian context people have used interesting words like 'cyber-proletariat' or 'cybercoolies.' The latter is for people who do not just this work: India has a lot of people who, for example, type and computerize the written notes of doctors in the United States. And they do similar work for insurance companies. In other words, work that would be too costly in the United States is sent to India, where people do it at a much lower price. This work is related to the world of electronic technology, but in a complicated way: one creates a kind of second or third class of cyberspecialists at the low end, as it were, not the value-adding end. India has been huge in this and similar spheres in the last five to eight years. Now other countries want to get a part of this too, and in places in Pakistan they're starting this kind of work.

It's interesting to see that for these countries this is also a way to get into some kind of membership in the global economy. If you're not in a place where you can play financial derivatives or get into high-level banking, what are you going to do? So this work is in a way a natural tendency: with relatively low investments you can take the thing you already have, which is an educated population, especially the English-speaking part of it, and find a kind of role. And it's double-edged, because on the one hand you're at the low end of a highly profitable world economy – hence the idea of a cyberproletariat – but on the other hand it may be putting you in a better life than you have already.

Now if we take the call centers with their demands for learning American accents, and think about the larger translocality question, there actually are similar examples, but less translocal, or translocal in a different way, like the growth of Domino's Pizza in Bombay. Here the young men and women are trained very carefully to take telephone orders, to make deliveries on a time schedule that's dictated by the Domino's worldwide system, and to perform a whole sort of retail social drama in exactly the way Domino's think is correct. They're not dealing with disembodied demands far away: the customers are nearby, they take the order, they get on a motorbike and deliver Domino's pizzas. But they're also players in a globalized kind of commercial etiquette, in which they have to learn how to wear a certain kind of hat, talk in a certain kind of way, ask for the order in a certain kind of way, etc.

The reason that I bring up this example is to say that people who get involved in what we might call out-of-body globalized performances are also keenly aware that these are just one thing among many things in their lives. It must always be remembered that when these cyberproletarians go home to a room with fifteen people in it at night, and take the train in Bombay, and buy some food on the way from their job, this virtual world is already quite far away. It must be remembered that these are partial identities, partial explorations. And for that reason I don't see them as so surreal as they might at first seem, because they're still part of a set of demands, constraints and requirements in social life, which place them in a more intimate scene of social reproduction.

At the same time, for the people doing these jobs I think it's quite a demanding and challenging exercise, because they're inhabiting multiple imaginary spaces. Especially for younger and poorer people, who are struggling for a place in the new economies and urban sociologies, it's not a single-focus enterprise. They don't spend the whole day thinking about how to seem more American; it's no different than learning how to do software, which in a place like India they don't even think of as alien, because it's simply what they do. Or to take a more distant example, it's no more strange than a fifteen-year-old in Holland or Germany who learns to play Bartok. You could say, 'How strange' – it's very abstract, very remote from everyday life – but we don't worry about it at all. If someone can learn to play Bartok or Webern when they're sixteen years old and at home, why can't they learn an American accent? After all, they have a lot of other knowledge about American identity, they see films, they read books. It's nothing bizarre.

This doesn't mean we have to say, 'This is great, this is the way of the future.' Because I have a position which I've been developing in India and in relation to India about the cyberproletariat, the software revolution, and in general about education. I think that a society like India needs to be very careful not to just become what I call the 'knowledge fodder' of the world, the fodder for the knowledge economy. But how do you do that so that every day you're not encountering a new fashion – today computers, tomorrow stock, the day after tomorrow insurance? How do you develop a global agenda for the regional and the local, instead of being pushed into the role of asking what the customer wants (and the customer is somewhere else)? So I think there's something to be changed in all this, but in the short run I don't think that these activities are as decontextualizing, alienating and artificial as they may at first seem.

Coming back to the translocality question in a broader way, what I wanted to stress in my book is that because of the degree of media penetration and saturation – which frequently also means media of many kinds and media from many places, particularly television, where it's available – people live, as it were, in layered places, which in themselves have a variety of levels of attachment, engagement and, if you like, reality. That goes back to my idea that in a world of migration and mass mediation, everybody is living in a world of image flows, such that it's not simply and straightforwardly possible to separate their everyday life from this other set of spaces that they engage with through the media, either as receivers, or as workers in call centers, or on interactive websites, etc. The work of the imagination allows people to inhabit either multiple localities or a kind of single and complex sense of locality, in which many different empirical spaces coexist. So one of these call center people is simultaneous living a little but in the United States and also living substantially in Bombay. But Bombay itself, because of films and so on, is not merely empirical Bombay.

In this sense you have a kind of creative, spatial form which isn't reducible to its empirical facts. Now those empirical facts – for example, that the trains in Bombay are incredibly crowded – must be faced at the end of the day. Even if you're inhabiting many localities, this one will always be present to you. But because I do believe in the work of the imagination, I believe your engagement with this empirical world can be somewhat different depending on what translocalities you inhabit mentally, in and through the imagination. So the train isn't the same for everyone, not only because there's a better part and a less good part of the train, but simply because the train is only one element of people's localized existence. Again I would say, remembering the urban poor, that the relationship of their experienced spaces to their imagined spaces is always at a disadvantage. And this must be changed. But the poor, too, negotiate a relationship between experienced spaces and imagined spaces. They're not only living in sheer experience while the rest of us live in the imagination, that's my sense of the political economy of these spaces.

AM: This brings us to the question of identity. How does an identity come into being in your view? Is it just a mixture of translocalities, or is it a more autonomous thing?

AA: I've come more and more to prefer the term 'identification' to the term 'identity.' Only because identity suggests something fairly formed, fairly fixed, fairly exclusive, fairly stable. In the classical sense of the word people have many identities, and there's a large portfolio: some are very recessive, others very active. We know this. But if you move to identification, you move to a kind of process, where people are engaging this menu of possibilities in the work of the imagination. In and through the work of the imagination, they are, as it were, trying out many possibilities – and in many cases they're forced to try out some possibilities. I'm very conscious right now of the brutal ethnic violence in Gujarat, where there's a continuing state-condoned and even state-sponsored pogrom which began in late February 2002 and is worse than anything since the partition of Pakistan in 1947. So I'm keenly aware that the identity that goes under the label 'Hindu' or 'Muslim' is not something most people can explore – they have no choice here.

What we see in Gujarat now, and in many parts of the world, especially since the 1990s, is a coercive politics of identification, in which ethnic plurality, secularism, and cultural hybridity are gradually placed under the pressure of ethnic nationalism, state insecurity and paranoia about migrants, in a way that produces coerced forms of identification. Identities which are the products of forced processes of identification are invariably fragile and mutually hostile.

AM: In *Modernity at Large* you describe the spreading of Indian culture around the globe, focusing on cricket, and you state that this culture is something which exists in a 'diasporic public sphere,' in 'delocalized transnations.' These spheres, then, have a 'cultural dimension,' distinguishing them from other such transnations. Would you define a city as a group of such transnations, as a crossroads of these diasporic public spheres? Or does a city have an identity of its own?

AA: As cities grow bigger and as the world grows more connected in a general, overall way, surely cities will contain more transnations. Also, as cities grow larger, people have begun to talk of them as 'city-regions' and even 'city-states,' because cities are becoming quasi-independent, with many of the features that we only think of as belonging to the nation-state. That is, they're great conglomerations of identity, of attachment, of space, and of governance. So in many ways cities have been floating out of national spaces and are becoming something of their own. Now the question is: What are they? Are they global? Are they national? Are they merely urban? Clearly, they're some of all of these. They are very complex junctions of these different spatialities, of these different zones and regimes of flow.

In them, something like transnations might exist in new and significant numbers. The point I would like to make, to relate to diasporic public spheres, is that we shouldn't only focus on transnations in a way that might fall back into thinking of them as separate formed nations, with their own traditions and so on. I want to keep my eye constantly on the interactivity of these transnations. And this brings us to the cultural dimensions. There are two different ideas of culture, which in the book I try to begin to separate. One is a dimensional idea, and the other is a substantive idea that culture is actually a set of traditions, substantive commitments, meanings, values. I want to see culture as dimension, which is first of all relational – that is, it only takes meaning from another culture, and not only by contrast, that's an old idea: I can be me only if you're you. But this isn't necessarily an us-against-them thing. There's always a conversation in which cultural difference emerges. Sometimes it becomes a bloody conversation, a violent conversation. But very often it's not. That, for me, is one aspect of the 'dimensional' sense of culture: it's structural and contrastive, in a Saussurean sense.

The other sense of the 'dimensional' has to do again with the imagination, in that culture is the dimension of social life and of collective identity in which the material conditions of actors, of subjects and agents, are constantly transformed by the work of the imagination. It's in the work of the imagination, I think, that the cultural dimension now really lives. Culture means not that you can simply say, 'I belong to this community.' I think it means, 'I inhabit a terrain of possibilities, constructed through the work of the imagination, in some social context which I inhabit, which allows me to infuse my life with meaning, with value, with belief.' These are well known features of the word 'culture,' but the twist here is that when I talk about the cultural dimensions of globalization, as in the title of the book, in the adjectival form, I somehow try to delink culture from place, and make it more an aspect of practice, of social life. Nevertheless, in the end, no idea of culture or even of the cultural dimension makes sense unless there is difference from something else. But in my approach, that difference is now very much ties up not just with static, spatialized communities but with flows and linkages. The differences are both constructed and reproduced through circulation, through traffic, through exchange and negotiations, rather then through simple exclusivity.

Now this is, again, the utopian side or the positive side of the term. We know that the dystopian side is precisely resisting this, and says: No, culture means something which is single, ethnic, exclusive and which is therefore violent, which requires other cultures to go. We know that this is one of the major trends in the modern world, to invent minorities through whom you can invent majorities, and through whom you can create communities through extreme violence. In a recent book by Philip Gourevitch on Rwanda, he has a great phrase: "Genocide, after all, is an exercise in community-building." A truly brutal aphorism, which precisely threatens any tendency moving in a utopian direction. Yes, when I talk about the practices of the imagination as a way in which meaning is infused into urban spaces, translocal spaces and so on, that's not just a one-way street to more flow, more mobility, more tolerance, more interaction, more peace if you like. It's frequently a road to the opposite.

Therefore I'm engaged constantly in a double task, which is widening the scope of the positive side, of the imagination as a source of horizons of possibility, while recognizing all the time that globalization produces the opposite of that also. This opposite is an excessive exposure of the racialized roots of nationalist thinking, which go back to Herder and others, and claim that culture is really about soil, space, folk – terms which are precisely, for me, the dark side. In Gourevitch's aphorism, that's what he is catching: that in some strange way, under certain circumstances, we can build communities by the extermination of other communities. How do we tackle these kinds of pathological forms of community building?

Going back to our original discussion of the word 'locality,' you could substitute 'locality' in his aphorism and say that genocide is after all a way of locality-building. Yes, but how do we find other methods of locality-building which are not only different but actually reduce the other tendency? This, to me, is the central challenge, both of global forms of governance and politics, and of governance and politics in megacities. How do you do it without opening the road to purification, cleansing and ethnocide, and instead open the road to something else?

In the end, this certainly has something to do with changing the gradual pauperization of the world's urban population and the world's population in general. Without that, all these potentials in the work of the imagination will remain sterile, or limited, or only for the very privileged, and in fact the spaces of the other kind of work of the imagination which Gourevitch is talking about will expand. So how to slow that down, or contest that, or give an alternative to it, may be the central challenge at both levels of properly global processes, flows and politics, and of urban politics, governance, planning, design, which have a powerful set of links, both of connectivity and of resemblance, to the global order. The city is where we have to do some trial and error. I don't have a formula for a solution, except for one thing. Let's, in seeking solutions, endorse the following principle: Even the poorest of the poor should have the capability, the privilege and the ability to participate in the work of the imagination. Can we create a politics that recognizes that? There is the question.

5.2 Zero Tolerance, Maximum Surveillance? Deviance, Difference and Crime Control in the Late Modern City
Nicholas Fyfe

Two journeys in New York City

Journey 1: In *The Conscience of the Eye*, the urban social theorist Richard Sennett guides us on a three mile walk from his apartment in Greenwich Village. The walk leads first through a 'drug preserve' just east of Washington Square, where addict-dealers in cocaine are never still, 'their arms jerky, they pace and pace; in their electric nervousness, they radiate more danger than the old stoned men' who used to occupy this area (1990: 124). Sennett then heads along Third Avenue to the edges of the Grammercy Park district ('the people who live here are buyers for department stores, women who began in New York as secretaries'); and then into the middle Twenties between Third and Lexington (where there are 'bars that cater to … leather fetishists, bars in run-down townhouses with no signs and blacked out windows' (1990: 129). In the upper Twenties along Lexington Avenue, Sennett observes the 'bags of spice [that] lie in ranks within the shops run by Indians and Pakistanis'; and then the 'last lap' of his walk passes through Murray Hill ('a quarter of the old elite in New York') and on to the east Forties between Lexington and First avenues from where one can see miles of burned out buildings and bricked up windows. 'This permissible belt of desolation in so rich a city', Sennett (1990: 131) concludes, 'is like a boast of civic indifference.'

Journey 2: The second journey is an account by William Bratton of arriving in New York City in 1990 as the new Chief of Police of the City's Transit Police Department:

I remember driving from LaGuardia Airport down the highway into Manhattan. Graffiti, burned out cars and trash seemed to be everywhere. It looked like something out of a futuristic movie. Then as you entered Manhattan, you met the unofficial greeter for the City of New York, the Squeegee pest. Welcome to New York City. This guy had a dirty rag or squeegee and would wash your window with some dirty liquid and ask for or demand money. Proceeding down Fifth Avenue … unlicensed street peddlers and beggars were everywhere. Then down into the subway where every day 200,000 fare evaders jumped over turnstiles while shakedown artists vandalised turnstiles and demanded that paying passengers handed over their tokens to them. Beggars were on every train. Every platform seemed to have a cardboard city where the homeless had taken up residence. This was a city that had stopped caring about itself.

(Bratton, 1997: 33–4)

Despite their contrasting backgrounds, Sennett and Bratton's accounts of difference and deviance in 1990s New York City contain some intriguing similarities. Both are deeply troubled by the sense of indifference that characterizes the city. Sennett's concerns stem from the way his experience of walking through a city seem so unlike that of the Parisian poet and flâneur, Baudelaire. The latter appeared engaged with the world around him, yet Sennett finds himself, as well as the others he observes, simply indifferent to each other:

> New York should be the ideal city of exposure to the outside ... By walking in the middle of New York one is immersed in the differences of this most diverse of cities, but ... [a] walk in New York reveals ... that difference from and indifference to others are a related and unhappy pair. The eye sees differences to which it reacts with indifference.
>
> (1990: 128–9)

For Sennett, however, there are emancipatory possibilities in this city of indifferent strangers. Developing an argument concerning the need for hetrogeneity in urban communities he first outlined in *Uses of Disorder*, Sennett contends that in 'A city of difference and of fragments of life that do not connect, in such a city the obsessed are set free' (1990: 125). Indeed, he goes on to declare that 'Deviance is the freedom made possible in a crowded city of lightly engaged people' (1990: 126–7). There are similarities here with Iris Marion Young's (1990: 241) arguments for the 'unoppressive city' where there is 'an openness to unassimilated others' and with Jane Jacobs (1961: 83) who, some 30 years before, celebrated 'the tolerance, the room for great differences amongst neighbours' within New York City. For Jacobs, however, it was not indifference that was the key to 'allowing strangers to dwell in peace together on civilised but essentially dignified and reserved terms' but the practices of 'do-it-yourself surveillance' (1961: 121), 'that intricate, almost unconscious network of voluntary controls ... enforced by the people themselves' (1961: 31).

For William Bratton neither Sennett's indifference nor Jacobs 'd-i-y' surveillance are sufficient to establish the city as a tolerant, emancipatory place. The deviance he detected in his journey through New York City requires a more robust response. Following his appointment in 1994 as Commissioner of the New York Police Department (NYPD), Bratton targeted the beggars, the drunks and the vandals with what became known as zero tolerance policing. Many on the political left have despaired at this strategy as an attempt to erase the diversity to be encountered in public spaces, which is so important to Sennett's view of the emancipatory possibilities of the city. According to Neil Smith (1999), for example, Bratton's zero tolerance approach exemplifies 1990s urban revanchism and is 'a chilling sign of potential urban futures'. But for those on the political right, Bratton's tough 'law and order' approach was about emancipation. 'Freedom', declared Rudolph Giuliani, the New York City Mayor who hired Bratton, 'is about the willingness of every single human being to cede to lawful authority a great deal of discretion about what you do' (quoted in Smith, 1999: 189). From this perspective, zero tolerance policing would help 'reclaim the streets for respectable law-abiding people and help overcome the "culture of fear" … characteristic of late modern urban environments' (Hughes, 1998: 112).

In this chapter I want to explore these tensions and anxieties around the inter-play of deviance, difference, and crime control in the city. For Sharon Zukin (1995: 27), 'the democratization of public space' is entangled with people's fears for their physical security. She warns that 'One of the most tangible threats to public culture comes from the politics of everyday fear' (1995: 38). Similarly, Ash Amin and Stephen Graham (1999: 16) note that 'the tensions associated with the juxtaposition of difference, perceived or real (such as the fear of crime or violence, racial intolerance, uncertainty and insecurity) often put into question the very definition and usage of the phrase "urban public space"'. Sennett, too, acknowledges this in his walk around New York City. 'There is withdrawal and fear of exposure', he observes, 'as though all differences are as potentially explosive as those between a drug dealer and an ordinary citizen' (1990: 129).

The roots of such fears and the ways in which they create and reinforce exclusion from social life in public spaces are complex. At one level, people may be excluded because of fears prompted by the experience of crime itself or as a result of sub-criminal acts such as racist, sexist, homophobic or ageist harassment (Pain, 2001). But fear can also reflect a more general sense of anxiety engendered through the confrontation of difference and difficulty and which, like the fear of crime, can lead to precautionary behaviour which restricts people's social activities, their employment opportunities and their freedom of expression (Bannister and Fyfe, 2001). However, it is not just fear and crime that constitute the 'new omens of urban calamity' (Baeten, 2001: 4). Often crime control itself is represented now as a major threat to difference and diversity in the city. Criminologists and left-leaning urbanists make much of how innovations in policing and crime prevention, like zero tolerance policing (ZTP) and closed circuit television (CCTV) surveillance, can be seen 'as tightening the ratchet of social control and as the forerunner of some new technologically sophisticated totalitarianism' (Young, 1999: 90). While supporters of such new crime control strategies believe they can bring about dramatic reductions in crime and the fear of crime, critics view them as little more than 'attempts to purify the public sphere of disorder and difference through the spatial exclusion of those social groups who are judged to be deviant, imperfect and marginal in public space' (Toon, 2000: 141).

These competing perceptions of crime control tactics and technologies have very different implications for our understanding of the emancipatory possibilities of the contemporary city. While proponents of ZTP and CCTV surveillance assert that reductions in fear mean people will enjoy a new sense of freedom in the city, opponents counter with claims that these initiatives are part of an oppressive 'criminology of intolerance' in which the prevailing concern is to exclude anyone 'that will disrupt the smooth running of the system' (Young, 1999: 46). In this chapter I explore these differing interpretations of crime control in the late modern city. Using ZTP and CCTV surveillance as case studies, I will argue that the nature and impacts of ZTP and CCTV surveillance appear far more complex than either their supporters or critics will allow for. To put ZTP and CCTV in context, however, it is first necessary to sketch out the emerging contours of crime control in the late modern city.

Visions and realities: crime control in the late modern city

According to David Garland, crime control in the UK and USA, currently exhibits two new and distinct lines of governmental action: 'an *adaptive strategy* stressing prevention and partnership and a *sovereign state strategy* emphasising enhanced control and expressive punishment' (2000: 348). The adaptive strategy involves the state withdrawing its claim to be the chief provider of security and instead emphasizes the use of preventive techniques, like increased surveillance, and the role of public–private partnerships in areas like policing and urban design. Yet, Garland argues, governments are 'deeply ambivalent' about this new infrastructure of crime prevention. At certain times in particular spaces and with respect to specific offences and offenders, government's reactivate 'the old myth of the sovereign state' with a strategy of more intensive modes of policing and punishment, like harsher sentencing, greater use of imprisonment and zero tolerance policing.

The reasons behind these new approaches to crime control are rooted in the complex social, economic, and political changes associated with late modernity. These include fiscal pressures on the state, the emergence of new forms of governance and the rise of new technologies, and, of particular importance here, a 'new collective experience of crime and insecurity' (Garland, 2000: 354). High crime rates have now become a normal social fact. Jock Young (1999: 122) notes how 'crime has moved from the rare, the abnormal, the offence of the marginal and the stranger, to a commonplace part of the texture of everyday life ... as well as extending its anxiety into all areas of the city'. Of course, the collective experience of crime remains highly differentiated both socially and spatially but significantly it is the middle classes who since the 1980s have experienced some of the most dramatic changes in the way crime features in their lives. 'From being a problem that mostly affected the poor, crime (and particularly vandalism, theft, burglary and robbery)' Garland contends, 'increasingly became a daily consideration for anyone who owned a car, used a subway, left their home unguarded during the day, or walked the city streets at night' (2000: 359).

Against this background of changes in the frequency and distribution of crime, the middle classes have 'scripted the official response to crime rates' (Smith, 1999: 199), resulting in new approaches to crime control that have left their mark in cities on both sides of the Atlantic. The adaptive strategy of prevention and partnership is evident in the growth in community policing initiatives, the proliferation of neighbourhood watch schemes in affluent suburbs, and the encouragement given to the 'fortress impulse' in architecture and urban design. Susan Christopherson (1994: 421), for example, describes cities dominated by 'security cages and a honeycomb of residential and business fortress', while Eugene McLaughlin and John Muncie (2000: 117) write of cities now riddled with 'sharply demarcated privatised walled and gated enclaves'. Traditional reliance on the policing by the state has given way to new 'security networks' (Newburn, 2001) based around private forms of policing and the proliferation of electronic surveillance. In terms of the 'sovereign state strategy', the repertoire of initiatives now being deployed in the US and UK is no less extensive: 'Harsher sentencing and the increased use of imprisonment; ... the revival of chain gangs and corporal punishment; boot camps and "supermax" prisons; ... community notification laws and paedophile registers; zero tolerance policing and sex offender orders' (Garland, 2000: 350). Although the visible imprint of this strategy might be less than the adaptive strategy, it is no less important to the fortunes of contemporary cities:

> In the world of global finances, state governments are allotted the role of little else than oversized police precincts; the quantity and quality of the policemen [sic] on the beat, efficiency displayed in sweeping the streets clean of beggars, pesterers and pilferers, and the tightness of the jail walls loom large among the factors of 'investors' confidence', and so among the items calculated when the decisions to invest or cut the losses and run are made.
>
> (Bauman, 2000: 216)

In the context of this chapter, the key questions raised by these two approaches to crime control concern their implications for regulating difference and deviance in the late modern city. Using ZTP and CCTV surveillance as case studies which exemplify the sovereign state and adaptive approaches, I will examine the contrasting discursive constructions of these tactics and technologies of crime control and their significance for anxieties about crime and anxieties about crime control in the city.

Zero tolerance policing (ZTP)

ZTP first came to public attention in the mid-1990s with the appointment of William Bratton as the Commissioner of the New York City Police Department (NYPD), where he introduced a policing strategy of targeting 'quality of life' offences. These so-called 'beer and piss' patrols focused on drunkenness, public urination, begging, vandalism, and other anti-social behaviour. Entitled 'Reclaiming the Public Spaces of New York' (New York City Police Department, 1994), this strategy was 'the linchpin of efforts ... being undertaken by the New York City Police Department to reduce crime and the fear of crime in the city' (Silverman and Della-Giustina, 2001: 950). The strategy was based on the claim that quality of life offences, like aggressive begging, squeegee cleaners, street prostitution, boombox cars, public drunkenness, reckless bicyclists and graffiti, restricted the use of public space and contributed to 'the sense that the entire public environment is a threatening place' (New York City Police Department, 1994: 5). The rationale behind focusing on quality of life offences was that 'strong and authoritative use of coercive police powers' in relation to these offences would reduce fear and prevent more serious types of disorder and crime from occurring (Innes, 1999, p. 398). This reasoning was leant academic credibility by the 'broken windows' thesis advanced by James Q. Wilson and George L. Kelling (1982):

> The presence of signs of dilapidation can instigate a feedback cycle, in which fear is engendered in the law-abiding members of the local population whose informal mechanisms of surveillance and control are the main guarantors of order in the locality. This fear leads to a general retreat from public interaction amongst the law-abiding groups and thus informal controls decrease and criminal and disorderly activities rapidly increase.
>
> (Innes, 1999: 398)

Bratton's crackdown on minor offences immediately seemed to deliver encouraging results. In New York City, the recorded crime rate between 1994 and 1997 dropped by 37 per cent, with a fall in homicide of over 50 per cent. According to Bratton (1997: 29) there was a simple explanation for this: 'Blame it on the police.' Not surprisingly, this 'triumphalist discourse' (Body-Gendrot, 2000: 117) quickly began to capture the attention of politicians and police chiefs in other countries with NYPD becoming the most visited and researched police department in the world. In the summer of 1995, the then UK shadow Home Secretary, Jack Straw, visited New York City and met Bratton. On his return, Straw promised that a Labour government would introduce ZTP and 'reclaim the streets for the law-abiding citizen' from the 'aggressive begging of winos, addicts and squeegee merchants' (quoted in Bowling, 1999: 532). Such moral authoritarianism has since been put into practice by the adoption of zero tolerance style policing in various parts of the UK, including the Kings Cross area in London, Cleveland in north east England and Strathclyde in the west of Scotland. In all these areas, advocates of ZTP have claimed dramatic reductions in levels of crime and the fear of crime (see Dennis and Mallon, 1997; Orr, 1997). Of course, any attempts to link directly falling crime levels to a specific policing initiative are fraught with problems. As Ben Bowling (1999: 551) concluded in New York City, for example, 'only a circumstantial case has been made for the link between aggressive policing and falling crime'. The fall in homicide in the city in the mid-1990s, he argues, had much more to do with the contraction in the crack cocaine market than any innovations in policing strategy. Moreover, in cities which did not adopt ZTP tactics in the US, crime also declined dramatically in the mid-1990s. In San Diego, for example, the policing approach adopted was very different to that in New York City and involved developing partnerships between the police, public and private sectors yet falls in crime have been comparable to those recorded in New York City (Body-Gendrot, 2000).

Despite these uncertainties about its impact, support for ZTP remains among some police officers and politicians in what increasingly appears as 'a last ditch attempt' by the state to 'make policing and legal regulation suc-ceed as a means of social control' (Hirst, 2000: 281). At the same time, how-ever, criticism of ZTP has grown. Indeed, condemnation of ZTP has yielded a surprising alliance of senior police officers, criminologists, and left-leaning urbanists, alarmed by its implications for public order, difference, and diver-sity in the city. Some UK police officers view ZTP as a return to the failed military-style policing tactics of the 1970s and 1980s, which contributed to serious public disorder in several cities (Hopkins Burke, 1998). For exam-ple, Charles Pollard (1997: 44), Chief Constable of the UK's Thames Valley force, is critical of the 'ruthlessness in dealing with low-level criminality and disorderliness ... and of the single-minded pursuit of short term results'. Some criminologists (e.g. Body-Gendrot, 2000; Greene, 1999) have echoed these concerns, highlighting the way in which any reductions in crime have come at a severe cost to public trust in the police, particularly among minor-ity communities. Others, however, go much further. Some describe ZTP as a 'Robocop version of beat policing [which] could quite easily destroy the "ballet of the street" and "benign disorder" that ... are so crucial to a vital street life' (McLauglin and Muncie, 2000: 130; cf. Merrifield, 2000: 484). Smith offers one of the most sustained attacks on ZTP. According to him, the publication of the NYPD's (1994) *Reclaiming the Public Spaces of New York* signalled 'the advent of a *fin de siècle* American revanchism in the urban landscape' involving 'a visceral identification of the culprits, the enemies who had stolen from the white middle class a city that members of the latter assumed to be their birthright' (1999: 187).

These anxieties about the implications of ZTP for difference and diversity are important not least because they challenge the complacent and self-interested claims of supporters of this policing strategy. Nevertheless, the radical totalitarian reading of ZTP offered by some critics, in which crime control rather than crime is constructed as the major threat to urban life and culture, can be as misleading and exaggerated as the utopian claims of advocates of ZTP. While the latter see it as some kind of 'easy miracle and instant cure' (Young, 1999: 130) to the problems of public space, critics simply invert this rhetoric and view ZTP as an unmitigated disaster delivering instant oppression and crushing any 'street spontaneity and vibrancy' (Merrifield, 2000: 485). But this interpretation places too much weight on a caricature of ZTP when even a casual inspection of the growing research literature reveals that ZTP is a far more complex set of practices than its popular image uncritically recycled by many of its opponents. In particular, while critical perspectives on ZTP focus on the everyday life of those on the street in all its kaleidoscopic detail, the police are simply portrayed as an 'abstract and systematic order which is responsible for oppression' (Thrift, 2000: 235).

Examination of police practices in New York City has revealed that enforcement of quality of life crimes served largely to help with intelligence gathering in relation to more serious offences (Greene, 1999). Moreover, rigorous enforcement was only one element in a wider set of reforms of management, communication and intelligence gathering designed to make the police more efficient, effective, and accountable. It is not surprising therefore that researchers like Eli Silverman and Jo-Ann Della-Giustina have concluded that ZTP has generated a series of myths that bare little relation to reality. In particular, they note that critics too often depict zero tolerance as 'leaving the police little or no discretion' when in reality zero tolerance cannot mean '24 hours, 7 days a week, perpetual enforcement of all quality of life offences' (2001: 954). This is even echoed by Bratton who has emphasized that discretion is a vital part of policing and that what happened in New York City was not zero tolerance policing. Indeed, Bratton has roundly condemned the concept, emphasizing that policing involves developing plans in consultation with local communities and taking action against a range of crime and incivilities (Young, 1999: 124). Moreover, critics leave 'little scope for the specifics of locality and difference' (Hughes, 1997: 158).

Comparative research within New York City has revealed, for example, the importance of local variations in zero tolerance policing styles. A study of two precincts in the South Bronx highlighted significant reductions in crime and civilian complaints against the police as a result of local styles of management adopted by police commanders which emphasized improved supervision of officers and greater community interaction (Davis and Mateu-Gelabert, 1999). Moving from the intra-urban to the international scale, there are also clear differences between ZTP in the US and the UK. Despite senior UK police officers engaging with the popular discourse of ZTP, policing in areas that claim to have experimented with ZTP has been orientated towards the cultivation of informants and information-based police action rather than aggressive enforcement. Indeed Johnston (2000: 67) concludes that ZTP in the UK context has more to do with risk-based policing (in the sense of information gathering and proactive intervention) than with addressing the problem of incivility.

There is a second difficulty for those who only see danger in 'the zero tolerance gospel' (Shapiro, 1997). An important insight provided by the broken-windows thesis underpinning zero tolerance strategies is that 'the cumulative effect of minor incivilities poses as much of a problem to the public as crime itself' (Young, 1999: 138). As Young argues, this was recognized over ten years ago when an Edinburgh women's domestic violence campaign first coined the term 'zero tolerance' in relation to violence against women. This demanded explicit recognition that rape or other forms of sexual violence represent 'the end-point of the continuum of aggressive sexual behaviour' (1999: 138) that might also including staring, touching, and verbal sexual abuse. Similar arguments could, of course, be made in relation to the abuses suffered by a range of other vulnerable social groups, including gays and lesbians, the young and the elderly, and ethnic and racial minorities. Few would dispute that failure to adopt a zero tolerance approach in these contexts contributes greatly to the exclusion of individuals and social groups. Some critics acknowledge that a democracy cannot 'allow all types of disorder to run amok', but this poses a dilemma for those who believe they have to 'fend off and contest Zero Tolerance tactics' (Merrifield, 2000: 885): how to differentiate between 'good' and 'bad' zero tolerance. What this suggests is the need for a greater engagement with the ambivalence of ZTP. On the one hand, some forms of zero tolerance may severely inhibit freedoms in the city; as Silverman and Della-Giustina (2001: 954) note, 'When zero tolerance changes into zealous pursuit of all quality of life offences, everyone loses – public and police alike in their ability to fight crime'. On the other hand, zero tolerance of particular incivilities may actually enhance the confidence of some groups in using the city. Thus, while critics of ZTP may wonder 'whether the baby of disorder might be getting ditched with the criminal bathwater' (Merrifield, 2000: 484) it is also important that these same critics don't simply throw the 'smart policing baby' out with 'the aggressive policing' bathwater (Bowling, 1999: 550).

Closed circuit television (CCTV) surveillance

While ZTP is largely associated with the cosmopolitan world of New York City, it is the relatively quiet, seaside town of Bournemouth on England's south coast which regularly features in discussions of CCTV surveillance. Bournemouth was the birthplace of the UK's 'surveillance revolution' (Williams et al., 2000: 169). Here in August 1985 the country's first public space CCTV system went 'live' and over the next ten years there was the piecemeal establishment of similar schemes in other towns and cities. From the mid-1990s, however, the diffusion of CCTV schemes accelerated. In 1994, 78 towns and cities in the UK had CCTV; by May 1999, 530 town and city centre schemes were either in operation or had funding allocated (Williams et al., 2000: 170). UK cities now have the most intensive concentration of electronic 'eyes on the street' in the world (McLaughlin and Muncie, 2000: 130).

The reasons for this rapid spread of public space CCTV systems are now well documented (Fyfe and Bannister, 1998, Williams et al., 2000). Economically, the spread of CCTV is bound up with urban regeneration agendas and attempts to revive the fortunes of the entrepreneurial city by 'managing out inappropriate behaviour in the new territories of consumption' (McCahill, 1998: 42). As Ian Toon (2000: 150) observes, CCTV is part of 'an attempt to reinvent public spaces, promoting the commercial functions of the street above all other uses'. Politically, the involvement of businesses and local government in financing surveillance schemes demonstrates how CCTV fits an agenda of developing public-private partnerships that enable the central state to pursue its 'responisibilization' strategy of off-loading certain crime control activities onto the local state and the private sector.

As with ZTP, there are no shortage of CCTV supporters willing to claim that this technology has brought considerable benefits to the city. 'Before' and 'After' studies of the impact of CCTV on the incidence of crime in several town and city centres suggest that crime rates have fallen dramatically and contributed to a so-called 'feel good factor' by 'reassuring town centre users that they are safer' (Home Office, 1994: 14). Opinion surveys also routinely reveal high levels of public support: 85 per cent of those asked in Sutton in south-east London said they would be in favour of town centre CCTV, rising to 95 per cent of those asked in Glasgow. CCTV surveillance therefore appears to be a cause for celebration: it 'increases public freedom, enhancing opportunities for people to enjoy public places' (Arlidge, 1994: 22). Yet, the utopian, deterministic rhetoric surrounding CCTV with its promise of a 'feel good factor' for those who use town and city centres is increasingly being questioned. Evidence for reductions in crime and the fear of crime is far from consistent (Fyfe and Bannister, 1998) and concerns remain that CCTV systems simply displace crime to areas out of the view of cameras, areas which may be less able to cope with the problems of crime. Nor is public support for CCTV as high or robust as is often claimed given serious methodological weaknesses in the ways in which opinion surveys have been conducted (Ditton, 2000). More generally, as Roy Coleman and Joe Sim (1998) cogently argue, the 'feel good factor' focuses on a particular conception of danger and disorder in city centre public spaces, marginalizing other areas of crime and anxiety, such as domestic violence experienced in private spaces.

While these uncertainties about the impact of CCTV on crime and deviance appear to have done little to stem popular and political enthusiasm for public space CCTV surveillance, a growing critical discourse of this 'silver bullet' of crime prevention has also developed informed by a similar radical totalitarianism to that underpinning criticism of ZTP. In *The Maximum Surveillance Society*, Clive Norris and Gary Armstrong (1999) note, for example, how the academic literature on CCTV is replete with allusions to Orwell's *Nineteen Eighty Four*, Big Brother, and Foucault's discussion of Bentham's Panopticon. 'The dominant cultural theme is tragic', they conclude, 'in which CCTV is placed in the context of those forms of surveillance which are deeply implicated in the structure of totalitarian rule' (1999: 5). More specifically, many urbanists focus on the contribution of CCTV surveillance to processes of social exclusion and the end of public space. Steven Flusty (1998: 59), writing in the context of Los Angeles, suggests that video cameras are now part of 'an infrastructure restructuring the city into electronically linked islands of privilege embedded in a police state matrix'. Jon Bannister and I have contributed to this apocalyptic vision of CCTV, warning that under the constant gaze of CCTV surveillance cameras, any claim that streets symbolize public life with all its human contact, conflict and tolerance would be difficult to sustain (Fyfe and Bannister, 1998: 265). More recently, Williams et al. (2000: 184) declared that CCTV is being used as an instrument to preserve 'the public spaces of our town centres ... for the consumer citizen, while those whose spending power is low ... are effectively excluded'.

Yet, as with ZTP, this dystopian vision of CCTV risks offering a misleading and exaggerated account of its implications for difference and diversity in the late modern city. The temptation to draw upon Foucault's reading of panopticism as a way of understanding the impacts of CCTV, for example, needs to be treated with caution. While there are some similarities, city streets are not the same as the bounded institutional spaces of the prison or asylum. Unlike prisoners and asylum inmates, people in cities do not 'suffer continuous confinement' (Hannah, 1997: 344), nor are those using the streets always aware they are being monitored with CCTV, whereas in the Panopticon the certainty of detection and therefore intervention meant conformity was a necessity. In CCTV systems detection and intervention are contingent on a range of social processes, including whether the screens are being monitored and whether an activity defined as deviant actually generates a response (Norris and Armstrong, 1999: 92). Indeed, opponents of CCTV, just as much as supporters, appear to share an 'unthinking belief that, such is the impressive technological power of those cameras ... that little or no human effort has to be added for them to be highly efficacious' (Ditton and Short, 1999: 39). This position is untenable. CCTV, like other technological innovations, doesn't create 'an electronic world swept of people' but 'hybrid "actor-networks" of people and electronic things' (Thrift, 1996: 1473).

Research into these 'actor-networks' of CCTV cameras, control room operators, and police officers is relatively rare. While critics are keen to revel in the exclusionary experiences of those subject to the gaze of the cameras, they are far less interested in understanding 'how the information generated by CCTV systems is selected, evaluated, used, and acted upon' (McCahill, 1998: 46). One study of CCTV surveillance frankly admits that 'the intention ... was not to collect the accounts of police officers and CCTV monitoring staff themselves on how they police teenagers in public environments, but rather to provide an account of prohibitions and constraints on activities from the point of view of the excluded' (Toon, 2000: 163). The latter is, of course, important, but so too (if one is to avoid the trap of technological determinacy) is the role of those operating CCTV systems. In one of the few published studies of the activities and inter-relationships between CCTV control room staff and police officers, Norris and Armstrong found that the deployment of police officers in response to activities witnessed in CCTV control rooms is a rare event. In 600 hours of observations in three control rooms there were only 45 deployments most of which were in response to crimes of violence. As these researchers conclude, 'Authoritative intervention is a relatively rare phenomenon, and few incidents result in deployment, fewer still in arrest' (1999: 168). The reasons for this are complex and reflect the interplay of organisational, structural and personal factors. CCTV operators can only request, rather than demand, police intervention and must be able to provide a robust justification for requesting police action. Indeed, without a specific legal mandate to intervene, the police are reluctant to become involved. For Norris and Armstrong (1999: 200) this suggests that the 'exclusionary potential' of CCTV, which has so concerned critics, is not particularly marked in practice, 'primarily because deployment [is] such a rare feature'.

The fact that intervention and arrest are relatively rare does not, of course, mean that 'significant social interaction, albeit remote and technologically mediated, has not taken place' (Norris and Armstrong, 1999: 151). For example, a study of young people's responses to the introduction of town centre CCTV in England revealed how they felt forced to find 'concealed interstitial spaces within, and "invisible" routeways through, the town centre' in order to escape the gaze of CCTV and 'reappropriate space for themselves' (Toon, 2000: 154). Nevertheless, it is also clear that CCTV surveillance, like ZTP, is 'much messier, contingent and open to contested interpretations than is implied in much of the literature to date' (Hughes et al., 2001: 333). Thus, rather than portraying CCTV surveillance in either utopian terms (as the silver bullet of crime control) or as part of a starkly dystopian discourse (of an Orwellian future of totalitarian control), a more nuanced position is required. Indeed, ambiguity and ambivalence are precisely the characteristics that now appear to inform local people's responses to the proliferation of CCTV. There is 'a grudging acceptance of the "need" for video surveillance with a range of (often diffuse) worries about how CCTV might come to be used and about the kind of world it signifies' (Sparks et al., 2001: 894). A sense of ambivalence is also central to Hille Koskela's examination of CCTV surveillance as an emotional experience:

> To be under surveillance is an ambivalent emotional event. A surveillance camera, as an object, can at the same time represent safety and danger. To be protected can feel the same as being threatened. A paradox of emotional space is that it does, indeed, make sense that surveillance cameras can make people feel both more secure and more fearful.
>
> (2000: 259)

In more concrete terms Young (1999: 193) makes the point that while CCTV is 'one of the most invidious of inventions' and something which can make Orwell's *Nineteen Eighty Four* a reality, in a different political context, it can be liberating and protective: 'The cameras can be turned around; their context and control can be changed'. Examples of the positive uses of CCTV include Newham in east London where it has been employed to provide protection against racist attacks using facial recognition software in order to identify known racist offenders on the street (Lyon, 2001: 58–9). Another is the way CCTV changes the ability of police officers to privilege their accounts of events given that cameras can now monitor their performance and activity on the street (Norris and Armstrong, 1999: 188). Rather than simply condemning CCTV as 'a product of some capitalist conspiracy or the evil effects of a plutocratic urge' (Lyon, 2001: 2) or uncritically accepting it as a 'silver bullet' of crime prevention, the real challenge is to find ways in which 'the new technologies of mass surveillance can be harnessed to encourage participation rather than exclusion, strengthen personhood rather than diminish it, and be used for benevolent rather than malign purposes' (Norris and Armstrong, 1999: 230).

Conclusions: futures of crime control

Debates over the tactics and technologies of crime control are increasingly polarized between utopian and dystopian visions of their implications for difference and deviance in the late modern city. Intriguingly, these debates have distinct echoes of arguments among historians about crime control in the modern city of the nineteenth century. 'Orthodox' accounts of the introduction of formal policing into urban areas as a means of 'solving the problem of order and checking the spread of lawlessness' (Reiner, 1992: 19) are pitched against 'revisionist' claims that the police were part of a 'centralised social system in which the state penetrated the depths of society' (1992: 34). Just as these revisionist accounts constitute an advance in understanding beyond orthodox views of the modern police, so too those critical of late modern methods of crime control have significantly expanded our understanding of ZTP and CCTV. Nevertheless, critics have often failed to engage with the complex and open-ended nature of crime control in the late modern city. Indeed, the radical totalitarianism which informs many of these critical perspectives tends to 'exaggerate the dystopian tendencies at work and the power of the intrusive social control machine' (Hughes, 1997: 157). As Gordon Hughes wryly notes, 'Glimpses of dystopia have a powerful appeal, not least to intellectuals who, doubtless, gain vicarious pleasure from being on the "edge", compared to the supposedly slumbering masses' (1997: 158). Yet the problem remains of how to address the tensions between anxieties about crime and anxieties about crime control at a time when crime is 'no longer a marginal concern, an unexpected incident in their life, but an ever-present possibility' (Young, 1999: 36). In part this means engaging with the ambivalence of crime control and the paradoxes and possibilities it entails.

It is also important to think beyond current approaches to crime control and look for ways outside of the criminal justice system of addressing questions of deviance and diversity in the city. In this regard there is a growing European radical communitarian vision of tackling crime by rethinking political and economic democracy to develop a progressive agenda of social inclusion and pluralism. Of particular importance here is the work of Paul Hirst (2000). According to Hirst, current strategies of crime control attempt to enforce hierarchical control on an increasingly heterogeneous and unequal society and to develop systems of surveillance based on norms that are increasingly contested. This results in a system of criminal justice that is both ineffective and inappropriate. In its place, Hirst argues for an approach to crime control informed by associationalism, of a society split into self-governing communities with different values and with publicly funded services devolved to self-governing voluntary associations. Groups would co-exist yet keep their own values by a mixture of micro-governance (special zones where different rules apply) and mutual extra-territoriality (self-governing communities sharing the same space but applying rules in matters of community concern to their members alone). As Hirst speculates:

> Imagine cities clearly divided into permissive and restrictive zones with regard to drug use. Imagine that if the rich can live in gated communities with security guards, that the metaphorical 'ghettos' of the USA became more like real ones with their own boundaries and their own local policing. Tell that to the LAPD? But the cost of their rule is immense, including the cost of riots, and its results ineffective.
>
> (2000: 291)

Elements of such strategies already exist in some cities. The Danes tolerate the anarchist enclave of Christiania in Copenhagen, and in the Netherlands there are marginal zones where prostitution and soft drug use are tolerated. Rather than looking for approaches to crime control that apply across the city and are delivered by one central agency, there needs to be a commitment to developing more diverse, decentralised and self-regulatory strategies. As Hirst explains:

> Outside a thin core of public morality – almost everyone will agree that murder, theft and fraud are crimes – groups will be better off setting and policing their own standards. Citizens would have to accept that different rules applied to different communities with informal self-regulation and arbitration.
>
> (2000: 279)

Intriguingly this view takes us back to the streets of New York City with which this chapter began. According to Jane Jacobs (1961: 31), probably the City's most infamous flâneur, the 'public peace' of cities is not kept primarily by the police but by 'an intricate, almost unconscious, network of voluntary controls and standards among the people themselves and enforced by the people themselves'. Although this might be dismissed as a utopian vision of crime control in the late modern city, is it any less utopian than the belief that we can control crime by 'changing the way it is handled within the formal system of criminal justice' (Currie, 1985: 229)?

References

Amin, A. and Graham, S. (1999) 'Cities of connection and disconnection', in J. Allen, D. Massey and M. Pryke (eds), *Unsettling Cities*. London: Routledge. pp. 7–47.

Arlidge, J. (1994) 'Welcome big brother', *The Independent*, 2 November, p. 22.

Baeten, G. (2001) 'Hypochondriac geographies of the city and the new urban dystopia: coming to terms with the "other" city'. Paper presented at the American Association of Geographers Conference, New York.

Bannister, J. and Fyfe, N. R. (2001) 'Fear and the city', *Urban Studies*, 38: 807–14.

Bauman, Z. (2000) 'Social issues of law and order', *British Journal of Criminology*, 40: 205–21.

Body-Gendrot, S. (2000) *The Social Control of Cities? A Comparative Perspective*. Oxford: Blackwell.

Bowling, B. (1999) 'The rise and fall of New York murder: zero tolerance or crack's decline?', *British Journal of Criminology*, 39: 531–54.

Bratton, W.J. (1997) 'Crime is down in New York City: blame the police', in N. Dennis (ed.), *Zero Tolerance: Policing a Free Society*. London: Institute of Economic Affairs. pp. 29–42.

Christopherson, S. (1994) 'Fortress city: privatised spaces, consumer citizenship', in A. Amin (ed.), *Post-Fordism: A Reader*. Oxford: Basil Blackwell. pp. 409–27.

Coleman, R. and Sim, J. (1998) 'From the docklands to the Disney store: surveillance, risk and security in Liverpool City Centre', *International Review of Law, Computers and Technology*, 12: 45–63.

Currie, E. (1985) *Confronting Crime: An American Challenge*. New York, Pantheon Books.

Davis, R.C. and Mateu-Gelabert, P. (1999) *Respectful and Effective Policing: Two Examples in the South Bronx*. New York: Vera Institute.

Dennis, N. and Mallon, R. (1997) 'Confident policing in Hartlepool', in N. Dennis (ed.), *Zero Tolerance: Policing a Free Society*, London: Institute of Economic Affairs. pp, 61–86.

Ditton, J. (2000) 'Public attitudes towards open-street CCTV in Glasgow', *British Journal of Criminology*, 40: 692–709.

Ditton, J. and Short, E. (1998) 'Evaluating Scotland's first town centres CCTV scheme', in C. Norris, J. Moran and G. Armstrong (eds), *Surveillance, CCTV and Social Control*. Aldershot: Ashgate. pp. 155–74.

Ditton, J. and Short, E. (1999) *The Effect of CCTV on Recorded Crime Rates and Public Concern about Crime in Glasgow*. Edinburgh: Scottish Office.

Flusty, S. (1998) 'Building paranoia', in N. Ellin (ed.), *Architecture of Fear*. Princeton, NJ: Princeton University Press. pp. 47–59.

Fyfe, N.R. and Bannister, J. (1998) ' "The eyes upon the street": closed circuit television surveillance and the city', in N. R. Fyfe (ed.), *Images of the Street: Planning, Identity and Control in Public Space*. London: Routledge. pp. 254–67.

Garland, D. (2000) 'The culture of high crime societies: some preconditions of recent "law and order" policies', *British Journal of Criminology* 40: 347–75.

Greene, J. (1999) 'Zero tolerance: a case study of police policies and practices in New York City', *Crime and Delinquency*, 45: 172–87.

Hannah, M. (1997) 'Imperfect panopticism: envisioning the construction of normal lives', in G. Benko and E. Strohmayer (Eds.), *Space and Social Theory: Interpreting Modernity and Postmodernity*. Oxford: Blackwell, pp. 344–59.

Hirst, P. (2000) 'Statism, pluralism and social control', *British Journal of Criminology*, 20: 279–95.

Home Office (1994) *CCTV: Looking Out For You*. London: Home Office.

Hopkins Burke, R. (1998) 'A contextualisation of zero tolerance policing strategies', in R. Hopkins Burke (ed.), *Zero Tolerance Policing*. London Perpetuity Press. pp. 11–38.

Hughes, G. (1997) 'Policing late modernity: crime management in contemporary Britain', in N. Jewson and S. Macgregor (eds), *Transforming Cities: Contested Governance and New Spatial Divisions*. London: Routledge. pp. 153–65.

Hughes, G. (1998) *Understanding Crime Prevention: Social Control, Risk, and Late Modernity*. Buckingham: Open University Press.

Hughes, G., McLaughlin, E. and Muncie, J. (2001) 'Teetering on the edge: future of crime control and community safety', in G. Hughes, E. McLaughlin and J. Muncie (eds), *Crime Prevention and Community Safety: New Directions*. London: Sage. pp. 318–40.

Innes, M. (1999) ' "An iron fist in an iron glove?" the zero tolerance policing debate', *The Howard Journal*, 38: 397–410.

Jacobs, J. (1961) *The Death and Life of Great American Cities: The Failure of Town Planning*. Harmandsworth: Penguin.

Johnston, L. (2000) *Policing Britain: Risk, Security and Governance*. Harlow: Longman.

Koskela, H. (2000) ' "The gaze without eyes": video-surveillance and the changing nature of urban space', *Progress in Human Geography*, 24: 243–65.

Lyon, D. (2001) *Surveillance Society: Monitoring Everyday Life*. Buckingham: Open University Press.

McCahill, M. (1998) 'Beyond Foucault: towards a contemporary theory of surveillance', in C. Norris, J. Moran and G. Armstrong (eds), *Surveillance, Closed Circuit Television and Social Control*. Aldershot: Ashgate. pp. 41–65.

McLaughlin, E. and Muncie, J. (2000) 'Walled cities: surveillance, regulation and segregation', in S. Pile, C. Brook and G. Mooney (eds), *Unruly Cities?* London: Routledge. pp. 103–48.

Merrifield, A. (2000) 'The dialectics of dystopia: disorder and zero tolerance in the city', *International Journal of Urban and Regional Research*, 24: 473–88.

Newburn, T. (2001) 'The commodification of policing: security networks in the late modern city', *Urban Studies*, 38: 829–48.

New York City Police Department (NYPD) (1994) *Strategy Number Five: Reclaiming the Public Spaces of New York*. New York: City of New York.

Norris, C. and Armstrong, G. (1999) *The Maximum Surveillance Society: The Rise of CCTV*. Oxford: Berg.

Orr, J. (1997) 'Strathclyde's spotlight initiative', in N. Dennis (ed.), *Zero Tolerance*. London: Institute of Economic Affairs. pp. 104–23.

Pain, R. (2001) 'Gender, race, age and fear in the city', *Urban Studies* 38: 899–913.

Pollard, C. (1997) 'Zero tolerance: short term fix, long term liability?', in N. Dennis (ed.), *Zero Tolerance*. London: Institute of Economic Affairs, pp. 43–57.

Reiner, R. (1992) *The Politics of the Police*. London: Harvester.

Sennett, R. (1970) *The Uses of Disorder: Personal Identity and City Life*. London: Faber and Faber.

Sennett, R. (1990) *The Conscience of the Eye: The Design and Social Life of Cities*. London: Faber and Faber.

Shapiro, B. (1997) 'Zero tolerance gospel', *Index on Censorship*, 4: 17–23.

Silverman, E. and Della-Giustina, J.-A. (2001) 'Urban policing and the fear of crime', *Urban Studies*, 38: 941–58.

Smith, N. (1999) 'Which new urbanism? New York City and the revanchist 1990s', in R.A. Beauregard and S. Body-Gendrot (eds), *The Urban Moment: Cosmopolitan Essays on the Late 20th-century City*. Thousand Oaks, CA: Sage. pp. 185–208.

Sparks, R., Girling, E. and Loader, I. (2001) 'Fear and everyday urban lives', *Urban Studies*, 38: 885–98.

Thrift, N. (1996) 'Old technological fears and new urban eras: reconfiguring the good-will of electronic things', *Urban Studies*, 33: 1463–93.

Thrift, N. (2000) ' "Not a straight line but a curve", or, cities are not mirrors of modernity', in D. Bell and A. Haddour (eds), *City Visions*. Harlow: Longman. pp. 233–63.

Toon, I. (2000) 'Finding a place in the street': CCTV surveillance and young people's use of public space', in D. Bell and A. Haddour (eds), *City Visions*. Harlow: Longman. pp. 141–65.

Williams, K. S., Johnstone, C. and Goodwin, M. (2000) 'CCTV surveillance in urban Britain: beyond the rhetoric of crime prevention', in J. R. Gold and G. Revill (eds), *Landscapes of Defence*. London: Prentice Hall. pp. 168–87.

Wilson, J. Q. and Kelling, G. L. (1982) 'Broken windows', *Atlantic Monthly*, March: pp. 29–38.

Young, I. M. (1990) *Justice and the Politics of Difference*. Princeton, NJ: Princeton University Press.

Young, J. (1999) *The Exclusive Society: Social Exclusion, Crime and Difference in Late Modernity*. London: Sage.

Zukin, S. (1995) *The Cultures of Cities*. Oxford: Basil Blackwell.

5.3   A Nigger in Cyberspace
Keith Piper

I was struggling to envisage a Rodney King computer game.

Initially, one would be confronted with an interface asking you to choose one of two options, to be a Controller or to be a Transgressor. However, in response to your privileged position as custodian of the system, the role of Controller is set as a default, whilst Transgressor is ghosted and inactive.

As the game opens on the first level you are alerted to the fact that your system has been infiltrated by a rogue 'virus', which you perceive to be crammed with transgressive algorithms. The 'virus' is moving at high speed along a communications bus, and you fear for the security of the cherished resources and privileged information stored in discrete locations elsewhere in the system. In response to this perceived threat you dispatch a series of devices programmed to 'protect and serve' and this level of the game develops into a scenario of cat and mouse. The object of the game at this point is to apprehend the 'virus' and return it to the part of the system which has been labelled the 'trashcan', a location within which all redundant, inconvenient, unsightly and transgressive elements are deposited, out of sight and out of mind. Once the 'virus' has been apprehended, this stage of the game is complete, and you are at liberty to move on to the second level.

The second level of the game borrows elements from 'Street Fighter II'. However, as the Controller you have up to eight agents at your disposal, arrayed against the single Transgressor. The object of the game is to determine an adequate response to transgressive gestures on the part of the 'virus'. If, for instance, the virus raises itself to an angle of twenty degrees or greater, you are presented with a choice of options ranging from administering a swift blow to the side of its head with a long handled baton, shocking it with an electrified prod, or placing your heel on to the back of its neck. This stage of the game is over when the 'virus' either assumes a position of absolute passivity, or lapses into unconsciousness.

On the third level of the game, you are confronted by the uncomfortable knowledge that the tactics employed on level two have been scrupulously logged in the system's memory and you are called upon to defend your choice of responses as measured against the perceived threat to the system posed by the transgressive 'virus'. If you succeed on this level, if you are able to create an argument which sufficiently demonises the transgressive 'virus' and amplifies the danger which it potentially posed to the continued smooth running of the system, then you are at liberty to play another game.

The first time the game was played, however, the logic broke down and transgressive viruses flooded out of the trashcan crashing the entire system.

Half a decade on, a Rodney King computer game may represent a marketing flight of fancy, but it does provide us with a convenient metaphorical entry point into wider set of debates. It provides us with a recognition that we are currently entering a scenario in which we are coming to occupy two parallel landscapes, separate but inextricably linked. Both are sites across which a range of contests of territory are being played out in earnest and, within these contests, we have all become both players and the played.

The first of these landscapes is the physical and social landscape of the city, both as a conglomeration of disparate neighbourhoods, and as key locus in a complex web of regional, national and international networks. The second is the parallel landscape which has come to be known as 'Cyberspace', the intricate and inextricably expanding universe of digital data; the 'virtual' spaces which it occupies and the channels through which it is disseminated.

Both of these landscapes historically came to be identified in modernist discourses as sites across which the optimism and opportunity afforded by the inextricable forward march of technology would inevitably bear their finest fruit. The city would become an arena replete with the technologies of economic, material and social enablement and recreation, and within this scenario of a brave new world, computer-based technologies would play a key role. The new citizen of the high-tech metropolis (the Technotropolis) would be at liberty to delve into Cyberspace at will, tapping into information networks and structuring lifestyles around the logical interaction between commerce, productive labour and entertainment.

The historical events surrounding the beating of black motorist Rodney King, the acquittal of the police officers who had been caught on video tape administering the beating and the subsequent rioting which gripped Los Angeles provide a symbolic point of dislocation, a key indicator marking the final and inextricable abandonment of any previously held scenarios of optimism.

Instead, what emerges is the notion of the 'dislocated city'. What emerges is a vision of the contemporary 'city' as a dislocated jigsaw of isolated and antagonistic communities entrenched within balkanised neighbourhoods. Disintegrating communications systems along with the entrenchment of privilege and disenfranchisement have not only created a dangerously volatile underclass, but also a disjuncture between the language systems with which these dislocated communities conceptualise the world around them. It is this chaos of language, this inextricable fragmenting of a 'common sense' which led the Simi Valley jury in the Rodney King beating trial of 1992, to accept the logic which framed excessive force on the part of the police officers as a justifiable protective measure. After all, these were individuals who had enlisted to guard the boundaries of those neighbourhoods of plenty, of good order and accumulated privilege from incursion by outsiders. The 'outsiders' being individuals from those other neighbourhoods: neighbourhoods of poverty, chaos and bedlam; neighbourhoods of the racial 'other'. These were their front line troops in the contest of territory between white wealth and the numerical expansion of black and other 'Third World' peoples. Here was a key point of struggle in the battle against the inextricable 'Africanisation' of the city. This language and the logic which underpinned it were lost on those black and 'Third World' folks and for three days the city burned.

The metaphor touched upon within the scenario of the Rodney King computer game which identifies the black as a rogue virus, as a conglomeration of transgressive algorithms whose presence must inextricably disrupt the smooth running of any system which it infiltrates, is useful only to the extent to which it parodies white racist discourses which frame the black as the cause rather than victim of urban depravation and decay.

The wider issues, however, around the particular in-roads and struggles for the visibility of a black theoretical and aesthetic presence within Cyberspace, and the sense to which it parallels the various struggles around black visibility and presence across the landscape of the postmodern city is of particular interest to us here. This is very much a contest of territory, a struggle around the colonisation of Cyberspace by various constituencies, and within this colonisation, a series of eclectic and expansionist 'Africanised' enclaves are emerging. These 'Africanised' presences are transgressive to the extent that the 'founding fathers' of Cyberspace very much replicated the social and economic interests of the enfranchised white status quo, and within their 'brave new world', as in the landscape of the affluent city, the black presence would always be a trespassing one. It is however the extent to which the black presence in Cyberspace uses its transgressive and trespassing nature as a tool of tactical engagement and struggle which I shall go on to explore in this text.

Transgressive behaviour has been a feature of Cyberspace since close after its inception. The so-called computer 'hacker', a technically literate data burglar, ensured an early entry into the lexicon of digital demonology, presenting himself as the swashbuckling scourges of the banker and the information manager. The image of the 'hacker' seemed to hover in the space between the rogue and disgruntled digital professional – using his insider knowledge of systems' architecture to roam Cyberspace at will – and the adolescent digital prodigy launching raids from a computer rig cobbled together amidst the clutter of an untidy and unventilated bedroom. Such an individual was conjured into celluloid life in the John Badham film *War Games* (1983) which sees a teenage boy hack his way into a military mainframe computer in order to play a game of 'thermonuclear war'. What becomes interesting about such characterisations is that the hacker is firmly located against a backdrop of middle-class white America. Whilst this may in fact be an accurate reflection of the background of progressive generations of digital technocrats and while the path from teenage hacker to corporate new technology yuppie may indeed be a well-trodden one, it has the net effect of recreating Cyberspace as a domain peopled exclusively by clever white males.

Moral panic around the dangers of allowing young people to immerse themselves into a Cyberspace universe as threatening as any inner city no-go area, replete with violent games and corrupting pornography has now become another favoured *cause célèbre* of the British tabloid press. ... It is interesting therefore to begin to examine how various aspects of black visibility, so often characterised as an almost essential cipher in the recasting of a space into a site of dangerous and transgressive activities have impacted upon the universe of Cyberspace.

With a few notable exceptions, the world of new technology has succeeded in projecting an image which either sees the black as placed outside of its domain, as being literally 'other', or frames the black as the 'subject' of the high-tech gaze. The so-called 'Third World' for instance, the world of underdevelopment and poverty, is seen very much as a pre-technological space. Its dark skinned peoples are characterised within the Western gaze as being unconscious to any notion of a digital realm of logic, development and privileged knowledge. ...

Their other potential interaction with Cyberspace would come only if they ever attempted to trespass into the so-called 'First World'. The perceived threat of the migration of peoples from the poor South into the industrialised centres of Europe and North America have resulted in an unprecedented escalation in investment in new technology as a means of monitoring and controlling their movements. At every port of entry, Cyberspace forms an invisible but all pervading barrier, scrutinising potential migrants and adding high-tech refortification to the fortresses of economic privilege which are now Europe and North America.

It is within the boundaries of the so-called 'First World', however, that the perception of the black as being either outside technology or passive subject of the technological gaze comes under its severest strain. Although often celebrated as the occupant of a more intuitive, physically reflexive space, a space in touch with the body, as opposed to the cerebral, coldly logical and physically detached space of new technology, the black presence has marked out a whole set of terrains in Cyberspace as sites of contest with the enfranchised status quo. Principal amongst these sites has been the terrain of new technology and music. In the track 'Caught, Can I Get a Witness!' rap group Public Enemy explore the legal minefield opening up around copyright ownership and the re-appropriation of black creativity through the use of the digital sampler as an act of political defiance.

> I found this mineral that I call a beat
> I paid zero
> I packed my load 'cause it's better than gold
> People don't ask the price, but it's sold. ...

The power which new technology gave to plunder the previously sacrosanct world of copyright ownership (the copyright of much popular music being in the hands of the record company as opposed to the artist) represented a major transgressive threat to the music recording establishment, initiating a form of digital looting. The realisation that the technology also allowed production capabilities, which were formally the exclusive domain of the enfranchised, to become available to individuals to use in their bedrooms redoubled its transgressive potential. The fact that the resultant musical movements of rap, house and acid house were all the products of the democratisation of Cyberspace and represented a significant creative entry into that technological domain by young black people is noteworthy. The recognition that around all of these movements has gathered a smokescreen of media demonology and hysteria – from panic around the violent, political and sexual lyrical content of rap to the spectre of British riot police storming 'illegal' acid house 'raves' – is testimony to the transgressive potential afforded by the colonisation of these spaces by black and black-derived cultural activities.

The key issue here is one of control. The contest has always been between those agencies which need to preserve Cyberspace as a tightly structured domain where information can be organised and accessed by the privileged and by so doing reinforce their control over the physical landscape of the city and the nation state, and those who find themselves the subject of that control.

In this sense I would argue that the enthusiasm on the part of Cyberspace insiders for so-called 'interactivity' has to be placed in perspective. True 'interactivity' – in the sense for example that African cultural forms have always displayed interactivity, allowing an unpredictable and intuitive interaction between presenter and spectator – would represent an anarchic nightmare to the enfranchised controllers of Cyberspace. The listeners' intervention into the griot's account, the traditions of 'call and response' in black cultural events and, more recently, the 'scratch, cut and paste' of some contemporary black music where the DJ is able to intervene with the received pre-recorded disc, creating a new 'interactive' collage of sound are all at odds with the artist and audience scenario of Western 'high culture'. Within this scenario one is presented with the work of the gifted 'maestro' as fixed and eternal. As the audience you are asked to spectate passively and applaud at the end, using a fixed set of expressive gestures. ...

Despite the fascinating progress towards user definable interactive tools as seen within the work of organisations such as 'AntiRom', it remains clear that many of the digital products presented as 'interactive' remain in many cases, by necessity, tightly structured matrixes through which one is allowed to navigate only along preordained pathways to a set of fixed destinations. In the case of many 'issue-based' or educational products, it must be acknowledged that a set range of destinations logically remains the very point of the exercise. However, in a broader sense it could be argued that many 'interactive' products become models (or at best parodies) of the orderly city of which the power structure has dreamed but failed to realise. As a pedestrain in this orderly city, one can only proceed along predetermined roadways, turning left, right or straight ahead at set junctions.

Within the truly interactive city on the other hand, the unruly pedestrian could jay-walk and trespass, cutting across wasteland and leaving graffiti on hallowed walls. Worse (or better) still, such a pedestrain could force a path through or over those walls and help him or herself to the treasured resources beyond. This becomes the interactive domain as riot zone with the user not as orderly citizen but as digital looter, disorderly and anarchic. Within this zone, treasured and privileged resources are redistributed and exclusive spaces are democratised. It is within this nightmare scenario for the controllers of Cyberspace that the digital equivalent of the disorderly black of urban chaos and transgressive behaviour steps into full visibility. It is at this symbolic point that Cyberspace changes from a sterile zone at

the service of the establishment into a free domain within which everyone becomes at liberty to seize a portion of terrain and reshape it to their
individual needs.

5.4   Cyborg City
James Harkin

William J Mitchell does not look much like a cyborg. When I meet him
in London, in the bookshop of the imposing Royal Institute of British
Architects building in Portland Place, he seems every inch the retiring, self-
effacing middle-aged family man, taking time out of his morning to buy
some books for his sons. But as soon as we walk outside he makes a slightly
eccentric observation. Across the road is the Chinese embassy and atop the
building, Mitchell points out, sits a vast nest of telecommunications aerials
and equipment. The thicket of wires and steel is imposing and a little sinis-
ter when you see it, but it is also strangely invisible.

Mitchell is the world's leading guru of how city life has changed in the age
of wireless communication, and author of the rather cultish book *Me++:
The Cyborg Self and the Networked City*. He hails from Sydney, Australia,
but is now a professor at MIT's super-futuristic Media Lab in Massachusetts,
where the technologies of the near future are given a test-run by some of the
brightest minds in academe. Granted a couple of hours of his time, I ask him
to take me on a tour of the digital, wirelessly connected world that is still
being built all around us – in a city that he doesn't really know.

We arrive at the top of Regent Street and pause for a coffee. While I
order, Mitchell tells me – in a dry, languorous voice not unlike that of his
countryman Clive James – how the new wireless technologies are making
much office space in cities redundant. If you go into corporate offices today,
he says, the private offices are closed and dark; the workers are out in hotel
rooms or on the move. The wireless laptop culture, he says, is increasing
the value of sitdown space just like this. 'Unassigned space, what used to
be thought of as non-productive space, is actually where all the real action
happens.' Like this coffee bar, he suggests, above the sound of Frank Sinatra
and the whirring of coffee machines.

Mitchell's theory is that the city has always been moulding us into
technology-dependent cyborgs, but that the new communications technologies
have made all this more vivid by overlaying on the urban landscape a kind
of central nervous system that plugs us deep into the wireless ether. Mobile

phones, for example, have become so intimately a part of ourselves that they are a kind of umbilical cord, anchoring us into the information society's digital infrastructure. A whole ragbag of new gadgets and wireless technologies hold up the promise of navigating our way through cities in exciting new ways.

The real impact of all this, argues Mitchell, is often better understood by culture and art. Take James Joyce's *Ulysses*, he says. The book opens our eyes to the romance and the hidden possibilities of Dublin as Leopold Bloom and Stephen Dedalus spend a day traversing its walkways, wandering in and out of each other's lives. The story is sustained by random encounters, and it progresses using the technology of the time – the characters are forever jumping on tram cars, for example. But if the characters had gone armed with mobile devices, says Mitchell, the whole structure of the novel would have changed. It is the kind of book, he reckons, that needs to be rewritten for the digital era.

We have finished our coffees, and are now running a little late on our own city stroll, so I suggest we catch the bus. We stand on upper Regent Street waiting for the No 453, headed south towards Trafalgar Square. I need change for the ticket machine, and ask him if I can cadge 20p. Mitchell does not have any change, but instead offers the helpful prediction that these ticket machines will soon have outlived their usefulness. Much preferable, he says, would be an electronic tag on your person that would do away with even an electronic ticket. But what about privacy? Technology already exists that could make all our digital transactions anonymous, he says. With a little will, technology itself could be used to keep us out of the clutches of marketeers and away from the tentacles of government. He is beginning to sound like a watery utopian.

On its slow route south, the bus crosses the magnificent thoroughfare at Oxford Circus. It is in retail hotspots such as these, says Mitchell, pointing up towards Oxford Street, that mobile phones are already quietly improving human coordination. Schoolchildren, for example, are increasingly going out comparison shopping by exchanging text-messages, like a little consumer army. The bus passes the famous neon billboard displays that frame Piccadilly Circus, and again Mitchell is exercised by the possibilities. If those billboards were programmed with a coherent artistic vision rather than just advertising, he says, they could be used, a little like the old Georgian squares of London, to give an aesthetic consistency and a unity to the area. It's already being done in various places around the world, he says – those in the know call it 'dynamic architecture' – and it's getting cheaper and more practical. The displays could be themed to change with the seasons or even at different times of the day. Piccadilly Circus could be made into a free speech zone, he says wistfully, a kind of digital speaker's corner activated by citizens dialling in from their mobile phones.

At this point, I feel compelled to throw a spanner into Mitchell's digital works. What about this guy, I say, pointing indelicately at a young man who is plugged into his iPod and staring blankly at the floor. He looks lost to the world. Well, yes, he says, but mobile devices can also increase your awareness of what is going on around you – people exchanging digital content, for example. Young people do it wonderfully, he says. They can switch attention, multitask, be involved in a real conversation at the same time as they surf the internet and send messages on their mobiles. But are they not not in danger of becoming permanently distracted? Not at all, says Mitchell. In his graduate classes at MIT, all his students bring in wireless laptops, and many of them check Google to verify and enrich what he's telling them. The result, he claims, makes lessons much more open-ended and dynamic.

The bus arrives in Trafalgar Square, and Mitchell is immediately impressed at how wirelessness has encouraged a more flexible use of the space. The large groups of teenagers we see on the square, he says, will have converged here by making shifting arrangements to meet via mobile phone – so-called approximeeting. When they get here, they have a choice of chatting with each other or having a conversation with someone else on the other side of the world. We spy a businessman working at a bench and Mitchell wonders, wearing his anthropologist's hat, what he might be working at and why. In the corner, a group of children are gamely chasing away pigeons, those unemployed relics from an earlier communications era.

When we leave the square and make our way up St Martin's Lane, Mitchell notices a sign on a lamp post reminding us that we are being watched by CCTV. It is chilling, he says, but he supposes that that is the point. In public space, you understand that you are going to be seen, so it shouldn't make much difference whether you are going to be observed by other people or on CCTV. In any case, there are ways in which we can get our own back on Big Brother. One student of his is in the habit of taking pictures of CCTV cameras in shops and retail spaces using his mobile phone. The idea is to make surveillance symmetrical and democratic – it also has the effect of driving shop owners crazy. In the Rodney King case, he reminds me, it was the use of a hand-held digital camera by a citizen that turned the situation around – a good example of how a democracy of surveillance can overcome the use of technology for political control.

Further up St Martin's Lane, we stop for lunch. I turn my digital voice recorder back on, and it prompts a conversation about how difficult it is to escape leaving behind a data trail. But if we remain committed to the robustness and the inviolability of public space, Mitchell says, there is no limit to what could be done in the cyborg era. We could, for example, create electronic clouds of information, gossip and graffiti and attach them to public places to be read by other passers by. He could even, he says, review this restaurant for an invisible, wireless magazine – tipping people off, for example, that 'this place sucks'. Mitchell has left his pallid-looking baguette nearly untouched, and I take his hint that the wireless future cannot come along too soon.

5.5   25 Instructions for Performance in Cities
Carl Lavery

The 25 Instructions for Performance in Cities listed below are of two varieties: general and specific. In both cases, however, there is sufficient space left for the student practitioner to appropriate the instruction for her own ends. The instructions are not designed to be a recipe. It is up to the performer to write the text, find the site, and decide on the medium of expression. The instructions have been inspired by what Fluxus artists such as John Cage, George Brecht and Jackson MacLow called 'event' or 'word' scores, written information that is meant, like a score of music, to take place in real time and to be performed by someone other than the composer or, in this instance, the instructor. It is expected that if the same score were given to ten groups of students, ten different performances would be created. As Anna Dezeuze writes in an essay on the Fluxus score: 'The notation [of the score] engenders a process, whether imaginative or physical, which will always be "too specific to approach in retrospect by any other person than the one who submerges herself in the process" ' (Dezeuze 2002: 88).

Despite the autonomy *25 Instructions for Performance in Cities* gives to students, the instructor has a crucial role to play. Although she has no aesthetic input concerning the activation of the score, the instructor is there either to encourage creativity or to caution against excessive ambition. But at no time should the instructor proffer specific advice on what form the performance should take. She is there to oversee the project and to make sure it happens. That's all. It goes without saying that these instructions can be used for collective or individual purposes and that they can be explored in a number of different performance modes: guerrilla theatre, invisible performance, walking, dance, performative lectures, installations, displays of documentation (video, photographs and DVD).

1.   Read everything you can about Sophie Calle's *Dangerous Game* (1988), Fiona Templeton's *You-The City* (1988) and *Mugger Music*

(1997) by Nick Crowe, Graham Parker and Ian Rawlinson. Meditate on what you read. Try to imagine what the work would be like and how it could be staged in your city. Then proceed to (a) plan your own version of the work; (b) find sites in your city or town that could accommodate the work; (c) rehearse and perform your version with a team of performers. You can, of course, add to (or change) the original.

2. Place an advertisement in a local newspaper asking for volunteer-participants to meet at a central location in your city at any time after dark. Make it clear that there is a limited number of places for the performance. Choose a master of ceremonies who will greet the participants when they arrive and provide them with a list of instructions. Three participants are then selected to get in a car and warned not to talk to each other or to the performer/chauffeur. A narrative or series of narratives about the city you have created out of newspapers or lies is then played on the car stereo. After ten minutes of travel, the car stops at a garage, ideally positioned on the outer ring-road of the city you live in. The participants are asked via a text message to change cars. After cruising on the outer ring-road (these exist in most British towns and cities) for forty minutes the participants are let out at a service station and instructed to carry out a series of tasks. They are then ferried back to the central location in the city and asked to share their experience of the city on a tape recorder, which may or, may not, provide the soundtrack to another performance.

3. Choose a play that is set in a city. Rehearse one scene from the play so that the cast are familiar with it. As the scene is being performed, project (on one of the adjacent walls) silent video footage in real time of cars travelling through the city. Each time the cars stop at a set of traffic lights allow the actors to speak.

4. Point a camera at a location in the city (say for two hours) so that it simply records what comes into view. Edit the footage. Screen the footage in a theatre or at a designated site. On microphones ask live performers stationed to the side of the screen to improvise stories about the people caught on the camera.

5. Create an installation of the city out of lost objects and the recorded testimonies of local people.

6. Perform a series of urban rituals in the city, paying particular attention to liminal sites and sacred spaces that are found in cities.

7. Explore different types of walking practices in the city: *flânerie*, drifting, wandering, *fuguerie*, nomadism and pilgrimage. Use these practices to create performance texts about the city, combining sound, image and text.

8. Produce a series of virtual postcards of your city and 'post' them on the Internet. You should choose a site that affects you strongly and perform the text you have written for a webcam. The task is to seek out and convey the 'urban sublime'.

9. Make the private public. Perform what you normally do indoors out-doors. This should include: cooking, eating, reading, washing, brushing your teeth, watching television and sleeping. Do this over a period of twenty-four hours. Stage it in a city square, theatre or shop window.

10. Compose a symphony in the city centre by coordinating the ring-tones of mobile phones. Do your best to involve strangers in this project.

11. Develop your own A–Z of the city grounded in personal experience. Distribute it on the street on a busy Saturday afternoon. Encourage other people to do the same.

12. Read Robert Smithson's essays on sites and non-sites in *Robert Smithson: The Collected Writing* (1996). Produce a series of site-specific works according to Smithson's dialectical methodology.

13. Study iconic paintings of city-life (see Edward Hopper's *NightHawks* (1942) and Seurat's *Un dimanche après-midi à l'Ile de la Grande Jatte* (1884–6)) and then stage these as living sculptures.

14. Produce a series of soundscapes of shopping malls, car parks, super-markets, ring-roads, alleyways, churches and playgrounds.

15. Carry a large table through the city-centre on a wet Saturday. Pick the busiest streets and busiest shops. Find a way of documenting the reactions of the people you encounter.

16. Familiarize yourself with the biblical 'Stations of the Cross'. At a variety of points throughout the city depict the events associated with the 'Stations' for a solitary spectator who makes her way through the city with a map. The performance should be in modern dress.

17. Create a forest in the city.

18. Sketch out smell maps, taste maps, audio maps, affective maps and geological maps of the city.

19. Take a video camera into the city and follow a dog or a cat for as long as you can. Make a film out of this.

20. Take your audience on a series of mythical journeys or quests in the city. Try to find kingfishers, sacred groves, fabled wells, underground streams, haunted houses, sites of healing, etc.

21. Situations designed for a mass audience of 'spect-actors':
    • Decorate a prominent multi-storey car park with wallpaper.
    • Perform mass acts of dowsing.
    • Arrange a wedding in the city centre.
    • Shower unsuspecting motorists with confetti from a road-bridge.

- At five minute intervals tell strangers how great they look.
- Leave messages of friendliness and enchantment on trees.
- Organize a mass map-making event in which participants are instructed how to make what Kevin Lynch in *The Image of the City* (1960) calls 'cognitive maps'. Encourage people to exchange maps.

22. Sit in a park, café or bar and listen to the stories spoken around you. Use this as the basis for a performance text.
23. Set up a series of booths in the city advertising palmistry, tasseography and tarot readings. Deliberately lie to your customers – predict futures of great happiness, collective joy and ecstatic being.
24. Draw a straight line through the city from north–south or east–west. Follow the line and produce a performance from what you encounter on the way.
25. Interview people in the street about their dreams. Use this information to transform the city into a dream space.

Reference

Dezeuze, A. (2002) 'Origins of the Fluxus Score: from Indeterminacy to the "Do-It-Yourself" Artwork', *Performance Research*, 7(3): 78–94.

Bibliography

The bibliography does not necessarily contain references relating to the texts used as samples in this publication. Full details of these texts are given at the beginning of each part of the book.

Acconci, V. (2004) *Vito Hannibal Acconci Studio*, Barcelona: ACTAR.

Adams, K. (2006) 'The Threshold of the Real: a Site for Participatory Resistance in Blast Theory's *Uncle Roy All Around You* (2003)', *Body, Space and Technology*, 6(1): http://people.brunel.ac.uk/bst/vol0601/home.html.

Alÿs, F., C. Lampert and J. Lingwood (eds) (2005) *Francis Alÿs Seven Walks, London, 2004–5*, London: Artangel.

Appadurai, A. (1996) *Modernity at Large: Cultural Dimensions of Globalization*, Minneapolis: University of Minnesota Press.

Artaud, A. (1974) *Collected Works of Antonin Artaud*, 4, trans. V. Corti, London: Calder and Boyars.

Augé, M. (1995) *Non-Places: Introduction to an Anthropology of Supermodernity*, London and New York: Verso.

Augé, M. (2002) *In the Metro*, intro. and trans. T. Conley, London and Minneapolis: University of Minnesota Press.

Auster, P. (1988) *The Invention of Solitude*, London: Faber and Faber.

Auster, P. (1993) *Leviathan*, London: Faber and Faber.

Bachelard, G. (1968) *The Poetics of Space*, trans. M. Jolas, Boston: Beacon Press.

Back, M. and M. Bull (2004) *The Auditory Culture Reader*, Oxford and New York: Berg.

Banksy (2005) *Wall Piece*, London: Century.

Barber, S. (1995) *Fragments of the European City*, London: Reaktion Books.

Barber, S. (2001) *Extreme Europe*, London: Reaktion Books.

Barber, S. (2006) *The Vanishing Map: a Journey from New York to Tokyo to the Heart of Europe*, Oxford and New York: Berg.

Barley, N. (ed.) (2000) *Breathing Cities: the Architecture of Movement*, Basel, Boston and Berlin: Birkhäuser.

Barthes, R. (1982) *Empire of Signs*, trans. R. Howard, London: Jonathan Cape.

Barthes, R. (1993) *Camera Lucida: Reflections on Photography*, trans. R. Howard, London: Vintage.

Bauman, Z. (2004) *Europe: an Unfinished Adventure*, Cambridge: Polity Press.

Benjamin, W. (1997a) *One-Way Street*, trans. E. Jephcott and K. Shorter, intro. S. Sontag, London and New York: Verso.

Benjamin, W. (1997b) *Charles Baudelaire: a Lyric Poet in the Era of High Capitalism*, London and New York: Verso.

Benjamin, W. (1999) *Selected Writings Volume 2, 1927–1934*, ed. M. W. Jennings, H. Eiland, G. Smith; trans. R. Livingston et al., London and Cambridge, MA: The Belknap Press of Harvard University.

Benjamin, W. (2002) *The Arcades Project*, ed. R. Tiedemann, trans. H. Eiland and K. McLaughlin, London and Cambridge, MA: The Belknap Press of Harvard University.

Berger, J. (2001) (untitled column), *Guardian*, 25 October: 7.

Blamey, D. (ed.) (2002) *Here, There, Elsewhere: Dialogues on Location and Mobility*, London: Open Editions.

Borden, I. (2001) *Skateboarding, Space and the City: Architecture and the Body*, Oxford and New York: Berg.

Borden, I. et al. (eds) (1996) *Strangely Familiar: Narratives of Architecture in the City*, London and New York: Routledge.

Borden, I., T. Hall and M. Miles (eds) (2000a) *The City Cultures Reader*, London and New York: Routledge.

Borden, I., B. Penner and J. Rendell (eds) (2000b) *Gender Space Architecture: an Interdisciplinary Introduction*, London and New York: Routledge.

Borden, I. et al. (eds) (2002) *The Unknown City: Contesting Architecture and Social Space*, London and Cambridge, MA: MIT Press.

Boyer, C. M. (1998) *The City of Collective Memory: Its Historical Imagery and Architectural Entertainments*, London and Cambridge, MA: MIT Press.

Brecht, B. (1976) 'On Everyday Theatre', *Poems 1913–1956*, ed. J. Willett and R. Manheim, trans. E. Anderson, London: Eyre Methuen: 176–9.

Brecht, B. (1978) 'The Street Scene', *Brecht on Theatre: the Development of an Aesthetic*, ed. and trans. J. Willett, London: Eyre Methuen: 121–9.

Brecht, B. (1993) *Journals 1934–1955*, ed. J. Willett, trans. H. Rorrison, London: Methuen.

Bridge, G. and S. Watson (eds) (2003) *A Companion to the City*, Oxford: Blackwell.

Brouwer, J., A. Mulder and L. Mertz (eds) (2002) *TransUrbanism*, Amsterdam: V2_Publishing/NAI Publishers.

Buck-Morss, S. (1989) *The Dialectics of Seeing: Walter Benjamin and the Arcades Project*, Cambridge, MA and London: MIT Press.

Bull, M. (2000) *Sounding Out the City: Personal Stereos and the Management of Everyday Life*, Oxford and New York: Berg.

Bunting, M. (2007) 'The Policing of the Artist', *Guardian*, 11 December: 28.

Burgin, V. (1996a) *Some Cities*, London: Reaktion Books.

Burgin, V. (1996b) *In/Different Spaces: Place and Memory in Visual Culture*, Berkeley and Los Angeles: University of California Press.

Calle, S. (2003) *M' as-tu Vue*, Munich, London and New York: Prestel Verlag.

Calvino, I. (1997) *Invisible Cities*, trans. W. Weaver, London: Vintage.

Christov-Bakargiev, C. (2001) *Janet Cardiff: a Survey of Works Including Collaborations with George Bures Miller*, New York: PS1 Contemporary Arts Center.

Cohen Cruz, J. (ed) (1998) *Radical Street Performance*, London and New York: Routledge.

Coles, A. (ed.) (1999) *The Optic of Walter Benjamin (de-, dis-, ex-)*, 3, London: Black Dog Publishing.

Coles, A. (ed.) (2000) *Site-Specificity: the Ethnographic Turn (de-, dis-, ex-)*, 4, London: Black Dog Publishing.

Cook, P. (2003) *The City, Seen as a Garden of Ideas*, New York: The Monachelli Press.

Coverley, M. (2006) *Psychogeography*, Harpenden: Pocket Essentials.

Crang, M. and N. Thrift (2000) *Thinking Space*, London and New York: Routledge.

Cresswell, T. (1996) *In Place/Out of Place: Geography, Ideology and Transgression*, Minneapolis: University of Minnesota Press.

Davis, M. (1984) *City of Quartz*, London and New York: Verso.

Davis, M. (2000) *Ecology of Fear: Los Angeles and the Imagination of Disaster*, London: Picador.

Dean, T. and J. Millar (eds) (2005) *Place*, London: Thames and Hudson.

Dear, M. (ed.) (2000) *The Postmodern Urban Condition*, Oxford: Blackwell.

De Botton, A. (2003) *The Art of Travel*, Harmondsworth: Penguin.

Debord, G. (1987) *Society of the Spectacle*, London: rebel press.

De Certeau, M. (1988) *The Practice of Everyday Life*, London and Minneapolis: University of Minnesota Press.

DeLillo, D. (1992) *Mao II*, London: Vintage.

Dennant, P. (1997) *Urban Expression ... Urban Assault ... Urban Wildstyle ... New York City Graffiti*, London: Thames University Press.

Derrida, J. (1982) *Margins of Philosophy*, trans. A. Bass, Chicago: University of Chicago Press.

Deutsche, R. (1996) *Evictions: Art and Spatial Politics*, London and Cambridge, MA: MIT Press.

Diamond, E. (1997) *Unmaking Mimesis: Essays on Feminism and Theatre*, London and New York: Routledge.

Doherty, C. and J. Millar (eds) (2000) *Jane and Louise Wilson*, London: Ellipsis.

Doherty, C. (ed) (2004) *Contemporary Art: From Studio to Situation*, London: Black Dog Publishing.

Dyer, G. (2006) 'An Explosion of Delight', *Guardian*, 14 October: 30.

Eccles, T., A. Wehr and J. Kastener (2004) *PLOP: Recent Projects of the Public Art Fund*, London and New York: Merrell.

Etchells, T. (1999) *Certain Fragments: Contemporary Performance and Forced Entertainment*, London and New York: Routledge.

Etchells, T. (2001) *The Dream Dictionary for the Modern Dreamer*, London: Duckworth.

Ferrell, J. (2003) *Tearing Down the Streets: Adventures in Crime and Anarchy*, Basingstoke: Palgrave.

Field, S., R. Meyer and F. Swanson (2007) *Imagining the City: Memories and Cultures in Cape Town*, Cape Town: HSRC Press.

Finkelpearl, T. (ed.) (2000) *Dialogues in Public Art*, London and Cambridge, MA: MIT Press.

Ford, S. (2005) *The Situationist International: a User's Guide*, London: Black Dog Publishing.

Freud, S. (1990) 'The Uncanny', in *Art and Literature*, 14, Harmondsworth: Penguin: 335–76.

Frisby, D. (2001) *Cityscapes of Modernity: Critical Explorations*, Cambridge: Polity Press.

Fyfe, N. R. (ed.) (1998) *Images of the Street: Planning, Identity and Control in Public Space*, London and New York: Routledge.

Gardner, L. (2007) 'What a Carry On', *Guardian*, 13 June: 26.

Garner Jr, Stanton B. (2002) 'Urban Landscapes, Theatrical Encounters: Staging the City', *Land/Scape/Theatre*, ed. U. Chaudhuri and E. Fuchs, Ann Arbor: University of Michigan Press: 94–118.

Gavin, F. (2007) *Street Renegades: New Underground Art*, London: Laurence King Publishing.

Gibson, K. and S. Watson (eds) (1995) *Postmodern Cities and Spaces*, Oxford: Blackwell.

Gibson, A. and J. Kerr (eds) (2003) *London: from Punk to Blair*, London: Reaktion Books.

Gilloch, G. (1997) *Myth and Metropolis: Walter Benjamin and the City*, Cambridge: Polity Press.

Glendinning, H., T. Etchells and Forced Entertainment (2000) *Void Spaces*, Sheffield: Site Gallery.

Gooding, M. (ed.) (1998) *Public: Art: Space*, London and New York: Merrell.

Gorman, S. (2003) 'Wandering and Wondering: Following Janet Cardiff's Missing Voice', *Performance Research*, 8(1): 83–92.

Grosz, E. (1992) 'Bodies-Cities', *Sexuality and Space*, ed. B. Colomina, New York: Princeton Architectural Press: 241–53.

Haedicke, S. and T. Nellhaus (eds) (2001) *Performing Democracy: International Perspectives on Urban-Based Community Performance*, Ann Arbor: University of Michigan Press.

Harkin, J. (2005) 'Cyborg City' (interview with W. J. Mitchell), *Guardian*, 26 November: 31.

Harvie, J. (2009) *Theatre and the City*, Basingstoke: Palgrave Macmillan.

Haydn, F. and R. Temel (eds) (2006) *Temporary Urban Spaces: Concepts for the Use of City Space*, Basel, Boston and Berlin: Birkhäuser.

Hayward, The (ed.) (2008) *Psycho Buildings: Artists Take on Architecture*, London: Hayward Publishing.

Helmer, J. and F. Malzacher (eds) (2004), *Not Even a Game Anymore: the Theatre of Forced Entertainment*, Berlin: Alexander Verlag.

Highmore, B. (2002) *Everyday Life and Cultural Theory*, London and New York: Routledge.

Hill, J. (ed.) (1998) *Occupying Architecture: Between the Architect and the User*, London and New York: Routledge.

Hill, L. and H. Paris (eds) (2006) *Performance and Place*, Basingstoke: Palgrave Macmillan.

Hoffman, J. and J. Jonas (eds) (2005) *Perform*, London: Thames and Hudson.

Hopkins, D. J., S. Orr and K. Solga (eds) (2009) *Performance and the City*, Basingstoke: Palgrave Macmillan.

Inura (ed.) (2004) *The Contested Metropolis: Six Cities at the Beginning of the 21st Century*, Basel, Boston and Berlin: Birkhäuser.

Jacobs, J. (1993) *The Death and Life of Great American Cities*, New York: Random House (Modern Library).

Jakovljevic, B. (2005) 'The Space Specific Theater: Skewed Visions' *The City Itself*', *The Drama Review*, 49(3): 96–106.

Jameson, F. (1998) *Brecht and Method*, London and New York: Verso.

Jestrovic, S. (2005) 'The Theatrical Memory of Space: from Piscator and Brecht to Belgrade', *New Theatre Quarterly*, 21(4): 358–66.

Kapur, G. (2007) 'subTerrain: Artworks in the Cityfold', *Third Text*, 21(3): 277–96.

Kaye, N. (2000) *Site-Specific Art: Performance, Place and Documentation*, London and New York: Routledge.

Keiller, P. (1999) *Robinson in Space*, London: Reaktion Books.

Keiller, P. (2005) *London* and *Robinson in Space*, DVD and sleeve notes, London: BFI.

Kingsnorth, P. (2008) *Real England: the Battle against the Bland*, London: Portobello Books.

Klein N. (2006) 'Fortress Continents', *Guardian*, 16 January: 23.

Knabb, K. (ed.) (2006) *Situationist International Anthology* (revised and expanded edition), Berkeley: Bureau of Public Secrets.

Kracauer, S. (1995) *The Mass Ornament*, London and Cambridge, MA: Harvard University Press.

Küppers, P. (1999) 'Moving in the Cityscape: Performance and the Embodied Experience of the Flâneur', *New Theatre Quarterly*, 15(4): 308–17.

Kwon, M. (2004) *One Place After Another: Site-Specific Art and Locational Identity*, London and Cambridge, MA: MIT Press.

Ladd, B. (1998) *The Ghosts of Berlin: Confronting German History in the Landscape*, Chicago and London: University of Chicago Press.

Lacy, S. (1995) *Mapping the Terrain: New Genre Public Art*, Seattle: Bay Press.

Large, D. C. (2002) *Berlin: a Modern History*, Harmondsworth: Penguin.

Lavery, C. (2005a) 'Teaching Performance Studies: 25 Instructions for Performance in Cities', *Studies in Theatre and Performance*, 25(3): 229–38.

Lavery, C. (2005b) 'The Pepys of London E11: Graeme Miller and the Politics of *Linked*', *New Theatre Quarterly*, 21(2): 148–60.

Lavery, C. (2006) 'Situationism', *Performance Research*, 11:3 (September): 111–13.

Leach, N. (ed.) (1997) *Rethinking Architecture: a Reader in Cultural Theory*, London and New York: Routledge.

Leach, N. (ed.) (1999) *Architecture and Revolution: Contemporary Perspectives on Central and Eastern Europe*, London and New York: Routledge.

Leach, N. (ed.) (2002) *The Hieroglyphics of Space: Reading and Experiencing the Modern Metropolis*, London and New York: Routledge.

Lees, R. (ed.) (2004) *The Emancipatory City? Paradoxes and Possibilities*, London: Sage Publications.

Lefebvre, H. (1996) *Writings on Cities*, ed., trans. and intro. E. Kofman and E. Lebas, Oxford: Blackwell.

Lefebvre, H. (1998) *The Production of Space*, Oxford: Blackwell.

Lefebvre, H. (2004) *Rhythmanalysis: Space, Time and Everyday Life*, trans. S. Elden and G. Moore, intro. S. Elden, London and New York: Continuum.

Lewisohn, C. (2008) *Street Art: the Graffiti Revolution*, London: Tate Publishing.

Libeskind, D. (2001) *The Space of Encounter*, London: Thames and Hudson.

Ligget, H. (2003) *Urban Encounters*, London and Minneapolis: University of Minnesota Press.

Lingwood, J. (ed.) (1995), *Rachel Whiteread: House*, London: Phaidon Press.

Lynch, K. (1960) *The Image of the City*, London and Cambridge, MA: MIT Press.

MacDonald, N. (2001) *The Graffiti Subculture: Youth, Masculinity and Identity in London and New York*, Basingstoke: Palgrave Macmillan.

McGonigal, J. (2004) 'Dark Play in Public Spaces: Confessions of a Flash Mob Organizer', http://www.avantgame.com/McGonigal%20DARK%20PLAY%20IN%20PUBLIC%20SPA CES%20PSi.pdf

McGregor, J. (2003) *If Nobody Speaks of Remarkable Things*, London: Bloomsbury.

McKinnie, M. (2007) *City Stages: Theatre and Urban Space in a Global City*, Toronto: University of Toronto Press.

McLeod, J. (2004) *Postcolonial London: Rewriting the Metropolis*, London and New York: Routledge.

Mason, M. (2008) *The Pirate's Dilemma: How Hackers, Punk Capitalists and Graffiti Millionaires are Re-mixing our Culture*, London: Allen Lane.

Massey, D. (1994) *Space, Place and Gender*, Cambridge: Polity Press.

Matzner, F. (ed) (2004) *Public Art: a Reader*, Ostfildern-Ruit: Hatje Cantz.

Miles, M. (1997) *Art, Space and the City*, London and New York: Routledge.

Miles, M. (2007) *Cities and Cultures*, London and New York: Routledge.

Miles, M. and T. Hall (eds) (2003) *Urban Futures: Critical Commentaries on Shaping the City*, New York and London: Routledge.

Mitchell, W. J. T. (1992) *Art and the Public Sphere*, Chicago: University of Chicago Press.

Mitchell, W.J. (1995) *City of Bits*, London and Cambridge, MA: MIT Press.

Mitchell, W.J. (2000) *e-topia: 'Urban life, Jim – but not as we know it'*, London and Cambridge, MA: MIT Press.

Mitchell, W.J. (2005) *Placing Words: Symbols, Space, and the City*, London and Cambridge, MA: MIT Press.

Moore, R. (ed.) (1999) *Vertigo: the Strange New World of the Contemporary City*, London: Laurence King Publishing.

Mumford, L. (1938) *The Culture of Cities*, London: Secker and Warburg.

Merrifield, A. (2002) *Metromarxism: a Marxist Tale of the City*, London and New York: Routledge.

Müller, H. (1995) *Theatremachine*, ed. and trans. M. von Henning, London: Faber and Faber.

Musil, R. (1979) *The Man without Qualities*, 1, trans. E. Wilkins and E. Kaiser, London: Picador.

Nancy, J.-L. (1991) *The Inoperative Community*, ed. P. Connor, trans. P. Conner et al., Minneapolis and Oxford: University of Minnesota Press.

Neuerer, G. (ed.) (2003) *Untitled (Experience of Place)*, intro. J. Verwoert, London: Koenig Books.

Nooteboom, C. (2002) *All Souls' Day*, trans. S. Massotty, London: Picador.

Öncü, A. and P. Weyland (eds) (1997) *Space, Culture and Power: New Identities in Globalising Cities*, London: Zed Books.

Paetzold, H. (ed.) (1997) *City Life: Essays on Urban Culture*, Maastricht and Amsterdam: Jan van Eyck Akademie/de Balie.

Parker, S. (2004) *Urban Theory and Urban Experience: Encountering the City*, London and New York: Routledge.

Parsons D. (2000) *Streetwalking the Metropolis: Women, the City and Modernity*, Oxford: Oxford University Press.

Pawley, M. (1998) *Terminal Architecture*, London: Reaktion Books.

Pearson, M. and M. Shanks (2001) *Theatre/Archaeology*, London and New York: Routledge.

Phillips, S. (1999) *Wallbangin' – Graffiti and Gays in LA*, Chicago: University of Chicago Press.

Pietromarchi B. (ed.) (2005) *the [un]common place: art, public space and urban aesthetics in Europe*, Rome: Fondazione Adriano Olivetti and Barcelona: Avtar.

Pile, S. (1996) *The Body and the City: Psychoanalysis, Space and Subjectivity*, London and New York: Routledge.

Pile, S. (2005) *Real Cities: Modernity, Space and the Phantasmagorias of City Life*, London: Sage Publications.

Pile, S. and N. Thrift (eds) (2000) *City A–Z*, London and New York: Routledge.

Pinder, D. (2005) *Visions of the City: Utopianism, Power and Politics in Twentieth-Century Urbanism*, Edinburgh: Edinburgh University Press.

Pradeau, J.-F. (2002) *Plato and the City: a New Introduction to Plato's Political Thought*, Exeter: Exeter University Press.

Puchner, M. (2004) 'Society of the Counter Spectacle: Debord and the Theatre of the Situationists', *Theatre Research International*, 29(1): 4–15.

Raban, J. (1998) *Soft City*, London: Harvill Press.

Rae, P. with L. K. Hong (2003) 'Nosing Around: A Singapore Scent Trail', *Performance Research*, 8(3): 44–54.

Read, A. (ed.) (2000) *Architecturally Speaking: Practices of Art, Architecture and the Everyday*, London and New York: Routledge.

Reader, J. (2005) *Cities*, London: Vintage.

Rendell, J. (2007) *Art and Architecture: a Place Between*, London and New York: I. B. Tauris.

Roach, J. (1996) *Cities of the Dead: Circum-Atlantic Performance*, New York: Columbia University Press.

Rogoff, I. (2000) *Terra Infirma: Geography's Visual Culture*, London and New York: Routledge.

Rykwert, J. (2000) *The Seduction of Place: the City in the 21st Century*, London: Weidenfeld and Nicholson.

Sadler, S. (1998) *The Situationist City*, London and Cambridge, MA: MIT Press.

Sandford, M. R. (ed.) (1995) *Happenings and Other Acts*, London and New York: Routledge.

Scheepers, I. (2004) *Graffiti and Urban Space*, Sydney: University of Sydney Press.

Sebald, W. G. (2002) *The Rings of Saturn*, trans. M. Hulse, London: Vintage Books.

Sennett, R. (1992) *The Conscience of the Eye: the Design and Social Life of Cities*, New York: Norton.

Sennett, R. (1996) *Flesh and Stone: the Body and the City in Western Civilisation*, Harmondsworth: Penguin.

Sennett, R. (2008) *The Uses of Disorder: Personal Identity and City Life*, New Haven: Yale University Press.

Sinclair, I. (1997) *Lights Out for the Territory*, London: Granta Books.

Sinclair, I. (2002) *London Orbital: a Walk Round the M25*, London: Granta Books.

Soja, E. (1989) *Postmodern Geographies: the Reassertion of Space in Critical Social Theory*, London and New York: Verso.

Speir, S. (ed.) (2002) *Urban Visions: Experiencing and Envisioning the City*, Liverpool: University Press and Tate Publishing.

Stevens, Q. (2007) *The Ludic City: Exploring the Potential of Public Spaces*, London and New York: Routledge.

Suderberg, E. (ed.) (2000) *Space, Site, Installation: Situating Installation Art*, London and Minneapolis: University of Minnesota Press.

Sudjic, D. (1992) *The Hundred Mile City*, London: Flamingo.

Tawadros, G. (ed.) (2004) *Changing States: Contemporary Arts and Ideas in an Era of Globalisation*, London: inIVA.

Tester, K. (ed.) (1994) *The Flâneur*, London and New York: Routledge.

Thomas, H. (ed.) (1997) *Dance in the City*, Basingstoke: Macmillan Press.

Townsend, C. (ed.) (2004) *The Art of Rachel Whiteread*, London: Thames and Hudson.

Ulmer, G. (1989) *Teletheory: Grammatology in the Age of Video*, London and New York: Routledge.

UN-HABITAT (2006) *State of the World's Cities 2006/07: the Millennium Development Goals and Urban Sustainability*, London: Earthscan.

Urry, J. (2002) *The Tourist Gaze*, London: Sage Publications.

Van Noord, G. (ed.) (2002) *Off Limits: 40 Artangel Projects*, London and New York: Merrell.

Van Treeck, B. (ed.) (1999) *Street-Art Berlin: Kunst im Öffentlichen Raum*, Berlin: Schwarzkopf und Schwarzkopf.

Vaßen, F. (1998) 'A New Poetry for the Big City: Brecht's Behavioural Experiments in *Aus dem Lesebuch für Städtebewohner*', trans. K. Hall, *German Monitor*, 41: 75–87.

Vidler, A. (1992) *The Architectural Uncanny: Essays in the Modern Unhomely*, London and Cambridge, MA: MIT Press.

Vidler, A. (2000) *Warped Space: Art, Architecture and Anxiety in Modern Culture*, London and Cambridge, MA: MIT Press.

Virilio, P. (1991) *Lost Dimension*, trans. Daniel Moschenberg, New York: Semiotext(e).

Watts, J. (2004) 'How Scratched Car Revealed Price of a Peasant's Life', *Guardian*, 8 April: 17.

Weber, S. (2003) '"Streets, Squares, Theaters": a City on the Move – Walter Benjamin's Paris', *Boundary 2*, 30(1): 17–30.

Whybrow, N. (2005) *Street Scenes: Brecht, Benjamin, and Berlin*, Bristol: Intellect Books.

Whybrow, N. (2006) 'Streetscenes: the Accident of Where We Walk', *Performance Research*, 11(3): 123–6.

Wilson, E. (1991) *The Sphinx in the City*, Los Angeles and Berkeley: University of California Press.

Winter, J. (2005) 'All the World's a Car Park', *Guardian 2*, 25 January: 14.

Wright, E. (1989) *Postmodern Brecht: a Re-presentation*, London and New York: Routledge.

Wrights and Sites (eds) (2003) *An Exeter Mis-guide*, Exeter: Wrights and Sites.

Wrights and Sites (2006) 'A Manifesto for a New Walking Culture: "Dealing with the City"', *Performance Research*, 11(2): 115–22.

Wrights and Sites (eds) (2007) *A Mis-guide to Anywhere*, Exeter: Wrights and Sites.

Young, J. E. (ed.) (1994) *The Art of Memory: Holocaust Memorials in History*, New York and Munich: Prestel Verlag.

Young, J. E. (2000) *At Memory's Edge: After Images of the Holocaust in Contemporary Art and Architecture*, New Haven, CT: Yale University Press.

Zukin, S. (1995) *The Cultures of Cities*, Los Angeles and Berkeley: University of California Press.

Themed journals/series

Advances in Art and Urban Futures, 1–4, Bristol: Intellect Books, 2003–5.

Art and Architecture ('Art in the Urban Context'), 62, June, 2005.

Cultural Geographies ('Arts of Urban Exploration'), 12(4), 2005.

Flâneur – an Online Journal (www.flaneur.org).

Liminalities: a Journal of Performance Studies ('On the City'), 4(1), 2008.

Performance Research ('On Tourism'), 2(2), 1997.

Performance Research '(On Refuge'), 2(3), 1997.

Performance Research ('On Place'), 3(2), 1998.

Performance Research ('On Memory'), 5(3), 2000.

Performance Research ('Departures'), 6(1), 2001.

Performance Research ('Maps/Mappings'), 6(2), 2001.

Performance Research ('Navigations'), 6(3), 2001.

Performance Research ('On the Road'), 12(2), 2007.

Public Art Journal ('A Place Between'), October, 1999.

Theaterschrift ('City/Art/Identity'), 10, 1995.

Theatre Journal ('Theatre and the City'), 53(2), 2001.

Transgressions: a Journal of Urban Exploration, 1–5, 1995–2001.

Index